The Virtues of Vengeance

The Virtues of Vengeance

Peter A. French

 University Press of Kansas

Published by the University Press of Kansas (Lawrence, Kansas 66049), which was organizd by the Kansas Board of Regents and is operated and funded by Emporia State University, Fort Hays State University, Kansas State University, Pittsburg State University, the University of Kansas, and Wichita State University

Library of Congress Cataloging-in-Publication Data

French, Peter A.
    The virtues of vengeance / Peter A. French.
      p. cm.
    Includes index.
    ISBN 0-7006-1076-6 (hardcover : alk. paper)
    1. Revenge. 2. Ethics. I. Title.
BJ1490 .F74 2001
179—dc21
                            00-049959

British Library Cataloguing in Publication Data is available.

Printed in the United States of America

10 9 8 7 6 5 4 3 2 1

For Sandra

CONTENTS

PREFACE

When I first conceived of this book I had just finished writing another book, *Cowboy Metaphysics*,[1] in which I used my favorite form of popular culture, major Western films, to work out the relationships between competing conceptions of death and ethics. In *Cowboy Metaphysics* I made a claim, one that I did not try to substantiate or elaborate, that vengeance could be virtuous under certain conditions and that a dominant theme of many of the better Westerns was the attempt to make that claim persuasive. The revenge plot appeals to very deep-rooted and, I think, very important, indeed crucial, intuitions about the foundations and point of morality. Contemporary moralists tend to express great discomfort with punishment, especially capital punishment, and even responsibility, but the revenge story, not only but famously in Westerns, attracts large audiences that leave theaters or rewind videocassettes with a sense of vindication, a sense that at least in the story, the film, things came out right, morally speaking. Victimizers were killed, and their victims, at least the ones who survived, can live in a morally restored locale. The avenger is a role often played by the heroes of Western films. One needs only to think of the Ringo Kid in *Stagecoach,* Shane in *Shane,* The Preacher in *Pale Rider,* Lassiter in *Riders of the Purple Sage,* Hannie Caulder in *Hannie Caulder,* William Munny in *Unforgiven,* Lin McAdam in *Winchester '73,* and, of course, Ethan Edwards in *The Searchers.* That list merely scratches the surface.

In the afterword to *Cowboy Metaphysics,* I promised a sequel that would again look at a selection of Western films with a view to explicating the virtuous elements of revenge, elements that I believe have been generally misunderstood or ignored by philosophers who write on issues in ethics, punishment theory, and related topics. My original intent was to write what is called a "nuanced study" of the films in the Western vengeance genre from which an account of virtuous vengeance would emerge. The book I have written, however, as a Westerner might say, is "rather a far piece" from the original intent.

The Westerns I admire occupy only a rather small, if significant, corner of our culture's interest in the virtues and vices of vengeance. I could not ignore certain landmarks of literature that frame much of our conception of vengeance. My interest in the conceptual terrain of vengeance soon dominated my thinking, and the Westerns became more occasions for illustrating the issues than the centerpiece of the study. Consequently, I did not write a nuanced study of representative examples of the Western revenge films. Instead, I have constructed a series of essays that, I believe, explore an important part of the moral conceptual terrain in which vengeance is situated.

Vengeance, though it is generally decried as barbaric by the standard moral theories and forbidden in its personal forms by most legal systems, lies close to the center of what it means for an action to be wrongful. Historically and mythologically its genesis lies in feelings of injustice and unfairness. Psychologically it responds to what are among our most basic moral emotions: resentment and indignation. It makes sense only within conceptual frameworks that include victimization, honor, and shame. Although it is rightly identified as historically primitive, the only cogent reasons put forth by moralists for prohibiting it have been more or less practical ones, and they are typically conjoined with what Jeffrie Murphy correctly identifies as sentimental clichés rather than arguments.[2] Vengeance, it seems, has fallen into disrepute without being seriously examined.

It is fashionable to describe one's theory of punishment or justice as prohibiting revenge or as definitely not countenancing vengeance. Vengeance, we are usually assured from the Stoic-Christian point of view that has dominated ethics, is impermissible. After all, bearing up under oppression and victimization, turning the other cheek, is the antithesis of revenge, and only God could be both pure enough and knowledgeable enough to administer vengeance in a morally fitting way. Leave it to heaven. Perhaps, but if God can play the part of the avenger, then vengeance cannot be all that bad. At least it cannot be evil per se to desire it or, perhaps, to engage in it. And what if there is no God or morally ordered universe, or if God has disengaged from the business of empowering morality?

Exiling vengeance into a distant dark corner of moral permissibility has robbed morality of one of its most potent and persuasive elements. Most moralists and ordinary people will agree that it is wrong to torture and rape another human being. But what follows from identifying those actions as wrong? Clearly, no one should do them. But if someone does torture or rape another person, what then? They should, no doubt, be rebuked or condemned or ostracized from the community of good people. Is that all that saying the actions were wrongful involves? I argue that the very concept of a wrong or evil action entails that it should be met with a hostile response. In many cases—including torture and rape—rebuke, condemnation, and ostracism are far from adequate hostile responses. The moral order itself is affronted if such responses are all that occurs.

Of course, the sustenance of the moral order might not be a problem if the moral qualities of our actions were in themselves casually efficacious in our lives, if the wrongfulness of our actions, in a dependable way, caused us to suffer fitting punishments and the goodness of what we do caused our happiness. But the universe is not such an ordered place, and the moral qualities of actions are not in themselves causally efficacious. Therefore, if there is to be a point to morality, it must be empowered, and we are the only known members of the moral community, the only moral persons, who can empower it.

Revenge is the technology of moral empowerment, a technology for the sustaining of morality. I do not claim that it is the only one or indeed that it is the best one, although in some situations it well may be the only available one. I do claim that in the absence of technologies of empowerment morality hangs on a thin meta-physical thread that is becoming thinner and thinner in the modern and postmodern world. It is in serious danger of being nothing but "words, words, words," and eventually, sooner or later, like Eliza Doolittle of *My Fair Lady,* we will be "so sick of words" and so of morality.

The book is organized into two parts. Part One affords me the opportunity to draw out certain features of vengeance from literary and film sources. Because I will be making reference to those sources, primarily for illustrative purposes, in the main body of the book, Part Two, I provide brief, but I hope helpful, ac-counts of the relevant aspects of those sources, and I explore some preliminary philosophical points on which the remainder of the book can build. In Part Two I attempt to map out the major features of what I identify as virtuous vengeance. Most of the essays that comprise Part Two were written so that they might, with some obvious modifications, stand on their own. In fact, I conceive of the work as a series of essays written around the general topic rather than as a sustained argument building to a conclusion. My intent is to be suggestive and, hopefully, provocative.

I have benefited greatly from discussions of the topics in the book and drafts of chapters and parts of chapters that I have had with my colleagues and gradu-ate students in the Department of Philosophy at the University of South Florida and at the Ethics Center. Discussions with faculty at Colby College, the Univer-sity of Maine, the United States Air Force Academy, and the University of Min-nesota were most valuable. Feedback from attendees at a national ethics conference in Long Beach, California, where I gave a keynote address that served as a trial run for a section of one of the chapters, also proved helpful. I owe a debt to the works of a number of philosophers with whom I also have had the opportunity to correspond. Their insights have been vital to the development of my position. As will be obvious at a number of crucial points in the book, I am indebted to John Kekes, Michael Slote, John Martin Fischer, Jeffrie Murphy, Robert Nozick, and T. E. Wilkerson. I am especially grateful to Margaret Walker, who continu-ally encouraged the project and often listened to my ramblings about vengeance and made helpful suggestions, many of which had an impact on the way the book took shape. I have learned a great deal from our many conversations on topics related to our various projects. I should also mention my debt to my friend, teacher, and colleague J. L. Mackie. Although John died too young at age sixty-four almost two decades ago, I continue to learn and benefit from his work and my recollections of our many conversations on topics that have engaged my interest throughout my career.

My wife, Sandra, was unfailingly supportive to the point of letting me work on the book for lengthy periods of time during our summer stays at our place in the Colorado Rockies. Even though the weather was beautiful and the temptation to be exploring off-road in the mountain passes and the nearly inaccessible ghost towns at eleven thousand feet was intense, she kept me at the task. In the same circumstances, my Shetland sheepdogs certainly exhibited less patience with me.

Finally, Nancy Scott Jackson, my editor at the University Press of Kansas, has been a constant source of encouragement.

PART ONE

Vengeance in Literature and Popular Culture

CHAPTER ONE

Some Literary Foundations:
A Survey

O what a brilliant day it is for vengeance!
Aeschylus[1]

When vengeance is mentioned in conversation, two expressions generally leap to mind. "Revenge is sweet" is probably the most common phrase associated with vengeance, and the other can be attributed to Sir Francis Bacon: "Revenge is a kind of wild justice."[2] As with many popular aphorisms, there is something basically true in both of these adages. They are also rather too broad to be of much help in trying to understand the concept of vengeance in a moral context. Revenge, of course, is sweet for the obvious psychological reasons. You, or someone close to you, has suffered an injury at the hands of another, an injury that you take to be unwarranted. You are filled with resentment or indignation. Then you devise a way to retaliate, to inflict a like, or greater, injury on your offender. The sense of accomplishment and moral righteousness at getting even or, better yet, at having legitimately, justifiably, righteously, inflicted a greater injury can be intoxicating, exhilarating, sweet. Charlotte Brontë writes: "Something of vengeance I had tasted for the first time. An aromatic wine it seemed, on swallowing, warm and racy." She then goes on to identify one of the culture's major difficulties with sweet revenge; "Its first after-flavor, metallic and corroding, gave me a sensation as if I had been poisoned."[3] Perhaps that reaction is prompted by the recognition of the wildness in the justice of it all.

Pietro Marongiu and Graeme Newman maintain that "all acts of vengeance arise from an elementary sense of injustice."[4] Vengeance is the way of making things right, of restoring the balance to the scales of justice. The extremely early appearance of vengeance as a moral theme in our cultural history suggests that even the most primitive societies had a sense of injustice. At least they appreciated the social and political value of feelings of resentment and indignation arising from not receiving what one believes to be one's due. In any event, the literary and religious story of Western culture is, in large measure, the tale of vengeance.

Any attempt to offer a thorough account of vengeance in the mythological and literary traditions of Western culture is beyond my abilities. It would be a task of enormous length because of the sheer volume of material. Whole libraries could be filled to their ceilings with books in which revenge is the dominant theme. Instead, I will survey some landmarks that, I believe, are representative of the development of the concept of vengeance in our cultural history and that set the stage for the philosophical discussion of the ethical status of the concept.

Freud argues that patricide is the primal crime from which the moral law emerges.[5] The primal patricide, at least for the ancient Greeks, was an act of revenge. On Hesiod's account, Gaia, the Earth, "coupled" with Ouranos (Uranus), the sky (whom she had given birth to "without mating in sweet love"), and gave birth to the Titans, the Kyklopes, and three grotesque giants, Koltos, Briareos, and Gyges. Ouranos hated those "awesome" children and imprisoned them in a deep hole in the earth, in their mother's womb. Gaia freed her children and begged them to punish Ouranos. She made a huge sickle that she offered to them as a weapon to be used against their father. All but the youngest, Kronos, refused to take up the sickle. Kronos grabbed his father's genitals while Ouranos and Gaia were engaged in sex and castrated him. The drops of blood that fell from the wound became the Furies, the goddesses that punish crimes against kin. Kronos tossed Ouranos's penis into the sea, and out of the foam the goddess of love, Aphrodite, was born. The symbol of Kronos with the sickle remains our icon of time. Kronos, however, was even more tyrannical than his father had been. Obsessed by the prophesy that he would succumb to a fate like his father's, he ate each of his children as they were born. All but one child suffered that fate. Kronos's wife, Rhea, hid that child, Zeus, from his father, and Zeus succeeded in chaining Kronos and exiling him.[6]

Vengeance was the underlying motive of the creation and the structuring of the Olympian hierarchy and thence the world order itself. In the earliest mythological explanations, acts of vengeance are represented as the only ways to rectify structurally unequal situations of tyranny, and from them, if only temporarily, may flow more reciprocal social orders and shifts in power that promise to be less tyrannical than were their predecessors. Certain themes also emerge in the early mythology that are replayed and developed in the later tragedies, notably the instigation or collaboration of a close relative, typically female (mother or sister), in the vengeful act of the son or brother against a close kin.

Of course, vengeance also is understood as the appropriate response to perceived personal injury. These are very personal matters, even if their provocation involves others with whom one is intimately related. They may stem as well from a sense of powerlessness[7] where one believes one should not be powerless, a sense of unwarranted victimization. This reaction is especially true in the case of Kronos, perhaps less true with Zeus, where the revenge is sought not only because he was the intended victim but also as both a response to familial victimization and as proactive insurance in his own case. Zeus, of course, while in exile on Crete probably felt the sense of unjust loss of status, of unwarranted deprivation, that is also a form of victimization. In the ancient Greek myths, resentment, wrath, honor, desert, deprivation, and reciprocity mark the conceptual landscape of vengeance.

Homer takes vengeance some considerable distance beyond the early myths. He begins the *Iliad* by telling us that "the Wrath of Achilles is my theme."[8] What would be closer to the truth is that the vengeance of Achilles (or the two episodes of Achilles' revenge on the plains of Troy) is the theme of the epic. Homer takes up the story of the siege of Troy in the ninth year of the enterprise, after the Greeks had raided Trojan villages and returned to camp with the spoils of their looting. Each of the princes of the Greek army had been allotted a portion of the booty. Agamemnon received the daughter of a local priest of Apollo. When the priest begged for her return and offered to pay a ransom, Agamemnon refused. The priest prayed to the god, and Apollo visited a deadly plague on the Greek army. Agamemnon agreed to relinquish the girl to satisfy Apollo, but he demanded immediate compensation: "You must let me have another prize at once, or I shall be the only one of us with empty hands, a most improper thing."

Achilles then asks, "And where does your majesty propose that our gallant troops should find a fresh prize to satisfy your unexampled greed?" Agamemnon's reply is to have his troops "pay a visit to your hut and take away the beautiful Briseis, your prize, Achilles, to let you know that I am more powerful than you, and to teach others not to bandy words with me and openly defy their King." Achilles rages and threatens that Agamemnon should pay for the taking of Briseis with his life. Rather than killing the king, however, he withdraws his force of Myrmidons from the battlefield and refuses to fight. "The day is coming when the Achaeans one and all will miss me sorely, and you in your despair will be powerless to help them as they fall in their hundreds to Hector killer of men. Then, you will tear your heart out in remorse for having treated the best of men in the expedition with contempt"(*The Iliad,* Book I).

That time is not long in coming. The Trojans mount a successful assault that drives the Greeks back to their ships on the beach. Without the courage and leadership of Achilles, the Greek cause seems lost and many Greeks are killed. Achilles sits in his hut and sulks. His refusal to fight is his vengeance against Agamemnon. His revenge, his wrath, is prompted by a deep sense of personal injustice, a sense that someone with more power has treated him unfairly and lowered his status in the eyes of those who lack his skills and courage. He explains to his friend Patroclus: "What has cut me to the quick is that a fellow no better than myself should want to plunder me and take away the prize I won, just because he has more power . . . I am served like some disreputable tramp" (*The Iliad,* Book XVI). Marongiu and Newman see the crux of the Achilles/Agamemnon controversy as focused on Achilles' demand to be treated "equitably." However, it is not so much that he wants to be treated equitably as that he wants to be treated as Agamemnon's equal, and he resents the fact that, given the structure of the army assembled by Agamemnon, he is in an inferior position. The resentment of those in inferior power positions who believe they are the equals of their superiors is typically the spur for acts of vengeance against the superiors. It is not uncommon in the workplace, for example, for petty acts of revenge to be perpetrated against supervisors by resentful workers.

Achilles' act of revenge is to refuse to fight and to withdraw his Myrmidon force from the fray. By doing so, he not only demonstrates to Agamemnon his value to the Greek army, but he also exposes Agamemnon's weaknesses as a commander. The depth of Achilles' resentment is revealed by his refusal to join the battle to save the Greek ships even after Agamemnon has apologized and agreed to return Briseis.

The revenge Achilles takes against Agamemnon is the theme of approximately the first two-thirds of the *Iliad.* Even a cursory reading of Homer's epic reveals that at least three types of mental states drive Achilles' actions (or inactions). In the first place, he harbors a deep and personal sense of unfair deprivation with respect to the distribution of goods (the unfair deprivation condition). Second, he feels powerlessness in the situation to do what he would most like to do—kill Agamemnon and reclaim Briseis—while believing he does not deserve to be in such an inferior position (the unjust powerlessness condition). And those feelings or conditions of unfair deprivation and unjust powerlessness foster in him such emotions as contempt, hatred, scorn, disdain, and loathing for Agamemnon (the disapprobative emotions condition). But there is more to it than that.

Achilles has been, or certainly believes himself to have been, affronted by Agamemnon. But of what does the affront consist? Certainly it is to Achilles' honor; and Achilles is a man of honor. In fact, as I shall argue in Chapter 5, he is a man of two distinct sorts of honor: one kind "is an intensely interactive phenomenon, gained and lost only by direct, conflictual interaction,"[9] while the other is not especially interactive.

Public honor, honor in the first sense, the sense with which it is most commonly identified, is an "attribute of free, independent men."[10] It is gained and protected by the achievement of victories over one's equals and one's superiors, "where 'victory' can mean anything from getting away with an insulting look to raping a man's wife or killing him."[11] At the beginning of the *Iliad,* Agamemnon appears to have gained in public honor at the expense of Achilles with much more than a mere insulting look. He has insulted him verbally and, by taking his prize from out of Achilles' own tent, physically and in both cases in the presence of others of stature in the social system. In the case of public honor, this latter condition is a requirement. It is not enough that Agamemnon or Achilles should humiliate one another in private; there would be no honor in it. They must be seen to do so publicly, before the eyes of those who matter to each in the company of Greek princes. The type of honor, public honor, that seems to be involved between them is not best described in a dyadic relationship. It is triadic because the audience is crucial. In this sense honor is akin to shame, a topic to be addressed in more detail in Chapter 5.

Public honor is also action-dependent. There would be no loss of such honor by Achilles or gain by Agamemnon, or vice versa, if their considerations of each other were played out on the field of envy. Achilles neither loses nor gains public honor if Agamemnon merely covets his possession of Briseis. Agamemnon neither loses nor gains honor if Achilles merely begrudges the fact that he is the commander of the Greek army. A slave may resent his master from afar, a neighbor may envy your new car, but these are not matters of honor. One can covet another's possessions without ever having met the owner because envy does not require one to interact with the owner. Elster calls envy an "external relation" and honor an internal relation. Envy can be provoked and enjoyed without interacting with the envier. For example, I can park my new sports car in the driveway, just to arouse the admiration and envy of any passerby, and I can enjoy the anticipation and the experience of having done so. I cannot gain or lose honor in so casual a manner. Neither Achilles nor Agamemnon would have thought he could lose or gain any honor by merely flaunting his material assets.

If public honor is a zero-sum game, as some have suggested, then the humiliation of Achilles may be seen as a significant loss by him that is equaled by a comparable gain for Agamemnon. Hence, Achilles tells the other Greek princes: "First he [Agamemnon] must pay me in kind for the bitter humiliation I endured." Honor, on the zero-sum conception, is a positional good. It is attached to standing or place in the social system, and as there are only so many places of honor at the table, there is only a limited amount of it to be distributed. If every place at the table were a place of honor, there really would be no place of honor at the table. The public honor game, on this conception, is zero sum with respect to a scarce commodity. It is a transferable good that can be acquired or lost by actions. Perhaps it can also be stolen.

Is honor a zero-sum game and is it only a positional good? Achilles does not seem to think so. His response is not to pay back Agamemnon in kind but to cause a far greater loss for him and the other Greek princes who continued to fight the Trojans. Achilles has, one might say, upped the ante of public honor, escalated its costs. But there is another sense of honor to be considered.

Suppose Achilles, using his superior weaponry skills, attacks one of his soldiers, an obvious inferior, for a minor infraction of the Myrmidon dress code and beats him to death. Achilles not only would gain no public honor by doing so, but he also would lose honor by the act. Thus, public honor can be lost even though no one achieves a comparable gain or any gain at all. That is not a zero-sum game. And, as Elster notes from a reference to Lincoln-Keiser's studies of feuding in Pakistan, if honor is conceived of as personal worth rather than as a positional good, personal rather than public, perhaps it can only be lost and never gained. (This, however, is a matter for discussion that I will postpone until Chapter 5.) In such a conception, if honor is not properly protected by honorable actions, it can be diminished or polluted. Personal honor is also not a transferable good.

The public or positional and the personal conceptions of honor are not incompatible. Achilles seems motivated by both, and appeals to him to end his campaign of revenge against Agamemnon incorporate elements of both. For example, Patroclus pleads with him as the Trojans are driving the Greeks back to their ships: "My lord Achilles, noblest of the Achaeans; do not grudge me these tears. The army is indeed in terrible distress. All our former champions are lying by their ships, wounded by arrows or spears . . . Surgeons are attending them with all the remedies at their command, and while they try to heal their wounds, you, Achilles, remain intractable. Heaven preserve me from the vindictive feelings you cherish, warping a noble nature to ignoble ends. What will future generations have to thank you for, if you will not help the Argives in their direst need? Pitiless man, you are no son of Thetis and the gallant Peleus. Only the gray sea and its frowning crags could have produced a monster so hard-hearted" (*The Iliad,* Book XVI).

The primary point of Patroclus's appeal, of course, is to the personal conception of honor that he believes Achilles is in severe danger of diminishing by his continued insistence on "one-upping" Agamemnon in the duel of positional public honor. Of special note is the personal conception of honor that prevails in the second act of vengeance undertaken by Achilles. In it, Achilles does not so much risk rank or position, as he responds to a personal responsibility to revenge (which is not to say that had he shrunk from the task of fighting Hector he would not have lost positional honor as well, in that case to Hector). If he were not to respond as the great warrior he is where revenge is expected, his personal honor (his nobility) would have been lost, but, as is often the case in our literary tradition, the cost of doing so is exceedingly high.

The second target of Achilles' vengeance is Hector, the greatest of the Trojan warriors. Patroclus entered the battle at the ships, with Achilles' permission, wearing the armor of Achilles and leading the Myrmidons. Achilles, however, had instructed him not to try to reach the walls of the city no matter how successful he might prove to be in driving back the Trojans, who no doubt would mistake Patroclus for the dreaded Achilles himself. Of course, Patroclus, heady with victory, does not heed the warning and is eventually killed by Hector, who appropriates Achilles' armor. Upon learning of the fate of his dearest friend, Achilles vows to take revenge on Hector, quite a different matter of vengeance than in the case of Agamemnon. Achilles does not feel a deep sense of injustice that Hector has killed Patroclus and more likely blames himself for letting his friend take the field in his stead. His vow presumes little of unfair deprivation with respect to the division of goods, though there is the matter of the lost armor that had been given to Achilles by his father.

Still, Achilles' vow is not to recover the armor, and in any event, he is outfitted with even more glorious armor that his mother arranges for Hephaestus to fashion for him. Achilles does not feel inferior to Hector or powerless with respect to him. In fact, he knows himself to be, and with good reason, the superior warrior of the two, and after all he is virtually invincible. In fact, his revenge mission aside, if this were just another skirmish between the armies, his status as the greatest of the Greek warriors would have required him to seek out Hector, the best the Trojans had to offer, in combat. Positional honor would require it. But this is not to be just another encounter between great warriors engaged in a larger military enterprise. It is a matter of blood revenge, the most basic and historically most important of the types of revenge in the Western cultural tradition. Achilles understands that the death of his friend requires the reciprocal death of Patroclus's killer, and that he must be the avenger. In fact, Achilles will not be satisfied with just the death of Hector. He will, he proclaims, also sacrifice twelve Trojan nobles in front of the funeral pyre of Patroclus. A death for a death is insufficient. Vengeance demands more.

Such escalating retaliatory responses to a killing pose moral and legal problems. The prospect of spiraling cycles of revenge with ever greater numbers of dead exacted at each instance apparently was a prime motivation for the talion law found in so many ancient law codes. How much is too much? What is enough? As J. L. Austin wrote in an entirely different context, "Enough is enough, it isn't everything."[12] Why thirteen deaths to avenge Patroclus? Why not thirty? Three hundred? What is enough?

The talion principle seems first to have appeared in the Code of Hammurabi. An application is found in section 229: "If a builder constructed a house, but did not make his work strong, with the result that the house which he built collapsed and caused the death of the owner of the house, that builder shall be put to death." In the biblical book of Exodus, the familiar formula is found: "If . . . hurt is done, then you shall give life for life, eye for eye, tooth for tooth, hand for hand, foot for foot, burn for burn, bruise for bruise, wound for wound" (Exod., 21:23–24).

Some legal historians view the talion principle *(lex talionis)* as barbaric, which, however, is something of a misunderstanding of its role in ancient legal systems. The talion principle played the part of a limiting or braking device on revenge-taking. The principle, as Hans Boecker notes, "originated in the administration of justice characteristic of nomadic tribes."[13] Its primary purpose was to control the extent of retaliatory response regardless of the tribal affiliations of the avenger and the target of vengeance. It says "only one life for a life, only one eye for an eye, only one tooth for a tooth, etc." Achilles, of course, will have none of that. To carry out his vow to avenge Patroclus, the deaths of at least thirteen Trojan nobles will be required. (The issue of revenge restraint, or proper proportionality, will be of concern in Chapter 7.)

Achilles' second act of revenge illustrates another very important element in the emerging picture of vengeance in Western thought: Homer brings the demands of responsibility to vengeance. Achilles must face a devastating choice before embarking on his mission of revenge. Quite simply, his death is the price of vengeance. This is not the mere risk of death that any warrior might court in facing a foe of Hector's ability and character. Achilles says to his mother, the goddess Thetis, "I have no wish to live and linger in the world of men, unless, before all else, Hector is felled by my spear and dies, paying the price for slaughtering Menoetius' son." This sounds like the boast of a warrior who we know, and he knows, is virtually invulnerable. After all, his mother dipped him in the River Styx, and all but his famous heels were protected from mortal wounds. But Thetis immediately responds to him, "If this is so, my child, you surely have not long to live; for after Hector's death you are doomed forthwith to die." Achilles, without pause, accepts his fate and tells her: "Then let me die forthwith . . . since I have failed to save my friend from death. He has fallen, far from his motherland, wanting my help in his extremity . . . I will go now and seek out Hector, the destroyer of my dearest friend. As for my death, when Zeus and the other deathless gods appoint it, let it come . . . But for the moment, glory is my aim. I will make these Trojan women and deep-bosomed daughters of Dardanus wipe the tears from their tender cheeks with both their hands as they raise the dirge, to teach them just how long I have been absent from the war. And you, Mother, as you love me, do not try to keep me from the field. You will never hold me now" (*The Iliad,* Book XVIII).

Achilles accepts his own death as the price of his revenge. Within the Greek conception of Fate, of course, one might think that this acceptance comes to no more than admitting that one cannot alter one's destiny. But there is far more to it than that for Achilles. Homer does not include in the *Iliad* the story that Achilles, before the expedition against Troy, learned that he was fated to die soon after he killed Hector and tried to avoid being enlisted in Agamemnon's force. There is, however, a hint of the issue in Patroclus's appeal to Achilles to rejoin the fighting. Patroclus wonders, "Is it possible that you are secretly deterred by some prophecy, some word from Zeus that your lady Mother has disclosed to you?" But within the *Iliad* Achilles learns from his mother only that "Fate has given you so short a life, so little time. But it seems that you are not only doomed to an early death but to a miserable life."

Later, however, Achilles tells the princes that came to "mend the fences" between him and Agamemnon: "My divine Mother, Thetis of the Silver Feet, says that Destiny has left two courses open to me on my journey to the grave. If I stay here and play my part in the siege of Troy, there is no home-coming for me, though I shall win undying fame. But if I go home to my own country, my good name will be lost, though I shall have a long life, and shall be spared an early death" (*The Iliad,* Book IX). If Thetis had said this to him, she would have been lying. She knew that Fate had destined him for a short life and had told him so. So he is lying to the princes when he leads them to think that he has a choice of a short or long life. In any event, Achilles accepts his destiny as the price he must pay to avenge the death of his friend. By accepting his fate, he makes it his own, taking responsibility for both the act of revenge and for its consequence: his own early death. He embraces his fate, does not resist it, and is not merely dragged along by it. In a world of Fate, this is the only way to be personally responsible, Nietzsche's "amor fati."[14]

Is Greek fatalism compatible with responsibility? I have argued elsewhere[15] that Harry Frankfurt's attack on the principle of alternate possibilities (PAP)[16] provides the grounds for reconciling fatalistic beliefs with the assignment of responsibility. Frankfurt's way of attacking PAP is to offer a number of counterexamples that depend on overdetermination. His examples are cases in which the circumstances make an outcome inevitable, yet they are not the cause of the outcome. Consider this account of Achilles' situation: Achilles decides for reasons of his own (his love of Patroclus) to avenge the death of Patroclus by killing Hector. However, if Achilles had decided not to avenge Patroclus but to commit suicide, the gods would have prevented his suicide and would have made sure that he killed Hector. In other words, Achilles cannot avoid killing Hector. He is fated to kill Hector to avenge Patroclus, and, we could add, he is fated to die shortly afterward. Could Achilles be responsible for killing Hector, in some more or less full-blown sense of responsibility, even though he had no alternative to doing so? Achilles will kill Hector, and he will do so either because he decided to do so or because the gods caused him to do so. In no case will he fail to avenge Patroclus by killing Hector.

The fact that Achilles could not have avoided killing Hector is a sufficient condition of his having done so. However, as Homer tells the story, that fact plays no role in explaining why he killed Hector. Someone "may do something in circumstances that leave no alternative to doing it, without those circumstances . . . playing any role . . . in bringing it about that he does what he does."[17] Achilles certainly was not motivated by the fact that he was fated to kill Hector; he was out to avenge Patroclus.

Fate is irrelevant to the responsibility status of Achilles' actions because Fate is irrelevant to explaining or accounting for his actions. That Achilles could not avoid avenging Patroclus by killing Hector does not help us understand what made him do it. Achilles tells his mother exactly why he is bent on avenging Patroclus, and Fate never enters into his explanation. Frankfurt's way of putting this is: "The fact that a person could not have avoided doing something is a sufficient condition of his having done it. But . . . this fact may play no role whatever in the explanation of why he did it . . . If someone had no alternative to performing a certain action but did not perform it because he was unable to do otherwise, then he would have performed exactly the same action even if he could have done otherwise . . . Thus it would have made no difference, so far as concerns his action or how he came to perform it, if the circumstances that made it impossible for him to avoid performing it had not prevailed."[18]

Certainly, in ascribing responsibility, we should not place much weight on a fact that is irrelevant to explaining a person's behavior. Typically we think that what matters are the reasons why a person did something, and the consideration of reasons is not incompatible with the fatalist's doctrine that whatever happens was unavoidable. Fatalism is not a causal theory or a theory about how things actually occur in the sequences they do. It is neutral with respect to how an action or event comes to happen. Suppose that the Fates or the gods know before any event that it will happen and how it will happen and even why it will happen. Such knowledge is not the cause or the reason why human actions happen as they do, why Achilles did what he did, although the Fates ensure that he will not do otherwise.

The fatalist will maintain that the reasons Achilles had to avenge Patroclus by killing Hector were also unavoidable by him. That does not make them any less Achilles' reasons for acting. In effect, Fate plays no significant role in whether or not Achilles should be held responsible for avenging Patroclus by killing Hector. He was fated to kill him, so he would have even if he had not chosen that course. The crucial fact is that even when told by his mother that he will die shortly after he succeeds in killing Hector, he proclaims that he will go and seek him out: "Glory is my aim." And he, rather remarkably for a fatalist, warns his mother, who is after all a goddess, not to try to interfere and stop him from his chosen task. How could she, for even Zeus is unable to prevent what Fate ordains?

A final point about vengeance in the *Iliad:* When Achilles and Hector meet beneath the walls of Troy in single combat, Hector tries to make a deal with Achilles about how the winner will treat the body of the loser. Achilles grimly refuses to agree to anything Hector proposes and concludes the conversation with the following: "So summon any courage you may have. This is the time to show your spearmanship and daring. Not that anything is going to save you now, when Pallas Athene is waiting to fell you with my spear. This moment you are going to pay the full price for all you made me suffer when your lance mowed down my friends." And when he has struck the fatal blow, Achilles pronounces over the dying Hector: "No doubt you fancied as you stripped Patroclus that you would be safe. You never thought of me: I was too far away. You were a fool. Down by my hollow ships there was a man far better than Patroclus in reserve, the man who has brought you so low. So now the dogs and birds of prey are going to maul and mangle you, while we Achaeans hold Patroclus' funeral" (*The Iliad,* Book XXII).

Revenge is a very personal matter, and when it is inflicted, it is important that the target grasp the reason why. If the target does not know that he or she is paying the penalty because of his or her specific prior harming or injuring of someone or of the avenger himself or herself, the act of revenge has misfired. Revenge, as will be discussed in Chapter 3, is, in very large measure, an act of communication. Hector may be just as dead, but Achilles would not have gotten vengeance. Hector must understand that Achilles is killing him for the sake of vengeance, that this is no ordinary battlefield meeting between two superb warriors. By the same token, it would not be revenge if, after he killed Patroclus, Hector were killed during a skirmish by a blow from an ordinary Greek soldier (even a Myrmidon), or if a Trojan arrow, aimed at a Greek warrior, were to fall shy of its target and find the opening in Hector's armor "at the gullet where the collar bones lead over from the shoulders to the neck, the easiest place to kill a man."

Vengeance takes center stage in the great Greek tragedies. I want to focus on only two that, for my purposes, extended the development of the concept in our culture. There is a party line in much of the writing and teaching about the *Oresteia* that its theme is the transition from the age of vengeance to that of justice.[19] Although true to an extent, what actually occurs in Aeschylus's trilogy does not really pose revenge against justice. Instead certain forms of vengeance are legitimized.

The trilogy recounts the revenge cycles of the House of Atreus. Two strands of vengeance join in the first play, *Agamemnon,* when Aegisthus, the only surviving child of Thyestes, and Clytaemnestra, the wife of Agamemnon, unite to kill the victorious returning commander of the Greek forces from the ten-year Trojan War. Aegisthus's motive is retaliation against Agamemnon, the son of Aegisthus's uncle, Atreus. Atreus had avenged the seduction of his wife by his brother, Thyestes, by killing all but one of Thyestes' children and feeding them to their father at a banquet. (The all-but-one theme, thus making the vengeance possible, reoccurs. Remember Zeus's escape from Kronos's dinner menu.)

Clytaemnestra is determined to avenge the death of her daughter Iphigenia, who Agamemnon sacrificed at Aulis to gain a favorable passage for the Greek ships bound for Troy. Clytaemnestra carries out the assassination of Agamemnon while he is in his bath. Aegisthus, who in the Aeschylus version does not participate in the actual slaying of Agamemnon, rejoices in the revenge: "Justice brought me home . . . I reached out and seized my man, link by link I clamped the fatal scheme together. Now I could die gladly, even I—now I see this monster in the nets of Justice" (*Agamemnon,* 1639–1643).

The second play, *Choephori* or *The Libation Bearers,* transfers the cycle of vengeance to the next generation. Orestes, Agamemnon's son, returns to Argos and discovers that his father has been murdered by his mother and that she and Aegisthus, from the hated other half of the family, are ruling the city. The god Apollo commands Orestes to kill his mother in reprisal. Overcoming his reluctance to commit matricide, he kills both her and Aegisthus. He is then set upon by the Furies and driven temporarily mad.

In the third play, *The Eumenides,* Orestes is pursued to Apollo's shrine at Delphi where Apollo purifies him of bloodguilt for the matricide, but Apollo cannot free him from the curse of the Furies. To achieve that result he must travel to Athens and gain the support of Athena. He does so, and Athena conducts a trial, the Areopagus, using ten Athenian citizens as her jury. The Furies act as prosecutors, and Apollo acts for the defense. The jury vote ends in a tie. Athena breaks the tie and frees Orestes from the curse of the vengeance cycle, the hounding of the Furies. She then convinces the Furies to become benevolent patrons of Athens and renames them the Eumenides, the Kindly Ones. Everything seems to turn out fine. In fact, the ending is rather reminiscent of the finales of Busby Berkeley or George M. Cohan musicals or Gilbert and Sullivan's *The Pirates of Penzance,* filled with "ain't we terrific" chauvinism.

Robert Fagles and W. B. Stanford, in "The Serpent and the Eagle: A Reading of 'The Oresteia,'" claim that the trilogy is a "rite of passage from savagery to civilization."[20] Fagles and Stanford (like too many literary critics to suit my tastes) wax on to greater and greater depths of painful hyperbole about the Aeschylean achievement. They write, for example: "*The Eumenides* sweeps us through a phantasmagoria of light and dark, of darkness breeding light, until the night brings forth torches of our triumph, like the torches of that Fury Clytaemnestra, 'glorious from the womb of Mother Night.' Night and day are the mother and daughter, suffering and the illumination it can bring. For the energy of the Furies is as great with order as the energy of Dionysus. They are his wild maenads gathering moral force. They are the Mean Dynamic. So they will become if we embrace them."[21] Does that description cast light or darkness on the play? My concern is that if one cannot make the theme and the elements of the play clearer to the reader than the playwright did within the text, little or nothing is accomplished by further obfuscating the work in purple prose. In any event, the attention of these authorities on the works of Aeschylus is clearly focused on the progression from tribal revenge to the celebration of Athenian jurisprudence on which the audience is taken by the playwright. Matters of vengeance move from the familial to the civil. Certainly there is much in the trilogy to commend such a reading.

Perhaps the most important element of the third play is that retaliation becomes a public issue to be decided by a representative jury of citizens. This aspect parallels the growth of the pollution doctrine that is utilized by Plato in the *Laws*. The idea was that a crime, especially a murder, even one committed within a family and behind closed doors, pollutes the community and becomes, thereby, a matter for the community to address. When I first encountered the pollution doctrine in ancient law texts, it struck me as a very primitive notion, relying on weird ideas, like *miasma,* that bring to mind images of a dank brown stench hanging over a town causing citizens to contract some virulent strain of influenza. But for the Greeks (and the Hebrews), the pollution doctrine was actually a significant step in *social*izing or *civil*izing vengeance. It made private, or family, murder everyone's concern, blazing the way for the criminal law to treat murder as a crime against society and thus for the public prosecution of those accused of the act. It should be noted, however, that the Furies, the wild goddesses of punishment for crimes against kin, only beset Orestes in Aeschylus's trilogy; they do not descend upon and infest and pollute the town of Argos, as do their counterparts, the flies, in Sartre's version of the story.[22] Hence there may be some legitimate concern about the publicity of the murder for which Orestes is tried and, most certainly, about the jurisdiction of an Athenian court in the matter.

The Eumenides provides some of the more interesting elements of the way vengeance takes shape (matures?) in our culture. Early in the play, Apollo confronts the Furies and tries to drive them away from Orestes and his shrine. "Go where heads are severed, eyes gouged out, where Justice and bloody slaughter are the same," he tells them. Obviously, he intends to draw a distinction between (at least idealized) justice and blood-feud vengeance, but the Furies respond by accusing him of instigating the revenge of Orestes, the murders of Clytaemnestra and Aegisthus: "Lord Apollo, now is your time to listen. You are no mere accomplice in this crime. You did it all, and all the guilt is yours . . . You commanded the guest to kill his mother." (Matricide and violation of the guest/host relationship were among the most heinous crimes an ancient Greek could commit.) Apollo corrects them: "Commanded him to avenge his father, what of it?"

Apollo, as he will do again at the Athenian trial, takes up the side of masculine vengeance against feminine revenge. The Furies are the avengers of kinship murders, crimes of blood. Clytaemnestra's assassination of Agamemnon was not a crime of blood, a destruction of one's flesh and blood, because she was only married to him. Of course, Clytaemnestra killed Agamemnon in retaliation for what was clearly a killing of her flesh and blood: the sacrifice of Iphigenia. She was then playing the part of the Furies. No wonder they have an affinity for her cause. Her act was an instance of the oldest form of justifiable homicide, revenge for a blood murder. If, as Athena will later rule, Orestes is to be acquitted for blood revenge, committing matricide to avenge the killing of his father, one would think that Clytaemnestra should have had at least a comparable exemption. In fact, her actions should be less reprehensible, and are in the eyes of the Furies, as she retaliated against a nonblood relative for the killing of her flesh and blood. Orestes killed a blood relative to avenge a blood relative. Had Orestes avenged the killing of his sister by killing his father, getting to him before Clytaemnestra, would he not have also committed blood revenge by killing a blood relative? Would he have been acquitted by Athena's court? Such logic, of course, did not move the playwright.

Marongiu and Newman, following the standard interpretation, maintain that the trial of Orestes "produces the early recognition in Western culture of 'moral suffering' as a means of atoning for a wrongful act. It marks the beginning of the idea of expiation, a central theme of many modern notions of vengeance that we call 'retribution.'"[23] The idea seems to be that the acquittal of Orestes, by acknowledging his atonement, moves the concept of punishment from a concern over the act to a concern about the person who committed the act. This sort of analysis of the play seems to me a bit too hasty. What is meant by "moral suffering" and has Orestes undergone it? Has he done sufficient penance, made suitable amends, adequately redeemed himself? Could anyone, having done what he did? Has he really *morally* suffered or *morally* suffered enough? Certainly Orestes suffered for murdering his mother by being hounded by the Furies, and earlier he went through a certain amount of mental anguish when he was convinced by Apollo and Electra to carry out the deed. But is any of that moral suffering? And even if it is, is it sufficient to expiate him from the crime and its punishment? The Furies do not think so.

What would we expect to uncover in a criminal to indicate that he or she had undergone moral suffering? Typically, we look for signs of sorrow and regret. Aristotle maintained that such emotions were essential to mitigating responsibility because they indicated the involuntary nature of the action (NE 1110b). But when the leader of the Furies interrogates Orestes about whether Apollo drove him to the killing of his mother, Orestes responds: "Yes, and to this hour I have no regrets." In fact, Orestes never talks of sorrow or regret at having committed matricide. His entire defense throughout the trial is to justify his killing of his mother. When describing to Athena how Apollo spurred him on, he makes it clear that he was far more concerned about the "pains I'd feel unless I acted" than he was the moral suffering he would endure after committing the murder. If the play does introduce the concern for the person who committed the crime into the judicial mix, it certainly does not do so at the cost of lessening the concern for the crime itself.

It is of further note that the trial never concerns itself with the killing of Aegisthus. That is, apparently, countenanced as a legitimate act of vengeance, although the victim is Orestes' blood kin, albeit only a second cousin. When he shows the bodies of his mother and her consort to the Chorus, Orestes says: "Aegisthus, why mention him? The adulterer dies. An old custom, justice." The idea seems to be that the killing of an adulterer was permitted by ancient custom and that no further retaliation was to be forthcoming. But if that is so, his mother was also an adulterer. And it should not be forgotten that Agamemnon was a philanderer who returned to Argos with one of his Trojan "conquests," Cassandra, thereby further infuriating his already vengeful wife. Is Aegisthus killed merely because of his commission of adultery? Or is that charge raised after the fact to remove the murder of Aegisthus from the indictment for which Orestes will stand trial? In any event, Aeschylus shows himself prepared to admit certain forms of vengeance without the need of civil proceedings to legitimize them, for example, the slaying by a son of the man who cuckolded his dead father. Is this an indication of a preference for masculine over feminine revenge in classical Greece, one that has been woven into our own culture and exploited in a number of Westerns and in such films as *Thelma and Louise*?

The case goes forth in the court of Athena in a ludicrous fashion. It would be comic were it not for the implications about vengeance that arise and that have found a home in our collective understanding of the concept. Apollo takes up the defense of Orestes, making the claim that Zeus is more concerned about the death of a man than a woman. In a famous passage that drips with misogyny, Apollo states: "The woman you call the mother of the child is not the parent, just a nurse to the seed, the new-sown seed that grows and swells inside her. The man is the source of life—the one who mounts. She, like a stranger, for a stranger, keeps the shoot alive unless god hurts the roots. I give you proof that all I say is true. The father can father forth without a mother. Here she stands, our living witness. Look—(he exhibits Athena)." Apollo's "logic" is that, as the mother is only a nurse to the child, she is not flesh and blood and so the matricidal act of Orestes is not a blood killing. On the same logic, however, the only blood killing in the sequence would have been Agamemnon's sacrificial murder of Iphigenia, and that is what Clytaemnestra was avenging.

Athena calls upon the jury to vote. Then she addresses Orestes and, more or less, gives away the outcome. "Orestes," she says, "I will cast my lot for you. No mother gave me birth. I honor the male, in all things but marriage. Yes, with all my heart I am my Father's child. I cannot set more store by the woman's death— she killed her husband, guardian of their house. Even if the vote is equal, Orestes wins." The vote of the jurors is equal, and Orestes walks away from the court free of the Furies and the bloodguilt for his mother's murder. Leaving aside the convenience of the tie that allows Athena to reconcile the Furies to the citizens of Athens and paves the way for her to turn them into kindly guardians of her city, the outcome clearly endorses male vengeance over female vengeance. Agamemnon killed his daughter, yet Athena will "set little or no store" by the avenger, Clytaemnestra, for two reasons: (1) she is a woman, and (2) to perform the act of revenge she must kill not only a man but her husband, the guardian of their house. Should Iphigenia's killing have gone unrevenged, perhaps because she was a female?

Fagles and Stanford valiantly try to rescue Aeschylus. With respect to Athena's judgment they write, "She may say, in effect, the murder of a husband by a wife is worse than the murder of a mother by a son, and so she may lend support to the ties of marriage, a civil institution, rather than the ties of blood."[24] That account, however, is not consistent with Athena's statement that she favors the male in all things except marriage. They go on to suggest that she really does not justify Orestes' act of matricide but only prefers it over his mother's killing of his father. Her judgment is one of "negative preference." Again, that analysis bends over backward to avoid the obvious: Aeschylus did not regard acts of vengeance performed by women as on a moral par with male revenge. Susan Jacoby is on target when she writes that "Aeschylus' *Eumenides* is more a dissertation on which forms of vengeance are sanctioned by the Olympian religion and which are not; it is also an explicit statement of civilized misogyny, equating female vengeance with slyness and male vengeance with justice."[25] Athena simply endorses the patriarchy of the Greek social system when she excuses Orestes. But the Greek view of feminine vengeance is taken much further in Euripides' *Medea*.

Medea murders her children as an act of revenge against Jason, her husband. Medea had aided Jason in the capture of the Golden Fleece and betrayed her family and homeland to save his life. She returns with him to Corinth and bears him two sons. Then he leaves her for a younger woman, a trophy wife, daughter of the king. Any children he has with his new wife would inherit the Corinthian throne. Medea has no legal or social recourse in Corinth, and Jason goes so far as to tell her that she should be happy with her situation because it is far better to be an abandoned wife in Greece than a princess in the savage lands of her birth. Medea can take no more of this treatment, and she murders not only her sons but Jason's second wife as well. She will not be treated as a mere chattel despite the social organization and legal structure of Corinth. Her barbaric origins, for the Greek audience, may have accounted for the viciousness of Medea's revenge, the heartlessness of the slayings. What can you expect from a savage?

Euripides, however, was doing much more than entertaining with the shock value of young male corpses strewn on the stage and the image of the princess of

Corinth burned to death in a magical robe. He was making it clear that, in a social scheme where women and wives are denied the opportunity of retribution for "crimes" against them, acts of vengeance are their only recourse, no matter how gruesome the outcome, and that there is a certain moral justice in their acting accordingly. In *Medea,* Euripides plays on the terror that the audience no doubt experiences from witnessing the lengths to which the disenfranchised, vengeance-minded female can go to rectify her perception of injustice. Medea is not only the quintessential woman scorned, but she is also a woman with nowhere to turn for redress but to her own murderous resources. She will be a model for feminine vengeance throughout the centuries, and one that is utilized in a number of female Westerns, such as *Hannie Caulder.*

Medea, of course, gains revenge on Jason, not in the manner of Clytaemnestra, by killing him, but by killing innocent children. Proportionality, at the very least, should be an issue. She also apparently gets away with it, making the message louder and clearer that revenge is at least permissible when the injured party has no other civil or social means of restitution. That message might well be directed not only at women but at any other marginalized group. It may be of some interest that within the Greek myths on which the play is based, Jason, in the aftermath of Medea's revenge, never recovers his status in society. There are different accounts of his utter downfall, but the most appropriate, at least the most ironic, has him, reduced to a bum, falling asleep under the remains of his once glorious ship, the *Argo,* and dying when a rotten plank falls on him.

The Mosaic code sanctioned personal revenge in a way that the Greeks, at least in Aeschylus's *The Eumenides,* clearly did not. Vengeance for the Hebrews was, it seems, more closely aligned with the communal pollution doctrine than it was in classical Greece. A killing shed blood into the soil and polluted the entire Hebrew community. The text tells the Hebrews that a murderer is not to be pitied: "Thou shalt put away the guilt of innocent blood from Israel, that it may go well with thee" (Deut. 19:13). A polluted community can only regain prosperity, be purified, by executing the murderer, and avengers of blood were granted the right, at least tacitly, to carry out the killings. It is unclear from Deuteronomy whether the avenger of blood was always a kin of the victim or whether the role became a professional one paid for by the family of the victim, a precursor of *Have Gun, Will Travel.* In any case, the elders of the city in which a murderer is hiding from an avenger of blood are instructed to "send and fetch him thence, and deliver him into the hands of the avenger of blood, that he may die." But the Hebrews placed an important restriction on the revenge that can be taken against a killer. Yahweh ordered the building of three cities (later to be increased to six when Israel expanded its own borders) distributed strategically throughout the land. These were to be cities of refuge for killers who killed "ignorantly" and who did not hate their victims before the slaying occurred.

The text takes pains to clarify what is meant by "ignorantly." We would probably use the term "unintentionally" or "accidentally" or "inadvertently." An example is provided: a person is chopping down a tree when the axe head flies off the handle and strikes and kills his neighbor. Blood has been spilled and vengeance on the part of the family of the victim is in order. An avenger of blood will be dispatched to kill the woodsman, but if the slayer is able to avoid the avenger and reach a city of refuge, he achieves sanctuary. Presumably, the avenger of blood will arrive at the city and ask the elders to produce the slayer. At that point, the elders of the city apparently must make a decision regarding whether or not the killing was done in ignorance and without previous hatred. We are not provided with how such a determination is to be reached, whether a trial of sorts is conducted, what sort of evidence is acceptable, and so on. What is clear is that the cities of refuge were created to prevent vengeance from occurring where the killing was "innocent," to prevent further innocent blood from being spilled on the soil and thereby polluting the land and the people.

The Mosaic code sanctioned vengeance while controlling it. It was not, as the talion law earlier stated in the Book of the Covenant in Exodus required, a life for a life. Instead was a life for a life that was not taken innocently, accidentally, or inadvertently. The cities of refuge conception is, then, a rather remarkable modification of the principles of *lex talionis*. It requires a determination of what we today would call intent, *mens rea,* before vengeance is sanctioned. On the other hand, it also makes clear that there is an absolute responsibility that falls on the family of the victim to avenge murder or the entire community will be cursed with pollution. No distinctions are drawn between types or kinds of intentional murders. The killing of a husband by a wife is not rated as worse than the killing of a mother by a son, for example. All intentional murders are proper causes of personal vengeance.

A number of biblical scholars have noted that although Yahweh places restrictions on the use of personal revenge by the Hebrews against each other, the general theme of the Bible is Yahweh's unlimited vengeance against the people of Israel when they commit acts of infidelity against him. Jacoby writes: "For the Jews of Biblical times, their position as the chosen people was accompanied by frequent, arbitrary displays of Yahweh's anger—a vindictiveness that was both collective and hereditary, punishing the innocent and the guilty alike. Yahweh was rarely as selective as he was in preserving Noah and Lot; most of the time, the just and the unjust perished together."[26]

Despite the traditional conception of unbounded communal and hereditary vengeance by Yahweh, the prophet Ezekiel assured his listeners of a more discerning divinity. The person, he claims, "that hath executed my judgments, hath walked in my statutes; he shall not die for the iniquity of his father, he shall surely live . . . The soul that sinneth, it shall die. The son shall not bear the iniquity of the father, neither shall the father bear the iniquity of the son: the righteousness of the righteous shall be upon him, and the wickedness of the wicked shall be upon him" (Ezek. 18:14–20). Ezekiel, in the face of the evidence of the Babylonian exile, seemed determined to convince his audience that Yahweh's vengeance would be as restricted to merit as was their taking of personal revenge. There is, after all, some sense to the analogy, because the relationship between Yahweh and the chosen people is always described in intensely personal terms, cycling from vengeance to forgiveness and restoration and back again to vengeance.

Within the Christian tradition, we typically are told that vengeance is to be reserved for God, which is a puzzling sentiment on a number of counts. In the first instance, the Christian God is usually described as all good, the very paradigm of virtue. If vengeance is an acceptable divine activity, it must not be incompatible with virtue; Jeffrie Murphy makes this point.[27] Perhaps more interesting, Saint Paul writes to the Romans: "Dearly beloved, avenge not yourselves, but rather give place unto wrath, for it is written, Vengeance is mine; I will repay, saith the Lord." He continues; "Therefore if thine enemy hunger, feed him; if he thirst, give him drink" (Rom. 12:19–20). That sounds as if revenge is a divine prerogative. Humans must "turn the other cheek," an admonition made by Jesus during the Sermon on the Mount. However, Saint Paul is not finished, adding, "for in so doing thou shalt heap coals of fire on his head." Now it looks as if the kindly acts of feeding one's hungry enemy and providing drink to him when he is thirsty are actually ways of taking revenge against him, that is, "heaping coals of fire on his head."

Perhaps all Saint Paul is doing is recommending a safe way of avenging oneself against one's enemies, given the fact that they are likely to be more powerful in the Roman society. One idea might be that, by providing drink and food to them when they have injured you, you will confound them. They will start to worry about why they are receiving succor from those they have harmed and they will feel bad, a form of self-inflicted punishment. Saint Paul calls that approach overcoming evil with good. Even if that is the real thrust of the message, the counsel is that vengeance is a good thing, an appropriate thing, morally and religiously, and the only important issue is one that focuses on the best means to accomplish it under the circumstances.

By the age of Dante, the Christians had sculptured and reformed the concept of vengeance into one with more moral power than even the ancient Greeks had conceived. *Lex talionis* became *contrapasso*. Dante's incredibly bizarre and seemingly inexhaustible imagination produced, in his vision of the deepest circle of Hell, an image of the Christian concept of revenge that likely would leave even Euripides dumbfounded.[28] The ninth circle of Hell is a frozen lake, Cocytus, in which Dante views the damned as they are "shrined in ice." He comes upon two heads that are "pent in one hollow, that the head of one was cowl unto the other; and as bread is raven'd up through hunger, the uppermost did so apply his fangs to the other's brain, where the spine joins it" (*Divine Comedy*, 136). What we have here is one man furiously eating the brains of another. Of course, this is Hell, so he will do so eternally. The scene is beyond grotesque, a corner of a Bosch painting, the equal of any Hollywood horror film moment.

Who are they, these macabre characters? The only one who speaks is the ravenous brain devourer. He informs Dante that he is Count Ugolino, and that the brain on which he is feasting is that of Archbishop Ruggieri. Dante probably assumes that his audience is acquainted with the story of the thirteenth-century machinations between the two, but he has the count provide some sketchy information about their part in the conflict in Pisa between the Guelphs and the Ghibellines. Letting the details of that factional matter slide, suffice it to say that Ugolino, who was a Ghibelline, betrayed his family to the Guelphs, but his plot was uncovered and he was exiled. He returned to Pisa when the Guelphs gained the upper hand and was appointed to a powerful public office. Archbishop Ruggieri, who had been Ugolino's friend before the betrayal and later became the leader of the Ghibellines, seized Ugolino and locked him in a tower. The plot sounds like a sequel to *The Godfather*. It is filled with betrayal, family honor, and, of course, revenge.

The count says that while Dante probably knows that he was executed by Ruggieri for his betrayal of the family, Dante may not have heard "how cruel was the murder . . . and know if he have wrong'd me." The tale is that, after a number of months in the tower, Ugolino's two sons and two nephews were locked up with him. They were not fed and soon realized that starvation was to be the means for their execution. The count gnawed at his hands in grief, but the children, thinking he was doing so because he was hungry "cried, 'Father, we should grieve far less, if thou wouldst eat of us.'" This response horrified Ugolino, and he fell into silence for three days. On the fourth day, one of his sons died, and by the sixth day all four children were dead of starvation. Ugolino was by then nearly blind, and he describes himself as wailing and groping about at the four dead bodies in his cell for a few days. "Then, fasting got the mastery of grief" (or in another translation, "Famine did what sorrow could not do"): the count ate the children. (The tale is told in the latter part of canto 32 and the first part of canto 33.)

In Hell, Ugolino is allowed his vengeance by perpetually eating the brain that hatched his own horrible death and that of the four children. But, of course, both the count and the archbishop are frozen in the deepest circle without hope. While the count is enjoying the revenge he is exacting on the archbishop, he is also being punished for his own traitorous sins. Ruggieri, we may assume, though he never speaks, is not relishing any of this, but he probably got a healthy measure of pleasure from having concocted Ugolino's horrific death and that of the four innocent children and having driven the count to cannibalism. Ugolino, however, must feel, and we get a sense of it in his retelling of the events in the tower, that the deaths of those children were also on his head. They would not have been there if he had not played the traitor in the first place. Although there is a certain balance in the meting of the revenge between the two antagonists, the deaths of the four innocent children, like the murder of Jason's children by Medea, tips the scales well past proportional reciprocity.

I want to suggest that Dante's vision, at least in this scenario, is to concretize the Christian concept of fit in vengeance. The punishment fits not only the crime but the criminal as a whole person. Graeme Newman notes: "One must match the despicable criminal sins with the punishments. In other words, one must go beyond the particular offense to the soul of the offender. By this model one is justified in matching the punishment to the criminal's entire person."[29] For Dante, the punishment cannot fit the crime in the strict talion sense because the punishments in Hell are eternal. They can have a qualitative match but never a quantitative one. The episode with Count Ugolino, however, reveals what Dante's conception of revenge really entails. The count, as he endlessly gnaws on the brains of his earthly tormentor, also must reflect on the nature of his sin. The damned cannot avoid reflection on their crimes, because each hellish penalty is arranged to constantly remind them, not always of the specific crime but of the type of criminal activities that have brought them to Hell. Hypocrites, for example, are forced to walk about wearing leaden capes that appear from the outside to be made of gold. In Dante's Hell there is no separation of the punished deed from the character of the person who committed it. Both the count and the archbishop are frozen in the deepest of Hell's circles because theirs were crimes of fraud. Both were traitors, Ruggieri to his friendship with Ugolino and Ugolino to the trust of his family and his city.

Dante breaks the category of sin into three distinct classes, paralleling Aristotle's analysis of three types of evil character: moral weakness, vice (or wickedness), and brutishness. For Dante the three types are incontinence, force, and fraud. Dante writes: "Of all malicious act abhorr'd in heaven, the end is injury; and all such end either by force or fraud works other's woe. But fraud, because of man's peculiar evil, to God is more displeasing; and beneath, the fraudulent are therefore doom'd to endure severer pang ... Three dispositions adverse to Heaven's will, incontinence, malice, and mad brutishness, and how incontinence the least offends God, and least guilt incurs. If well thou note this judgment, and remember who they are, without these walls to vain repentance doom'd, thou shalt discern why they apart are placed from these fell spirits, and less wreakful pours justice divine on them its vengeance down" (canto 11).

Aristotle's evil character types and Dante's sinners virtually match. For both, the incontinent seem the least evil. Aristotle's brutes are, by and large, Dante's sinners of force. The wicked in Aristotle's typology closely (but not quite) and in an important way resemble the fraudulent in the *Inferno*. The crucial difference is that the Christian Dante's conception of evil not only does not exclude membership in the class of the preferentially wicked but also locates a significant number of despicable characters in that class, and it punishes them in the deepest circles of Hell with exquisite forms of revenge.

Ronald Milo[30] suggests that it is helpful to think of Aristotle's distinction between moral weakness and vice in terms of "cases where the agent has good moral principles but fails to act on them and cases where the agent acts on bad moral principles."[31] The first type is typically described as lacking in self-control, Dante's conception of incontinence. The belief states of the agent, however, also are crucial to drawing the distinction between the morally weak and the wicked. The morally weak person believed that what he or she did was wrong. The wicked person, on Aristotle's view, believed incorrectly that what he or she did was right. The wicked person was ignorant of the general moral principles that applied in his or her case, and such ignorance, Aristotle insists, is not exculpatory.

The picture of evil in Aristotle and, I think, Dante, is much more complicated than these distinctions suggest. Imagine that each of Aristotle's three types of evil character is subdivided in terms of the criminal's (or sinner's) belief states with respect to the rightness or wrongness of the actions undertaken. At least six types or classes of evil persons will emerge: persons lacking self-control who believed (wrongly) that what he or she did was the right thing to do; persons lacking self-control who believed that what he or she did was wrong; persons who acted on morally bad preferences or principles believing them to be morally good or right; persons who acted on morally bad principles or preferences believing them to be bad or wrong; persons who acted brutishly believing that what they did was the right or the good thing to do; and persons who acted brutishly while believing that what they did was wrong or bad. The first two types are treated both by Aristotle and Dante as rather less serious than those of brutishness (force) or wickedness (fraud). Brutishness, that is forceful, violent acts of harm against others, might be thought to command greater punishments than acts of deceit, treachery, and treason, but that is certainly not Dante's idea, nor is it Aristotle's.

Aristotle distinguishes between two types of brutishness (NE 1148b), but he says remarkably little on the subject. He tells us that brutishness is typically found in barbarians, where he attributes it to nature. Then he allows that civilized folk may be afflicted with brutishness as a result of habit. His example of the latter is startlingly modern: "when someone has been sexually abused from childhood" (NE 1148b). The idea seems to be that if one is abused as a child, one may develop a brutish disposition that makes such behavior habitual. Aristotle is clear that those who are brutish by nature should not be categorized as morally weak or incontinent. He adds that those who are brutish by habit are also not morally weak of will. It is, however, a morally praiseworthy accomplishment to master one's natural or habitual brutishness. Hence, it is a kind of moral weakness to be under the domination of either kind of brutishness, but it is not the same sort of moral weakness that Aristotle contrasts with wickedness (vice) and brutishness. He draws the distinction in the following way: "It is, accordingly, clear that moral weakness and moral strength operate only in the same sphere as do self-indulgence and self-control, and that the moral weakness which operates in any other sphere is different in kind, and is called 'moral weakness' only by extension, not in an unqualified sense" (NE 1149a).

It seems reasonable to assume that those who are naturally brutish do not believe that what they are doing when behaving brutishly is wrong or bad. Perhaps they never think of what they are doing in moral terms; after all, they are brutes. They are natural amoralists. The habitually brutish do not care that what they are doing when behaving brutishly is not the morally right thing to do. Because of the experiences that ingrained the brutish habit, they are indifferent to the demands of morality, at least over some range of their behavior. Their weakness lies outside, as Aristotle might say, the "sphere of self-indulgence and self-control." It is not as if they are indulging themselves in some desired behavior over which they know or believe they should exercise control. Brutes, whether natural or habitual, just do what they do. Aristotle's examples of natural brutishness, however, are at least as vividly grotesque as Dante's depictions of the stories of the damned. Interestingly, he talks of people who devour their children, but they do so due to natural brutishness, not in the manner of Count Ugolino or even Thyestes. The sheer repulsiveness of an act, he would caution, is never to be confused with a trustworthy sign of its source in natural brutishness or in habitual brutishness, for that matter.

Wickedness takes quite a different description for Aristotle. Following the schema I have suggested above, a person of wicked character is one who acts on morally bad principles and either believes that what he or she did was the right thing to do or believes that it was the wrong thing to do. Aristotle's account, however, requires excluding the second type, while that is the type permanently sequestered in Dante's lower circles of Hell. For Aristotle, because the agent of the evil deed acted in accord with what he or she perversely believes to be good moral principles, he or she does not believe that what was done was wrong or immoral or evil. Ignorance (broadly and variously understood) of the right principles accounts for the perverse belief state. But, insofar as that ignorance is not excusable in the mature person, as noted earlier, that person is held responsible for his or her wicked deeds. Suppose we call this sort of Aristotelian wickedness "perverse wickedness."[32] Its description captures the sense of the Socratic dictum that no one does evil willingly. Plato writes that "Polus and I felt we had no choice but to conclude that no one wants to do wrong, and that every wrong act is done unwillingly."[33]

On one reading of "unwillingly" Aristotle may be taken as attacking the Socratic dictum because he maintains that "wickedness is voluntary" (NE 1113b). By that he means that we are the sources of our own actions and so acting wickedly is not acting inadvertently or accidentally or the like. However, he does make it clear that "every wicked man is in a state of ignorance as to what he ought to do and what he should refrain from doing, and it is due to this kind of error that men become unjust and, in general, immoral" (NE 1110b). Acting in ignorance, of course, is not acting involuntarily or not voluntarily, but it might be understood as unwilling, in that one turns out not to be doing what one believes one is willing oneself to do: the right thing. The ignorance of or mistake in moral principle leads one to do something one would not do if one were not ignorant or mistaken.

Milo notes that the other type of wickedness, the sort that Aristotle does not seem to admit, should be identified with the standard Christian conception of evil. It is certainly Dante's conception of the most wicked. For the Christian, "wickedness consists in knowingly doing what is morally wrong without any compunction or scruple."[34] This sort of wickedness is preferential: doing what is wicked is preferred to doing what is morally right. Typically acting in the wicked fashion is calculated to gain some desired end, and achieving that end is incompatible with behaving in a manner that is consistent with good moral principles that the evildoer may even abide by in some part, or in much, of his or her life. Count Ugolino's desire for wealth and power led him to calculatedly betray his family to the Guelphs. Ruggieri gains his revenge against the count at the intended horrible cost of the killing of four innocent children.

Much of our current thinking about wickedness seems to reflect an Aristotelian rather than a Christian/Dantean conception. Evildoers come off in our media as doing what they do in the belief (albeit a perverse one, probably caused by some condition outside of their control) that it was the right thing to do. Not infrequently, they are described as brimming with righteousness while carrying out atrocities. Some sociological or psychological story and popularized theory will be trotted out to make the perversity of the wrongdoer plausible. Such is our retreat to Aristotle when it comes to wickedness. We seem to think that where evil is concerned, perversion is far easier to understand and to accept than preference.

Perverse wickedness, as Milo notes,[35] can be conceived from either a cognitivist or a noncognitivist perspective, making it more attractive to a legion of moralists. Cognitivists can maintain that "the agent of a perversely wicked act does something that is morally wrong because he is ignorant that acts of this sort are morally wrong and falsely believes that such acts are right."[36] Noncognitivists can tell us that a perversely wicked act "consists in doing what is morally wrong because of one's acceptance of *bad* moral principles."[37]

Either of these accounts might appear to be cogent. Think of a murderer, as revealed on the nightly news broadcast, who raped, tortured, and mutilated his victim before killing her. A noncognitivist would reject the notion that this murderer acted out of ignorance. For the noncognitivist, moral principles are not objects to be known or mistaken about or ignorant of; they are expressions of attitudes. So the noncognitivist will focus full attention on the sort of principles that the murderer holds most deeply. Those, by definition, are his moral principles. Among them we would expect to find some principle that condones or encourages, perhaps even requires, him to rape, torture, and murder women. Now we can understand him. His wickedness is perverse but also—and this is the moral rub—thereby conscientious. On some formalist accounts conscientiousness may be a mark of integrity.[38]

The cognitivist's defense of the possibility of perverse wickedness, on the other hand, will focus on the murderer's ignorance. It is crucial that his ignorance is not what Aristotle would have called an ignorance of particulars (NE 1111a). He cannot be "in the dark" about some important fact or facts of the matter concerning his victim. Were that the case, his behavior might be, to some extent, excusable. Aristotle, for example, maintains that ignorance of the particulars (or at least some of them) may be involuntary and therefore pardonable: "A person who acts in ignorance of a particular circumstance acts involuntarily . . . especially if he is ignorant of the most important factors. The most important factors are the thing or person affected by the action and the result" (NE 1111a). He does add the condition, mentioned earlier in another context, that "an action upon this kind of ignorance is called involuntary, provided that it brings also sorrow and regret in its train" (NE 1111a).

Aristotle's point is that only factual ignorance whose cause is external to the agent is excusable. It is hard to imagine of which particular important circumstances the murderer may be ignorant due to conditions that are external to him. He surely knows that the person on whom he perpetrated the rape/torture/murder is an unwilling woman, and he knows the result of his actions: she is dead. He may not know her name, where she lives, whether she is married, a mother, and so on, but these are less important particular circumstances. If he is ignorant of anything important, it must be moral principles. And that sort of ignorance, Aristotle insists, is not pardonable. His perverse wickedness reflects a bad moral character. In fact, it is precisely because he has a bad moral character that he is ignorant of proper moral principles.

Why, however, should the possession of a bad moral character render him ignorant of moral principles? Milo asks, "If one adopts a purely cognitivist account of the nature of moral beliefs—i.e., if one holds that to believe that a certain act is wrong is to accept as true a proposition to this effect, then how does one explain why having a bad character . . . prevents a person from grasping the truth of this proposition?"[39] What blocks a person with a bad character from granting the truth of propositions to the effect that what he or she is doing, or did, is morally wrong? Aristotelians might say that perversely wicked people are so morally sick that their intellectual capacities are impaired. They are afflicted with a cognitive blindness or cognitive myopia. There is something quite appealing in the imagery, but it really provides no insight into how perverse wickedness (bad character) produces ignorance, or prevents knowledge, of moral principles. If that cannot be explained, then it is conceivable that someone could have a preference for doing something while believing the proposition that the thing preferred is the morally wrong thing to do in the circumstances or under any circumstances. Some people, I am convinced, just do what they prefer doing regardless of the fact that they believe it to be morally wrong or improper. Dante's inhabitants of the frozen lake of Cocytus are, or rather were, such people. There is nothing of incontinence about it. Short of providing a knockdown argument to the effect that such people are not conceivable, the standard cognitivist line on perverse wickedness is not very persuasive.

As Milo notes, the basic problem for a cognitivist's (and, it should be added, a noncognitivist's) conception of perverse wickedness links to the beliefs cognitivists ascribe to the evildoer.[40] Cognitivists must assign to the murderer, for example, beliefs to the effect that it is morally right to rape, torture, and murder women, that committing such atrocities on women is not morally wrong but morally permissible or even morally required. That defense may even sound plausible. How else could he do it? How indeed! To make accounts of this sort plausible, one must maintain that it is possible to believe that there are no kinds of acts such that if one knows what it is for an act to be morally wrong, one *must* believe that acts of that kind are morally wrong. For any act, it must be possible to believe that it is either morally right or morally wrong.

Surely the murderer knew that he was forcing sexual intercourse on, torturing, and killing his victim. If someone knows what it is for an act to be morally wrong, one would think, at least, that the person should also know that acts of that sort are prima facie morally wrong. It is hard to imagine a person who understands what it is for an act to be morally wrong denying the relevance to the moral status of his actions that what he is doing is forced sexual intercourse, torture, and killing. The murderer, we may suppose, has command of a perfectly adequate moral vocabulary. Therefore, I think we need to admit that either he does not care that he acted in violation of moral principles, or that he cares more about performing the immoral and criminal acts he did than about acting in accord with moral principles that forbid such actions.

Aristotle departs from a defense of perverse wickedness because he cannot adopt the position that there are no kinds of acts such that if one knows what it is for an act to be morally wrong, one *must* believe that those acts are morally wrong. He tells us that, for example, there are some types of actions "whose very names connote baseness, e.g., . . . adultery, theft, and murder. These and similar . . . actions imply by their very names that they are bad . . . It is, therefore, impossible ever to do right in performing them: to perform them is always to do wrong. In cases of this sort, let us say adultery, rightness and wrongness do not depend on committing it with the right woman at the right time and in the right manner, but the mere fact of committing such action at all is to do wrong" (NE 1107a).

If Aristotle is correct, and I think he is, then one cannot know both what it means to believe that some action is morally wrong and also believe that raping, torturing, and murdering a defenseless woman is not morally wrong. But this then should have profound effects on Aristotle's conception of wickedness and that of other cognitivists. It would seem that on Aristotle's account, at least where murder, adultery, and theft are concerned, a person cannot be perversely wicked. If you know (or believe) you are committing adultery, for example, you must know (or believe) it is wrong or bad to do it. Only those adulterers who do not know what adultery is, and so do not know that what they are doing is adultery, can be perversely wicked. If you know it is adultery, you know it is wrong to do it. Thus, if you do it, you are preferentially, not perversely, wicked. But there are not supposed to be any preferentially wicked people, because "no one does evil willingly."

Further, if you do not know what it means to believe that some action is morally wrong, you cannot have beliefs about the rightness or wrongness of what you are doing in the first place, so you cannot properly be described as perversely wicked. The most we could say about you is that you (sometimes) just prefer to do things that you should know are morally wrong or bad. Again, that would make you preferentially wicked, not perversely wicked.

Thus, perverse wickedness on a cognitivist's account, despite its original attraction to explain the behavior of people like the murderer on the nightly news report, loses its persuasive power. Cognitivists may have to concede that such evildoers are preferentially wicked, which seems to make them more reprehensible than if they were understood to be perversely wicked. Perhaps cognitivists will opt to shunt them off to Aristotle's habitual brutishness category and leave the lower circles of Hell vacant. But that, I think, would reflect a certain moral spinelessness, a trait that certainly is not legitimately attributable to Dante.

A noncognitivist position might, however, preserve perverse wickedness. Then, at least, we can recognize in some evildoers the potential saving grace of conscientiousness and ascribe to them a pitiable ignorance of the proper moral principles. Noncognitivists hold that "believing an act to be morally wrong consists . . . in having a certain kind of con-attitude towards it."[41] The attitude or the disposition to choose one way rather than another is the extent of the matter. There is, as Milo points out, "nothing to be ignorant of or falsely believe."[42] One's moral principles simply are one's pro or con attitudes toward actions. For the noncognitivist, it may look as if preferential wickedness is not possible, at least as long as choice is determined by pro-attitudes. Only the degenerate or mentally disturbed would act counter to their pro-attitudes. Wickedness should always be perverse. Or so one might be led to think.

In a famous passage encapsulating the noncognitivist's position, Nowell-Smith writes: "If a man consistently, and over a long course of years, tries to get the better of his fellows in all transactions of daily life or if he is never moved by the consequences of his actions for other people, we might say, colloquially, that 'he has no moral principles.' But this clearly means, not that he has no moral principles or that he has good ones and continually succumbs to temptation to act against them, but that he has bad moral principles."[43] Revelation of a person's preferences is revelation of his or her moral principles. And some person's moral principles are perverse.

But an account like Nowell-Smith's overlooks equally acceptable alternative readings of the situation that are still within the scope of noncognitivism. Why should we describe the murderer as having bad moral principles rather than as having morally bad principles? (A point suggested by Milo.[44]) If we adopt the latter reading, then his wickedness is preferential, not perverse, for he is, after all, in either case acting on his preferences, his pro-attitudes. Noncognitivists must call those preferences "his moral principles" and then judge them to be bad ones. Noncognitivists, however, need not maintain that people who are acting on their preferences, their pro-attitudes, must believe that they are doing what is morally right even if they are doing something so despicable as raping, torturing, and murdering. They just might prefer to promote their own ends by doing something they believe to be morally wrong, though not giving a damn that it is. Is that so hard to believe? Dante didn't think so! Of course, if one's dominant pro-attitude is to rape, torture, and murder women, one has extraordinarily perverse preferences.

The noncognitivist's position, like that of the cognitivist, seems doomed to collapse perverse wickedness into preferential wickedness. A noncognitivist, trying to rescue the category of perverse wickedness, might maintain that a person, doing evil deeds because of his or her dominant pro-attitude toward the pursuit of his or her own ends, must believe that he or she is morally bound to do so, that failing to do so would be a serious moral failing. Did Count Ugolino feel that way when committing his traitorous acts? There is, however, as much reason for a noncognitivist to maintain that the evildoer believes that what he or she is doing is morally wrong while preferring it to all other possible actions in the circumstances. Why hang the belief that what he or she is doing is morally right around the neck of the wicked person? Dante and the Christians do not. In fact, what makes a person truly wicked for them is that he or she knows that what he or she is doing is morally wrong and prefers to do it anyway. The noncognitivist's perverse wickedness amounts, it seems, to nothing more than the cognitivist's preferential wickedness, absent the knowledge element. Both have wicked people perversely preferring their own ends even when those ends conflict with such standard moral prohibitions as Do not rape, torture, or murder fellow human beings.

A pathetic naiveté seems to afflict those who believe that if the murderer could have been convinced that he was raping, torturing, and murdering his victim, he would have just stopped doing it. But he knew he was raping, torturing, and murdering, and that is what he preferred doing. He is not that morally ignorant. He is a living moral monster, one who does evil willingly, the possibility of whose existence has been denied by a legion of moral philosophers from ancient times to the present. Yet our history books and our newspapers and our nightly newscasts are replete with accounts of him and his kind.

Preferential wickedness does not have the potentially morally redeeming feature that is typically associated with perverse wickedness: conscientiousness. The preferentially wicked cannot claim that, had they known or believed that what they were doing was wrong, they would have refrained from doing it, that they were just doing what they sincerely believed to be the right thing to do. They knew it was wrong, and they preferred it. Dante rightly treats them as fully morally responsible for the evil they do, and in Hell they receive perfectly appropriate punishments for their immoral behavior. And because they are punished for eternity, they have an unlimited amount of time to reflect on their preferences.

Vengeance, the centerpiece of Dante's Hell, is constructed so as to give the idea of fit a richer sense than the talion law required. The preferentially wicked in the lower circles of Hell are guilty in a much fuller moral sense than the targets of revenge in the Greek myths, epics, and tragedies. Dante's sinners, because they are preferentially wicked, not only did the terrible things for which they are punished; they did them with knowledge that they were doing evil. Each has what in legal parlance is called *mens rea,* a guilty mind. By "guilty mind" I do not mean that they are filled with the sorrow and regret for which Aristotle was looking as signs of mitigation. They performed their wicked deeds because, in the circumstances, that is just what they wanted to do. It is their preferences that have made their minds guilty, not any sorrow or regret that may be a consequence of their surveying of their actions after the fact.

Dante grasps that vengeance cannot be complete, that it cannot truly fit the crime, if the punishment does not respond to both the crime and the guilty mind of the criminal. Taking an eye for an eye, a life for a life, might have no appreciable effect on the guilty mind of the criminal. The exquisitely devised punishments of the deeper circles of Hell are intended to demonstrate the depths of revenge to which an avenger must go to conjoin the crime and the guilty mind, the preference or disposition for wickedness, in an effective way. Achilles tells Hector why he is killing him, and, presumably, Hector has a moment or two to reflect on how he came to such an end. Hector, however, does not have a guilty mind for killing Patroclus, nor should he. The characters in Dante's *Inferno,* however, have eternity to reflect on their wicked preferences in life, and that reflection is a crucial part of their punishment. Without it, the punishment would not fit the crime; vengeance would not be complete.

It is not hard to see why Christians, following the admonition of Saint Paul, might, given Dante's vision of fit, reserve vengeance for the divinity. Only God, it may be assumed, could know enough of the preferences of sinners to concoct eternal punishments that fully fit both their crimes and their guilty minds. Vengeance, fully and completely realized, Dante shows us in the punishments of the fraudulent, is a divine art form. Little wonder that humans have shrunk back to the less creatively demanding rules and procedures of what they call justice to deal with criminality. How much easier it is to treat evil as either perversion, brutishness, or incontinence and to explain it, or explain it away, with the latest fashionable sociopsychological theory, freezing the virtues of vengeance in a Cocytus on that part of the moral conceptual terrain whose maps have been lost.

The literature on the revenge tragedies of the sixteenth and seventeenth centuries is enormous, and I have no intention of adding to it. It should be noted, however, as has Jacoby[45] (among others), that the extraordinary outpouring of domestic vengeance stories dramatized in the period reflects the deep and widespread concern of the time with the control of private and political revenge cycles. The Protestant Reformation and the associated religious wars and rebellions provided strong motivations for revenge-taking. Monarchy was thriving but was threatened regularly by the potential uprising of nobles who might regard the merest royal slight as a pretext for vengeance. Private revenge was in Christian doctrine, as Jacoby writes, "a mortal sin not because of its human consequences but because it usurped the divine prerogative . . . Kings, too, could be guilty of the mortal sin of private vengeance if they acted from personal rather than divinely authorized public motives."[46] But that prohibition, clearly, fueled the fires of vengeance because it is, then as now, extremely difficult to discern whether or not one's cause is personal or public. Also, if the legal mechanisms of the state are ordained to take retribution and they grind exceedingly slowly, or hardly at all, a lifetime could pass without the proper redress of the grievance. God can take an eternity, and often seems to, to get around to meting out punishment where it is deserved. The pleasure of revenge, its sweetness, is deeply rooted in the human psyche, and its repression requires extremely persuasive argument or demonstration. The appeal to God and thereby the casting of it as a mortal sin restrains only to a degree.

The dramatists of the period took up the challenge by, typically, portraying the taker of private revenge as altered in moral stature by his or her acts of vengeance. The avengers in their plays change before the eyes of the audience into creatures as ugly and morally loathsome as those on whom they wreak revenge. Thus, as Jacoby makes clear,[47] although the tragedies of the period are chock-full of all manner of private vengeance, there is more than a hint of the grave moral consequences of taking revenge.

Shakespeare's achievement in his great tragedies is that he so convincingly portrays the internal tension of a person who has ample cause for vengeance and a sense of the enormity of the moral cost of taking it. Lesser playwrights, and there were a fair share of them in the Elizabethan and Jacobean eras, luridly paraded the religious message across the stage—private revenge is divinely forbidden, and those who engage in it suffer the fate of their targets (a message that one could have read in large bold letters from Archbishop Ruggieri's fate in Dante's *Inferno*)—but their dramatic shortcomings are exposed in their inability to evoke the internal tension in the protagonist. The emotional and moral demands of taking revenge wrack the consciences of injured parties and conflict with their acceptance of the validity of the religious prohibition. Shakespeare, perhaps better than anyone else, sustains that tension in his tragic characters and thereby reveals the price, in very personal terms, of taking responsibility for vengeance.

Hamlet is the prime example of what I have in mind. I would not presume to offer anything approaching an analysis of the play. There is, most assuredly, a great deal more in the play than concerns me. My interest is simply to draw out one, but a thematic, element that enriches the story of vengeance in our culture. For my purposes, the most important line in the play is the one uttered by Hamlet after he has been given the assignment to avenge the murder of his father. Hamlet is visited by the ghost of his father and told that his father's death was actually a murder and that his uncle, Claudius, who has subsequently married his mother and claimed the throne of Denmark, was the perpetrator. When the ghost departs, a distraught Hamlet sighs: "The time is out of joint: O cursed spite. That ever I was born to set it right!" In an important sense, of course, Hamlet was born to set things right, and setting them right would have been within the bounds of religiously sanctioned revenge. He is the rightful heir to the Danish crown and should have the full backing of the church and the moral order of the Elizabethans and Jacobeans if he were to instigate public vengeance against the usurper and claim the throne. Shakespeare has us, and Hamlet, overlook this point, and we are set about on a circuitous journey through Hamlet's mind in search of enough proof to justify his assignment, for in another sense, he was not born to set things right. He is far from equal to the task his lineage imposes on him.

According to Jacoby, "The real greatness of *Hamlet* lies in its depiction of a man undone by the responsibility of carrying out a vengeful assignment unsuited to his nature."[48] Goethe sees Hamlet, as we should see him, as overwhelmed with astonishment and trouble rather than as ready to take on the important task to which he has been assigned. He is not "a young hero, panting for revenge . . . who feels himself fortunate in being called out against the usurper of his crown."[49] The pressure of the responsibility of vengeance drives him to avoidance rather than action. Unlike Achilles, who immediately faces up to the fact that the cost of avenging Patroclus will be his own early death and carries out the task, Hamlet seems to find every way under the sun to put off the job. The differences between Achilles and Hamlet, of course, are great, and perhaps the most important is that Achilles does not face the religious prohibition against private revenge that might play on Hamlet's mind and slow his vengeful reflexes. It does, however, remain something of a mystery to me that Hamlet might think that his assignment flies in the face of the prohibition against private revenge. I am more inclined to side with Goethe who writes, "Shakespeare wished to describe the effects of a great action laid upon a soul that was unequal to it."[50]

One of the important things we learn about vengeance from Hamlet is that the responsibility of performing it can overwhelm a person unsuited to the task. When one takes on the role of the avenger, especially in matters that the Elizabethan would regard as private, one risks a greater personal loss than the gain in successfully avenging the injury. The Christian risks his or her immortal soul by the commission of a mortal sin. If the religious superstructure is removed and a more contemporary judicial one substituted, a comparable loss is risked, hence the typical contrast of vengeance with justice and Bacon's reference to vengeance as "wild justice." Acts of revenge might remove one from civilized society and the comforts that entails.

The avenger, when all is said and done, stands outside the law, outside civility, outside the community, outside, and the ring of vengeance can sound hollow when rung in the name of justice. That's what courts and penal systems are for. They are designed to remove the personal from revenge and turn the whole process into state retribution, the impersonal, socially sanctioned meting of punishment to those adjudicated as deserving of it by a disinterested body representative of the community in which the offense occurred. But where is the individual responsibility, where are the personal virtues, in that? The responsibility is shifted from the individual to a social institution, from something very concretely personal to something litigiously procedural. The virtues of courage and fortitude and loyalty and friendship, virtues identified in the earliest literature in our culture and intimately intertwined with vengeance, are replaced with legal protections, rules of evidence, and concerns about cruel and usual punishments. Hamlet, it might be thought, should have taken his complaint against Claudius to an appropriate court, had there been such a venue. He could have saved himself, Ophelia, Laertes, Polonius, Gertrude, Rosencrantz, Gildenstern, and the whole rotten state of Denmark quite a lot of grief! And we would have learned a great deal less about vengeance and the costly toll on the individual that the responsibility to avenge typically charges.

In concluding this brief overview of some of the literary roots of the concept of vengeance, I want to mention the contribution of a philosopher, John Locke. In the influential *Second Treatise of Government,* Locke includes the right of individuals to punish wrongdoers for injuries suffered among the rights of those in the state of nature. Locke writes: "The execution of the law of nature is in that state [the state of nature] put into every man's hand, whereby everyone has a right to punish the transgressors of that law [the law of nature] to such a degree as may hinder its violation . . . And if anyone in the state of nature may punish another for any evil he has done, everyone may do so . . . Every man hath a right to punish the offender, and be executioner of the law of nature."[51] Locke does argue that there must be a limit to the extent of punishment meted out in nature. That limit is set by "calm reason and conscience."

Locke distinguishes two rights in nature that relate to revenge. One is the right to punish an offender. As just noted, everyone has this right regardless of the identity of the victim of the offense. Locke reasons that everyone in the state of nature is empowered to kill a murderer because everyone can punish an offender against the law of nature and murder is a crime "which no reparation can compensate." The second is the right to take reparations from the offender. That right is reserved only for the victim and is, according to Locke, very likely to be abused by those naturally inclined to favor their own cases by exaggerating their losses and injuries. Enforcement of the reparations right also is likely to cause great inconvenience, so at the making of the social contract individuals will be willing to transfer this right to the state.

To summarize this rather sketchy survey, there seem to be at least fifteen conceptual elements in the literary sources (and one philosophical source) that reflect our cultural understanding of revenge and that will require further elaboration in an account of the virtues of vengeance:

1. Vengeance, mythologically, was conceived as the efficient way to rectify structurally unequal situations in the human social world and in the realm of the gods.
2. Revenge can be an appropriate, sanctioned response to a perceived personal injury or a sense of unwarranted victimization or both.

3. The conceptual landscape of vengeance is marked by such concepts as resentment, indignation, reciprocity, desert, fit, and honor.

4. The perception of an unfair distribution of goods, an unfair deprivation, or a feeling of unjust powerlessness typically provokes vengeance. And these conditions foster disapprobative emotions toward the target of revenge.

5. Honor dominates the field of vengeance. There are at least two distinctively different conceptions of honor that support revenge behavior. In one, honor is an intensely interactive phenomenon that can be gained and lost in direct public confrontations with others, usually one's equals or superiors. Considered in that way, honor may be the prize in a zero-sum game.

6. Honor also may be understood as a personal measure of merit as judged by the individual with or without the endorsement of others.

7. The cost of taking revenge often threatens the material self-interests of the avenger and thus restrains most people from undertaking acts of vengeance.

8. For vengeance to be successful, the target must understand that he or she is suffering injury or being killed as a penalty for his or her actions that triggered the revenge behavior of the avenger.

9. In ancient cultures male vengeance was generally regarded as having a higher moral status than vengeance performed by females. Feminine vengeance was morally suspect.

10. Revenge is morally permissible if the avenues of civil redress of serious grievances are blocked.

11. Proportionality or fit is a major concern in assessing the moral acceptability of vengeance.

12. Fit involves not only the punishment suiting the crime but also fitting the criminal's guilty mind, the mind that preferred the particular form of wickedness that triggered the revenge.

13. Early in the evolution of the conception of justifiable vengeance, it was established that inadvertent or accidental killers should not be targets.

14. Taking revenge typically provokes extreme psychological tensions in the avenger that may be so difficult to bear that they render him or her incapable of effective action. Successful avengers most likely will be persons with the emotional composure and physical stamina necessary to weather the personal pressures and losses that are likely to be endured.

15. Punishing of offenders can be conceived of as a natural right possessed by everyone, though it is not to be confused with compensation or reparation rights.

CHAPTER TWO

The Western Vengeance Films

"Sweet is Revenge—especially to women.
Lord Byron[1]

All is not lost—the unconquerable will, And study of revenge, immortal hate,
And courage never to submit or yield.

John Milton[2]

Although the revenge or vengeance plot can be found in virtually every genre of film, it has dominated American Westerns. There are some obvious reasons for its frequent use in these films. The locale and temporal setting of the Western lend themselves to individuals having to punish wrongdoing if it is going to be punished at all. The Western generally takes place on the frontier, at some distance physically and conceptually from the trappings of civilization. Or it is set in communities in which civilization has only just arrived and in which the administration of law and justice is undependable or corrupted by special interests or cruel and "uncivilized" men. Because the technology of harm-causing available within the Western's plot is dominated by one tool, the gun (the pistol or the rifle), the attempt to administer just deserts is typically a very personal matter, usually one-on-one, the shoot-out. What in the history of English law was the trial by combat is often the only trial available in the Western. Towns in which one might expect to find a representative of law and order are small and far apart. If the town has a sheriff or a marshal, the chances are that he is either corrupt, lazy, old, or understaffed and outgunned, sometimes all of the above. A great deal of wrongdoing can be visited on good folks in the wide open spaces, and little if any retribution is likely to be exacted from the offenders unless the victim or the victim's representative sets about the task.

It is, no doubt, a cliché to note that the structure of the American Western film provides a wealth of opportunities for the filmmaker and the audience to explore the implications and subtleties of revenge, if not always its virtues. Cliché or not, with respect to this book, Westerns reward examination. I am neither a film critic nor an analyst of the nuances of film; I am a fan of Westerns. What I want to say about them (or rather a limited assortment of them) relates them to my more general philosophical concerns about the concept of vengeance and the conceptual terrain in which it is located. I find many of the Westerns helpful in clarifying the concept, though they may not add significantly new elements to those that appear in the literary works discussed in Chapter 1. Perhaps they are no more helpful than examples from other genres of film or elements of popular culture would be, so I make no claim for a special status for Westerns in this regard. My use of them is idiosyncratic, a product of my love of them. I know them rather better than some other sources that might offer as much toward furthering the understanding of vengeance.

Westerns represent a particularly American use of the technology and art of film. They may be the most American contribution to the art form. I am not prepared to back up such a claim with an argument. Nonetheless, the Western's century-long popularity with American, indeed world, audiences despite the official and philosophical rejection of the stance it takes on revenge is, for me, a compelling reason to take these films seriously, to see what they have to impart about vengeance. The Western, after all, when stripped to its core, is a self-conscious morality play that seldom wanders far from an investigation of the social, psychological, political, and moral implications of revenge.

I have assembled a collection of vengeance Westerns for examination but make no claim to have exhausted the various types of plots within the genre. Some of the films to which I want to draw attention cannot be ranked among the best the genre has to offer. Some are indisputably minor works. A few are masterpieces of the genre. One is widely recognized as among the five greatest films ever made.

The biography of Hans Kohlhaas, a mid-sixteenth-century German horse trader, was turned into a novel by Heinrich VonKleist and published in 1806. The real-life Hans in VonKleist's novel became Michael Kohlhaas, and since his literary appearance Kohlhaas has served as a model for a number of characters in literature and film. Coalhouse Walker in E. L. Doctorow's *Ragtime,* for example, is modeled on Michael Kohlhaas. The Kohlhaas story inspired a Western that is rather enigmatically titled *The Jack Bull* (1999, directed by John Badham). The film stars John Cusack as Myrl Redding and features performances by John Goodman and L. Q. Jones. The latter plays the villain of the piece, Henry Ballard. The story follows the Kohlhaas plot with little modification. Redding is a respected horse trader who sets off for Casper, Wyoming, with a string of horses that he will be offering at auction. Included in the string are two matched blacks that he has promised to a rancher. Ballard has purchased the land through which Redding must pass if he is to get his horses to the auction. He sets a toll of ten dollars for passage, but Redding cannot pay the toll in full. He offers five dollars but is refused unless he leaves the two black horses as security. Reluctantly, Redding does so and also leaves one of his men, a Crow Indian named Billy, to tend the horses.

When Redding returns to pay the additional five dollars, he discovers that his two horses have been horribly abused. They are nearly dead and covered with open sores. Billy is also severely injured, Ballard having set his dogs on him. Redding insists that Ballard restore the horses to their original condition and pay fifty dollars to Billy for his pain and suffering. Ballard refuses to do so, telling Redding to take the horses as they are. Redding refuses. He will only take back the horses if they are restored to the condition they were in when he left them as security.

Redding goes to his lawyer to file suit against Ballard, but the local judge, who is one of Ballard's business partners, refuses to hear the case. Incensed, Redding decides to take his case to the attorney general at the capital. "If people are going to kick me, I'd rather be a dog than a man," he tells his wife. She intercedes and volunteers to go to Cheyenne, the capital, to bring Redding's petition to the attention of the attorney general. She believes that her brief acquaintance with the attorney general's wife might gain her the needed attention. Not only does she not get to present the petition, but she is killed on the streets of Cheyenne by a runaway wagon that is started by an attack on Redding's man instigated by some of Ballard's men.

After Redding buries his wife, he proclaims that he is taking over the administration of justice in his case and that he is giving Ballard seven days to restore the horses and pay Billy. There is, he decides, no law in Wyoming, so he must make his own and will do so consistent with his understanding of the basic principles of justice. His appeal is to a theory of natural law and justice. He has been unfairly deprived of what is rightfully his and has been rendered powerless to do anything about it by a corrupt legal system. He organizes his own posse and sets after Ballard. Failing to find him on his ranch, he burns down Ballard's stable. Then he burns down other properties of Ballard's relatives, in effect terrorizing the region in search of Ballard, who is hiding out in Cheyenne.

Things move from bad to worse for Redding. During an encounter with the sheriff he kills one of Ballard's men to save Billy. Then, when a homesteader is shooting at Redding who is distributing flyers denouncing Ballard, the homesteader's wife rushes into the line of fire and is accidentally killed by her husband. Ballard files charges of murder against Redding in the court of the corrupt judge. Under a decree of amnesty from the governor, Redding agrees to come to Cheyenne to settle matters. However, he is charged with the murders and with insurrection and is brought to trial. As could be expected, the witnesses against him lie, and his only defense is that all he wants is justice. He is acquitted of one count of murder but convicted of the other and of insurrection. The sentence is death by hanging, but Judge Toliver, who has been sympathetic throughout to Redding, sentences Ballard to restore the horses in excellent condition to Redding before the execution of the death sentence. Ballard is also sentenced to two years in jail for perjury. In the end, Redding is hung, his young son gets the horses, Ballard is carted off to jail, and the army slaughters Billy and his small band of Crow Indians.

The title, *The Jack Bull,* is an allusion to a comment made by Redding's man when he describes his boss as "like a Jack Russell bull terrier." He claims that a jack bull terrier will clamp his jaws on somebody and never let go. That is both Redding's virtue and his vice. He will not retreat from his attempt to gain justice even when there is little or no practical point in continuing. He is warned at every stage of the way that his quest for justice has gotten way out of proportion with respect to the offense. Nonetheless, he continues to escalate matters until, like Michael Kohlhaas, he has become an arsonist, a killer, and an insurrectionist. The very law he purports to be upholding is the law he is willfully breaking, and he gains his revenge only at the cost of his own and his friend's life. His son is left an orphan with two matched black horses.

Milton has Satan express something of what might have been the sentiments of Redding at the end of *The Jack Bull*. Milton writes: "Thank him who puts me, loath, to this revenge / On you, who wrong me not, for him who wronged . . . / Honour and empire with revenge enlarged . . . / compels me now / To do what else, though damned, I should abhor."[3] The cost of vengeance for Redding far exceeds whatever benefit he might at first have expected. In fact, Redding is so swept up in the campaign of vengeance for his unwarranted victimization, the mistreatment of the horses, the injuries inflicted on Billy, and then the accidental killing of his wife that he loses all sense of proportionality. The warnings of the majority of moralists that vengeance once unleashed is nearly impossible to control go unheeded.

The Jack Bull does not condemn revenge. In fact, it speaks for the need to administer justice where those legally appointed to do so have not and will not. This point is made particularly clear at the end of the film when Judge Toliver tells the corrupt judge that he will prefer charges to remove him from the bench because people like Redding deserve the administration of impartial justice. In its absence, they have no recourse but to act on the law they carry within them, the law declared throughout his campaign by Redding, a natural law of restitution and compensation. Redding was wronged and Ballard deserved punishment. Redding's failure in virtue, his vice, was one of proportionality. He grasped the moral necessity for a hostile response to the wrong done to him and to Billy and the horses, but not the extent to which he should go to exact it.

The matter of proportionality in punishment is, in no small measure, the theme of the Academy Award–winning film *Unforgiven* (1992, directed by Clint Eastwood). In this film a group of prostitutes in Big Whiskey, Wyoming, pools their financial resources to offer a substantial financial reward, a bounty, for the killing of two cowboys because one of them mutilated the face of one of the prostitutes when she commented on the size of his penis. The sheriff (played by Gene Hackman) had ordered the offender to compensate the saloon/whorehouse owner for damaging the earning power of the prostitute by giving him a string of horses. The prostitutes regard such a fine as utterly inappropriate, far from what their sense of justice demands. They will settle for nothing short of death. They do not see the matter as one of compensation, an issue in tort; they see it as a criminal matter requiring a severe, indeed the severest, retributive sanction.

The reward lures a number of itinerant gunfighters and bounty hunters to the area, making it open season on the two cowboys. The sheriff, in his attempt to prevent what he regards as a miscarriage of justice—the assassination of the cowboys—savagely beats one of the gunfighters, English Bob (played by Richard Harris), as a lesson to any others intent on collecting the bounty. When William Munny (Clint Eastwood) and his partner Ned Logan (Morgan Freeman), ex-outlaws with profligate pasts who have been reduced to pig farming, arrive in town, Munny is also a victim of the sheriff's brutality. He is savagely beaten and is nursed by the prostitutes.

Munny and a myopic young braggart who calls himself the Schofield Kid succeed in killing the two cowboys, in both cases under less than heroic circumstances, one while he is relieving himself in an outhouse. During the killing of the first cowboy, Ned Logan discovers that he cannot play the role of an assassin, and he decides to abandon the mission and return home. He is captured, tortured, and killed by the sheriff for the murders committed by Munny and the Schofield Kid, and his body is displayed in front of the town saloon. While Ned was being beaten to death, we see the distraught faces of the prostitutes, shocked at what their demand for vengeance has wrought, aware that their revenge has spiraled far beyond their control and is out of proportion with the offense. Actually, the prostitute's bounty has ceased to be an important factor. On learning of the death of his partner, and with the help of prodigious quantities of whiskey, William Munny is transformed from the bounty-driven pig farmer–assassin into the moral avenger. He enters the saloon to kill the sheriff, the saloon owner, and anyone else who had anything to do with Ned's death and the exhibition of his corpse. The final scenes of *Unforgiven* are among the most memorable in the history of film vengeance.

The title of the film reminds us that the characters will not and cannot be forgiven. Munny brags, "I've killed women, and children . . . killed just about everything that walks or crawls at one time or another." Now he has come to kill the sheriff and the others responsible for the killing and desecration of Ned. Death is Munny's way of life, the only occupation at which he has ever been any good. He kills six men who are gathered in a saloon, a relatively small space. (Beauchamp, the writer of dime-store Western novels, says that he killed five, but Beauchamp seems not to be counting the owner of the saloon, who was killed by Munny before the gunfight erupts.) Bullets are zinging around, yet Munny is not even wounded. In *Cowboy Metaphysics,* I maintained that Munny is in a state of grace during the gunfight. It is not a religious state. Hardly. His grace is not a gift of God. It is self-conferred, a product of his ruthlessness and cold-bloodedness, the whiskey, and his willingness to be the avenger, not for money but for his friend. He knows, as he earlier tells the Schofield Kid, "It's a hell of a thing to kill a man. You take away everything he's got . . . and everything he's ever going to have." He does not shrink from performing such "a hell of a thing" when the matter is not a bounty but the honor and the dignity of his friend.

There is a radical difference between Munny the assassin hired by the whores and Munny the avenger of Ned, and it is portrayed for us with crystal clarity. Munny the assassin is virtually inept. He cannot shoot straight, he cannot mount a horse without falling off, he is battered to a pulp by the bullying sheriff, and he sends a boy to do a man's work. He is closer to a buffoon than a hero. Munny the moral avenger displays grace, dignity, poise, dexterity, and power. He moves with a purposeful, easy elegance (another definition of "grace"). He is everything that Munny the assassin is not. He is self-reliant, confident, a man of honor, yet one who clearly recognizes the costs to his own character of what he is doing. Munny the assassin is in it for the money; Munny the avenger is in it because "I'm here to kill you, Little Bill, for what you did to Ned." His pronouncement of his intention is reminiscent of Achilles' informing Hector that he is killing him because of what was done to Patroclus. The target needs to unambiguously understand why the harm is being inflicted by the avenger. There appears to be a moral reason why the message embedded in the act of vengeance needs to be made explicit to the target.

As the film ends, an epilogue scrolls by in which we are told that two years after the action of the film the mother of Munny's wife made the journey to the pig farm only to find that Munny and his children had left. She paid her respects at her daughter's grave, but nothing on the marker explained "to Mrs. Feathers why her only daughter had married a known thief and murderer, a man of noto- riously vicious and intemperate disposition." But we have seen the moral avenger emerge from behind the mask of the vicious murderer, and we may know the virtue that the late Mrs. Munny saw in the man with the well-earned reputation for killing women and children and "everything that walks or crawls at one time or another."

Arguably, Munny's revenge for the killing and desecration of Ned lacks proper proportionality; it does not fit the offense. It seems exorbitant. However, given the fact that the sheriff's deputies probably participated in some measure in the torture of Ned, and they were responding to the sheriff's order to kill Munny, it is difficult to see how Munny could have avoided returning the fire of those who fired on him. That may be what makes the six corpses in the saloon a morally satisfying act of vengeance despite the apparent excess, whereas the killings of the two cowboys are but paid assassinations, both utterly lacking in anything approaching a high moral character. The first is shot in an ambush, the second in an outhouse. It might, of course, be argued that the cowboy who mutilated the face of the prostitute was the one ingloriously killed while defecating, and there is something of poetic justice, at least, in that outcome. Poetic justice, how- ever, does not make for virtuous vengeance. Worse yet, it is the nearsighted young- ster, the Kid, who opens the outhouse door and fires three shots into the cowboy at close range. The act might well be described as one of cowardice. In fact, the ambush killing of the first cowboy is hardly courageous either. It is only after Munny takes up the revenge of Ned that he behaves in what can comfortably be called a courageous or heroic manner.

Revenge of the murder of friends is also central to the plot of *The Missouri Breaks* (1976, directed by Arthur Penn). This film, in some respects, defies explication. I have found it impossible to locate someone who has seen the film who is neutral about it. It appears that it is either greatly admired or vehemently detested. For some, it is a near cinematic masterpiece; for others, it is so wrapped up in a cast of perverse characters that the story line is often undecipherable. Both poles of criticism fit the film. Undeniably, it is seriously flawed and incoherent in places. *The Missouri Breaks* is cluttered with unique, eccentric characters whose histrionics shove the plot to the background, but it does have a discernible plot, one that engages the loss of the frontier to capitalist exploitation with the personal vengeance theme.

Tom Logan (played by Jack Nicholson) is the leader of a small band of affable horse thieves who are harassing the Montana ranch country near the Breaks of the Missouri River, a geological formation. The rustlers' primary target is the wealthiest rancher in the district, David Braxton. Logan sets up a small farm near Braxton's spread to use as a relay station for his band's raids. But Logan discovers that he greatly enjoys farming, and his gang soon becomes disenchanted with his leadership. Logan befriends and then falls in love with Braxton's daughter, further complicating his relationship to his gang and the man from whom they steal. The gang continues their rustling activities, and Braxton's foreman is killed, which provokes Braxton to hire a regulator, a private policeman, to track down and kill the rustlers.

The regular, Robert E. Lee Clayton, is a professional killer. Marlon Brando's Clayton is an utterly bizarre character, one of the weirdest ever to appear in a serious Western. Not only does his every appearance unnerve Logan and the gang members, but he leaves everyone, including the audience, dumbfounded as to his persona. Clayton is a protean person, never the same from one appearance to the next. He arrives at the Braxton ranch dressed as an Indian, but we later see him outfitted as an effete Southern fop, then in the hat of a Chinese laborer, then as a circuit-riding minister, and then, craziest of all, in what Philip French describes as "the fantastic drag get-up of an old pioneer lady in a poke bonnet."[4] In each of his costumes he manages to hunt down and murder the four members of Logan's gang, and he does so more for his own satisfaction than to please his employer. Untold hours might be spent trying to determine the relationship between Clayton's choices of costume and his targets. One thing is common in each of his murders: they are all accomplished at long range.

Clayton uncovers the fact that Logan, who is pretending to be a farmer by being a farmer (an example of pretense that might have intrigued J. L. Austin[5]), is the gang's leader. Logan has had enough and vows to avenge the murders of his friends by killing Clayton and Braxton, the man who by hiring Clayton has destroyed not only his friends but the farming life he now cherishes. He will do it although it means that he will have to desert his precious farm and lose the woman he loves. Clayton uses an accurate Creedmore Sharp rifle; Logan takes his revenge at close range by slitting the sleeping Clayton's throat. "You know what woke you up? Lee, you just had your throat cut."

When Logan confronts Braxton, he finds a pathetic old man who is being fed porridge by his servant. Braxton's daughter tells him that her father has come unraveled and lost himself. Logan tells her, "All I can say is you'd better leave the room because I'm goin' to do it regardless." He cocks Clayton's rifle, then realizes he cannot achieve the desired vengeance by killing a demented old man. He throws the gun out of the window. He perceives Braxton to be morally and mentally incompetent and thus incapable of grasping the revenge message he is about to deliver. In the absence of the target's understanding, the act is murder, not moral revenge. But Braxton rises out of his chair with a pistol drawn and fires five shots at Logan, hitting him once. Logan returns fire, killing Braxton. The film ends with Logan leaving his farm without Braxton's daughter. She tells him, "I don't want to spend the rest of my life trying to get back at somebody." He responds, "Why'd you say that?" "No reason." "Why hell, neither do I." They ride off in different directions with only a vague hint that they may someday get together north of the Breaks. Although there are undoubtedly many symbolic meanings to be read into the title, it is enough to understand that it is an ironic comment on the fate of even the justified avenger.

The heroes of *Shane* (1953, directed by George Stevens), *Pale Rider* (1985, directed by Clint Eastwood), and *The Tall T* (1957, directed by Budd Boetticher) also avenge injuries and threats of injury of friends. In *Shane* and *Pale Rider,* the friends have formed a surrogate family for the avenger, made him virtually a member of their households. In *The Tall T,* Pat Brennan (Randolph Scott) avenges the murders of three friends, a father and son who run a stage swing station and Rintoon, a stagecoach driver. Brennan and the recently wed and then widowed Doretta Mims (Maureen O'Sullivan) are held captive by the gang, led by Frank Usher (Richard Boone), that murdered his friends, awaiting the arrival of ransom money from her father. Brennan and Doretta escape by killing the gang member who was left to guard them. They can clearly ride away and let the remaining two gang members divide the ransom money. Doretta begs Brennan to do so. "I'm gonna finish this. They come, I'm gonna finish this once and for all," he tells her. "Oh, but why?" "Some things a man can't ride around." One of the gang returns and Brennan kills him. Then Usher rides up carrying saddlebags filled with the ransom money. Brennan surprises him. Usher, however, raises his hands and will not turn around to face Brennan. "You won't do me with that scatter gun," he correctly predicts as he walks to his horse and mounts. Usher and Brennan share a sense of integrity that will not let them kill a defenseless person.

Earlier in the film, Usher refused to allow his gang members to kill Brennan and throw his corpse down the well at the swing station with those of their three other victims. Brennan won't shoot Usher in the back. His sense of self-respect restrains him, and, of course, Usher counts on that being the case. Usher rides off, leaving Brennan, Doretta, and the ransom money behind. However, when he gets to the top of a hill, he turns his horse, unsheathes his rifle, and rides down on Brennan, who shoots him down, killing him. Brennan appears not to be surprised at Usher's return, although it is unclear whether it is the money or pride or both that provokes Usher's decision when he could have ridden away unscathed. Brennan's commitment, however, to "finish this once and for all" suggests that if Usher had not returned, Brennan would have tracked him down and taken revenge. Otherwise, he would have "ridden around" the most significant perpetrator of the murders of his friends.

The Westerns that James Stewart made with director Anthony Mann are dramatic studies of the conceptual interstices within vengeance and the broader conceptual landscape in which it is situated. Indeed, the physical landscapes of Mann's Westerns are integral players in defining the conceptual field of the action. Although *Bend of the River, The Man from Laramie,* and *The Naked Spur* take Stewart's characters into the depths of moral hatred when they are wronged, a hatred that motivates extraordinary behavior in order to gain revenge (especially in *Bend of the River*), it is from the first collaboration of Stewart and Mann that much is to be learned about the relationship between vengeance and honor. That film is *Winchester '73* (1950), a magnificent film and a classic Western. (The screenplay is based on a story by Stuart Lake, who was also the author of a fictionalized "biography" of Wyatt Earp entitled *Wyatt Earp: Frontier Marshal,* originally published in 1931, that is still a popular seller among the Westerns at *Amazon.com.*

The plot of *Winchester '73* seems relatively simple. Lin McAdam, Stewart's character, rides into Dodge City in search of the man who murdered his father by shooting him in the back. The town is celebrating the Fourth of July with a shooting contest. The prize is a perfect Winchester rifle, the Winchester '73 of the title. McAdam's strongest competitor in the contest is Dutch Henry Brown (played by Stephen McNally). McAdam immediately recognizes Dutch Henry— who is really Lin's older brother, Matthew—as the murderer of his father. Lin is unable to kill Dutch Henry (Matthew) in Dodge because Wyatt Earp, the marshal, has confiscated all the guns in town. The two face off in the shooting contest, and Lin wins the Winchester. Dutch Henry, however, waylays his brother in Lin's hotel room, reminiscent of his cowardly shooting of their father, and steals the prize rifle. The remainder of the film recounts Lin's quest to recover the rifle and avenge the death of his father by killing his brother. The rifle changes hands a number of times, and Lin seems always a step or two away from regaining it. The two brothers finally meet, and Lin kills Dutch Henry. He rides back into town with the Winchester '73, ready to begin a new life, a new family, with Lola Manners, the prostitute who has also meandered through the story and changed hands almost as frequently as the prize rifle.

Winchester '73, however, is much more than a Western version of a standard chase or quest film. It has the thematic elements of a Greek or Shakespearean tragedy implanted in an Odysseyian adventure whose goal is the restoration of a family and its honor. It probably also is no accident that the family in question is named McAdam. Lin and Matthew are sons of Adam, recalling the first biblical murder. This version is a Cain and Abel story with a significant twist: Cain did not murder Abel; instead he murdered "the old man," and Abel eventually will kill him to avenge the patricide. To make matters worse, this Cain stole the family honor from Abel, not once but twice. The patricide occurs before the film begins, and it is not confirmed that this is a matter between brothers until just before the final shootout. All we learn is that Lin is dedicated to avenging the murder of his father and that Dutch Henry is the murderer.

We first acquire that information during a remarkable scene that occurs when Lin and his partner, High Spade, enter a Dodge City saloon with Wyatt Earp. Lin spots Dutch Henry sitting at a table, and both men instinctively crouch and go for their guns. They slap leather simultaneously, drawing "with a demoniacal frenzy."[6] But, of course, they have no guns to draw. They are in a civilized town, not a place where family revenge can be exacted. Nonetheless, in that single scene we learn something very crucial about the hero, the avenger, Lin McAdam: he is not the calm, collected, self-controlled gunfighter usually associated with Westerns. The very sight of his target, his brother, transforms him into a near psychotic, "a flipping maniac."[7] At the very least, the scene calls into question the character of the avenger and reveals him as teetering on a psychological precipice fully prepared to perform an irreparable act of fratricide, motivated by the urgings of the McAdam family demons within him. Or by the Furies? Yet, there is also something vaguely humorous in the pasquinade showdown. Murderer and avenger are rendered impotent by civilization's confiscation of their weaponry. Both look and feel foolish.

The saloon scene is followed by the shooting contest, which becomes a one-upsmanship match of sharpshooting prowess between the two brothers. As such it serves as a communally sanctioned, though morally and emotionally deficient, surrogate for the act of vengeance that Lin plans for his brother. Insofar as their murdered father trained both brothers, they display virtually equal ability as they vie for the perfect rifle. The rifle stands as the symbol for the contestants of both the honor of the family McAdam and their father. The contest evokes the sibling rivalry for the attentions of their father that undoubtedly typified the motherless McAdam family life.

The competition for the prize rifle is held under controlled conditions, conditions set by Wyatt Earp, the first of a number of father figures that appear in the story. Under Earp, Dodge is a very civilized town. Children play in the streets, and women of ill-repute, such as Lola (played by Shelley Winters), are sent packing out of town on the next stage. Earp's Dodge City is a well-ordered and safe community and is contrasted with the wild and woolly and out-of-control town of Tascosa, where the streets are unsafe for women and children, in which Lin's odyssey ends. The shooting contest for the Winchester also is in celebration of the Fourth of July and the Founding Fathers of the country. More fathers and father figures, and more to come!

Lin wins the rifle, but, remindful of their past familial relationship in which the older brother bullied away everything Lin possessed, including his father,

Dutch Henry jumps Lin and steals the prize. The remainder of the film recounts Lin's quest for both the murderer and the perfect rifle. We follow the rifle's movement through the plot, but it is not in the end what the story is about. When Lin rides back into Tascosa after finally killing Matthew, he has the Winchester '73, but it is not the possession of the gun that matters. What counts is the recovery of his personal and family honor that the gun has come to symbolize. The brother that went bad is dead. The recovery of the family honor also makes possible for Lin the formation of a new family with Lola. It quells the McAdam family Furies. The act of vengeance for him is both backward-looking, serving just deserts for past offenses, and future-oriented, restoring family honor and his own sense of worthiness for the future. The latter seems to be at least as important as the former in motivating Lin's quest.

Lin's relationship with Lola is progressively more tender, always moving toward family, and all the while the rifle is traveling from hand to hand across the Western landscape until it returns to a McAdam. One journey is linear, the other cyclical, but both will terminate in the restored McAdam family. Lola is the human symbol of family that is near but always just out of Lin's reach. She offers the potential of a real home. The two symbols, the rifle and Lola, family past and family future, impel Lin's adventures to their conclusion.

The rifle, however, is perfect, and Lola is anything but flawless. She is the imperfect potential partner who has been targeted if not sullied by his brother and his brother's outlaw friends, especially the sociopathic Waco Johnnie Dean (Dan Duryea). Lin first sees Lola as she is being run out of town, and he makes an effort to defend her but is deterred upon learning that he would have to deal with Wyatt Earp. Lola next appears during the migration of the rifle. She is about to make an utterly inappropriate marriage with Steve Miller, a cowardly Easterner. Lin and High Spade ride into the hollow where a band of Indians are preparing to attack Lola, Steve, and a small cavalry troop. Lola asks Lin, "Did you have a home?" He responds, "Sort of . . . with my father." During the attack, Lin gives Lola a gun, and she assures him that she knows that the last bullet in the gun is for her. When the Indians have been routed, she gives the gun back to Lin but asks if she can keep the last bullet. He replies, "If you want it." She wants it.

The gift of the bullet, according to Jeanine Basinger, is symbolic at a number of levels. "The bullet was a symbol of his protection of her, his concern, but also of her independence and courage in a moment of crisis. It represents her ability to choose for herself—and she chooses him. When she takes the bullet from him, she is both accepting his offer and making one herself."[8] The offer is, or at least includes, family and a real home, the very reason she is with Steve. Later in the film, she is hit by a bullet that is fired at Lin by Dutch Henry. She lies wounded, but protecting a child, in the streets of Tascosa while Lin rides after Dutch Henry for the final showdown between the brothers.

The prize rifle passes into the possession of a panoply of Western film types. Matthew (Dutch Henry) loses it to a gunrunner, he to an Indian chief, who drops it in the dust during an attack on the cavalry band, where it is discovered by a soldier (Tony Curtis in his first film) after Lin has left and given to Steve Miller. Waco, who is subsequently shot down by Lin in a gun battle, kills Miller. The Winchester is, however, again snatched away by Dutch Henry, setting the stage for the final confrontation between the brothers.

Family, as in the Greek tragedies, lies at the motivational core of *Winchester '73*. As noted earlier, throughout the story an assortment of father figures (Earp and the sergeant major of the cavalry troop) put in appearances. Both Earp and the sergeant major are portrayed as caring and successful fathers to their broods, the townspeople and the young cavalry recruits. Potential families—Lola and Steve, Lola and Waco, Lola and Lin—are formed at various stages in the plot as a reminder that this business has its roots in a dysfunctional family unit, in a son who "went bad" and a father who would not play the part of the doting parent upon the return of the prodigal, in another son whose sense of personal honor demanded that he avenge the patricide and make things right. In case the point about the centrality of family is missed, Waco terrorizes an innocent family, the Jamisons, and the sheriff burns down the Jamison house, which was to be the family home for the ill-fated Steve and Lola union, when he tries to capture Waco. Lola and Steve Miller's wedding, an event whose occurrence was earlier cast into doubt by Steve's display of cowardice, is cancelled when Waco kills him in cold blood.

Vengeance is the means for both retribution and restoration for Lin. The resolution of his dual quest for his brother's life and the perfect rifle cannot occur in the public spaces of civilization, not even in the rowdy streets of Tascosa. The brothers confront each other "in the brutal landscape outside the community."[9] The shoot-out with rifles, Matthew with the prize Winchester, is magnificent cinema. It occurs on rocky cliffs above the desert, a dead landscape, charged with ricocheting bullets blasting dust and chips of rock around the combatants. As they fire on each other, Matthew higher on the cliffs than Lin, they punctuate each shot or volley with familial commentary. "You're caught below another man's gun." "I guess I forgot, Matthew." "I could smoke you outta there easy." "Shoots real pretty, wouldn't you say?" "I didn't get a chance to use that gun, Matthew. But I intend to." "There's something you forgot, too. The old man taught you never to waste lead. Now you're short." Each of their verbal retorts echoes their relationship to their father, the old man. They chide each other as he no doubt would have chided them, and they make it perfectly clear to each other that this deadly encounter is about him and the fact that Matthew shot him in the back. By killing not only his father's murderer but his wicked brother who is that murderer, Lin regains self-esteem and the value of a good name on which he can build his future social relationships. Cesare Beccaria writes, "When deprived of the esteem of others the man of honor sees himself exposed either to become a merely solitary being, an insufferable state for a social man, or else to become a butt of insults and infamy."[10]

Lin McAdam, of course, need not fear that he will lose the esteem of others because of the actions of his brother. His brother has, conveniently, changed his name to Dutch Henry Brown. It is the fear of losing personal esteem, worthiness, if he does not avenge his father's murder and restore the good name of his family, that motivates Lin. He has discovered something he cannot ride around. He would, at least to himself, feel dishonorable and unfit to found his own family, to make a home. That he will do so with Lola, the proverbial prostitute with the heart of gold who was willing to marry the cowardly Steve, who was forced by Waco to wear an apron and serve coffee, is an irony of the story. She certainly is no Penelope. Lin is, of course, also motivated by the animosity he feels toward Matthew for depriving him of his home and his just rewards. With respect to the latter, his resentment mirrors that of Achilles toward Agamemnon.

The business of the names of the characters is something of a mystery. Why does Matthew choose the alias Dutch Henry Brown? Unhappily, there is no way of learning the answer, and it never is explained in the film. Lin's name, however, is also open to speculation. It appears to be a shortened form of some other name, but what other name? Again, we never find out. Matthew, of course, has Biblical origins, but Lin has no such roots, at least as far as I can discern. The name could be short for Merlin or Lindell or something of that sort. Following the fending off of the Indian attack, the sergeant major expresses his thanks to Lin and High Spade by telling them that he and his Union outfit could have used them at Bull Run and other Civil War battlefields. Lin's response is that they were with them at Bull Run. They were on the other side. The recollection of the Civil War, of course, echoes the theme of brother against brother, the McAdam civil war. But it also might suggest that Lin has changed his name. Perhaps it was Lincoln. That, of course, is idle conjecture, as nothing especially turns on it, and it should be noted that Lin, whatever the younger son's longer name is or if he had a longer name, was probably the name he was called by his father. But then, why is Matthew called Matthew and not a comparably shortened Matt by Lin when he is "speaking for the father" during the brothers' verbal accompaniment to their deadly shoot-out on the cliffs? Again, idle if entertaining speculation, I suppose.

Winchester '73 locates the victim, the avenger, and the target within the same family. The more typical revenge Western places the victim and the avenger in the family and the target as an intruder. In plot structure it more closely resembles a Norse saga, such as the *Saga of the Volsung,* than a tragic drama by Aeschylus. The revenge theme is played out along such lines in, for example, *Once Upon a Time in the West, The Outlaw Josey Wales,* and *Riders of the Purple Sage.* In *Once Upon a Time in the West* (1968, directed by Sergio Leone), the victim is an older brother, and the avenger (Charles Bronson), who is variously referred to as the "Man with the Harmonica" or just "Harmonica" or "The Man Who Makes Appointments," is his younger brother who, when just a child, is forced to balance his brother on his shoulders while the latter is being hung by the villain, Frank (Henry Fonda).

Although *Once Upon a Time in the West* involves many interrelated themes that are familiar in Westerns—the supplanting of the wilderness with towns, the end of the frontier, the Easterner capitalist's confrontation with the free-spirited Westerner, and so on—the film is centrally about families or the loss of them. Early in the film we witness the brutal mass murder of a family that strands the heroine, Jill (Claudia Cardinale), who has arrived too late to take on the role of wife and mother, in an isolated ranch house. She is a would-be mother in search of a family. Ultimately, she, with the help of two orphans, Cheyenne and Harmonica, will "give birth" to a town beside the railroad track, and she will be both mother and sexual fantasy to the workers who are constructing it. Cheyenne, a sympathetic outlaw (Jason Robards), talks of his dead mother and unknown father.

Harmonica finally confronts Frank, and in flashbacks we see Harmonica's recollection of the hanging of his brother, his loss of family. In Frank's eyes we see only the steely sizing up of a competitor, a check for the location of the sun, and so on. He is the ultra villain who has no family, who murders families for financial gain. They draw and Harmonica fires the mortal shot. Frank, dying in the dirt, asks for the real name of the avenger. Harmonica responds by jamming a harmonica into Frank's mouth. At the moment of death, Frank's eyes suggest that he remembers the vicious hanging of Harmonica's brother, though it was just one of so many murders in his career. His face seems to express approval of the revenge taken on him. It is a way of life he appreciates, and it contrasts with the life of commerce and business into which he tried to enter but that he could not fathom. It is the way of life, he and Harmonica earlier had agreed, of "an ancient race" that soon will be wiped off the face of the earth by the advance of civilization with its procedural conception of justice and demands of profit-making. It is a way of life focused in honor, a notion unknown to the capitalist.

Despite the building of a town and a railroad in close proximity to the location of Frank and Harmonica's final face-off, the matter of personal vengeance between them is settled privately without an audience. Despite the wide-open spaces of the West, it is a very interior moment. Robert Cumbow writes about the final shoot-out between Harmonica and Frank: "The memory of what happened to the little boy who became the Man with the Harmonica haunts us long after the satisfaction of Harmonica's revenge on Frank has faded . . . When he falls—and he will fall, it's only a question of how soon—his brother will hang from the noose affixed to the peak of an arch in the middle of a desert limbo."[11] The focus of the film comes to rest on the predicament of that younger brother and how as a man he will finally resolve it, exact an adequate amount of revenge, sufficiently punish the man who compelled him to participate in the murder of his brother. The scene is filmed in excruciatingly extreme close-ups of the faces of the combatants. Closer and closer, more and more interior, until we are inside the eye of the avenger and see his pain.

Much of the action of the film, though it may not be apparent until seen as a whole, that is, from the perspective of the revelation of the hanging, is manipulated by Harmonica's intent to do more than just shoot down Frank in a face-to-face duel. Harmonica will successfully foil Frank's grand business plans and discredit him in the eyes of his henchmen and the capitalist railroad builder for whom Frank works. He will strip away all pretenses from Frank's persona and in the end leave him as nothing but what he is, a child-killing, family-destroying, degenerate, steely-blue-eyed gunman, an appropriate target for the avenger.

The plot of *Outlaw Josey Wales* (1976, directed by Clint Eastwood) has many of the elements of *Winchester '73*. It is an odyssey driven by the need to avenge a murdered family. In this case, the husband and father, Josey Wales (played by Clint Eastwood), pursues the murderers of his wife and children. He is especially concerned with taking revenge on Captain Terrell, the leader of the band of Union raiders, Red Legs, that slaughtered his family and burned his farm. Like Lin McAdam, Josey Wales's vengeance is the prelude to the establishment of a new family. A major difference between the two is that Wales is already being co-opted back into the farmer/family patriarch role of his past by his new commune family before he has completed the task of revenge to which he has directed his energies. Also, unlike Lin McAdam, he is the target of various bounty hunters. He is both a pursuer and the pursued. He is an outlaw on the run as well as an avenger.

In the end, when he confronts Terrell face to face, he corners a pathetic figure hardly worth the effort of vengeance. He clicks off empty rounds at Terrell from three pistols. The cowering Terrell pulls out a saber, but Josey shoves it up into his guts. Some commentators on the film, such as Phil Hardy,[12] maintain that the new family life had made the idea of revenge ridiculous to Josey. But that reading is not quite consistent with the film. During his humiliation of Terrell, Josey sees flashbacks of the murders of his family. Clearly, revenge is still central to his intentions, and it again becomes morally viable when Terrell draws his saber in an attempt to kill Josey. It is the same saber with which Terrell rendered Josey incapable of defending his family during the raid, the saber that left a deep scar down the right side of Josey's face, a constant reminder of his task of revenge. Arguably, during the clicking off of the empty chambers, Josey is satisfied that humiliation is now sufficient vengeance. The issue for him seems more, what is suitable revenge at this point in time and given the condition of the villain—rather than a choice between vengeance or no vengeance.

Riders of the Purple Sage (1995, directed by Charles Haid), based on the famous Zane Grey novel, was filmed twice: as a silent and then in the talking era in 1931 and 1941. None of the earlier versions captures Grey's story as well as the 1995 version starring Ed Harris and Amy Madigan. Lassiter, a notorious gunman (played by Harris), is the avenger in search of the three men and a preacher who kidnapped his sister and her baby. After thirteen years on the trail he has found each of the three men and killed them. He has learned that the location of the grave of his sister, Millie Urn, is known only by Jane Withersteen (Madigan), a woman trying to run a ranch in the face of violent attempts by her male neighbors to destroy her business and marry her off to one of them. Lassiter becomes Jane's protector and they fall in love. He tells her that he has come to kill the preacher who persuaded his sister to abandon her home, her husband, and her God.

Preacher Dyer, who dominates the ranching community, pays a call on Jane to order her to marry the rancher he has selected for her. He spots Lassiter and draws his gun on him. Lassiter wings him and Dyer leaves. Jane admits to Lassiter that not only is Dyer the preacher he is seeking, but also that Dyer had procured Millie to be her father's wife. Millie refused, and she and Jane's father fought. Millie grabbed his gun and shot Jane's father, then she committed suicide. Lassiter is stunned but declares that he has "given up his purpose" because of his love for Jane. "Hate is not the same with me since I loved you," he tells her.

Dyer and the men of the community continue their terror campaign. In order to prevent Jane from marrying the rancher selected by Dyer, this time coerced by their threat to hang Jane's most loyal rider, Lassiter rides to the church to kill them. "It ain't vengeance now, it's justice," he shouts to Jane. He explains that his killing of Dyer and at least five other men is "not for what happened in the past, but for what is happening right now. It's for you." Of course, it has the same effect. Lassiter shoots down Dyer, killing the last, and the worst, of the men who destroyed his sister, Millie Urn. Jane loses her ranch and her herds, and she and Lassiter seal themselves in a canyon, taking refuge forever from the rest of the human race.

In my opinion, the greatest director of film to stand behind the camera referred to himself simply as "a director of Westerns."[13] When asked to name the three greatest directors, Orson Welles is reputed to have answered, "John Ford, John Ford, and John Ford." Welles reportedly spent long hours studying Ford's *Stagecoach* in preparation for the making of *Citizen Kane.* I admit to being among that growing number of people who regard Ford's *The Searchers* (1956) as the greatest American film yet made, a film that both depicts the American dream and unflinchingly dissects that dream, revealing that it rests on violence, vindictiveness, and vengeance. The film is fifth on the list of the world's greatest films ever made, according to *Sight and Sound*'s worldwide poll of film critics.[14]

So much has been written about *The Searchers* that it is surely folly for a philosopher to add more. However, because I want to make references to it in Part Two, it will be useful here to provide a bare outline of this masterpiece. The plot is wrapped tightly around the concept of family, and, as with most of Ford's Westerns, it is also concerned with the costs of civilization contrasted with its potential benefits. Ethan Edwards (played by John Wayne, in his finest performance) returns to the home of his brother at the edge of the Texas frontier two years after the end of the Civil War. He provides his brother with no information about his whereabouts since the surrender except that he did not relinquish his sword and holds himself still bound by his oath to the Confederacy. He has a bag of newly minted Yankee dollars but does not explain how he acquired them. In short, there are reasons to believe that Ethan has not been operating within the law since the end of the war. The captain of the regional Texas Ranger unit says that Ethan fits a number of descriptions on wanted posters, but nothing further is made of his exploits prior to his return to the Edwards family home.

Robert Frost wrote, "Home is the place where, when you have to go there, they have to take you in."[15] That sentiment seems to apply to Ethan and his brother Aaron. There is a recognizable discomfort in the family, at least among the adult members, about his return home. Martha, Aaron's wife, welcomes Ethan, but with a distinct glint of loss in her expressions as she does so. There is more than a hint that she is Ethan's unrequited love. Aaron is rather less cordial. He worries about Ethan's exploits and why Ethan had not gone to California as had been reported. There is an unstated tension in the family's opening of their home to the dashing prodigal, a heavy understatement of apprehension that he is planning to stay too long and that the family is at risk because of his presence.

The Edwards family appears to be, in large measure though not intentionally, a product, or rather a by-product, of Ethan's adventures, of his leaving the homestead. And not just to fight in the Civil War. Again, as in *Winchester '73,* the Civil War lurks in the background and suggests the past disruption or destruction of potential familial relationships. On a remote Texas ranch, the delayed aftermath of the Civil War—Ethan's return, dressed partially in uniform and with his sword—threatens the stability of the household. Martha married Aaron no doubt because she felt she could not depend on Ethan to secure and sustain a home for her. He was always too much of a wanderer. We can hear the theme song of the film in her mind questioning, "What makes a man to wander? What makes a man to roam?"

The motivation of escaping the life of a wanderer's wife, despite loving him, will tempt Laurie Jorgensen, the daughter of the Edwardses' neighbor, later in the film. Events, unlike in Martha's case, will intervene and prevent her marriage of convenient stability. But the point will be brilliantly made when her suitor, Charlie McCorry, serenades her with "Gone again, slip to my lou." Martin Pawley (Jeffrey Hunter), the real object of Laurie's affections, was adopted into the Edwards family when Ethan found him after an Indian raid that had killed his parents. He is raised as a brother to the other Edwards children. Martin is described as being one-eighth Cherokee, a matter of lineage that is no small matter to Ethan, but a fact that is of no consequence to the family or to the other white settlers on the frontier. For instance, Martin is welcomed by the Jorgensens as a suitor for their daughter Laurie.

Ethan is both the founder of the family and a threat to it. Martha's marriage to Aaron has excluded Ethan from the family home, and although he is welcomed back by her, in the evening we see him outside the house looking in as Aaron follows Martha into their bedroom and closes the door, excluding Ethan from her. Ford's camera angles make the point that, despite his being the outsider, Ethan is the central figure of the family. In one scene, Aaron and Martha are talking with Ethan, and we see the three of them from a low camera angle so that the cross-beams of the house appear above Ethan's head. He stands as if he is the pillar of the house and its future rests on his head. The image is, as matters unfurl, ironic, for he will leave the home at a crucial moment and it will collapse.

A small company of Texas Rangers arrives at the Edwards ranch. They are tracking down cattle rustlers. Ethan agrees to accompany the Ranger patrol in exchange for his brother remaining at the home to protect the family. Martin joins Ethan and the Rangers. Forty miles from the Edwards ranch they find the cattle slaughtered and realize that they have been hoaxed, drawn away from the family by a band of Comanches on a murder raid. Ethan, Mose Harper, an old and rather simpleminded man who will be far more important to the plot than first appears (a stellar performance by Hank Worden), and Martin Pawley ride back to the Edwardses' place while the other Rangers head toward the Jorgensen's ranch. They find that the Edwards home was the target of the raid and that the house has been burned and the family slaughtered. Martha has been raped, mutilated, and murdered. Lucy and Debbie, the two Edwards girls, however, are missing and presumed to have been taken captive by the Comanches. After the funeral for Aaron, Martha, and their son Ben, a funeral cut short when Ethan strides away from the gravesite shouting "Put an amen to it," the Rangers, Ethan, Martin, and Brad Jorgensen, who intends to marry Lucy, set out to find the girls. Mrs. Jorgensen pleads with Ethan to promise her not to let the boys waste their lives in vengeance. Ethan does not answer her, casting her only a brief look that suggests contempt for her plea.

Ethan will not be deterred from his mission to find his nieces and kill the leader of the Comanche raiding party, Chief Scar, the man who desecrated Martha. Vengeance, for him, is necessarily associated with self-respect and personal and family honor. He is riled with moral anger and hatred for the Comanche chief who has murdered his brother and, probably more important to him, raped, mutilated, and murdered the woman he loved, his sister-in-law. Undoubtedly, Ethan also feels a sense of personal failure and shame for having been misled, for having fallen for the hoax, for having left his beloved Martha inadequately protected.

The Rangers' search for the Comanches is a failure, and Ethan vows to pursue the Indian band alone. Martin and Brad, however, insist on joining him, and the three set off as the Rangers return home. Ethan finds Lucy raped and murdered, and Brad, in despair, dashes at the Comanche encampment and is killed. Ethan and Martin continue the search for Debbie. Ethan is aware that Debbie is young and that as she gets older she will probably be married into the tribe. This concern gives birth to Ethan's second motivation to find Chief Scar and Debbie: not only is he consumed with the need to avenge Martha, but he now also wants to kill Debbie.

Ethan has, from his first evening back in the Edwards home, evinced racism with respect to Indians. He makes a point of commenting on Martin's Indian ancestry, much to the general discomfort of the rest of the family. His intention either to find Debbie while she is still young or to kill her if his search is unsuccessful until she has matured is fueled by his very deeply seated belief that if she has slept with an Indian, she has lost her white purity and dishonored the Edwards family. He may well see his mission of death to Debbie as demanded by his allegiance to Martha, who Debbie favors in terms of physical features. Martha was violated, forced to have sexual intercourse with her murderers. (Ethan finds her torn dress before he finds her body.) In his eyes, Martha died disgraced and that also disgraced him. Ethan will kill Debbie if she has had sex, whether or not under duress, with those same murderers. We are told on a number of occasions that Martha would never want Debbie to become the wife of a Comanche. Death would be preferable.

Ethan clearly shares the racist sentiments attributed to Martha and dedicates himself to the death of Debbie. Laurie, who is to marry Martin when the search is completed, also holds similar views. She tells Martin that Martha would want Ethan to put a bullet in Debbie's brain. The racism of the white settlers is an important element in the film, and John Ford does not shy away from portraying it. Importantly, through the deepening viciousness and near psychic behavior of Ethan, Ford demonstrates the evil of racism. But he is also portraying America carving itself out of the wilderness with that morally corrupt blood coursing through its veins. A very convincing case can be made that John Ford uses *The Searchers* to indict and attack the racism that he identifies as an indelible feature of the American character and experience. That he does so through a character played by one of the most American of film icons, John Wayne, strengthens the interpretation, for Ethan Edwards is a dark, driven, antisocial, and brutal racist.

The searchers are Ethan, a fanatical avenger of his family's slaughter who also is intent on killing the last surviving member of that family, and Martin, a young man who is postponing his own marriage and family to "fetch Debbie home." It may be no coincidence that the first four letters of Martin's name are the same as Martha's and that Ethan's relationship to Martin teeters tenuously between hatred and familial affection. The goal of Martin's search is, in some respects, more puzzling than Ethan's, because Debbie has no home to which to return. Her family, her home, has been destroyed years before, and she has established a new family in the tent of Scar. Her only blood relative, Ethan, the man dedicated to killing her, disinherited her when he discovered she was living as one of Scar's wives. Ethan writes a will giving all of the Edwards estate, such as it is, to Martin, who is appalled that Ethan has disowned Debbie, his natural legatee.

After five years of searching, Ethan and Martin find Debbie in Scar's camp, they are attacked, and Ethan is wounded. They return to the Jorgensen's home without Debbie only to interrupt the wedding ceremony of Laurie and Charlie McCorry. The ceremony is also interrupted by Mose Harper, who informs the wedding guests that he has been in Scar's camp, and has seen Debbie, and that the camp is nearby. The Rangers reassemble to attack the Comanche camp. Martin is convinced that Ethan's plan is to kill Debbie during the attack. He gets permission from the Ranger captain, over Ethan's objections, to try to sneak into the camp and rescue Debbie. Martin succeeds in getting into Scar's tent and kills him. Debbie escapes. When Ethan discovers that Scar is already dead, he scalps the corpse and then chases down Debbie and catches her. Instead of killing her, he raises her over his head as if she were a child and rides back to the Jorgensen's ranch with her. The scene of Ethan sweeping the mature Debbie up over his head in one motion is a virtual mirror image of the scene when Ethan first arrived at the Edwards ranch and greeted the young Debbie by lifting her up over his head. The next day she was kidnapped and her family was slaughtered.

In what may be one of the most famous scenes in the history of film, the Jorgensens walk into the house with Debbie followed by Laurie and Martin, arm in arm. Ethan, however, stands for a moment framed in the open door, then as the door closes he walks away into the desert landscape. The ending is foreshadowed at the beginning of the search when Ethan and the Rangers discover a dead Comanche. Ethan shoots out the eyes of the corpse. The Ranger captain, who is also the frontier minister, asks Ethan what good that did, and Ethan tells him that, by the Comanche's beliefs, if "he ain't got no eyes, he can't enter the spirit land. He has to wander forever between the winds. You get it, reverend." Ethan will never be restored to a home life, to a family. His fate is that of the Comanche he condemned to wander forever between the winds. He is the avenger of a destroyed family, making a new one possible. In doing so he also destroys another family, Scar's family, and he will not be welcome in the new family. The uneasiness with which he is greeted when he first returns to the Edwards ranch becomes the closed door of the Jorgensen's home. The story begins with an open door to a family that will be annihilated in only a few more minutes of film. It ends with a closed door on a family that may well realize Mrs. Jorgensen's dream that "someday this land will be a good place to live." But not for Ethan Edwards. This is not his home, and they do not have to "take him in."

Arthur Eckstein[16] has persuasively argued that Ethan should not be seen as walking away from an accomplished mission and off to other adventures while those left in his wake plead for him to stay. Ethan is no Shane who, after saving the settlers from the villainous Rikers, rides back up into the mountains as Little Joey calls after him to come back. Nor is he like The Preacher of *Pale Rider,* riding away toward the mountains while a teenage girl, Megan, who earlier in the film had asked him to sexually initiate her into womanhood, pleas with him to return. The theme of *The Searchers* is far more pessimistic than mythic. According to Eckstein, "While Shane has saved the settler community, the only person Ethan has saved is Debbie from himself. It is hardly surprising that when the silhouetted Ethan walks away at the end of *The Searchers,* no one tries to call him back."[17]

Ethan Edwards is not a mythological hero at peace with himself at the end of the search. He is a deeply disturbed avenger who, as the refrain of the theme states as Ethan walks into the desert, "may search his heart and soul, go searchin' way out there. His peace of mind he knows he'll find, but where, O Lord, Lord where?" Ethan's interior search, the song suggests, has just begun, and it will not be as easy as the external one for Scar and Debbie because his psychological scars are large, deep, and jagged and his trail of vengeance has only partially revealed them to him.

Scar is often depicted in analyses of the film as Ethan's alter ego. They have lived similar lives. Scar tells Ethan that he takes white scalps because his sons were killed by whites. He is also an avenger. The killings of the Edwards family were a part of his vengeance, just as Ethan intends to kill Scar to avenge the slaughter at the Edwards ranch. The two are bound together on interlocking vengeance cycles. Both Scar and Ethan reject any sort of proportionality in their quest to get revenge. Scar takes numerous scalps; Ethan is excessive in killing Comanches even when they are carrying off their dead. He kills buffalo just in the hope that Comanches might starve if they cannot hunt them. Scar kills the settlers' cattle in order to make his murder raid against their families possible.

Ethan probably sees in Scar the person who was able to do what Ethan might only have dreamed of doing: destroy the home his brother had made with Martha and have sex, albeit rape, with his unrequited love. Scar is the successful invader of the family Ethan can only visit and from whose bosom he is excluded. Scar is Ethan's scarred psyche, and "the 'search' of the film thus becomes the seeking out and destruction of Ethan's unacceptable desires, and only after Ethan's ritualized mutilation of Scar can he finally accept Debbie."[18] Whether or not such an interpretation is persuasive with respect to Ethan's change of heart, Ethan is denied a final encounter with a live Scar.

Martin's killing of Scar is not an act of vengeance. It is an act of self-defense. The epic of vengeance terminates in an act of self-defense! Deprived of the opportunity to kill Scar, Ethan emerges from the tent holding Scar's scalp with the same sort of crazed look he had when he discovered the body of Martha after the Comanches' murder raid at the beginning of the film. That brutal act of mutilation is all that Ethan accomplishes. His beloved Martha is not avenged, and Debbie, who has for all intents and purposes become a Comanche, is allowed to live and rejoin the white community, despite what Martha would have wanted.

Eckstein writes: "The threat of incestuous adultery on Ethan's part is soon replaced in the film by the even more frightful threat of his murder of a child—his niece, the Martha-like Debbie. By the end of *The Searchers,* one can therefore well understand why Ethan is excluded from community and family. And even though Ethan ultimately does not kill Debbie (an unspeakable act that would have plunged him completely into the abyss), civilization still needs to shut Ethan out, for it would be too simple to believe that his last-minute decision to spare Debbie has suddenly 'cleansed' him of all his previous sinister impulses."[19] Ethan's motivation to kill Scar is always clear. It is to avenge Martha, the only member of the family he seeks out in the ruins of the ranch. His motivation to kill Debbie is less persuasive unless we see Debbie as a young Martha who has also been taken from Ethan and used by Scar. I think it can be argued from the film that Ethan's wanting to kill Debbie is an extension of his avenging the brutal rape and murder of Martha. It is more than his hatred of miscegenation; it is racism bound up in barely repressed sexual jealousy.

A great deal of argument could be focused on the question of who is the real hero of *The Searchers*. Ethan Edwards, the failed avenger, is indubitably the central character. But Ethan is a most unlikely hero. It is difficult to list his admirable qualities. Martin Pawley is far more virtuous. And neither of them really finds Debbie despite their years of searching. Debbie is found twice in the film, both times by the person whom Geoffrey O'Brien calls the "secret hero" of the film. She is found by old Mose Harper, "the man who can cross all boundaries and who intuits or randomly picks up the information that counts. The others search without finding; he finds without searching."[20]

Mose wanders throughout the film not in search of Debbie but for the right to sit in the "hospitality" of the Edwardses' family rocking chair. That rocking chair is a crucial symbolic element of the plot. On Ethan's arrival evening, the rocker dominates the scene. It sits in the foreground of the interior shots of the house facing the fire. Ethan sits in it, then he jumps out of it when he is incensed over Aaron's remark that Ethan before the war had evinced a desire to leave the ranch. Ethan never again sits in the chair.

Mose rocks away in the chair before heading out with Ethan, Martin, and the Rangers on that first fateful mission to catch the rustlers. When Mose and Ethan arrive back at the burning ruins of the ranch, Ethan looks for Martha, but Mose finds the rocker, miraculously undamaged, straightens it up, and sits in it. Finally, Mose's price for finding Debbie is the rocking chair, and in the last scenes of the film we see him rocking on the Jorgensens' porch. The rocking of the chair is motion going nowhere. It is home, comfortable, secure. Ethan's life of wandering forever between the winds is also motion ultimately going nowhere, but it is far from comfortable and certainly not secure or safe.

Alasdair MacIntyre notes that in "the high medieval scheme a central genre is the tale of the quest or journey. Man is essential *in via*. The end which he seeks is something which if gained can redeem all that was wrong with his life up to that point."[21] *The Searchers* gives the appearance of being a quest, a quest at first to fetch Debbie home and later to kill her, but it utterly fails the medieval point of the quest motif. At the end, Ethan is unredeemed, excluded, condemned to wander between the winds. The only person who clearly gains what he desires from the outcome of the search is Old Mose. Martin saved Debbie's life, but he gains nothing that he could not have had if he never had joined Ethan on the search. Even Debbie, who is restored to the white civilization, does not seem to gain more than she had with the Comanches, a point she makes to Martin when the searchers first find her in Scar's camp. The quest genre is a progress, perhaps modeled on the Hebrew exodus to a promised land. Ethan Edwards has only the vast, torturous desert before him, the desert of his corrupted soul. There is no redemption, no progress. However, Ethan's plight is not the cost of vengeance. It is the just deserts of the character he has molded.

Revenge for the murder of a family member drives the plot of another John Wayne Western, the one for which he finally won an Academy Award, *True Grit* (1969, directed by Henry Hathaway). *True Grit,* however, is far less complex than *The Searchers,* and despite a number of memorable scenes and superb photography, in my view it is a minor film. My interest in it in the context of the present subject is that the avenger in *True Grit* is a woman, indeed, a young woman. Played by Kim Darby, she is Mattie Ross. Tom Chaney kills her father, and she sets out to find him and avenge her father's death. "I won't rest until Tom Chaney is sparking in Hell," she says. She hires a marshal, Rooster Cogburn (John Wayne), to pursue Chaney in the Indian Territory and to bring him back to Fort Smith for trial and hanging or to kill him. She makes her meaning plain: "I intend to kill Tom Chaney if the law fails to do so."

The avenging woman in Westerns is rare, but there are notable exceptions. For example, there is Molly Riordan (Janice Rule) in *Welcome to Hard Times* (1967, directed by Burt Kennedy), based on the novel by E. L. Doctorow. Molly, unlike Mattie, is not avenging an offense against her family or a family member. She is the victim who takes up her own cause when the men in the town of Hard Times are unwilling to do so. Early in the film, Mayor Will Blue, played by Henry Fonda, makes what is clearly a rational decision not to stand up to the vicious Man from Bodie (Aldo Ray), who burns the town. During his destructive rampage, the Man from Bodie beats, rapes, and leaves Molly for dead, her back burned. She recovers under the care of Blue, but she is both embittered and filled with vengeance; hatred dominates her life. Blue describes her as having turned cold like the wintry wind. She publicly and privately tries to humiliate Blue for his failure to defend her or to avenge her, telling him that he will "always be hiding behind words and a woman's skirt." He tells her that he won't be a man in his own eyes until he is a man in hers, but she can only chide him, "How would you know anything about being a man?"

Because Molly cannot get Blue to avenge her and because she is certain that the Man from Bodie will return, she decides to turn Jimmy Fee, a young boy, the orphaned son of the only man in town who had gone up against the psychopathic Man from Bodie, into her protector. She preaches to him about male courage and skill in the use of firearms, a reversal of the usual role of women in Westerns. She buys him a shotgun and trains him to kill on her command. When the Man from Bodie returns to again savage the town, Blue manages to overcome his own pacifist beliefs and kills him, albeit after the Man from Bodie had expended his bullets. Blue carries the corpse into Molly's room to show her what he has done. As he tosses the body on a table he asks, "Molly, is this what you wanted?" The Man from Bodie's eyes briefly open and Molly screams. Thinking Molly is in danger, her young protector, Jimmy, rushes in with a gun. Blue tries to stop him, but the shotgun is fired and Molly is killed.

Her obsession with producing an avenger costs Molly her life; in fact, she lives the wasted life in the vengeance that Mrs. Jorgensen in *The Searchers* fears is in store for Brad and Martin if they follow Ethan. There is no honor for Molly Riordan. There is only bitterness. She is consumed with hatred in many forms, not all of which are moral, directed at different objects, some of which are undeserving. Although we are constantly told by a string of characters that there is a spirit of life in Hard Times, there is only death in Molly.

Another Molly is also the main character of a woman's revenge Western. Molly Parker in *Molly and Lawless John* (1972, directed by Gary Nelson) is played by Vera Miles (Laurie of *The Searchers*). She is the downtrodden and unappreciated wife of the sheriff of a small southwestern town. She falls in love with a young outlaw, Johnny Lawler (played by Sam Elliott), who, unlike her husband, flatters her and shows her affection. He convinces her to help him break out of jail, and she leaves town with him. She cares for him and makes love with him, but he is only using her, though more cleverly than her oafish husband. When he cheats on her with a woman closer to his own age and then threatens to kill the baby of a dead Indian that Molly is raising as her own, Molly kills him. She then returns to her husband, but her acts of revenge have liberated her. She is a new woman with a strong sense of self-respect, riding into town with the baby and the body of Johnny Lawler, a gun at her side. She demands the $2,000 reward for Lawler and assumes the dominant role in the family. She hands the baby to her stunned husband, then rides off toward their home, the sheriff walking behind her carrying the baby. Molly Parker has taken revenge on two men: her husband, by deserting him with a younger man and then returning to take control of their relationship, and Johnny Lawler, by shooting him down, a man who had played on her kindness, her motherliness, and her desperation for attention and affection, who used her, physically and emotionally, and then cheated on her. Molly Parker's revenge restores her sense of worth and dignity.

Perhaps no Western portrays the victimized woman as avenger with less subtlety than *Hannie Caulder* (1971, directed by Burt Kennedy), a minor though not entirely unrewarding addition to the genre, starring Raquel Welch. Hannie is married to a stage-line station manager in the desert near the Mexican border. The three sociopathic Clemons brothers, one a homicidal lunatic played by Strother Martin, ride into the station. They have robbed a bank and are being pursued by the Mexican army. They murder Hannie's husband, and when they discover her in the house, each of the three violently rapes her. They then set the house on fire and leave her for dead. Wrapped only in a blanket, she staggers from her burning home to find her husband's corpse. She buries his body and then a famous bounty hunter, Thomas Luther Price (Robert Culp), appears leading a horse on which is tied the corpse of a man he has killed and is carting to a town to collect the bounty.

Hannie tries to negotiate with Price to kill the Clemons brothers for her. "You're a bounty hunter." "I am." "You kill men for money." "You know a better reason?" "Sure as hell do." He will not accept her proposition to sleep with him if he will avenge her against the Clemons. "What ever it is that happened to you, you'll forget it." "The hell I will."

Hannie convinces Price to train her as a gunfighter so that she can take revenge on the Clemons brothers herself. They go to Mexico to a master gunsmith who designs a gun for her. After lengthy practice sessions to improve both her marksmanship and her prowess in facing another person who will be intent on killing her, she and Price ride out to find her targets. Price, however, meets them first in the streets of a dusty border town, and he is killed. Hannie then systematically takes on the three Clemons brothers seriatim and kills them. In the final scene, having wreaked the vengeance for which she endured so much, Hannie twirls and holsters her gun while Price's voice is heard, apparently in her memory, saying, "Win or lose, you lose, Hannie Caulder." She rides off with a taciturn gunman dressed in black who she originally mistook for a preacher. Apparently she will embark on the life of a bounty hunter, and her life will end, no doubt, in a manner similar to her mentor's.

Hannie has nowhere to turn other than her own resources if the Clemons brothers are to be adequately punished for what they did to her. The legal authorities are of no help. The sheriff tells her that the Clemonses are "only walkin' around wanted." He has no intention of arresting them and bringing them to trial. Furthermore, the brothers are not wanted for raping Hannie or for killing her husband. If they are killed or punished for their other crimes, including bank robbery and other murders, that cannot satisfy Hannie's need for revenge. She must take on the task herself and make the Clemons brothers understand that she is killing them for what they did to her, not because they deserve a death penalty for their lives of crime.

Hannie does not lose her sense of self-worth so she does not use acts of vengeance as a way of restoring her dignity or self-value. In other words, she does not seem to believe that she must kill the rapists in order to reassert her moral merit over theirs. She intends to kill them because they deserve it. Her hatred is far more retributive, indeed moral, than it is malicious. Of course, the rapes physically and emotionally devastated her, and her emotional wounds, unlike her physical ones, never heal. But she does not track down and kill the rapists for spite or to work off a grudge. Hannie is not resentful of the Clemons brothers in the sense that she thinks that she has been made lower than they are on some social scale. They are scum and she knows she is not. Their violation of her requires a hostile response, in and of itself, one she will deliver because no one else will.

A further point is worth noting: Hannie Caulder does not believe that, after she has killed each of the three degenerates who raped her, she has been compensated for enduring their sexual assaults or, for that matter, the murder of her husband. Whatever satisfaction she feels after killing them can be only a sense of accomplishing the administration of just deserts. She has gained nothing by way of offsetting her injury. She kills them because that is what they deserve, not because she deserves something from them. Whatever pain they might experience when she guns them down is utterly incommensurate with her suffering and could never "even the score."

Nietzsche famously claimed that the revolt of slaves against their masters has its motivational origin in what he called *ressentiment*. By that term Nietzsche seems not to have intended the psychological state of resenting another for slights or injuries received at his or her hand, but the state of not acting on legitimate resentment, holding it inside, letting it fester, until it poisons the victim. In effect, *ressentiment* makes one a victim twice over. It identifies the potential for self-destruction that hatred that is not productive of responsive action can produce. To sublimate one's justifiable hatred is a form of self-abuse. Nietzsche described the person filled with *ressentiment* as "neither upright nor naïve nor honest and straightforward with himself."[22] A noble person "consummates and exhausts" hatred "in an immediate reaction and therefore does not poison."[23] Indeed, Nietzsche's noble "shrugs off" many occasions of hatred.

Price's attempt to persuade Hannie from her mission because she will eventually forget what the depraved Clemons brothers did to her is a typical male response to a rape victim. But after he witnesses Hannie experiencing a flashback of the attack, he relents and agrees to teach her how to use a pistol and how to kill a man. We may suppose that he has concluded either that Hannie is the sort of person who will not allow her justifiable hatred to fester inside her, that she will act with or without proper training (better she be trained by a professional), or that unless she makes some attempt to avenge the Clemons brothers' violation of her person, she will continue to suffer and ultimately "poison" herself, a fate he does not wish for her. He decides that she will need training to have any hope of success in a showdown with the rapists. I suspect that his somewhat patronizing response to her indicates that he is acting from the latter and not the former analysis of the situation, though he does acknowledge and admire her commitment, which he has tested by making her walk barefoot for miles in the scorching desert.

Hannie's moral hatred is not Nietzschean *ressentiment*. Admittedly, she cannot shrug off the "vermin that eat deep" into her, but she also does not poison herself with the sublimation of her hatred. She acts, first by trudging relentlessly through the desert dressed only in a blanket and then by undergoing days of practice with the gun before setting out on her mission of vengeance. Her revenge is in deeds. She is not among those slave moralists who "compensate themselves with an imaginary revenge."[24] Hers is a triumphant affirmation of the moral order. She accepts the task, demonstrating that justifiable moral or retributive hatred need not descend into the poisonous depths of *ressentiment*.

Hannie discovers that there are substantial costs to be paid by the virtuous avenger. She is comparable in this regard to Lin McAdam, Myrl Redding, and most of the other avengers in Westerns. However, unlike Lin McAdam, Hannie

Caulder will not return to a lifestyle comparable to the one before the assault. She will not form a new home. She is rather more like Ethan Edwards after she has successfully avenged herself on the Clemons brothers. She will wander between the winds. She will never be a wife and housekeeper again. The physical strain and emotional drain of first learning to kill and then killing irrevocably alter her character and her future. She has become a bounty hunter, a paid killer, barely inside the law and moral permissibility.

At the end of the film, Price's voice echoes the theme that Alaisdair MacIntyre identifies in the Homeric epic: "Winning too may be a form of losing."[25] In Price's terms, there is no "may be" about it. Built into the basic structure of the Western, as I argued in *Cowboy Metaphysics,* is the idea that death is both inevitable and annihilation. It sets the moral boundaries, and how one lives and dies is all there is or ever will be of a person. Death is the defeat that no one can avoid; all winners ultimately lose. But her ultimate death is not, I think, the loss that Price predicts for Hannie. He identifies the fact that Hannie's decision to get revenge by killing the Clemons brothers is one of those existential moments, to which Sartre referred in *The Flies,* from which there is no retreat.[26] They occur at the "far side of despair," and although Sartre maintained that "human life begins" there, it also ends there. Nothing can be the same again.

Hannie's life-choice determines an irrevocable pattern in which her mentor's death foreshadows her own end. Her loss will be a loss of a lifestyle, a loss of innocence, a loss of home. She fashions the blanket from her burning home in which she had wrapped her bruised and naked body into a serape, and she wears it in each encounter with the rapists. She carries this remnant of her home and family with her, but all that family and home will ever be to her are vestiges of her past. She has learned firsthand of her capacity to kill another human being; she may even enjoy it. That is the enormous risk in revenge: it can be life-transforming and not for the better of the avenger, which perhaps is the strongest reason for objecting to it, despite its virtuous aspects.

I noted in Chapter 1 that in the classical literary texts male vengeance was generally regarded as having a higher moral status than acts of revenge carried out by women. *Hannie Caulder* quite self-consciously disavows that idea. Hannie not only holds the moral high ground from the beginning to the end of the film, but she also exercises what could be called her Lockean right to punish without going to excess. She works hard to gain the expertise necessary to succeed at her task, and she directs her efforts at, and only at, the appropriate targets. There is nothing of Medea about her. She is also morally superior to Molly Riordan of *Welcome to Hard Times* and perhaps even to Mattie Ross of *True Grit.* She accepts the task of revenge as her own, while the other two enlist males to do the job for them, albeit Mattie insists on accompanying Rooster on the mission. It seems fair to say that, with the exception of Molly Riordan, the female avengers, or at least the ones in the Westerns I have discussed, are on the same moral footing as their male counterparts.

At the close of Chapter 1, I identified fifteen conceptual elements of vengeance that appeared in the literary examples surveyed. The revenge Westerns, by and large, evidence the same set of features but draw attention to some that I did not catalogue, though they may appear, sometimes prominently, in the literary tradition. The Westerns make clear that vengeance is a very personal matter. The emotions that give rise to revenge motives are close to home. In fact, home, family, and friendship are dominant points of reference in the Western vengeance films. Only in the women-as-avenger stories (particularly *Hannie Caulder, Molly and Lawless John,* and *Welcome to Hard Times*) are the injuries being avenged physically incurred by the avengers. In all of the others, emotional injuries are deeply felt by the avenger as a result of death and destruction visited on others with whom the avenger has very personal bonds of affection.

Family, home, and friendship are intensely personal motivations, and they give rise to what may be called "nonvoluntary obligations." You fall into them or are born into them or they are imposed or dumped on you. John Rawls notes that "certain natural attitudes underlie the corresponding moral feelings."[27] Such moral feelings and related senses of obligation are significant elements in *The Iliad, The Oresteia, Medea,* and *Hamlet,* but they are vivid and unvarnished with conceptions of social roles, monarchical succession, and so on, in the Westerns. A voluntarist, of course, would argue that nonvoluntary relationships should not be regarded as sources of moral obligation. Only those relationships entered into willfully can generate real moral obligations. But such a view flies in the face of common practice and understanding, and it is the commonplace view that is reflected in the Westerns. Of course, marriage is usually a voluntary arrangement and friends are typically chosen. So even on a voluntarist interpretation, spouses avenging the murders of their husbands or wives and friends avenging the injuries suffered by their friends could be acts fulfilling moral obligations. The voluntarist's restriction would, of course, exclude from the scope of moral obligation children avenging their parents, siblings avenging each other, uncles avenging their brothers' families, and anyone avenging unrequited or unconsummated love interests.

Rawls seems to think that we can account for what he calls the "morality of association" in terms of an individual's learning about ideals that are defined in terms of respective social roles. On an account that Rawls might favor, Lin McAdam of *Winchester '73* feels morally obligated to avenge the murder of his father because he internalized the ideal of the good son, he had a productive association with his father as they played out their familial roles, and out of that association bonds of mutual trust, respect, and friendship grew. Lin would be stricken with guilt if he failed to uphold the obligations of his side of the association. Hence, he avenges his father's murder primarily to avoid that guilt.

I suppose it is possible to persuasively employ such an analysis to interpret the actions of many of the Western avengers, but the films portray these issues as far more basic, more primitive. Lin McAdam does not hunt down his father's killer because he understands what it is to be a good son and he enjoyed a mutually beneficial relationship with his father. He hunts down the killer because his father was murdered, his family violated. His home, even though it was only "sort of a home," was destroyed. Ethan Edwards searches for Scar and the Comanche band because they raped and murdered Martha and slaughtered his brother and nephew. He does not do so because he had internalized an ideal of uncle and had built up an association of trust and other cooperative virtues productive of mutual benefit with the deceased members of the Edwards family.

Family, home, and friends are the conceptual reservoirs of many of our deepest moral emotions. We don't need to explain how obligations arise within them by reference to psychological covering laws based on a conception of individual rational self-interest, as Rawls does. Feelings of trust and obligation and fidelity and loyalty and the like do not only arise from one's appreciation of the fact that one is a member of a mutually beneficial association in equilibrium. The cooperative virtues and their related obligations may have, and the Westerns portray them as having, roots that are not captured in the individualist's schema. Such associations may simply be boldface facts of the human condition, the bedrock of a human life. D. H. Lawrence wrote: "I am part of the sun as my eye is part of me. That I am part of the earth my feet know perfectly, and my blood is part of the sea. My soul knows that I am part of the human race, my soul is an organic part of the great human race, as my spirit is part of my nation. In my own very self, I am part of my family."[28]

Home is where they have to take you in, but it is also where the heart is. Being part of a family anchors a person in the world, and that attachment is integral to the structure of the plots of the revenge Westerns. Even the Western mythic wanderers like Shane, albeit temporarily, anchor themselves to a family and reformulate their sense of personal honor to encompass its defense. Excluded from family, devoid of friends, one is condemned to wander forever between the winds. I suppose that conclusion is one of the profoundly antimodern, anti-Enlightenment, antiliberal individualist insights of the revenge Westerns and perhaps why they strike a meaningful chord with so many people. They affirm a view of the moral life in which core human relations are not negotiable, not matters of contract, not even voluntary.

The virtues of vengeance arise from a far older and richer sense, a relational sense, of what it is to be a particular person than individualist contractarian conceptions of social organizations and institutions suggest. Families, just as individuals, however, are prone to be fragile, and they are especially so when their homes are located on the edges of civilization, as they always are in Westerns. There are inestimable emotional costs associated with family loss, home loss, loss of friends. Little wonder that when one's family or home is invaded, one's loved ones harmed or murdered, one is filled with the strongest feelings of resentment, indignation, hatred. And little wonder also that these feelings fuel revenge. The revenge reaction is visceral; that is the general theme of the revenge Westerns.

Importantly, although family or friendship is the focus of or the reason for vengeance on the part of the hero of the Westerns, the avengers are self-reliant persons who set their own moral parameters. They are not communitarians. They may be emotionally anchored in home, family, or friends, but their moral sense and confidence are drawn from an inner strength, a physical and moral self-sufficiency. They are self-reliant and motivationally independent. Their sense of honor is personal, not public, and honor for them is decidedly not a zero-sum game.

The Western avenger's judgments of personal obligation lack a necessary connection to any conception of the common good or, for that matter, to any telos. They are nonconsequentialists in every fiber of their motivations except personal honor; they act to ensure and sustain. They are not champions of the good life or the good of the community. They are also not deontic universalizers. When Brennan, in *The Tall T,* says that he is going to stay to face the return of the murderous gang because there are some things a man can't ride around, he is not making a universalizable moral claim. He means quite clearly that here and now are some things he cannot avoid doing and still have self-respect. What matters to him is his sense of who he is; no one else enters into the equation. He is not saying that all men in his circumstances ought to stay and fight. His is a very personal decision, a distinctively particularist credo. He has internalized his moral judgmental audience. He does not see his actions as Doretta might see them, and he does not stay to fight for her benefit or for her approval. He has internalized a detached observational point of view that evaluates actions in terms of the appropriateness of their being described as evidencing the inner strength of the agent, his inner strength. In large measure, that is the wellspring of his moral authority qua avenger.

PART TWO

Philosophical Analysis
of Vengeance

CHAPTER THREE

The Concept

Vengeance as Communication

If you wrong us, shall we not revenge.
William Shakespeare[1]

Robert Nozick, while attempting to distinguish between revenge and retribution,[2] provides a useful account of what is involved in vengeance, though some of his distinctions between revenge and retribution are less than convincing.[3] Acts of revenge, Nozick tells us, need not be done for a wrong. They may be done because of an injury or a harm or a slight. Retribution is taken only to redress wrongs. But on what basis can a clear distinction between wrongs and harms, slights or injuries, be drawn? If "wrongs" is understood as prohibitions codified in law and prosecutable by state authorities or through civil legal proceedings by offended individuals, Nozick's distinction becomes rather uninteresting because it would confine retribution to legally defined violations. A community could not retributively punish a member for slighting behavior, for example, if such behavior is not against the law in that community. It could only be said to be taking out revenge against the slighter. All communal as well as individual enforcements of moral precepts that are not actionable in law would be acts of revenge.

Nozick also insists that, in the case of revenge, there is no internal limit on how much of an injury can be inflicted on the offending target. Retribution, supposedly, is governed by internal limits. In Chapter 7 I will dispute this idea in terms of the concept of fit. In this chapter I will investigate some of the norms of revenge that exist in a number of societies and that were also operative in the historical/literary foundations of revenge in our culture, as noted in Chapter 1. Where such norms exist, however, they seem to set both external limits—for example, practicality—and internal constraints on revenge.

Nozick is surely right, however, in emphasizing that revenge is typically more personal than retribution. The avenger often is linked in some crucial way to the person or persons who were injured, harmed, slighted, by the target. The avenger might be the injured party or a relative or friend of the injured party. The business of linkage to the injured party is interesting for many reasons and seems to have a great deal to do with the standard negative response among moralists to the very idea of vengeance. Impartiality has been all the rage in moral circles since the Enlightenment. Admittedly, the linkage of the avenger to the injured party usually dictates the type of revenge that is taken. If person X did something injurious to me, then I am most likely to believe that successful revenge will require me to do at least the same to him. However, if X did something injurious to my sister, I might regard doing the same to X's sister as appropriate vengeance. On the other hand, the avenger might say to X, "I'm going to kill you because of what you did to my sister." After all, X may have no siblings. Still, the avenger could say, "Because of what you did to me by harming my sister, I am going to harm your sister in a similar fashion," assuming, of course, that X has a sister to harm.

The personal aspect of some acts of vengeance does set them apart from the standard acts of retribution on, as Nozick notes, two counts. In the first place, revenge of that type can be desired only by the injured party or by someone who is closely linked to the injured party. Retribution, on the other hand, can be desired by anyone, or rather anyone can hope for, wish for, want to see retribution carried out against the offender. Suppose I read about the death of a factory worker in Pittsburgh and believe that his death was caused by the criminal negligence of the owners of the factory. I can desire that those owners be punished to the full extent of the law and/or I can desire that a family member or friend of the dead worker revenge his death by killing the owners, but is my desire, in this matter, really a desire for revenge? It certainly is a desire that acts of revenge be successfully performed by someone, that revenge be done. I will have stronger feelings of this sort, no doubt, if I also believe that the criminal justice system probably will be circumvented by the owners, that their lawyers will find the loopholes to get them off the penal "hook." Should I, a few days later, read that revenge was taken against the owners by a close friend of the deceased, I probably will at least feel a sense of approval. I may applaud, if only in private, the friend's action. Such is the filmmaker's expectation in vengeance films such as the *Death Wish* series. The audience desires that revenge be done, but is that a desire for revenge or for retribution?

I believe that Nozick's second point of difference between revenge and retribution—that revenge can only be inflicted by a person with a personal tie to the victim—is wrong. The state does not punish the criminal for the sake of revenge, though it can, depending on the penal theory one adopts, punish for the sake of retribution. The state is impersonal. On Nozick's account, I cannot head to Pittsburgh to revenge the dead worker I never met and who has no personal ties to me, though I could, if I were in an appropriate position in the judicial system, visit retributive punishment on the owners for having caused the death of the worker. The *Death Wish* series, following Nozick's distinction, when it ran out of personal ties for the hero to avenge, became a series about vigilantism. Its lead character started killing any criminals he happened to meet in the city. He was, no doubt, convinced that the law would never prosecute and punish the muggers, rapists, and other offenders that were inflicting themselves on the public, so he took the matter of punishment, capital punishment, into his own hands.

His acts in that regard, however, cannot, if Nozick is correct, be acts of vengeance. (I think that too much has been made of the personal linkage in understanding vengeance, or what I will call "virtuous vengeance," but I will postpone examination of the issue until Chapter 5.)

A very important point that Nozick makes, and one that is evident in the literary roots of vengeance, is that the avenger must somehow communicate to the target the reasons for the infliction of the punishment. The relationship between the avenger and the target becomes a remarkably intimate one. Nozick mentions the "emotional tone" of revenge.[4] I suppose that what he means is that the avenger typically wants, in fact needs, to savor the sweetness of revenge in order to bring closure to his or her act of vengeance: "Therefore, the thirster after revenge often will want to experience (see, be present at) the situation in which the revengee is suffering."[5] This response is reminiscent of Cable Hogue's remark to Josh, in the Sam Peckinpah film *The Ballad of Cable Hogue,* when he is told to leave vengeance to God: "That's okay with me as long as he does it soon and I can watch."

Vengeance is warm, retribution is cold, poetic justice is frigid.

The taking of revenge usually produces an emotional or psychological state in the avenger, a feeling of pleasure, a sense of accomplishment, a high. That state cannot be fully experienced if the villain has met his or her end in some natural occurrence, for example, by being buried in an avalanche, unless, of course, the avenger triggered the avalanche with the intent to kill the escaping villain. There is little satisfaction in the villain's death for the would-be avenger who has not been the direct or proximate cause of his or her demise. A feeling of personal failure to achieve an important moral task is likely to grip the would-be avenger. This reaction seems to occur to Ethan Edwards, in *The Searchers,* when Martin Pawley has already killed Scar by the time Ethan has entered the tent. He is left only to mutilate the Comanche chief's corpse. The same is true in the less drastic cases where one's thirst for revenge will only be slaked by the villain's downfall. Unless the avenger is the direct or proximate cause of that ruin, vengeance will not have occurred, and he or she will be left lacking the sense of accomplishment, the sweetness, even if in the regular course of events the villain is "brought low."

Nozick mentions that "there need be no generality in revenge."[6] By that he means an avenger is not committed to treating all similar acts done to any other people in the same manner in which he or she treats the act he or she is avenging. Avengers who commit themselves to a generalization principle with respect to what they are about are likely to become vigilantes. There is a significant noncognitive element in vengeance that Nozick identifies as a dependency on how the avenger "feels at the time about the act of injury." Retributivists are committed to the adoption of general principles that require certain punishments under certain conditions and to the promulgation of those principles. I wonder if the move in our culture away from vengeance and toward retributivism does not track a wider movement in our thinking about ethics toward cognitivism and away from noncognitive conceptions of morality and values. In any event, if the avenger does not have con-attitudes toward the harm or injury to be avenged that are sufficiently strong to motivate his or her taking direct, personal, action against the wrongdoer, even virtuous vengeance will gain no foothold. The matter will have to be left for the courts and the penal system of the community.

Aside from the noncognitive element that distinguishes vengeance, retribution and revenge share a common structure. Nozick writes, "A penalty is inflicted for a reason (a wrong or injury) with the desire that the other person know why this is occurring and know that he was intended to know."[7] The structure is as old as Achilles' meeting with Hector beneath the walls of Troy. Nozick fills out the structure for retribution. Using his schema as a model and making necessary modifications to fit the distinctions previously drawn, vengeance may be profitably seen to have the following structure:

> Avenger Y succeeded in avenging X's act A (in the best-case scenario) if the following conditions held:
> 1. Y felt that A, an act that inflicted a harm or injury on someone, possibly Y, was, to some degree or extent, wrong,
> 2. And imposed a penalty on X,
> 3. That reflected, at the time, how strongly Y felt about the wrongness of A,
> 4. Intending that the penalty be exacted because of the wrong act A,
> 5. And in virtue of the wrongness of A,
> 6. Intending that X realize that the penalty was visited on him or her because he or she did A,
> 7. And in virtue of the wrongness of A,
> 8. By someone who intended to have the penalty fit and be executed because of the wrongness of A,
> 9. And who intended that X would understand that the penalty was inflicted on him or her so that 1–9 are satisfied.

A basic metaphysical condition of virtuous vengeance is the belief that its moral quality, its rightness or wrongness, is not, in any direct or proximate sense, one of the causally efficacious properties of a person's actions. Performing an action that has a moral quality does not automatically trigger an appropriate reward or punishment for the actor. Only the recognition of that moral quality and the intercession of a "rewarder" or "punisher" can establish a moral link between the actions of a person and what he or she deserves. Revenge is one way to ensure the linkage between wrongful behavior and penalties; penal sanctions and other forms of communally adopted or approved punishments are another. Vengeance and karma are not close relatives.

In *Responsibility Matters* and in other writings, I drew a distinction between what I called spatial and temporal moral theories.[8] I want here to draw attention to another distinction that distinguishes types of moral theories. It turns on whether the moral qualities of actions are understood to be causally efficacious in the life or lives of their agents. Some moral theories endow the moral qualities of actions with the causal power to award deserts to agents, either directly or, more typically, in some mediated way. Others see the moral qualities of actions as causally impotent. Moral theories of the first sort I will call karmic, the others nonkarmic. Karmic moral theories might be naturalistic or supernaturalistic. (Might some be nonnaturalistic?)

The term "karma," of course, evokes Asian philosophical and religious theories. Although the term comes from that source, what I am calling karmic moral theories appear in both Euro-American as well as Asian versions. Karmic moral theories respond in roughly the same way to the same sorts of concerns in moral psychology. In the classical Hindu literature, the doctrine of karma takes shape around the idea that for every thought or deed that has a moral quality, there is a corresponding reward or penalty that will be visited on the agent in either this life or in a future life. Bruce Reichenbach provides a list of the basic presuppositions of a karmic theory.[9] For my purposes, four of the five metaphysical doctrines cited by him are foundational in the identification of karmic moral theories of either the Euro-American or Asian variety. Those are: all actions that have moral qualities have consequences; those consequences occur according to the formula that right actions have good consequences, wrong ones have bad consequences; although some of those consequences might immediately follow the actions, some may be separated from their causes by considerable temporal distances; and karmic effects "can be accumulated."

Karma, in the Hindu conception, is not a law that operates on all human actions. It is activated only with respect to actions that had a certain sort of intention or that reflect or manifest certain types of attitudes. Some actions, as noted in the *Bhagavad Gita,* are done to bring about specific or expected outcomes desired by the actor. In other cases, the actor may have no personal interest in the results of his or her actions. Actions of the latter sort are done selflessly or from a motive that is not self-aggrandizing or without ill will toward the object of the action. The distinction is crucial in the causal metaphysics of a classic Hindu karmic morality. "Set thy heart upon thy work, but never on its reward. Work not for a reward; but never cease to do thy work," Krishna advises. "Work done for a reward is much lower than work done in the Yoga of wisdom . . . How poor those who work for a reward!"[10]

In the last book of the *Gita,* Krishna tells Arjuna that, in order to avoid the karmic forces, works of "sacrifice, gift, and self-harmony," even though they are morally required, must be "done in the freedom of a pure offering, and without expectation of reward."[11] The reason for the renunciation of actions done from personal inclination and hope of personal reward is that only such actions have karmic powers, only they will produce like effects. Krishna makes this point clear when he says, "He who is free from the chains of selfishness, and whose mind is free from any ill-will, even if he kills all these warriors he kills them not and he is free."[12]

The karmic law, in the classical Hindu conception, is not the moral law, although it is inextricably linked to ethical considerations. It has no moral content and provides no moral guidance. It is, purely and simply, a causal law of desert, saying only that right actions will produce good consequences and wrong ones will produce bad ones. It does not state what actions are right or wrong. It is also not a law of compensation. A Lockean-like distinction between punishment and reparation appears to be made in the classic Hindu understanding of karma.

The law of karmic causation in the ancient Hindu texts is not strictly identical to the law of event causation, nor is it only a special case of ordinary event causation. To render karma sensible, apparently some sort of dualistic causal story needs to be adopted. I think it goes something like this: All human actions occur in an ordinary, physical, extensional causal-event sequence regardless of their moral character. Some actions, however—those with a moral quality, those describable as done with certain intentions or attitudes—have causal effects in another causal sequence that I am tempted to call intensional, but I suspect that is not quite right. In any event, the second sequence must necessarily link to and map onto the extensional physical causal sequence. It is not as though the dual causal sequences run parallel to each other. The second sequence, apparently, frequently twists and turns its way into the first and must create some of the conditions in which the first operates. Killing other human beings selflessly and killing them selfishly might well look like similar actions on the first sequence. They produce virtually identical effects in the ordinary causal order of events: the battle is won and the bodies of many warriors are lying about dead. But the actions of a warrior killing another warrior selfishly or with ill will also cause karmic effects that are not generated by another warrior's selfless killing. The karmic effects, however, do not necessarily have an impact on the immediate or proximate physical causal sequence, the ordinary causal sequence. Where they do occur and how they weave back into the ordinary causal sequence, however, is a major metaphysical problem for the Hindu karmic theorist.

Moral qualities attach to actions that are associated with intentional and attitudinal states, and those actions are captured by the law, or on the wheel, of karma. They will have consequences in the life (lives) of the agent but not on those affected by the agent's karmic actions. The selfless killer, on the other hand, will experience no karmic consequences, good or ill, from his or her homicidal deed. Krishna talks of killing warriors as not (morally) killing warriors as long as the killing is done without attitude or "ill-will" or for selfish reasons. The action of killing renders the warriors dead in accordance with ordinary causal law; for example, slicing off their heads causes their vital organs to cease to function and they are dead, but it has no moral impact. It has no effect on the moral status and, hence, on the life (or lives) of the killer. The killer (in this life or another) will be neither better nor worse off because of it.

This idea may be reminiscent of the standard Western moralist's notion that lack of intention should at least lessen the moral responsibility for a deed. Aristotle, for example, argues that a person is only responsible for what he has done voluntarily (or intentionally), "hekousion."[13] But I think that very little should be made of this position because it does not seem to be the case that the selfless killer cannot be described as acting voluntarily or intentionally. It is just that the selfless killer does not have certain intentions or attitudes. He or she certainly still intends to kill the other person. After all, that is what warriors do. We might, however, associate nonkarmic or selfless killing with what is referred to in the criminal law as the absence of *mens rea*.

Karmic moral theories of the classical Asian sort and, I think, of the more modern Euro-American variety are responses to the ancient, though still troubling, nontheological problem of evil. This is the problem that so perplexes Job in the Bible. It is the problem of trying to explain why, if the universe is either a good place or in the control of a good god, good people suffer and evil people prosper. Why isn't virtue invariably rewarded and wickedness always punished? There seems to be something capricious, random, at best amoral, about the distribution of happiness and unhappiness, pleasure and pain, success and failure, misery and joy, profit and loss in human life.

There sits Job, a genuinely good man, his world in ruin because of a cosmic game between God and Satan, "afflicted with loathsome sores from the sole of his foot to the crown of his head" (quotes are from the King James Version), cast out among a heap of ashes and dung. Along come his friends who ask him, "Who that was innocent ever perished? Or where were the upright cut off?" Then they intone the standard theory: "Those who plow iniquity and sow trouble reap the same." And Job responds: "Make me understand how I have erred . . . How many are my iniquities and my sins? Make me know my transgression and my sin." Of course his friends cannot, because he has not transgressed. He has not sinned. But they fall back on the old formula, asserting that on the evidence of his current condition, he must have sinned: "The wicked man writhes in pain all his days, through all the years that are laid up for the ruthless . . . in prosperity the destroyer will come upon him . . . Do you not know that . . . the exulting of the wicked is short, and the joy of the godless but for a moment?" But Job cannot be persuaded. He reminds them: "Why do the wicked live, reach old age, and grow mighty in power? Their children are established in their presence, and their offspring before their eyes . . . They sing to the tambourine and the lyre, and rejoice to the sound of the pipe. They spend their days in prosperity . . . Behold, is not their prosperity in their hand?"

Karmic moral causality is the Hindu response to a lament like Job's. The answer, however, is far subtler than that of Job's friends. It does not deny that the wicked prosper or that the virtuous often suffer. It explains current suffering and prosperity in terms of the karmic effects of previous wickedness or virtuousness that might well have been committed in a former life of the person. Further, it assures that in the future, whether in this life or another life of the agent, all wicked-ness will be punished and virtue will be rewarded. Cosmic moral order is main-tained, and the apparent randomness of the distribution of good and bad states is revealed to be only apparent and not really the case. In other words, the karmic moralist sides with Job's friends but modifies their account of universal justice by extending karmic causality over rather considerable temporal distances.

But how does karmic causality work? The naturalistic account, apparently pre-ferred in the classical Hindu literature, might best be described as dispositional. The action with a moral quality causes an event on the ordinary event causal chain, and it also causes the actor to form a disposition. The dispositions so formed, or karmic residues, will cause the actor, at a propitious future occasion, to behave in a way that will produce in him or her happiness if the originating action was virtuous or unhappiness if it was wicked. These dispositions, or *samskaras*, are tendencies to act, think, experience, interpret, and so on, in such a way as to have the morally appropriate effect on the actor. The idea that the law of karma allows enormous temporal distances between cause and effect is, then, not quite on the mark. The action has an immediate causal effect on the actor: the production of the residues or dispositions. Of course, as with any disposition, *samskaras* will only manifest themselves when conditions are favorable, and that may be many years or lives removed from the originating action.

This *samskaras* account of karmic effects, though it may better satisfy our intuitions than an account of causation over extreme temporal distance, runs afoul of those intuitions in another important respect. Karma not only is sup-posed to implant dispositions in us to do things that will make us happy or unhappy in the future, but it also is supposed to affect the very environment in which we will live and in which the *samskaras* will manifest themselves. The bodies of our future lives, the environments in which we will live, our health, genetic structure, wealth, social status, and so on, have to be influenced by our karmic residues. The environment must be "affected in such a way that in some future life it will be instrumental in rewarding or punishing us according to the merit or demerit resulting from our actions."[14] But how is that supposed to work? How can karmic causality, on such a naturalistic account, affect the objective (nondispositional) as well as the subjective conditions of a person's life? How, for example, do *samskaras* cause floods, earthquakes, and tornadoes?

No fully satisfactory naturalistic direct causal answer seems to emerge in the literature, although many were formulated.[15] The naturalistic dualist causal story of Hindu karma arrives at the same sort of impasse that confronts all dualisms: the Humpty-Dumpty argument, as Passmore once called it.[16] The point, cap-tured by Passmore's phrase, is that once a system has been torn asunder to ex-plain it, it becomes "quite impossible to put the pieces together again in a single situation." Yet, unless the system can be put back together, it was meaningless to break it up in the first place.

Naturalistic approaches are deserted by Sankara and those in the Nyaya system of thought in favor of a mediated and supernatural causal account. They argue that there must be a god to supervise or administer karmic effects in the material world. Only a theistic administrator can guarantee the union of virtue with happiness and wickedness with unhappiness. The law of karma and the karmic residues *(apurva)* are unintelligent and unconscious, so "there must be a conscious God who knows the merits and demerits which persons have earned by their actions, and who functions as an instrumental cause in helping individuals reap their appropriate fruits."[17] Nyaya, in fact, regards this need as the basis for a proof of the existence of a god. Udayana Acarya's *Kusumanjali* (with a commentary by Hari Dasa Bhattacarya) contains the following argument: "from dependence,—from eternity,—from diversity,—from universal practice,—and from the apportionment to each individual self—mundane enjoyment implies a supernatural cause [i.e., desert] . . . It is only the conviction that they do produce heaven, etc. as their fruit, which makes men engage in sacrifices, etc.; and these [passing away when the action is over] cannot produce this fruit unless by means of some influence which continues to act after the rite is over,—and hence is this invisible influence, called merit and demerit, established."[18]

Sankara argues in a similar fashion for the intermediate causal role of the Highest Lord, Isvara. He writes: "There arises the question whether the threefold fruits of action which are enjoyed by the creatures in their *samsara*-state—viz. pain, pleasure, and a mixture of the two—spring from the actions themselves or come from the Lord.—The *Sutrakara* embraces the latter alternative, on the ground that it is the only possible one. The ruler of all who by turns provides for the creation, the subsistence and the reabsorption of the world, and who knows all differences of place and time, he alone is capable of effecting all those modes of requital which are in accordance with the merit of the agents; actions, on the other hand, which pass away as soon as done, have no power of bringing about results at some future time, since nothing can spring from nothing."[19] Sankara summarizes his account of the role of Isvara in karma: "The final conclusion is that the fruits [of action] come from the Lord acting with a view to the deeds done by the souls, or, if it be so preferred, with a view to the *apurva* springing from the deeds."[20]

Sankara's position is not that the Highest Lord arbitrarily assigns pain, pleasure, and so on (the "fruits of action"), but that Isvara is caused to assign the fruits of action by the moral qualities of the actions themselves, either directly or because of the residues they produce. The moral qualities of actions are still causally efficacious, and the power of the Highest Lord further ensures the environments appropriate to what the agent deserves, that is, those in which the karmic dispositions will be instantiated in the life of the agent. Sankara thereby overcomes one of the major problems of the naturalistic accounts, although at the cost of adopting theistic postulates that must restrict the god's scope of actions by excluding forgiveness, mercy, and grace as divine attributes. Clearly, if the Highest Lord has the discretion to forgive or be merciful, then karma would not be an inviolable causal law. It would be contingent and not necessary.

But a conceptual problem emerges: we should expect that a god as powerful and knowledgeable as would be required to administer karma, the Highest Lord as described by Sankara, also should not be incapable of interventions on the karmic wheel. Still, the god's scope of actions must be limited, for if the god could intervene by, for example, showing mercy, the whole point of karma as a causal law would be lost, the connection between an agent's past actions and that agent's present condition would be severed. At best, that connection then would only be one between the actual world and a possible world that is prevented from actualization by the intervention of a merciful deity. If the god were permitted interventions, the focus of the problem of evil would shift to questioning why the god intervenes in some cases but not in others, or in all others. The nontheological problem of evil would morph into the theological problem of evil: how can we understand a god that allows so much human suffering when divine intervention could alleviate it? Although karma dissolves the problem of evil on the human level, it is of no help with the issue when it transports to the theological plane.

In various guises, karmic morality can be identified in Euro-American thought. Plato, in the *Republic* (as the philosophers at Colby College reminded me) can in places be seen as something of a karmic moral theorist, a nonmediated one. The Myth of Er that concludes the dialogue recounts the tale of the choosing of next lives: "'Souls that live for a day, now is the beginning of another cycle of mortal generation where birth is the beacon of death. No divinity shall cast lots for you . . . The blame is his who chooses. God is blameless.' . . . And there, dear Glaucon, it appears, is the supreme hazard for man . . . It was a strange, pitiful, and ridiculous spectacle, as the choice was determined for the most part by the habits of their former lives."[21] Plato seems to be suggesting that as we act we form habits that causally will affect the way we choose our next lives. Wicked people, despite what pleasures they may have enjoyed in their previous life, will be disposed to choose future painful lives. It is not much of a stretch to see this interpretation as a rendition of a karmic residues story.

Descartes seems to have been aware of the karmic leanings of the audience to whom he addressed the "Dedicatory Letter" of the *Meditations*. He explains that his work is intended to persuade those without faith to accept moral virtue by means of natural reason. To do that, he is convinced that he needs to prove the existence of God and the immortality of human souls. "Since in this life one frequently finds greater rewards offered for vice than for virtue, few persons would prefer the just to the useful if they were not restrained either by fear of God or by the expectation of another life."[22] A not far-fetched reading of his remarks could see them as supporting the view that a supernatural mediating causal force that is driven by moral considerations of just distribution combined with the immortality of the human soul are prerequisites for moral motivation. Although both are karmic conceptions, I am too uncertain about Descartes's moral theory to make very much of a comment that may be intended only to garner support from his liturgical audience.

Kant's ethics, at least through the writing of the *Critique of Practical Reason,* however, makes for rather a clearer case. Kant's moral theory is seldom thought of in these terms, but I believe he provides a paradigmatic example of a medi-ated supernaturalist karmic moral theory. The typical focus of discussions of Kant's ethics is on the Categorical Imperative and duty for its own sake. Brad-ley, for example, takes the "duty for its own sake" mantra to be the sole distin-guishing characteristic of Kantian ethics.[23] Kant, as is well known, stresses that true moral motivation excludes the desire for personal goods, e.g., happiness. Doing one's duty, however, is no guarantee of personal happiness.

For Kant, respect for law is respect for form. It cashes out as a feeling, borne of the awareness of the moral law as the Categorical Imperative, which is invariably sufficient to incite us to act rightly. It is also a motive that is available to all of us all of the time. Hence, it is radically different from other motives. For example, other motives might lead one to act rightly, but there is no guarantee that they will do so in every instance. Being moved by the dictates of moral duty, under-stood in terms of the Categorical Imperative, is not pursuing one's good, though it is also not to be acting irrationally. The latter claim is, however, not at all self-evident if rationality is understood in standard economic or hedonic terms. The echo of the Krishna in the *Gita* is not difficult to discern. Actions motivated by duty without personal interest or attitude—in other words, selflessly—are mor-ally superior to the standard motives.

Kant, however, was well aware that his dutiful moral person is more than likely to confront Job's problem. So his response, as J. B. Schneewind points out, is that although "morality requires each of us to make ourselves perfectly virtuous— to give ourselves a character in which the dictates of the Categorical Imperative are never thwarted by passions and desires . . . it also requires that happiness be distributed in accordance with virtue."[24] But these two requirements of moral-ity, the perfection and the distribution requirements, create problems that Kant believes can only be solved by appeal to metaphysical postulates: immortality of the human soul and the existence of God.

To satisfy the perfection requirement, Kant's version of one of Jesus' commands during the Sermon on the Mount, humans require far more than a finite life-time. Kant writes: "The realization of the *summum bonum* in the world is the necessary object of a will determinable by the moral. But in this will the perfect accordance of the mind with the moral law is the supreme condition of the *sum-mum bonum.* This then must be possible, as well as its object, since it is contained in the command to promote the latter. Now, the perfect accordance of the will with the moral law is *holiness,* a perfection of which no rational being of the sen-sible world is capable at any moment of his existence. Since, nevertheless, it is required as practically necessary, it can only be found in a *progress in infinitum* towards that perfect accordance, and on the principles of pure practical reason it is necessary to assume such a practical progress as the real object of our will. Now, this *endless* progress is only possible on the supposition of an endless duration of the existence and personality of the same rational being (which is called the immortality of the soul)."[25]

The second requirement of morality (the distribution requirement), the achievement of the summum bonum, entails the "distribution of happiness in exact proportion to morality (which is the worth of the person, and his worthiness to be happy)."[26] The summum bonum is the perfect goal of a human life. Reason prescribes it, or, as Theodore Greene notes, "the inclusion of happiness as an element in the *Summum Bonum* is reason's demand and the *Summum Bonum* is man's rational ideal."[27] If the summum bonum is not achievable by the virtuous, if those who have attained "worthiness to be happy" are not happy, Kant's ethics would be rather pointless. Bradley's criticisms would then be devastating. (Perhaps they are in any event!) The summum bonum's potential achievement is necessary to sustain moral belief. "It is, as it were, a pledge that the universe is systematically ordered according to moral purposes."[28] Without such a pledge, Kant believed, the motive of duty for its own sake will fall on deaf ears.

The two elements of the summum bonum, happiness and moral virtue, in Kantian ethics are clearly distinct. They are not analytically related: Job's problem. If they stand in any relationship at all, it must be a synthetic one and "must be conceived as the connexion of cause and effect."[29] But they cannot be related by cause and effect because, as Job was painfully aware, virtue does not cause happiness, nor does happiness cause virtue. Naturalistic accounts fail. There can be, Kant concludes, no necessary connection between virtue and happiness. But the realization of that fact could lead to utter moral depression and denial: Job's state. "If the supreme good is not possible by practical rules, then the moral law also which commands us to promote it is directed to vain imaginary ends, and must consequently be false."[30]

Kant's solution is that "morality of mind should have a connexion as cause with happiness (as an effect in the sensible world) if not immediate yet mediate (viz.: through an intelligent author of nature), and moreover necessary."[31] In effect, Kant opts for a solution remarkably similar to Sankara's mediated karma. Kant writes, "Happiness proportioned to that morality, and this on grounds as disinterested as before, and solely from impartial reason . . . must lead to the supposition of the existence of God, as the necessary condition of the possibility of the *summum bonum*."[32]

Acting in accord with the Categorical Imperative produces moral worthiness, and moral worthiness is the supreme good; but, as Schneewind notes,[33] it is not the summum bonum, the complete or the perfect good. That end requires that the achievement of virtue is the criterion for the distribution of happiness. The job of Kant's God is to serve as the mediate causal link between human virtue and happiness. Kant's argument is that we have a duty to promote the summum bonum. Our only way of doing so, however, is to act always from the motive of duty for its own sake. But such morally meritorious behavior does not have the causal capacity in itself to ensure happiness. It can only ensure the achievement of virtue, one—but only one—part of the summum bonum. Yet, because the promotion of the bipartite summum bonum is a duty, its realization must be possible. It can only be possible, however, if God exists to forge the mediate causal link between our achievement of virtue and our happiness. Morality, for Kant, is "not properly the doctrine how we should make ourselves happy, but how we should become worthy of happiness."[34] Our worthiness causes God to distribute happiness in the appropriate proportion to us. Hence, Kant's moral theory in the *Second Critique* is karmic. The moral qualities of actions have a causal, albeit mediated, effect on the life of the agent, even if in a life after death, the existence of which is founded on the postulate of the immortality of the human soul.

It is worth a brief mention that apparently Kant's work in ethics after the *Second Critique* seems to discard the summum bonum and with it the moral proof of the existence of God and the immortality of the soul. Moral duty, in the latest of his works, is enthroned as the only and supreme moral motivation. No external ends, including the summum bonum, are allowed, and the experience of doing one's duty for its own sake even may be identified as "an experience of the Divine. May it not be that the virtuous individual experiences directly, in the categorical imperative, the voice of his God and that he apprehends Him, with the certainty of a personal faith, as a transcendental reality?"[35] Perhaps the karmic as well as the hedonistic and heteronomous elements of the *Second Critique* disturbed Kant. In any event, the post–*Second Critique* moral theory in which God is revealed in the moral law per se hardly addresses the moral motivation challenges that the earlier karmic version met head-on.

Nonkarmic moral theories deny that the moral qualities of actions are necessarily among their direct or mediate causally efficacious properties with respect to the agent. Utilitarian theories seem to fall in this category. For example, those who do right are not assured that the rightness of their actions will cause, directly or in some mediated way, their own happiness or living the good life. Doing right may be to act so as to maximize general happiness, but the agent's happiness itself may not be increased. In fact, just the opposite might occur. Mill makes this point very clearly when he writes: "The utilitarian standard . . . is not the agent's own greatest happiness, but the greatest amount of happiness altogether . . . Utilitarianism, therefore could only attain its end by the general cultivation of nobleness of character, even if each individual were only benefited by the nobleness of others, and his own so far as happiness is concerned were a sheer deduction from the benefit."[36]

Vengeance responds to our nonkarmic moral intuitions. It (and most retributive systems of punishment) forges an intermediate causal linkage between the moral quality of an act, its wrongness, and an appropriate penalty. According to Nozick, "If something is to happen to someone because of the moral quality of his act, this must occur through another's recognition of that moral quality and response to it."[37] Y recognizes the wrongness of X's act and responds with revenge.

The intention conditions (4–9) are crucial to vengeance. If the penalty befalls a villain accidentally or inadvertently or mistakenly, even if it perfectly fits the wrongness of the act and the bad character of the villain, vengeance has not been accomplished. (Nor, for that matter, would retribution have occurred.) For example, suppose that X deserves to die for having done A, and avenger Y is pursuing him. Z has committed an equally heinous crime, and X's and Z's paths converge. Y takes aim and fires at X, but just as he does, X stumbles and falls, and Y's bullet hits Z in the head, mortally wounding him. No act of revenge has occurred, but a fitting penalty has been visited on Z.

Bounty hunters are not, strictly speaking, avengers. They are, typically, in the chase for the money and lack the requisite intentions of vengeance. In the film *The Missouri Breaks,* for example, Marlon Brando's character, Lee Clayton, is a regulator, a kind of bounty hunter, hired to rid the range of a band of horse rustlers. He devises perverse ways of killing his prey, but he is not set on revenge. He tells Braxton, the rancher who hired him, that he is just doing his job. On the other hand, Jack Nicholson's character, Tom Logan, titular leader of the gang, seeks revenge against the regulator for the deaths of his buddies and against Braxton for hiring Clayton. He achieves his first goal by slitting Clayton's throat. His attempt to wreak vengeance on Braxton is, however, thwarted when he finds that the rancher has become enfeebled and demented and probably could not understand what is going to happen to him or why. Braxton is afflicted with what, explained in Chapter 6, I will call a "moral handicap," which would constitute a failure of conditions 8 and 9. When Braxton pulls a pistol and attempts to kill him, Logan shoots back in self-defense, but the rancher's death is not a satisfactory form of vengeance.

The avenger, Y in the schema above, is the causal conduit by which the wrongness of A is recognized and identified as morally requiring a response, a response that Y must make. "There are some things a man can't ride around!" The recognition of the moral quality of another person's acts gives rise to the moral obligation to respond to that person in a morally appropriate way. Sometimes that may mean rewarding him or her or patting him or her on the back. Other times it means killing him or her. The only power that morality has to affect human affairs resides in the response of moral people, members of the moral community, to the recognition of the moral quality of actions and characters. Recognition without appropriate response is an unmistakable indication of, at best, a weak character. In our so-called civilized times, we have removed the personal recognition and response obligations from the shoulders of individuals and created institutional mechanisms as substitutes. And we call it justice. In large measure, what we have done, however, is to strip morality of its most effective and involving element: individual action provoked by the recognition of evil, the resentment drive to set things right.

It is a basic fact about humans, noted by Peter Strawson,[38] that we have certain attitudes toward those who do not treat us with goodwill and respect or esteem or who act toward us with contempt, indifference, or, especially, malevolence. Such things matter to us. We attach "very great importance" to "the attitudes and intentions towards us of other human beings, and the great extent to which our personal feelings and reactions depend upon, or involve, our beliefs about these attitudes and intentions."[39] When we perceive or recognize that someone has injured or slighted us or failed to render to us what we regard as proper respect, we resent the offender. In effect, our reactive attitudes are essentially human responses to the way we perceive ourselves to be treated by others as measured against standard sorts of expectations.

Those expectations of treatment are bound up in our conceptions of right and wrong, our morality. How much or how many of those expectations are "hardwired" and how much or how many are the result of cultural forces is not of interest to me. If they are not "hardwired," at least the disposition to husband them and abide by them seems to be. In any event, we have expectations that others will display toward us, to use Strawson's phrase, "a reasonable degree of good will or regard." We demand, in effect, a certain degree of reciprocity in terms of respect and even esteem from those with whom we interact. John Wayne's character in his final film, *The Shootist,* J. B. Books, concisely summarizes these expectations: "I won't be wronged, I won't be insulted, and I won't be laid a hand on. I don't do these things to other people, and I require the same from them."

The reactive attitudes such as resentment are responses to the perceived moral quality of another person's actions as they affect the reactor directly. Those attitudes, as Strawson notes, can be generalized or can take the form of vicarious analogues of the personal instances when our expectations are extended to cover other people, especially those with whom we have some affinity. In such cases, one does not so much feel resentment as indignation. The difference between the two cases, of course, is that, in the latter, one's own interests are not directly injured or offended. And there is a third type as well: when one turns one's moral scrutiny on oneself and recognizes or perceives oneself to be morally wanting. In such cases, the feeling is neither resentment nor indignation. It is either guilt or shame.

Strawson persuasively argues that the three types of reactive attitudes are not only logically connected, "they are connected humanly."[40] Suppose, for example, that someone manifested the first type of reactive attitudes but neither of the other two types. Such a person would believe that only offenses to his or her own person mattered morally. Such a person would be a moral solipsist of the first order, an utter egocentric, and he or she would still be so if, in addition to the first type, he or she also manifested the third type. Then he or she would believe that only personal offenses against himself or herself morally mattered and that only he or she could feel shame or guilt when not behaving in a morally proper way toward others. Such a person might feel shame for not having protected a weak person from being bullied, while feeling no moral indignation toward the bully. It is, I suppose, also imaginable that someone who might be called a saint could exist who has no personal reactive regard but whose life is bound up in the offensives and injuries suffered by others, a person who only manifests the second type of reactive attitudes. Such a person, however, would certainly be a social deviant and should likely be treated as morally repressed or morally self-repressive, "for all these types of attitude alike have common roots in our human nature and in our membership in human communities."[41]

My point, developed from this Strawsonian base, is that the reactive attitudes, especially resentment, indignation, and shame, trigger the response mechanisms that give the moral qualities of actions causal power in human affairs. Consider the personal reactive type of case. X does A to Y. Y's reactive attitude R, resentment of X, is founded on two prior judgments or, to use J. L. Austin's terminology, two verdictives[42] that are typically embedded in a basic expression of blame. For example, "X is to blame for A," when used verdictively, has the illocutionary force of pronouncing that A was wrong or condemnable and that X is bad or evil or inconsiderate or disrespectful for having done A; in effect, that X has no acceptable exculpating excuse for having done A.

The verdictive, whether or not verbalized, supports the behabitive, "I blame X," whose illocutionary force is the verbal manifestation of moral disapproval of X. It is the adopting or the "taking up" of an attitude toward X. Although neither the verdictive nor the behabitive actually needs to be uttered, the avenger, to satisfy the conditions of successful vengeance, must communicate another sense of "blame," again within Austin's illocutionary framework, to the target. The avenger must use a blaming expression, or some comparable communicative behavior, with the illocutionary force of an exercitive. Exercitives are "sentences as opposed to verdicts."[43] For example, "I blame *you* for doing A" (recall Achilles telling Hector why he is about to kill him).

Similar stories can be told for Strawson's vicarious analogue cases and for the self-reactive cases. In the latter, however, the exercitive is spoken, if at all, in soliloquy, although some people, particularly the guilt-ridden who find confession an effective guilt-management tool, will say to others such things as "I am to blame for A," sentencing themselves, as it were, and typically hoping for absolution. The primary point, however, is that the reactive attitudes expressed—for example, in the behabitive use of "blame," moral resentment, moral disapproval, moral indignation, shame, guilt, and so on—depend on the behabitive blamer having reached prior verdicts regarding the act in question and the actor in the circumstances. Elizabeth Beardsley's way of putting this is that "the representations in verdictive blame form one of the building blocks used in constructing the concepts of exercitive-blame and behabitive-blame."[44] The recognition of the moral qualities of both action and actor is, therefore, essential to virtuous vengeance.

Think again of Hamlet. One way to look at a central element of the play is to see Hamlet as undergoing two sorts of moral recognition problems. The first concerns the identification, to a degree of certainty, of the murderer of his father. The ghost had identified the murderer as King Claudius, but Hamlet realizes that the gravity of the indictment requires a penalty of death, and he wants more certainty than the word of an apparition, even that of his father, can provide. Hence, he concocts the play within the play "to catch the conscience of the King." That device provides him with the sort of confirming evidence that leaves no room for doubt in his mind.

His second recognition problem is to find the proper time and place to take his revenge. With respect to the second problem, Hamlet is close to a total flop. The perfect opportunity presents itself when the king is kneeling in his chapel. Hamlet approaches him from behind, prepared to kill him, then stops himself and withdraws. His reason for not administering the fatal blow then and there, however, indicates his failure to grasp the extent, the limits, of his role in the vengeance job that the ghost of his father set for him. He decides not to kill Claudius because he believes the king is praying and that if killed while in prayer his soul will wing its way to a heavenly eternity. Hamlet wants to send him to Hell. The irony of the scene, however, is that after Hamlet leaves, we learn from Claudius that his conscience is so wracked with guilt that he is unable to pray, no matter how hard he tries.

That fact is, however, irrelevant to the matter Hamlet has been born to set right; it is just a nasty joke on the inept assassin. Whether Claudius spends eternity in Heaven or Hell is none of Hamlet's business. Hamlet's job is to revenge the murder of his father by killing the usurper. The act of murder has an obvious moral quality that requires a confident, steadfast, moral person to embody it, to empower it, to be its agent in the course of human events. Hamlet is ordained to be the means by which the moral quality of his father's murder gains genuine causal power. Vengeance should be taken, and Claudius should be penalized according to some morally defensible conception of adequate punishment.

Hamlet, it could be contended (though not based on the text), might have refrained from killing Claudius by stabbing him in the back in the chapel scene because performing the execution in that manner would not satisfy all of the conditions of a best-case revenge. If he were stabbed in the back without warning, Claudius would not understand that the penalty was inflicted on him so that the other conditions of vengeance were satisfied. That, however, is not Hamlet's reason for failing to perform the deed. He, of course, could have informed the king of his intentions and then killed him, but, as noted earlier, Hamlet does not have the strength of moral character to efficiently and effectively meet his obligation. Instead he "rides around it." His failure, odd as it may sound with respect to a character who gets to mouth some of the most eloquent and memorable speeches in the history of the theater, is a failure to communicate at the crucial moral moment. He has reached the verdict, he manifests the appropriate reactive attitudes, but he cannot bring himself to exercise the sentence.

The intention conditions (4–9) in the revenge schema ensure that Y's act of vengeance means something, that it is a communicative act. Revenge delivers a message, or, rather, revenge is a message. The message is sent, delivered by Y to X. But what message?

There are a number of possible answers to that question. Some might say that the message is an educative one. X is being educated as to the wrongness of A or as to right and wrong in some general way. Call this the E answer. Alternatively, it might be supposed that the message is one of deterrence. Call that the D answer. Yet another possibility is that the message is one of reform, the R answer. Each of these answers, E, D, or R, to the "what is the message?" question requires that we treat the vengeance act as one of purposive communication, in the sense that the avenger intends or expects some further or future consequences from performing the act. Another way to characterize these consequentialist types of revenge is that they are versions of what Braithwaite and Pettit call "target retributivism."[45] For the act of revenge to be regarded as successful, some additional target, e.g., education, reform, or deterrence, must be hit. There may be target-retributive avengers of this sort—Nozick might call them "teleological avengers"—and we could work out the conditions that must be met for their acts of vengeance to be felicitious along lines akin to Austin's account of performatives.[46]

In order to prevent a misfiring of revenge for an E-type, D-type, or R-type target-retributive avenger, there must be a certain type of uptake on the part of the person on whom the act of vengeance is being visited. In each case, the message of revenge must have a beneficial effect on its target, its recipient. For the E-type, the villain must become better educated about what is right and what is wrong. For the D-type, he (or she) must be deterred from future performances of A despite having the inclination to do A. For the R-type, he (or she) must undergo a change in character, perhaps a radical one, to rid himself (or herself) of the inclination to do A. For the teleologist, the target-retributive avenger, without such perlocutionary results, the vengeance communication will not have been successful.

The crucial element in target-retributive vengeance is acceptance. But acceptance is a rather tricky business and can mean different things for E-type, D-type, and R-type vengeance. Suppose the telos of E-type vengeance is to get the wrongdoer to accept that what he (or she) did to someone else was wrong. We can do unto him (or her) what he (or she) did to the other person, an eye for an eye, but how do we show the wrongdoer the wrongness of what he (or she) did? Does it hurt? Does it leave one disabled? Yes. But will he (or she) accept that it is wrong, its wrongness? For the vengeance target to grasp the wrongness of the act he (or she) did to the victim, Nozick notes, the target must already be a member of the moral community, one who grasps the difference between right and wrong.[47] But even so, there is no guarantee that the target will make the connection from the talionic penalty to the wrongness of the matched act. If the penalty is not talionic, for example, incarceration, freedom deprivation, will it be easier or harder to bring about the educational goal? R-type avengers, of course, take the E goal further to reform. If the E goal is not achieved, genuine reform seems unlikely.

I suppose that a certain superficial reform might occur if the revenge target no longer does the offensive act, though only out of fear of punishment. That would associate the R-type with the D-type. D-type avengers assume that their targets are not likely to grasp the wrongness of their actions by undergoing comparable injuries or harms. For them, the point of the penalty is to get offenders to stop doing the objectionable acts by placing so high a personal price on doing them that any rational person would desist rather than pay that price a second time. Or, upon learning of the price paid by others for doing such things, offenders will calculate that their interests are served by ceasing the practice. For the D-type avenger, the wrongness of an act is literally cashed out in terms of the price that likely must be paid to engage in it.

All of these forms of target-retributive revenge depend on what Nozick calls "an optimistic hypothesis"[48] about the object of revenge accepting the fact that the act of revenge was appropriate, that what he or she did was wrong and deserving of the penalty. The avenger, however, has generally little or no reason to be so optimistic. In fact, there is no reason for the avenger to try, in any way, to make the offender a better person. His or her acceptance of the wrongness of what he or she did is not crucial. It is incidental. What matters is that he or she understands that the penalty is being inflicted because of the wrongness of the act as perceived by the avenger. The avenger need not have the slightest hope that the act of revenge will change the offender, make him (or her) a better person. Understanding, not acceptance, by the offender is the crucial element of the communicative act of vengeance. Understanding need not result in any change in character or behavior. If, however, the avenger is convinced that the offender is not capable of understanding, then revenge is pointless, as Tom Logan decides in the case of Braxton in *The Missouri Breaks.*

Nozick's way of putting the matter is that the offender has become disconnected from correct values and the penalty is a way of forcibly imposing a reconnection.[49] I would rather say, as suggested earlier, that the avenger shoulders the moral duty of empowering what is morally right. No character transformation on the part of the offender is required for that to be successfully accomplished. The act of vengeance is an expression of the effect of morality in and for itself. Morality has been mocked by the offender, but, through the avenger's agency, morality will yet have a very significant effect on the offender's life. It may well end it.

The conditions do not make reference to whether or not the offender acted freely when he or she flouted morality (that issue will be discussed in Chapter 6). It is, to use Nozick's term, "disconnection" from morality ("correct values" for Nozick) that is important. If vengeance is to be morally felicitous, the message (some form of "you are disconnected and this penalty serves as a reconnection" typically expressed in a less prosaic fashion) must be delivered and understood—understood, not necessarily accepted. The offender has not empowered morality in his (or her) life, so the avenger takes on the moral duty of giving morality an effect in the offender's life. Although the offender resists, he (or she) cannot avoid the impact of morality when "hit over the head" (to use Nozick's phrase)—perhaps literally—with what is right and what is wrong. Morality qua morality is transmitted in the message of vengeance. The avenger is the agent of an otherwise impotent morality, which is enabled, through the avenger, to communicate a significant impact in the life of the offender, even if the offender never accepts morality, never guides his (or her) life by its principles, never has the chance.

The temptation for the avenger, motivated by appropriate reactive attitudes of resentment or indignation, is to exact a penalty far in excess of the magnitude of the mocking of morality that was manifested in the behavior of the offender. The proportionality problem for the avenger (to be dealt with in more detail in Chapter 7) is to determine the limits of what the offender deserves. The talionic principle, according to Nozick,[50] should set the upper limit on the penalty. But although that view seems to have recommended itself to ancient legal code writers, I cannot find any convincing rationale in its favor. The penalty exacted by the avenger is the message of morality that the offender is supposed to understand though not necessarily accept or embrace.

The problematic should not be to match the penalty with the offense, an eye for an eye, but to, in Walker's terms, "maximize the probability that offenders will understand the message."[51] One of the more ineffectual things our contemporary penal system has done to reduce the likelihood that the message will be understood is to stereotype sentences for offenses so that they lack the connection with the offense and the message is, at best, muddled. After all, how is a fine of $10,000 related to the message that polluting the local water supply is morally unacceptable? Perhaps talionic penalties dependably get the message across, but sometimes they may be insufficient and something more draconian would be more effective. The moral message may be diminished or lost altogether if penalties are standardized.

The avenger needs to be especially concerned about what will maximize the probability of the moral message being understood. We might refer to that as one of the major moral obligations of the virtuous avenger. Maximizing the probability that the message is understood might not always require as much as a talionic response, but sometimes even the talionic response may be inadequate. The success of the communication depends, in large measure, on the offender's receptive abilities and therefore on the avenger's ability to correctly access them (I will return to this issue in Chapter 7).

It might be suggested that the avenger casts himself (or herself) into the inferno of moral condemnation by performing the very acts that reconnect the target to morality. Nozick sees the problem in terms of "flouting the value" of the offender.[52] The idea is that morality requires that all people be treated as having worth, as being of value, a value Kant captured in the second formulation of his Categorical Imperative in which we are required to treat all people as ends and never as means only.[53] Such a concern would seem to be especially striking if the avenger kills the offender. Nozick writes, "The person may deserve to die, may deserve correct values having that significant effect on his life, but this cannot be done at our hand if we are to be connected to (his) value and not flout it."[54] One way that a number of philosophers, at least back to Plato, have dealt with the problem is by slipping a teleological element into the justification of punishment. For Plato that element was education. Of course, Plato did allow that capital punishment would be appropriate if the offender is incorrigible. In such a case, however, there is the saving grace of having ended a morally worthless life. In cases of monstrous offenders, Hitler is typically cited as the example, we might be convinced that all value has been removed from the individual and that administering the death penalty solely for nonteleological purposes cannot flout the nonexistent value of the offender.

The metaphysics of human worth that underlies Nozick's need to link teleological vengeance (target retribution) with nonteleological vengeance (or retribution in his case) might recommend itself in light of the fact that the motivation for revenge is triggered by a transgression of the worth or dignity or respect of someone. Even if we are not prepared to adopt a worth or rights metaphysics, it would still be the case that the very sort of act that started the vengeance ball rolling is being replicated in the act of revenge. Avengers who cannot wash away the moral stains from their administration of penalties with the cleanser of teleological results will not avoid morally "dirty hands," unless it is possible to distinguish on moral terms between an act of revenge and a transgression of the worth of the offender.

There is something appealingly noble and romantic, in a sacrificial sort of way, about such a "dirty hands" result. Certainly my favorite form of popular culture, movie Westerns, has milked this outcome. The hero, morally sullied by taking on the bad guy and satisfying the conditions of best-case moral vengeance, cannot remain in the community, must ride off into the mountains, into the West. But the assumption that underlies the "dirty hands" result is that the act of vengeance, even if it involves killing, is morally bad.

The "dirty hands" problem seems to owe its origin in the literature to Machiavelli. Michael Walzer concisely defined the problem as one in which a person is "forced to choose between upholding an important moral principle and avoiding some looming disaster."[55] Acting to ward off the disaster can only be accomplished by violating moral principle, and so the hands of the person who acts to do so are morally sullied. Montaigne, picking up on the same theme, tells us that sometimes "a man must do wrong in detail if he wishes to do right on the whole."[56] The moral price paid for doing "wrong in detail" is the loss of one's morally good character.

The "dirty hands" problem in the case of vengeance, however, could only really get started if the avenger must do something morally wrong in order to do right on the whole. What seems to make deadly revenge wrong, for Nozick, is that killing people, for whatever reason, affronts their moral worth. People have moral worth or value independent of their moral merit that is, for Nozick, protected by rights, natural rights, notably to freedom and well-being. Moral merit is gained or lost by their behavior, and though desert with respect to penalties and rewards is determined in virtue of actions, deadly punishment collapses worth into merit and destroys worth. In effect, it sends the dual message that the offender has no positive moral merit and no further moral worth.

John Rawls,[57] Ronald Dworkin,[58] Gregory Vlastos,[59] and Alan Gewirth[60] defend similar or related views. Vlastos provides the motto of human worth egalitarians: "The human worth of all persons is equal, however unequal may be their merit." Moral desert, if there is to be any such thing (Rawls explicitly excludes desert from his principles of justice[61]), has to be based on merit. As I reject moral worth egalitarianism, moral merit is the sole grounds on which the moral justification of even deadly punishment can rest. Although I will have more to say on this subject in Chapter 6, a few further comments may be appropriate here.

Those basic human rights to freedom and well-being are believed by the worth egalitarians to be necessary for people to develop their moral qualities and thereby gain moral merit. John Kekes spells out the foundations of the position: "The heart of the egalitarian case is that human worth attaches to selves, while moral merit depends on qualities. One reason why human worth ought to be independent of moral merit, according to the egalitarians, is that selves are distinct from their qualities. Since people possess selves necessarily and universally and qualities only contingently, people also have human worth necessarily and universally and moral merit only contingently."[62] Moral merit is scalar, but there is no continuum of moral worth.

The worth egalitarians typically cite Kant when searching for an authority to support their position, and, indeed, Kant's second formulation of the Categorical Imperative would seem to stand them in good stead. But Kant is not as good a poster child for worth egalitarianism as is usually thought. He writes in *The Metaphysical Principles of Virtue:* "Lying is the . . . obliteration of one's dignity as a human being. A man who does not himself believe what he says to another . . . has even less worth than if he were a mere thing."[63] Kant certainly seems to be implying that human worth is directly proportional to moral merit.

Nozick is also less than consistent, as he allows that in cases like Hitler we would be morally permitted to exact deadly vengeance, implying that it is morally permissible to penalize with death those people who have by their own acts reduced their own moral worth to nil. But how does one diminish one's moral worth if there is no proportional relationship between worth and moral merit? If deadly vengeance is morally justifiable, indeed morally required, in certain cases, then there cannot be a distinction with a difference between moral worth and moral merit. Offenders earn their fates by their actions; they merit them by virtue of being evil and have "even less worth" than if they were mere things. People, as I will argue in Chapter 6, have unequal moral merit and thereby unequal moral worth. The virtues of vengeance are founded in that inequality and would not exist if the worth egalitarian's conception genuinely reflected human social (or rather antisocial) behavior. The worth egalitarian, a metaphysical optimist, despite being assaulted by the enormity of the evidence to the contrary, is an indomitable believer in the basic goodness of human beings. Vengeance theorists are realists who deny any such conception of the goodness of humans. The defenders of the moral virtues of vengeance endorse the view that recommends itself in even a cursory study of human history, literature, popular culture, or the daily newspapers: that there is an unbridgeable moral chasm between people who regularly do wicked deeds and those who typically do good deeds.

RATIONAL VENGEANCE

Vengeance is a dish that tastes best when eaten cold.
William Ian Miller[64]

Jon Elster has succinctly spelled out what might be called the aspects of revenge that appear to be governed by norms in those societies in which feuding is practiced. They cover: "What constitutes an affront that must be avenged? Who are allowed or required to exact revenge? What means can legitimately be used in taking revenge? How soon is vengeance allowed or required to take place? Whose death shall expiate an affront? What fate is reserved for those who fail to take revenge when the norms require it?"[65] In different cultures these questions may be answered rather differently. The affront that requires retaliation might be very slight in some communities, perhaps only a perceived failure to exercise some social grace, a breach of etiquette. In other communities the provocation of revenge may have to be a rather significant injury, including physical harming. In any event, in many societies, there are some affronts for which retaliation by or for the affronted person is expected, and failure to act appropriately is treated as a serious violation, perhaps one with moral overtones.

In some societies, there may also be norms concerning who must carry out the revenge. If the affront is something less than a killing, typically the vengeance requirement falls on the injured party. But when a death has occurred, it needs to be clear whether the father, the oldest son, the uncle, or whoever has the obligation. Sometimes the norm might only specify the kin of the deceased or affronted as having the duty. How the task is then assigned may be of no concern to the norms, and each family may allot the job as it sees fit. Also, the matter of determining the appropriate target is generally not left to the discretion of the avenger. If the male head of a family kills the eldest son of another family, the norms of revenge may forbid retaliation by killing the wife of the killer, although killing either him or his eldest son might be sanctioned. In some cases, however, all such controls on the choice of target are suspended. In Montenegro, as Elster notes, special norms come into play during the first twenty-four hours following a killing, the period of "boiling blood": "Only during this period could expiators for a crime be chosen outside the household of the killer."[66]

Consider Milovan Djilas's account of the emotions generated by vengeance in the Balkans (as quoted by Elster): "Revenge is the greatest delight and glory. Is it possible that the human heart can find peace and pleasure only in returning evil for evil? . . . Revenge is an overpowering and consuming fire. It flares up and burns away every other thought and emotion . . . Vengeance . . . was the glow in our eyes, the flame in our cheeks, the pounding in our temples, the word that had turned to stone in our throats on our hearing that our blood had been shed . . . Vengeance is not hatred, but the wildest, sweetest kind of drunkenness, both for those who must wreak vengeance and for those who wish to be avenged."[67]

The emotions run high and are sweet, and where norms of revenge exist, the failure to take proper retaliatory action is met with rigorous social sanctions. One is denounced as a coward and ostracized from the community. In Corsica, the reluctant avenger is exposed to the *rimbecco*, public reproach: "The *rimbecco* can occur at any moment and under any guise. It does not even need to express itself in words: an ironical smile, a contemptuous turning away of the head, a certain condescending look—there are a thousand small insults which at all times of day remind the unhappy victim of how he has fallen in the esteem of his compatriots."[68]

Social norms, for Elster, have two necessary features. One is that a social norm must be shared by the members of the community and sustained by their regular and dependable approval and disapproval. That feature is hardly controversial. After all, it is what makes them social norms, and, in fact, that feature is taken to be sufficient by other writers, e.g., Philip Pettit.[69] The other feature identified by Elster is that a social norm must be an imperative that is either unconditional or, if conditional, not future-oriented. What I will call "Elster social norms" (those with both features identified by Elster) cannot be adopted for rational reasons because rational choice is concerned with outcomes and is conditional. (If X is what you want, then do Y.) "Elster social norms" simply and straightforwardly command that something be done or forbid the doing of it, and they acquire their obligatory sense from communal enforcement. Revenge certainly has the retrofocus of an "Elster social norm." It will be recalled that the message communicated in vengeance is not teleological. No impact intended to alter the future life of the target, except perhaps to end it, is involved. As long as it is understood as the avenger's imposing of suffering on someone who harmed the avenger solely because that individual harmed the avenger, revenge will lack the sort of outcome orientation that would be amenable to rational choice.

For vengeance to be rational for the avenger, he or she must expect to realize a gain or prevent a loss in his or her own interests. Vengeful persons are often described as consumed with a passion to make the past "right" even at the expense of any future for themselves. Hume notes that "vengeance, from the force alone of passion, may be so eagerly pursued as to make us knowingly neglect every consideration of ease, interest, or safety."[70] The suggestion appears to be that the avenger who is set on the administration of suffering to the target often does so not only without hope of reward but also at a significant loss with respect to what the avenger values. On first blush, if such an account is correct, vengeance seems capable of satisfying the nonoutcome orientation condition of an "Elster social norm." Still, rational persons might perform acts of vengeance if they were convinced that other people (indeed, rational people) are typically cowered by those who reveal themselves as prepared to avenge the slights and injuries they experience. It may therefore be rational (i.e., in one's material self-interest) to establish a reputation as a revenge norm adherent, an avenger, in order to gain competitive advantages over others in the community.

This argument, or what might be called an indirectly rational account of revenge (that it can sometimes be rational to appear to be irrational), gains a foothold, however, only if people know that not all of the members of their community are rational and that they cannot be sure which ones are and which are not. Only under such a condition of uncertainty could a rational person expect to gain from appearing to act irrationally, for example, by avenging an affront. If all members of the community are rational and known to be so, no one would take the threat of revenge seriously, and the competitive advantage would be lost. As Elster states, "Faking adherence to the norm cannot be a rational strategy unless some people genuinely adhere to it."[71]

The communal enforcement condition in the case of revenge is somewhat problematic. Can it be sustained in the absence of an outcome-orientation for the members of the community? Why would the members of a community enforce sanctions against revenge norm violators? What's in it for them? The problem is one of cost to the enforcers. Why should they—why would they—expend their own time, energies, and funds to ensure that victims or the relatives of victims retaliate against victimizers? It might be suggested that there is an "Elster social norm," a supernorm, in the community that ordains that members punish nonavengers, those who violate the revenge norms, and so they enforce sanctions thereby avoiding the imposition of sanctions on themselves.

Elster himself, however, provides convincing reasons to think that such a second (or any higher order) norm is not likely to gain a foothold in a community: "Expressing disapproval is always costly, whatever the target behavior. At the very least it requires energy and attention that might have been used for other purposes . . . As one moves upward in the chain of actions, beginning with the original violation, the cost of receiving disapproval falls rapidly to zero. Empirically, it is not true that people frown upon others when they fail to sanction people who fail to sanction people who fail to sanction a norm violation. There do not appear to be fourth or fifth order norms."[72] At best, they might sanction just because that is what they do and have always done in that community. It is "the way." In effect, they internalize the enforcement rules[73] and do not expose them to rational evaluation, either individually or as a group. If that is the case, and in some places it probably is, and revenge is always and only retrofocused, then both of Elster's conditions are satisfied outside of the reach of rationality in that community. Perhaps the *rimbecco*-ridden culture of Corsica is, or was, such a place.

But if community members do apply the test of individual rationality to their sanctioning behavior, they are likely to determine that it is inconsistent with the enhancement of their material self-interest (though in the absence of a dominant protection agency—as described by Robert Nozick[74]—they might determine that it is in the material interest of the community at large). And this determination will be true for the vengeful as well as the nonvengeful members. Suppose that I am a normally vengeful person; would I have much reason to approve of your taking vengeance against a third party or to disapprove if you fail to do so? I think not. In fact, I have a far stronger reason not to approve of your taking revenge and to disapprove of your doing so, as do my fellow community members: my own (or their) taking of revenge will not likely set off cycles of vengeance that will endanger me and my family when I avenge affronts.

This view certainly suggests that in the case of revenge the community enforcement feature of "Elster social norms" is unlikely to be sustainable in a community in which most of the members are rational. Elster writes that "sanctions cannot sustain a norm of revenge unless some of the sanctioners are genuinely moved by the norms." To be "genuinely moved" by an "Elster social norm," however, is to be, on his account, irrational. But perhaps the members of a community can be "genuinely" rationally moved by a social norm, though not an "Elster social norm," of vengeance. That response could occur if an account of revenge as directly rational can be persuasively made.

An account of revenge as directly rational[75] will have the following form: (a) there is a particular end in view, an outcome orientation, that is consistent with rationality and also is capable of generating the approval/disapproval element; (b) revenge is a possible mechanism of producing the outcome; therefore, (c) revenge behavior will be rational for the avenger.

Suppose we grant that vengeance for its own sake, purely retrofocused revenge, is not a rational form of behavior. For it to be rational there must be some outcome orientation, some end in view, associated with it that provides the hook on which rationality hangs. The first place one naturally would look for such a future-oriented element is to an effect on the target. But for that result to be productive of the end in view for the avenger, it would have to be the case that the avenger experiences a material gain from the infliction of pain and suffering or death on the target. That could well be the case with sadists and probably defines them as a class, but the virtues of vengeance should not rest on the avenger having a sadistic disposition. It might be argued that the delivery of the message to the target, as discussed in the previous section, satisfies the condition, but that criterion will not stand the test of consistency with rationality, for the message alone is neither outcome-oriented nor is its delivery and understanding by the target, in itself, in the material self-interest of the messenger. The standard nonretributive punishment theories offer candidates, but none are especially convincing when applied to the vengeance situation. For example, avengers typically do not take revenge in order to deter the harm causer from future attacks. nor do they avenge only to rehabilitate the target. The basic point is that we will need to focus directly on the avenger for the desired outcome. When we do, we typically find the candidate that answers to (a): it is honor.

When honor is identified as the individual outcome, the argument falls into place, at least it does in some communities, cultures, societies, forms of life. There revenge behavior is one of the acceptable mechanisms for the production and the maintenance of honor. Where that is the case, it will be rational for individual members of the community to be avengers, unless, of course, the costs of doing so far outdistance the benefits that accrue to the individual avenger. Elster's norms of revenge, on a reading like the one I am proposing, however, are actually norms of honor in which revenge is a means, an executive virtue.

This social normative account of honor appears to capture only one type of honor, what I will call public honor. Honor may also be private. When honor is private, (personal) acts of vengeance may not generate communal approval, failing the social aspect of norms, but they may well generate self-approval and, in some cases, a sense of restoration of worth and merit. In cases of private honor, I will maintain, revenge behavior will be both rational and an executive virtue for the avenger. Neither type of honor, however, will qualify, because of their outcome orientation, as "Elster social norms."

Although I will devote considerable discussion to honor in Chapter 5, one point is appropriate in this context. I do not claim that honor is rational. It may be a primitive or basic human motivator, even an innate psychological tendency for which an evolutionary explanation can be supplied, and Elster claims that a genetic polymorphic explanation may be the most promising.[76] The point is that honor serves as the needed outcome-oriented end that can render revenge behavior amenable to a directly rational choice interpretation. The argument takes the following form: (a) honor is a particular desirable end in view that is consistent with rationality and is capable of generating the approval/disapproval element; (b) revenge behavior is a way of producing or maintaining honor in some communities, cultures, societies, forms of life, and so on; therefore, (c) revenge behavior is rational in such communities. Simply, the light of honor illuminates the rationality of revenge for the avenger.

In 1721 Edward Young wrote in his play *Revenge,* "What is revenge, but courage to call in our honour's debts?"

Moral Anger and Hatred

> If I be not angry, the punishment of an adversary is totally indifferent to me.
>
> *David Hume*[77]

Aristotle devotes section 5 of book IV of the *Nicomachean Ethics* to a discussion of the virtues of anger. Anger itself is not a virtue because it is a passion (NE 1105). It can be virtuous when it involves choice, or rather when one is disposed to it "in a particular way," when it reflects or is a certain state of character. Aristotle tells us that "good temper is the mean with respect to anger" (NE 1125). The good-tempered person is not anger-free. Good temper lies on the spectrum of anger; it is the virtue of anger. Anger, as is the case with a number of other passions, is to be regulated by the rule of the mean, regulated but not exorcised. Anger and malice are very different passions. There is no such thing as virtuous malice; malice has no mean.

Aristotle joins Aeschylus in endorsing the view that anger at the right things or people at the right time is praiseworthy, and, more important, not getting angry at the things or persons at which one should be angry reveals a serious character flaw. The Furies are not banished but instead are guaranteed an honorable place in the Athenian system of justice at the end of the *Eumenides*. Persons deficient in anger at the appropriate times, Aristotle tells us, are "thought not to feel things nor to be pained by them." Further, such people are unlikely to defend themselves and will endure being insulted or their friends being insulted. Persons deficient in anger are no better than slaves.

Aristotle does worry that it is difficult to determine how, with whom, at what, and for what duration one should be angry because he fears that the anger to which a person of good character is disposed can slide down a slippery slope into obsessive anger, bad temper, if not kept in check by reason. He counsels erring on the side of the deficiency but surely not adopting a Stoic or Christian stance. The crucial point, however, is that getting angry and acting on that anger not only are not flaws in character but also can be indications of a good character. This is not the place to embark on a tangent track in the discussion of Aristotelian ethics. However, Aristotle's account of the "virtue of anger"—i.e., that it can be praiseworthy in certain circumstances, that those unable to raise their passions to its level in such situations are blameworthy, that it should be provoked by insults and injuries to friends as well as oneself—would seem to support the view that the ethical person, for Aristotle, is the involved social animal and not merely the contemplative individual.

Anger is an essential passion of successful social life. As Jeffrie Murphy has noted, it is at the foundation of "the moral order itself."[78] It is an indicator of care, of honor, of self-respect and respect for others. If we do not react angrily when our values are attacked, our friends are harmed, our family members are injured or insulted, who are we but, as Aristotle says, slaves without moral fiber?

Any moral theory that would counsel total restraint of anger under such circumstances is, in Aristotle's terms, foolish.

Seething anger in the face of evil that does not motivate rectifying action is not only morally impotent, it is dangerously self-consuming. Moral anger, which we may define, following Aristotle, as the virtuous anger provoked in the good-tempered person by the wicked actions of others and, perhaps, oneself, demands action; it is morally incomplete without it. It is a sign of good character to have the passion in the circumstances, but a failure of character, perhaps a lack in another virtue, such as courage, not to try to take appropriate action. Those who get angry when they or their family or friends or community are attacked, harmed, insulted, treated with disrespect, and so on, and restrain themselves, do nothing in response, are moral failures, not, as the Christians would have it, to be praised for "turning the other cheek."

There is a rather wide range of "anger emotions" or, to use the term popularized by Strawson and mentioned earlier, "reactive attitudes and feelings" that can occur when one believes that the intentional behavior of others has had a negative impact on oneself, one's family, friends, community. Resentment, hate, rage, fury, indignation, and contempt are examples. Resentment "is typically felt toward another you believe has wrongfully harmed you."[79] In fact, resentment typically involves the belief that you, the person resenting, have been personally injured or slighted or deprived of something you desire by the behavior of someone else. Often resentment is petty, perhaps even a form of jealousy. I will call such cases examples of "simple resentment." They are buttressed by a conception of self-worth that the resenter feels is being diminished. But what raises resentment to the level of what may be called personal moral anger?

I follow Hughes in treating moral anger as "a reactive attitude characterized in part by the belief that a moral subject has been wrongfully harmed."[80] By "wrongfully harmed" I mean to exclude cases in which the harm was accidental or inadvertent. If I believe that your advantage over me was gained by your superior skills, I may be envious or jealous but not morally angry with you. If I believe that you broke my arm because you tripped and fell against me, I may consider you a klutz but I would not be morally angry with you. That is not to say that in both cases I may not be angry, if only for that time period in which it takes me to adjust my beliefs about your behavior to the facts. I certainly may be angry, very angry. After all, I lost the job. My arm is broken. What do you expect me to be, happy?

Such anger, however, is a manifestation of simple resentment. It lacks the appropriate belief states to rise to the level of moral anger. My anger in such cases is what Joseph Butler called "hasty anger."[81] It is impulsive and does not involve beliefs about how you wrongfully treated me. Moral anger is clearly a Strawsonian reactive attitude or feeling. It is comparable to what Butler called "settled or deliberate anger" and wells up upon further consideration and interpretation of the situation. A moral subject has been intentionally and wrongfully injured and/

or put at risk of harm and/or "has been or is the object of an intended wrongful harm or has been or is the object of an intended wrongful risk or harm"[82] by another.

Within the class of moral subjects, I include anything that can be a subject of a moral responsibility ascription or can have moral claims made in its behalf to protect its interests.[83] I regard myself as a member of the class of moral subjects. If my resentment toward someone was generated by my belief that I was wrongfully harmed or put at risk of harm or made the object of an intended harm or risk of harm by that person, my resentment is no longer simple; it is a form of moral anger. And insofar as I am the injured party, it may be called "personal moral anger." (The term is owed to Hughes, but the point was made by Strawson.[84])

If my anger is aroused on behalf of a moral subject other than myself, the attitude or feeling is what Strawson calls "the vicarious analogue of resentment," and I may be described as morally indignant or morally disapproving, though not resentful. It is vicarious moral anger. Of course, I may be both personally and vicariously angry with regard to the same occurrence of harm. Someone may wrongfully harm me and my family or friends with the same action. I then will both resent and be indignant toward the offender. Anger, especially moral anger, is one of the great motivators for undertaking hostile actions against the offender. I suppose, but have no supporting evidence, that personal moral anger moves most people to retributive responses with rather greater speed than does vicarious moral anger. The avenger who is sparked to react aggressively to unambiguous feelings of vicarious moral anger may be said to have a more sensitive moral response mechanism than the average run of humans and thus deserves moral plaudits.

On the account I am adopting, resentment, not simple resentment, is the reaction one feels in cases when the wrongful harm or injury occurs to oneself, and indignation or disapproval is the reaction when the wrongful harm or injury occurs to others. Actually, the latter is a generalized version of the former in the sense that both rest on the same set of expectations of respect, goodwill, and the protection of personal dignity. As I noted in Chapter 3, Strawson makes the point that the personal and the impersonal reactive attitudes are connected "not merely logically. They are connected humanly . . . and also with yet another set of attitudes,"[85] the self-reactive attitudes.

The personal and impersonal reactive attitudes involve "demands on others for oneself and demands on others for others." But the self-reactive attitudes involve "demands on oneself for others," for example, feeling ashamed or guilty for having caused harm or having been disrespectful. According to Strawson, "All these types of attitude have common roots in our human nature and our membership in human communities."[86] In effect, it is constitutive of who we are that we react with anger, hatred, disdain, disapprobation, and hostility to what we regard as wrongful harm-causing, whether suffered by ourselves or others with whom we are associated or feel a kinship or common bond.

A further point is worth mention. Anger is moral if it is provoked by an action in the circumstances toward which one would have the same Strawsonian reactive attitude regardless of who performed it. This is my version of G. E. Hughes's account of moral condemnation of an action necessarily involving a commitment to condemn any other action one regards as relevantly similar to it.[87]

Hostility is where passion manifests in punishment. Adam Smith makes the point that the sentiment that "most immediately and directly prompts us to punish . . . is resentment."[88] By "resentment" Smith means, as Murphy has observed, what might better be called "retributive hatred," not simple resentment. He goes on to say that resentment (for which we should read its Strawsonian vicarious analogue, "indignation") interests us in the misery (as gratitude does in the happiness of other human beings in a more direct way than any other passions to become instruments of punishment (and reward). Smith writes: "Though dislike and hatred harden us against all sympathy, and sometimes dispose us even to rejoice at the distress of another, yet, if there is no resentment in the case, if neither we nor our friends have received any great personal provocation, these passions would not naturally lead us to wish to be instrumental in bringing it about."[89]

Personal and vicarious moral anger can be and ought to be placated by hostile responsive action taken against its cause. Wrongful actions require hostile responses. That is the basic form of the rule of retaliation, the principle of positive retribution. That, despite its seeming lack of fit with the body of moral principles upheld in our culture, is actually one of the primary foundations of morality. It is a foundation that is settled in passions, attitudes, emotions, and sentiments, not in reason. It embodies our concept of moral wrongness, provides the muscular element without which moral wrongness, wickedness, evil, and like concepts would be without impact in our lives. It links our cares, the noncognitive aspects of our moral lives, our expectations and beliefs, and our ideals to action. And because of it vengeance may be a virtue and is sometimes necessary to maintain the moral order.

J. L. Mackie, in a paper that provoked my thinking about these matters some years ago,[90] quoted Edward Westermarck: "It is one of the most interesting facts relating to the moral consciousness of the most humane type, that it in vain condemns the gratification of the very desire from which it sprang." Westermarck is correct; getting even (here and now, or at least as soon as possible), as even the karmic moral theories allow, is noneliminatable from a moral system. Forgiveness and reconciliation may be admirable, but they make sense only in a moral system that admits that wrongful actions require hostile responses. After all, condonation of wrongful actions, of evil, is morally impermissible. It is no better than collusion. My claim then is that if we have a concept of moral wrong at all, it includes the notion that whatever is morally wrong must be met with an antagonistic response from the members of the moral community. As Mackie states, "It is involved in the very concept of wrongness that a wrong action calls for a hostile response."[91] That we may also have reasons in certain circumstances to control the level of hostility, to mitigate punishment, even to forgive, is an entirely different matter.

Mackie explained the need for a hostile response principle in our morality, a principle requiring harming embedded in a collection of other principles that generally forbid harming, in terms of "an ingrained tendency to see wrong actions as calling for penalties." That is, he attempted to account for what he called the "paradox of retribution" in the form of a sociobiological explanation. Although I did not reject Mackie's account, in an earlier book I made a stab at justifying the presence of a moral retaliatory rule on other grounds.[92] I made use of some Hobbesian assumptions about the state of nature and the strategic rationality analyses of game theory. I associated the retaliatory rule with the adoption of a Tit For Tat strategy in human relationships that mirror the matrixes in iterated Prisoner's Dilemma games. The match with Tit For Tat, however, proves far from perfect on many counts. Although I was at first enthusiastic and applauded Peter Danielson when he wrote that "it would not be an exaggeration to say that TIT FOR TAT is a natural moral law,"[93] I, along with Danielson, came to reject such a characterization and elsewhere have discussed a number of reasons for doing so.[94]

For purposes here, however, it may be sufficient to add another: Tit For Tat clearly departs from the primary thrust of the rule of retaliation in that it justifies hostile action solely on forward-looking grounds. What I mean is that although the occasion for noncooperation is the previous noncooperation of the opponent, the sole rational reason for one's move is to rehabilitate the opponent back to a cooperative strategy. Positive retribution is not, in Tit For Tat, a rational reason. If one learns that the opponent cannot be rehabilitated, Tit For Tat collapses into unproductive mutual hostility. Although I argued in Chapter 3 that revenge can be rational for the avenger only because it may have certain desirable future-oriented outcomes for him or her, it most certainly is driven by its backward-looking element.

Moral anger, whether personal or vicarious or a hybrid of both, is an effect of a previous wrongful action by another, and it is that action that, according to the retaliatory rule, calls for a hostile response. As previously argued, there are no compelling reasons to believe that the hostile response will produce a future situation vis-à-vis the target that is favorable to the avenger. Honor (as I hope to show in Chapter 5), in the sense that I think it is relevant to revenge, is neither a zero-sum game nor something that can only be lost.

I now think Mackie was right when he insisted that the apparent dilemma of a moral system focally containing a principle counseling harm-causing, the paradox of retribution, is dissolved when we stop looking for a foundation of morality in reason. The task of the moral philosopher is not to explain why wrongful actions deserve aggressively antagonistic responses from the affected members of the moral community or their representatives. It is to work from the basic fact, the bedrock as Wittgenstein might have called it, that moral distinctions and

concepts and principles are founded in human sentiments, passions, and emotions, reactive attitudes and feelings, and to try to understand what Jeffrie Murphy
aptly refers to as "our shared common sense beliefs"[95] about appropriate "reactions to the quality of others' wills towards us (and others), as manifested in their
behavior."[96]

In effect, I ignore Mackie's sociobiologic attempt to provide a hardwired answer to the question of the origin of our adoption of a rule of positive retribution, not so much because I think it unconvincing or wrongheaded or bad science,
but because I think it is irrelevant. I agree with him that our very conception of
a wrong action, arguably the most central notion in any morality, must involve
a positive retributive principle: wrong actions call for, are to be met with, hostile
responses. But that principle is sufficient for a theory of morality that is consistent with Hume's regularly resisted discovery of the natural, emotional, sentimental basis of our moral conceptions and practices. We do not require a further
intellectualizing by way of a sociobiological theory of facts of life of which we
are all aware.

This is how we are, what it is to be human. I do not care why we are this way
or that if we had evolved differently we would have other sorts of emotions,
feelings, and sentiments. Strawson makes my point. He writes: "The vital thing
can be restored by attending to that complicated web of attitudes and feelings
which form an essential part of the moral life as we know it . . . Only by attending to this range of attitudes can we recover from the facts as we know
them a sense of what we mean, i.e., of all we mean, when, speaking the language of morals, we speak of desert, responsibility, guilt, condemnation, and
justice. But we do recover it from the facts as we know them. We do not have
to go beyond them . . . The existence of the general framework of attitudes itself
is something we are given with the fact of human society. As a whole, it neither
calls for, nor permits, an external 'rational' justification."[97]

Anger can become or be conjoined with hatred. The two passions may be
associated, even conflated, but hatred is not a form of moral anger. I can hate
someone or something but not believe that I was wrongfully harmed or put at
risk by the object of my hatred. I might not even be angry at it, let alone morally
angry, while still hating it. For example, I hate Kit Carson. I suppose that requires something of an explanation. Carson, while serving as the Indian agent in
Taos, New Mexico, instigated what appears to be the first use of biological warfare in American history. He invited a number of Ute leaders to a conference at
which he gave each a blanket that had been previously used on the beds of people
who died of smallpox. The recipients of his "gifts" contracted the disease. I suppose I am also vicariously somewhat morally angry with Carson, though it is a
very temperate anger, as I am unmotivated to do anything in response to it. I
would like to see his generally stellar status in American history severely down-
graded. It seems closer to the truth, however, to say that I hate him and what he
did and for what he did. And I also hate genocide and biological warfare, although

I have done virtually nothing because of these hatreds, making me, I suppose, a case in point for Hume.

Hume, in his discussion of the passions in the *Treatise*, notes that love and hatred are not, in an important respect, like pride and humility. The latter are what he calls "pure emotions." By that he means they are not attended with any desire and so do not immediately excite to action those who possess them. Love and (for my purposes), more importantly, hatred "are not completed within themselves, nor rest in that emotion, which they produce, but carry the mind to something farther."[98] Hatred, Hume tells us, "produces a desire of the misery and an aversion to the happiness of the person hated."[99]

Hatred appears to have a tripartite nature. It has a cause (the pain one feels on suffering the injury), an object (the person who did the injury, the target), and an end (the inflicting of misery on the target). One might surmise that hatred is nothing but the desire to inflict misery on the target or that hatred is constituted by the desire to inflict misery and an aversion to the happiness of the target. But, Hume points out, although we do not hate without desiring the misery of the target—the two only can be observed as typically or constantly conjoined—that particular desire is not absolutely essential to hatred. It does not constitute the emotion. It is possible to imagine haters who express their passion in some other way or who harbor hatred for "a considerable time" without "reflecting on the . . . misery of their objects."[100] In my case with Kit Carson, though I may desire that his reputation be stained, I certainly cannot sensibly desire his misery. His misery and happiness are well beyond my reach, although a karmic moralist might take comfort in the belief that the desire for his misery and the aversion to his happiness will be satisfied at some future time or in some other place (cold comfort, if you ask me).

Hume suggests that someone could hate another person yet have no desire to inflict misery on that individual and so fail to be motivated to perform actions calculated to cause the misery of the hated. The absence of an essential link from the emotion to the action requires an intentional machinery within the hater to empower the emotion. Apparently, on Hume's account, some (perhaps many, even most) people typically have at least the requisite desire, although it may not be sufficient to generate action, while others may have the emotion and lack or indefinitely repress the desire and so never act on it.

There are a number of different types of hatred according to Jean Hampton.[101] Simple hatred, she tells us, is an intense dislike or strong aversion for some person or thing that one perceives to be unpleasant or discomforting. Such hatred is accompanied (always?) by a desire to see the offending person or thing removed or eliminated from one's environs. Her examples of simple hatred are, appropriately, prosaic; for example, the hatred one has for a boring colleague. You can't stand her and wish she would go away, take another job, inflict her inane chatter on someone else. Hating in this way, she opines, is not unlike hating the change in the weather that wrecks one's plans for an outing in the park. Such hating amounts to disliking something or someone because of some objectionable but nonmoral characteristic or quality that it or the person exhibits.

Although Hampton says very little more about simple hatred, I wonder if her example is not quite as simple as she suggests. That is, hating the weather for becoming stormy is one thing; one dislikes the change because, though nothing can be done about it, one's plans have been disrupted. Hating one's boring colleague, if it is supposed to be analogous to the weather case, should suggest that the colleague cannot help being a run-on-at-the-mouth bore and that being boring is a nonmoral characteristic. I suppose that, if one believes that she cannot help being a bore, hating her comes to no more than wishing she would go away. Are people both boring by nature and unable to prevent themselves from inflicting their boring chatter on others? Perhaps some are. But if one thinks that the boring colleague could improve her social skills if she worked at it and that not wasting the time of other people has even a modicum of a moral rule of thumb about it, then the matter may be somewhat disanalogous to the weather example. In any event, one's hatred then might demand more of an expression or one might fail in respect to the virtue of courage. Someone ought to tell her; and who better than someone who can't abide her presence? This is, of course, a very minor matter, and I do agree with Hampton that some occasions of hate fit her category of simple hatred. More important for the present discussion, Hampton identifies two other categories: malicious-spiteful hatred and moral hatred.

As should be obvious from the names she has chosen for them, one is to be encouraged, or at least not discouraged, the other definitely shunned. Let's consider the malicious version first. Hampton's account of malicious-spiteful hatred associates the hatred whose object is the injury or diminishing of the status of the hated with "nursing a grudge against a wrongdoer." It is personal animosity generated by a "*competitive response* to *that person*," the wrongdoer. Hampton links this sort of hatred to the kind of resentment that is fueled by a "shaky sense" of self-worth in the hater. Her idea is that, insofar as resentment relates to self-worth and a competitive situation may cast in doubt one's own sense of self-worth, one may resent the success of the other and translate that resentment into the hatred that desires the downfall of the victorious other. Malicious hatred involves the regular assessment of rank and value in the social system to which one associates oneself.

Malicious-spiteful hatred, Hampton tells us, depends on the belief that humans can and do differ in rank.[102] It is founded in an "anti-Kantian theory of worth." Here I think Hampton makes a crucial mistake of conflating moral worth with merit, not necessarily moral merit. It is an undeniable fact of life that humans do differ in rank—where rank is calibrated in terms of merit—in a number of ways that are crucially important with respect to this sort of hatred. Some are wealthier, healthier, better athletes, better writers, better carpenters, more successful managers, politicians of higher rank. Some academics are better teachers, better researchers, better scholars than other academics. The list can go on and on. Almost every profession and subprofession, nearly every line of human endeavor, has a merit ladder of more than one rung. It is natural for anyone engaged in a human activity to assess his or her status vis-à-vis that of others engaged in one's line of endeavor, whether that be in work or play or human relationships.

The inspection of how one is doing against the field or against a specific opponent is liable to lead one, naturally favoring one's own case, to be envious or jealous of the advancement of others or a specific other one regards as, at best, one's equal. The worth or self-worth of the competitors in Kantian terms may not be at stake. When someone maliciously hates an opponent (or a perceived opponent) because he or she is being treated as more meritorious in the line of endeavor in question, that hatred need not touch on issues of moral worth or moral merit. (The difference between moral worth and moral merit will be discussed in Chapter 6.)

I want to suggest that Hampton is, in large measure, right about malicious-spiteful hatred, but I think there are two types of malicious-spiteful hatred. The first is the sort that emerges from envy or jealousy of rank in competitive human endeavors in which merit, skill, luck, and so on, play a role. The hater, in such cases, recognizes that a difference in ranking does exist and feels resentment at not being ranked higher or at least as high as the object of hate. The resentment indicates a belief that one is undervalued in that line of endeavor, and this belief can, but need not, lead to self-doubt. The belief and so the hatred, in fact, may be well founded, as errors in merit evaluations do occur and favoritism not infrequently raises its ugly head in human relations. The malicious hater hopes, perhaps sets out to try, to diminish the value of the competitor along the scale of merit appropriate to the endeavor in question and, usually, to elevate the regard in which his or her own accomplishments are viewed.

The potential does exist, as noted by Hampton, that in the process of degrading the opponent, the malicious hater also weakens his or her position. Being elevated over a competitor that one has substantially degraded may not amount to much of a rise in rank. Importantly, this sort of malicious hater's desire for a higher ranking does depend upon his or her awareness or belief that he or she is ranked lower on the merit scale relative to the endeavor in question than the object of hatred. But, of course, the hater, in these sorts of cases, has correctly perceived the situation. He or she has been assigned less merit, is ranked lower, and quite possibly for very good reasons. I agree, however, with Hampton, that the malicious hater's typical strategy of diminishing the merit of the higher ranked opponent is most unlikely to produce the outcome the hater desires. Malicious hatred in merit cases is not necessarily immoral, but it may well be counterproductive and so foolish. Of course, should the strategy involve false attributions, or fabrications in the effort to destroy the reputation of the higher ranked competitor, there would be no question about its moral status.

Hampton attempts to support her case for the futility of malicious hatred in merit cases by referring us to Western movies, where she claims this is a popular theme. I am unclear, as she does not specify, exactly which films she has in mind.

On her account, the theme is that the avenger masters the hated wrongdoer in order to diminish him and thus to elevate the avenger above the wrongdoer. Eventually, however, the avenger realizes how pathetic the wrongdoer is, gets no pleasure from his victory, and "drops his gun."

Try as I might, I cannot think of a major Western that actually follows Hampton's theme. Western avengers do not deal with hated wrongdoers in order to shore up their own shaky sense of self-worth. They deal with them because, in the words of the famous "Texasism," "He needed killing." And they do so because "there are some things a man can't ride around." A Western that might come close to Hampton's superficial description is *The Outlaw Josey Wales*. In its final sequences, Wales corners the vicious Red Leg leader responsible for killing his family and destroying his homestead. He does come to view his long-hated adversary as a pathetic low-life creature and disdains to kill him, until the wrongdoer makes an attempt on his life and then Wales kills him. Never, however, does Wales lose his own sense of self-worth and seek revenge in the form of the groveling and death of the wrongdoer as a means of worth restoration. He wants retribution for the murders of his family, and he sees himself as the only instrument able and, perhaps ordained, to achieve it. His momentary decision not to kill the target outright but to let him suffer in his own humiliation may be a lapse provoked by a misguided evaluation that he had already gained his goal. The wrongdoer's vicious responsive actions, however, bring back into focus the fact that the retributive end has not been satisfactorily achieved so Wales kills the bastard.

The second sort of malicious-spiteful hatred is related to moral worth. A malicious hater of this type does not set out to diminish the merit evaluation of the object of hate. Instead, the hater focuses on the moral worth of the individual and attempts to destroy his or her moral status. This is not malice based on competition for a rung on the merit ladder in a specific human endeavor. It involves a sort of misguided conception of moral worth in competitive terms and attempts to lower the standard of moral worth in order to accommodate one's diminished sense of self-worth within the category.

Hampton provides a case that may help to illustrate the way this sort of malicious hatred functions. She tells us of a woman who has contracted AIDS and who purposefully sets out to have sexual relations with men she meets at parties. When she leaves her victims' rooms in the morning, she writes with lipstick on the mirror, "Welcome to the Wonderful World of AIDS." A reasonable analysis of her behavior is that she believes she has lost her moral worth or standing as a person to the disease, and in some general way she hates all of those whom she believes still have moral worth. She sees herself in some sort of competition with them for moral worth, perhaps conceiving of moral worth as a zero-sum game, an obstacle that has been set too high for her, but not for most others, to vault. By infecting them with her disease, she will lower them to her level; they will not be able to hurdle the bar, and it will have to be lowered. She will, as it were, rerack the category of moral worth, which is more than misery liking company. She might, and according to Hampton does, believe that by infecting enough people she will change the "worth curve" and restore herself to the realm of moral worth or moral value. The competitive element, such as it is, is for her to "defeat" the worth of others that she regards as above her in order to restore worth equality.

The malicious hater, of this sort, accepts the notion of moral worth egalitarianism that there is only one level of worth, one rung on the worth ladder, but believes that due to some factors, perhaps beyond her control, she has fallen below fellow humans in worth, fallen off the single-rung ladder. She aims to restore herself by lowering the standard of worth. It is a version of the strategy of destroying what others have in order to make them equal with me who does not have what they have. Of course, it utterly misunderstands the notion of moral worth egalitarianism, conflating it with moral merit evaluation. Hampton writes, "One who has a scarred face cannot become more beautiful by throwing acid in the face of everyone she meets; all she succeeds in doing is making everyone as ugly as she."[103] Certainly worth-reduction malicious haters are immoral as well as self-defeating.

Hampton's other type of hatred is moral hatred, which, on her account, does not necessarily involve competitive impulses nor is it directed at damaging or hurting persons. It is an aversion to a person because he or she has identified himself or herself with a cause or practice the hater deems to be immoral, and it is conjoined with "the wish to triumph over him (or her) and his (or her) cause or practice in the name of some fundamental moral principle or objective."[104] Moral hatred is not directed at the harm of the individual. In fact, no personal hatred of the individual seems to be directly involved, on Hampton's account. The cause or practice is the primary target. The object of hate is the "message in the insulter's action," the "immoral cause her action promotes,"[105] or whatever part of her is identified with the immoral cause. Hampton tries to explain the relationship between the individual and the immoral cause by use of the highly visual notion of rotting, recalling the ancient Greek and Hebrew idea of pollution, or *miasma*. The infected person is said to be rotten, gone bad, spoiled, decayed. Some, of course, have become rotten to the core. The metaphor conjures up the picture of a good person by nature who has been fouled by association with evil causes. In fact, in her attempt to explain the idea of rotting by degrees, Hampton uses the example of the spoiled child, the brat.

I have a number of difficulties with Hampton's moral hatred. The first has to do with the underlying notion that humans are by nature good and that association with evil causes befouls them. As I shall argue later, I have no sympathy for the notion that humans are by nature either good or bad. We become evil by doing evil things, and we may do so either because we choose to do so or because we have become unconsciously habituated to it. All wickedness is preferential. Evil is not a vast menacing cloud somewhere in the universe inexorably engulfing us, as some horror stories would have it. Hampton seems to think that, insofar as evil infects and rots people, it is "the evil" that deserves our hatred and, supposedly, our attack, not the poor infected people.

My view, as noted earlier, is that wrongdoing requires a hostile response and wrongdoing is done by people. Admittedly, people sometimes do wrong because they do not have the strength of will to do right, though they know what the right thing to do is. Reasons for weakness of will might be provided that could persuade us that an offender has a psychological problem that requires therapeutic treatment. But not all evil is explainable in terms of *akrasia;* I think only a small portion is. Also, Hampton seems to be committed to what John Kekes calls "choice morality."[106] The offender is rotting because of the association with the evil cause, but the association may not have been avoidable, not a matter of choice. In such cases, perhaps they constitute most cases of evil, she rejects the notion that the offender is fully responsible for the evil. Moral haters, as she would have it, go after the evil, not the wrongdoer, or not the wrongdoer per se. They hate the sin, not the sinner.

My second concern with Hampton's account is that it seems committed to a version of the doctrine of double effect. Although one desires to triumph over the infected (rotten) individual, that is only a second effect of the real reason for responding with hostility. It is the cause or the practice that is the target. Should the individual suffer a severe penalty, even death, that was not the primary intent, although perhaps it could not be helped when attacking the evil cause. Her account sounds remarkably similar to what Plato says about punishment in the *Laws:* "The unjust man is presumably bad, but the bad man is involuntarily so. Now it never makes sense that the voluntary is done involuntarily. Hence the man who does injustice appears involuntarily unjust . . . Everyone does injustice involuntarily."

Punishment for offenses can only be justified, Plato believes, if it is noble, but it would not be noble to inflict pain and suffering on someone who acted wrongfully involuntarily. Plato's "ingenious" solution to the problem is to admit that punishment is a morally unacceptable way of dealing with such offenders but to argue that therapy is appropriate. If what we do to wrongdoers is therapy intended to cure their diseases and rehabilitate them, then the principles of justice and nobility will be satisfied. However, as far as Plato is concerned, it is irrelevant that the form of the therapy adopted to do the job may amount to inflicting severe injury on the wrongdoer.

Hampton talks of the pleasure the moral hater receives when achieving victory over the immoral cause: "The pleasure a moral hater has in seeing his opponent defeated and his cause victorious can be accompanied by at least two others. If *you* are the one who effected the victory, then in addition to enjoying the thrill of your cause's prevailing you can take pride in the fact that you have accomplished it. And if the victory has to do with combating injustice against *you,* then you can enjoy not only the impersonal benefits that come from the assertion of your moral cause, but also the personal pleasure that comes from the fact that its victory involves the assertion of *you* and your worth. (But you have not pursued your fight in order to get this personal pleasure; it is only a side effect confirming your belief in yourself, albeit a welcome one.)"[107] Impersonal moral hatred opens the door for Hampton to forgiveness of the wrongdoer. Of course, the forgiving moral hater never stops hating the cause or practice and its manifestation in the character traits or behavior of the wrongdoer. But the forgiving moral hater acknowledges the inherent worth and goodness of the wrongdoer. None of this would be possible, Hampton suggests, if the primary target of the moral hater were the rotten person, if the moral hater had been acting on the desire to inflict injury on the wrongdoer *simpliciter*.

Murphy makes a strong case for another kind of hatred that is a hybrid of Hampton's moral and malicious hatred. The desire to injure the hated person, identified by Hume and central to Hampton's account of malicious hatred, may not be the result of a feeling of competition in which one's worth or status is at stake. The desire, Murphy maintains, may be motivated by retributive feelings, which are feelings that their object's current status or well-being is ill-gotten or undeserved. These feelings have to do with redressing the imbalance in desert, restoring the appropriate moral balance, making the wrongdoer pay for the disruption, the harm, caused by his or her actions. This response is much more than a moral hatred, and it cannot be placated in the hater by an attack on only the cause or the practice with which the wrongdoer is affiliated. The matter is intensely personal.

Consider Hannie Caulder. Three men have viciously raped her. She hates them; well she should. She does not only hate rape and all that it means in human relations. And further, a characteristic of the retributive hater noted by Murphy, she has earned a sense of righteousness, in which she can publicly express her hatred and her intentions to kill the rapists. Her emotions are not spiteful. She does not resent the rapists because she feels she has lost her self-worth or questions her self-esteem, nor does she view her relationship to them in a competitive way. Instead, she wants to kill them, purely and simply because they deserve it for what they did to her. Her hatred is almost entirely retributive.

Is retributive hatred ever morally permissible? That question can only be answered if a further question is answered affirmatively: Is punishment, the inflicting of harm on someone, ever morally permissible? I have said enough so far about our conception of wrongness including the need for a hostile response to make clear that I believe, at least in some cases, that it is morally permissible to inflict harm on someone because what they did was wrong. I do not think that utilitarian concerns should be taken into consideration in cases of the moral permissibility of the hostile response to wrongdoing. Moral permissibility in these cases is governed solely by desert, which is an essential element of our conception of moral responsibility. Obviously, if inflicting harm on a person is sometimes morally permissible, then on those occasions it is morally permissible to retributively hate that person.

Moral permissibility should not be confused with something being morally mandatory. Murphy reminds us of two biblical admonitions regarding retributive hatred that require consideration before we are secure in pronouncing it morally permissible. One may be called the epistemological admonition and the other the moral status admonition. The epistemological admonition, supposedly implied in "Vengeance is mine; I will repay, saith the Lord" (Rom.12:19), is also expressed in a number of ways in the philosophical and religious literature. This admonition is grounded in the undeniable fact that humans are not endowed with the divine ability to know all the facts, especially those regarding why people act as they do, their "hearts." Hence, we may typically lack the knowledge necessary to justify retributively hating someone; better leave it to Heaven!

Certainly we are far from divine. We can and do make mistakes. (Which reminds me of a line in the film *The Witches of Eastwick:* "When God makes mistakes, they call it nature. When we make mistakes, they call it evil.") But the epistemological admonition does not tell us that we must have all knowledge about why people act as they do before we can justifiably get morally angry at them and retributively hate them. It can, and Murphy suggests that it should, be read as a caution that reminds us that we can make serious mistakes, deadly mistakes. The point of *The Ox-Bow Incident* is not that cattle rustlers should not be hanged. It is that those doing the hanging had better be as certain as is humanly possible that they are hanging the right people.

The epistemological admonition can be read as reiterating Aristotle's position in his discussion of the virtues of anger: it is always better, morally, to come down a bit on the side of the deficiency, to be prepared to extend the benefit of the doubt in cases of apparently complex motivations. Such a position, of course, reflects the demeanor of the heroes of Westerns who are slow to anger, measured in their immediate responses, and do not allow themselves to be pushed into deadly combat before they have fully assessed the situation and their opponents' moral responsibility. Think of Shane, The Preacher in *Pale Rider,* Will Kane in *High Noon,* Patrick in *The Tall T,* and a number of others.

The moral status admonition, as Murphy reminds us, also has a biblical home. It is popularly phrased as "Let him who is without sin cast the first stone," but the biblical passage actually states,"He that is without sin among you, let him first cast a stone at her" (John 8:7). In any event, this admonition suggests that we are all morally corrupt to some degree and so lack the moral superiority to judge fellow sinners and administer penalties for their behavior. Even if there never were epistemological concerns, "even if it were possible to be absolutely sure of the iniquity of another person, possible to know exactly how much suffering his evil deserves,"[108] this admonition is supposed to restrain us from punishing out of fear that we are not morally pure enough to "cast the stone."

The moral status admonition, even more than the epistemological admonition, either takes refuge in a karmic moral theory or destroys the concept of moral responsibility altogether. At the very least, it seems to insist that matters of punishment for wrongdoing—even if, for example, the "beyond a reasonable doubt" standard is met—must be left to a morally pure entity. Insofar as no human qualifies as a morally pure entity, no human is qualified to retributively hate, and therefore no human is justified in punishing a wrongdoer. The appropriateness of punishment and its severity must be left to a divine entity. Interestingly, the admonition does not condemn vengeance or retributive punishment. It only takes such things out of the hands of humans and trusts them to the morally pure entity. How bad can vengeance and retributive punishment be when performing them does not sully the hands of God, who remains morally pure? The moral status admonition clearly reads like a version of an intermediary karmic moral theory, not unlike Kant's.

Even if the moral status admonition does incorporate some sort of karmic moral resolution to the problem of reward and punishment, it still entails the view that the human use of moral responsibility ascriptions is ultimately unjustifiable, even meaningless, an empty exercise. All of the passion and emotion that accompanies, indeed provokes, responsibility ascription must be no more than a mark of the moral inferiority of the human species. The moral status admonition, when looked at in this way, collapses the "house" of morality, as we know it, by blasting away its very foundation—ordinary human moral responsibility—and renders our language of morals unintelligible at its core. God, the pure moral entity, presumably would have to make some sort of moral responsibility ascriptions with regard to our behavior, or the karmic theory would crumble. But what guarantee do we have that we could understand God's judgments, lacking as we do both moral purity and the divine insight?

At best, the moral responsibility ascriptions we make must, in the end, have no more force than recommendations, exhortations, or suggestions. But suggestions to whom? Surely not to a morally pure and all-knowing God. Analogies might be drawn to petitionary prayer, leading then to arguments about the blasphemous nature of that sort of exercise, but I will refrain from traveling in that direction. Suffice it to say that moral responsibility ascriptions, if the moral status admonition is taken seriously, may be understood as human exercises in divine pretense or guesswork, a sort of game of estimating how people and their actions are being judged by the divine. If that were all that holding people morally responsible for what they do is, then I suspect that moral responsibility ascription would have no clout in our lives, and the passions and emotions, especially those of moral anger and retributive hatred, that give rise to responsibility ascription would have become extinct in human experience. We would not be the creatures we are.

When God in the whirlwind tells Job that humans cannot hope to understand the ways of the divine, that should have been a warning to intermediary karmic moral theorists who still make ascriptions of moral responsibility. It is one thing to believe that evildoers eventually will be punished by God, but quite another to presume to know the content of the divine conception of evil. "Shall he that contendeth with the Almighty instruct him?" (Job, 40:2).

What would a social world without human moral responsibility ascription be like? Edmund Pincoffs[109] identifies three types of social practices to which moral responsibility ascription is related. One involves the identification of appropriate subjects of blame (and praise). These are the character evaluation practices. The second type may (but perhaps need not) relate to the first and is the type with which we are herein centrally interested: the identification of those who merit punishment (or reward), the desert practices. The third involves the setting of targets of (usually financial) burden shifting, the compensatory practices. These practices and the institutions that embody them provide the glue that bonds our conception of a moral community.

Our concept of moral responsibility derives its practical sense from the fact that it is both integral to and dependent on those practices and institutions. If all three types were terminated, moral responsibility ascription would have no point, and without moral responsibility those practices cannot even be conceived. That is, there is a necessary conceptual link between the concept of moral responsibility and the existence of those social practices. If one or two of the practices were eliminated, perhaps because we took the second admonition to heart, the concept of moral responsibility, though truncated and hardly a shadow of its former self, could survive. But, we should wonder, wouldn't skepticism about moral status take all three down with it?

If we accept the view that one must be morally pure before one can retributively hate and act on that hatred by responding with hostility toward its object, the desert practices are unjustifiable. But can the morally impure justifiably blame people for their misdeeds and manifestations of bad character? Can they, with any degree of assurance, identify character types from mere observations of behavior? Again, the "Let he who is without sin cast the first stone" admonition would seem to block the character evaluation practices. Could the compensation practices survive the admonition? I don't see how.

How can we, without being hypocritical and presuming to understand the judgments of the morally pure entity, the divine, hope to allocate adequate compensation for injuries that we may, in other cases, have inflicted? The moral humility that the admonition requires could, if taken literally, remove us altogether from the arena of moral responsibility and either throw all such matters into the hands of a divine judge or some universal force, or collapse the tent of moral responsibility in which we huddle for social security and stability and turn us out into something like Hobbes's state of nature. Insofar as I am convinced that the metaphysics of the former requires more blind faith than I believe reasonable persons should muster, the latter is all that can be expected. That outcome is morally unacceptable, irrational, and unnecessary.

Another way to read the moral status admonition, as suggested by both Murphy and Michael Moore,[110] is that it tells us to use occasions of retributive hatred to introspect, to discover the potential for wrongdoing in ourselves. Who could object to that? But is such moral introspection really supposed to stop revenge responses in their tracks? Hopefully it will make most of us less self-righteous, more humble, and that result is good. But even if we were to discover the potential for evil within us, which of course we will, why should that discovery deter us from following the path of revenge on which our justified moral anger and retributive hatred have set us?

The most reasonable reading of the moral status admonition is that it be taken as a caution against self-righteousness. It requires a healthy helping of humility, but not a cessation of desert practices. In this sense it is comparable to the epistemological caution, but no more. It allows righteous retributive hatred and hostile actions motivated by it, but not self-righteous retributive hatred. In effect, it sets an Aristotelian-like mean on the spectrum of retributive hatred that runs between humility and self-righteousness. And, I suppose, like the epistemological caution, it counsels erring on the side of humility (the deficiency) rather than self-righteousness.

Perhaps the major moral saving grace of retributive hatred is that the retributive hater not only desires to injure, even kill, the target, but he or she also desires to restore the moral balance in the community that has been disrupted by the actions of the target. In this sense the morally angry retributive hater is very much like the hero—Hercule Poirot, Sherlock Holmes, Inspector Morse, Lord Peter Wimsey, et al. —of detective fiction.[111] Restoration is the primary motivation, not revolution.

Acting on moral anger and retributive hatred, as both Hampton and Murphy warn, despite its moral permissibility and even if moderated by the two cautions, might have an extremely negative impact on the avenger. It can consume the avenger's life, leaving everything else to go to rack and ruin, including psychic well-being. In that sense, the avenger can become his or her own victim. Think of *The Searchers*. The avenger also, perhaps typically, may have to perform morally repulsive acts to adequately punish the target. Ethan Edwards, although unable to kill Scar to avenge the horrific death of his beloved Martha and his brother, nephew, and niece, mutilates his enemy's corpse by scalping him. James Stewart's character in *Winchester '73* kills his brother. Hannie Caulder kills the three rapists. Certainly the fortitude needed to perform such repulsive acts should assault the sense of decency of the avenger, and most would-be avengers, we can expect, will discover that they are not up to the task of adequately acting on their retributive hatred. Their moral anger and retributive hatred is, in Murphy's terms, "doomed by one's own better nature to go forever unfulfilled."[112] They may settle for doling out less than the full measure of revenge the wrongdoer deserves.

Because considerations of decency—and probably cowardice—constrain most of us, state institutions of retribution have been created and charged with taking over the retributive task. In this assumption I differ radically from the party line in that I do not find very persuasive the notion that concern about spiraling cycles of vengeance provoked the impersonal institutionalization of punishment. I am far more convinced of what may be a version of a Lockean view of all of this. That is, I suspect that assessment of the trackdown costs coupled with cowardice pointed the way to institutionalization. Fear of vengeance out of control, wild justice, it seems to me, likely would have been a minor concern in communities. It could easily be quelled by revenge norms, including talion principles. The greater fear would have been of all sorts of wrongdoers practicing their transgressions with impunity due to the economic rationality and cowardice of the general populace.

From the moral point of view, I do not think we should worry that much about good people occasionally responding with hostility to evildoers in a disproportionate manner to the harm they suffered. We should worry about good people, anesthetized by moral insensitivity, moral cowardice, and/or economic considerations, not taking responsive actions and bearing their wrongful losses stoically, brimming over with Christian forgiveness. If I am right in my surmise, then the creation of punitive legal systems would lend some credence to the view that karmic moral theories might not have been as widely accepted as may be believed or that they were thought to be morally inadequate. Karmic moral theories placate lingering concerns in the moral community that too few of its members have the courage to act on their legitimate feelings of moral anger and retributive hatred, and that institutional mechanisms are bound to be flawed in their administration of appropriate penalties. I am not arguing against state systems of "justice" and punishment, but I do think the fact that most of us have so readily turned these important matters over to impersonal, procedurally structured technologies should not be exhibited as one of our great moral accomplishments. The substitution of the institutionalized punishment systems, however, comes with psychic and moral costs for victims.[113]

I do not mean to suggest that trackdown costs are a small matter. The toll, economically and psychically, that they take out of the avenger can be substantial. That is one of the major themes of such westerns as *Winchester '73, The Searchers, True Grit, Hannie Caulder, Two Rode Together, Gunfighter, The Streets of Laredo, The Outlaw Josey Wales*, and so many others. My point, however, is that taking revenge that is constrained by the epistemological and moral status cautions, although perhaps not morally mandated, is both morally permissible and a manifestation of a good moral character. This point raises another issue. Earlier I associated the moral avenger with the "dirty hands problem." If I am right that it is morally permissible to avenge retributive hatred as long as it is done within the constraints of the cautions and is in proper proportion to the wrongdoing being avenged (a matter to be taken up in Chapter 7), then the hands of the avenger are not dirtied by performing the deed. That, however, does not alter the fact that avenging retributive hatred in cases of personal or vicarious moral anger requires moral courage, the taking of a risk to which most of us are adverse.

To teach morality is not just to teach kindness and a number of prohibitions; it is to teach when and how and at whom to be angry, who and when to retributively hate, and when and how to act because of one's moral anger and retributive hatred. We hear a great deal these days about an ethics of care. Care ethics typically makes the virtue of care sound like it has everything to do with forgiveness and mercy and nothing whatsoever to do with preserving the moral community by acting with hostility toward the evil people who invade it. I would like to think of the virtues of vengeance as an essential part, albeit not the soft side, of a care ethics.

CHAPTER FOUR

The Conditions

It is a condition that confronts us—not a theory.
Grover Cleveland[1]

One of the main points of the previous section was that a basic, and I believe noneliminatable, tenet of morality is that wrongdoing requires a hostile response. But a hostile response from whom, toward whom, and how hostile? There are three sorts of conditions, in addition to the communication condition (discussed in Chapter 3), that must be met for the morally legitimate use of harm in dealing with a wrongdoer. I will refer to them as the authority condition, the desert condition, and the fit condition. I think of these conditions in something like the way J. L. Austin conceived of the felicity conditions for performatives.[2] When the conditions are satisfied, the harming of a wrongdoer is morally legitimate, a "happy" performance.

Austin, it may be recalled, developed a schematic structure for the sorts of things that are necessary for the felicitous functioning of a performative (actually an explicit performative, but that is of no particular relevance to my proposal regarding virtuous vengeance). Austin separated his conditions into three categories. The first concerns the existence of a conventional procedure and then focuses on the appropriateness of particular persons invoking that procedure in the circumstances.

In effect, when trying to determine whether a particular performance is or is not felicitous, we first need to establish that a conventional procedure exists of which the performance is an instance. Then we need to ascertain whether the people invoking or using it have the appropriate authority to do so. This is a matter of some current importance in the Arab world, as reported in the *New York Times* (June 20, 1999). Apparently, the rate of familial homicide of nonvirginal daughters is alarmingly high in Jordan, Egypt, and among the Palestinian Arabs. It is generally assumed, especially by the poorer Muslims in those regions, that family honor is destroyed if a daughter has had sexual relations outside of wedlock, even if she were violently raped. The father or the brothers of the young woman can only reclaim the family's honor by killing her. If they do not kill her, they literally cannot hold up their heads in public. The taboo against premarital sex by young women is, according to the report, ascribed to the Koran. Therefore, the killing of the offending daughter is taken to be both a familial and a religious duty, and, in fact, the courts typically go very lightly when sentencing those who commit honor-restoring killings of women. Thus it would appear that a conventional procedure exists and that the authority to perform the murders falls to the fathers and brothers.

Some scholars of the Koran point out that the religious obligation that purportedly backs the familial murder convention does not really exist in Islam. Women, of course, are to enter marriage chaste. It is of some note that in the Arab countries that are religiously conservative, the incidence of honor killings of daughters is very small. That does not mean that familial honor is not thought to be at risk on the bridal bed. It is. But the religious directive against premarital sexual relations is, most likely, taken much more to heart by the young women in such communities. In any event, social norms regarding honor are powerful wherever they appear. In the regions noted, the machinery of government and justice seems to turn a blind eye to the practice, if not straightforwardly endorsing it. Prison sentences of three months for killing a nonvirginal daughter are typical. So, regardless of the interpretation of the Koran, a social convention, a norm of revenge, undeniably exists, and it includes the conveying of authority to perform the deed. And fathers and brothers, reportedly in the name of family honor, brutally murder their unmarried daughters and sisters who are not virgins or even are suspected of having lost their virginity.

Austin's second category requires correct and complete execution of the procedure. The third insists that those using the procedure have the appropriate thoughts, feelings, and intentions to conduct themselves in keeping with the procedure and that they actually conduct themselves subsequently in the prescribed way. Failure to meet these or any of these conditions, on Austin's account, renders the performative utterance, or I will say conventional practice, "unhappy," although failure in the case of the third type of conditions, the mental state conditions, does not void the performance. It only makes it insincere. For example, to promise without intending to keep the promise is not to have failed to promise, but it is to have deceitfully promised.

Another of Austin's examples helps to make his schema clear. Suppose that a recently built ship, to be called the *Olympic,* is on the chocks prepared for the christening ceremony. An hour before the ceremony is to begin, I walk up to the ship, grab the champagne bottle that is hung at the bow, smash it across the side of the ship, and proclaim, "I hereby christen you *Titanic.*" For good measure, to follow Austin's version, I kick out the chocks and the ship starts to glide into the harbor. Has the ship been named *Titanic*? Clearly not. Why? Because I am not the person designated to do "the honors." I do not have the authority. There is a conventional procedure for ship naming, and it goes roughly as I performed it. But without authority, my performance has no effect. The ship will not be called the *Titanic,* no matter how sincere I was in my "performance." What I have done is a travesty, a misplay. My recital of the ritual words is but a misinvocation.

Another example actually occurred to my brother Thom and me during his wedding ceremony. The minister pronounced that Thom's bride and Peter were now man and wife. Thom and I and my wife, of course, took notice of the slip, but it had no effect on the performance of the marriage. I suppose it might have insofar as the procedures were not executed by all parties correctly (a version of Austin's second condition), but the relevant parties chose to overlook the minister's having flawed the ceremony. His error will, of course, always glare out at those with enough patience to watch the wedding video (perhaps there was some effect, as the marriage ended in divorce). Might Thom have success-fully maintained that he was never properly married and avoided the tribulations of the divorce proceedings? Probably not, since, subsequent to the flawed cer-emony, the standard civil procedures were completed without a comparable flaw.

Austin took the first two sorts of conditions as the determining factors of whether the act had been performed or achieved at all. Failure to satisfy condi-tions of the third sort, as previously noted, does not prevent the achievement of the act, but makes it an insincere performance. Infelicitous performances in which one of the first two conditions is violated, according to Austin, are mis-fires, while those of the third type are abuses. Misfires are not performances of the intended or apparent sort at all. Something, of course, happened, but it was not the outcome ensured by the ceremonial or ritualistic practice. Austin went on to sort the types of misfires into misexecutions, misapplications, flaws, hitches, and the like. He divided the abuses into insincerities and, according to a note appended to the text of *How to Do Things with Words* by J. O. Urmson, dissimulations and such things as disloyalties, breaches, and the like.

A point that is worthy of our attention is that the felicitous invocation of a ceremonial or ritualistic practice will usually be at least morally permissible, but if that is so, then at least certain misfired invocations of the same practice may be morally forbidden. For example, if my brother were already married at the time of the ceremony, he would not have satisfied the condition of being "appropriate for the invocation of the particular procedure invoked."[3] The marriage ceremony would have been void, a misfire. But, of course, it would not have been without effect. My brother most certainly would have done some-thing, and something that is both legally and morally forbidden in our cul-ture: he would have committed bigamy. Although I admit to knowing little of the Arab cultures in which the killing of unchaste unmarried daughters or sis-ters is practiced, I assume that if the mother or sister carried out the killing, it would be a misfire of the practice and would probably be treated as a murder.

It is of some interest, I suppose, that in most cases where the misfire is be-lieved to be of moral import, we have specific names for the deed. In less egre-gious cases, we tend to bundle the misfires under general categories, such as the "slip" committed by the minister. Also, abuses of procedures or practices in cases where we place a good deal of moral import, such as promising, are morally for-bidden and thus legitimate reasons to morally blame the abuser. I am not clear what we should say in my ship christening case. The act was certainly a prank, perhaps a spiteful one; in that it was a misfire. The intended procedure, the one for which all was in ready before I arrived on the scene, did not actually occur. I did not abuse that procedure. What did occur, however, is something for which I should be held responsible. I deserve moral blame and punishment. It is not as if I did nothing because what I appeared to be doing, christening the ship, was a misfire. I did something, and it had untoward consequences; it just was not naming the ship *Titanic*. It was trespassing, malicious mischief, interference with property, and so on.

Insofar as acts of vengeance are acts of communication and certainly have, at least superficially, a great deal in common with what Austin identified as performatives, the temptation to assimilate the analysis of what counts as a justified act of revenge to some sort of account of the felicity of performative utterances is difficult to resist. In fact, I cannot wholly resist it. Austin is encouraging in this regard: "A great many of the acts which fall within the province of Ethics are not, as philosophers are too prone to assume, simply in the last resort physical movements: very many of them have the general character, in whole or in part, of conventional or ritual acts, and are therefore, among other things exposed to infelicity."[4] Acts of revenge, or at least those for which moral justification is claimed (and that probably includes the vast majority of them), are certainly conventional (even norm-governed) and ritualistic.

The communication condition is, I have maintained, one of the constitutive conditions of vengeance, and it in fact can also be viewed, in Austinian terms, as a kind of performance whose success is dependent on its own set of felicity rules or conditions. Therefore, in the performance of vengeance, there is an embedded subperformance that can go wrong in a number of different ways, as suggested in Chapter 3.

I do not wish to imply or suggest that the three additional conditions for virtuous vengeance, conditions on which I focus the remainder of the book—authority, desert, and fit—are to be construed as somehow matching up with Austin's three categories of felicity. They are all constitutive conditions, or conditions comparable to Austin's A and B categories, not his Γ category. Failure to meet any of the four "Virtuous Vengeance Conditions" constitutes a misfire, not an abuse. There is, however, a dependency relationship between the conditions. The fit condition must be dependent on the desert condition. Obviously, if no penalty is deserved, there are no issues of proportionality with respect to the penalty administered. The same also might be said about authority. We do not consider whether an avenger has legitimate authority until the wrongdoer's desert is settled. Thus, chronologically and logically, desert takes priority in the Virtuous Vengeance Conditions. But it is, as are the others, a necessary and not a sufficient condition of virtuous revenge.

Abuses of vengeance occur when avengers are insincere, when they are disrespectful of the practice in one way or another. In such cases, revenge has been successfully and legitimately taken, but the act will be hollow, and even the avenger may subsequently view it as such. The important point, however, is that it is not an abuse of vengeance to harm someone who does not deserve it, or to harm a person who does deserve it beyond what is proportional to the wrongdoing, or to harm a wrongdoer when one does not have the appropriate authority to do so. In all such cases, the performance is not one of vengeance, but a misfire, a misexecution, a miscarriage of the practice. Austin, according to Urmson, in some such cases might have called it "a non-play" with respect to the practice or convention. If the avenger kills a wrongdoer who does not deserve a penalty of death or, although deserving such a penalty, the avenger does not have the proper authority to administer the fatal blow to the wrongdoer, then the act is murder. It is not revenge.

In *Unforgiven,* William Munny carries out two distinct acts of revenge. For the first, he acts as a paid surrogate for the town prostitutes, who want revenge against two cowboys who mutilated the face of a young prostitute. The prostitutes will settle for nothing less than the death of the cowboys. Arguments could well be raised, and they are in the film, in support of the position that although the cowboys deserve some penalty, indeed a severe one, they do not deserve death. Desert is not an issue. Let us grant, against the objections of the sheriff, that the prostitutes have the appropriate authority to administer the deserved punishment, whatever it is, and that they can exercise it through the actions of hired guns or bounty hunters. I realize that this is a highly contentious surmise, both in itself and in the movie, but that is not the issue with which I am herein concerned. In effect, let us grant that the authority and desert conditions are not at issue. Fit, as the sheriff argues early on in the movie, is the issue. In fact, the whole movie might be described as about fit. Killing the cowboys just does not fit their offense. It is murder and therefore it is not morally permissible. The desert, authority, and communication conditions may be satisfied, but without fit the act of revenge cannot be virtuous. It is a misfire.

The sheriff and the men of the town capture Munny's friend Ned, who has not actually killed either of the cowboys, and they torture and kill him. In this case, the sheriff may have legitimate authority had Ned been the killer, but since he was not, Ned did not deserve to be tortured to death. Munny determines to avenge his friend's death, and he does so in spectacular fashion. He enters the saloon where Ned's corpse is displayed, and, after announcing his intention to avenge the unwarranted death of his friend, he kills six men and wounds the sheriff. His is not merely an impulsive act driven by passion. He knows what he is doing and what it is to kill someone. As he earlier told the Schofield Kid, "It's a hell of a thing to kill a man. You take away everything he's got . . . and everything he's ever going to have." The Kid, in reference to his killing of one of the targeted cowboys, says, "I guess he had it coming." To which Munny responds, "We all have it coming, Kid." Fair enough, we all have death coming, but do we deserve to die at the hands of a specific killer? It is unclear whether Munny is answering that question.

Back in the saloon at the end of the film, Munny notices the wounded sheriff stirring, trying to get a gun. Munny points a shotgun at the sheriff's head. "I don't deserve to die like this . . . I was building a house," the sheriff says, and Munny spits out, "Deserve's got nothing to do with it." He fires the gun. This last remark might seem rather incoherent in the circumstances, a conceit of the author. The sheriff does deserve to suffer a penalty for his torture and murder of Ned; deserve has everything to do with it.

As noted above, however, the film is not about desert. It is about fit and, to a lesser degree, authority. The issues should be whether death is fitting punishment for the sheriff and whether Munny, as Ned's best friend, has the legitimate authority to administer the penalty. Unless Munny's final words to the sheriff are read as claiming that there can be no question as to desert, they would seem to negate somewhat his communicating the appropriate message of vengeance as he did when he entered the saloon and pronounced it in Achillean fashion. He is there to punish those who mutilated and killed Ned. What they did was wrong, and they deserve to be punished for doing it. Any other reading of "Deserve's got nothing to do with it" introduces a doubt about the satisfaction of both the communication and the desert conditions, conditions that Munny clearly believes are satisfied as he takes revenge. Desert is crucial to perhaps the only morally legitimate act of vengeance Munny did, or ever will, commit.

CHAPTER FIVE

The Avenger:
The Authority Condition

VIRTUE AND MORAL ORIGINALITY

> What! . . . no sympathy with art, no pretension of philosophy; only a simple knowledge
> of the secret that has puzzled all the philosophers, baffled all the lawyers . . . : the secret
> of right and wrong. Why, man, you are a genius, a master of masters, a god! At twenty-
> four, too!
>
> *George Bernard Shaw*[1]

Moral philosophers typically talk about the differences between action-and agent-based theories. Some moral theories are said to focus their attention on the evaluation of actions, while others are concerned with the way agents or people or their characters should be morally evaluated. Kant and the utilitarians are usually classed as action-oriented, while Aristotle is primarily interested in agents or the characters from which their actions flow. The recent interest in virtue ethics that has been fostered by neo-Aristotelians such as Alasdair MacIntyre and feminists such as Nel Noddings suggests still further ways to draw the distinctions. We might distinguish between character-or virtue-oriented ethicists and obligation- or duty-oriented ethicists. The latter tend to focus on actions and the former on agents. Ethicists of the former sort typically look to Plato or Aristotle as their philosophical forefathers, those of the latter to Kant or Mill. My interests are not, however, in the agent/action ethics distinction, but in an internecine one in virtue ethics.

What makes a person virtuous? Any number of answers could be proffered. On one account, the one that is typically read out of Aristotle, a person is virtuous because he or she does virtuous things, because he or she performs virtuous actions. That was a departure for Aristotle from the Platonic conception of virtue. Plato's virtuous or just soul (for example, in the *Republic*), the soul in harmony, appears to be something which is good in and of itself and quite apart from any human activity it might engender or that might express it. For Aristotle, on the other hand, virtue is always in action. If it is not expressed in human affairs, it just is not. Sarah Broadie's way of putting this is that "Aristotle constantly reminds his readers that happiness is activity: it is virtue in action, not virtue unused."[2]

Aristotle, according to Broadie, makes it clear that to act well is to act "in accordance with excellence (or virtue)."[3] From where, however, does he substantiate the virtues or excellences in accord with which the virtuous person is to act? MacIntyre writes, "The virtues are precisely those qualities the possession of which will enable an individual to achieve *eudaimonia* and the lack of which will frustrate his movement towards that *telos*."[4] In the same vein, Rosalind Hursthouse[5] reads Aristotle as maintaining that we determine what acts are virtuous by applying a test for virtuousness that is derived from a conception of *eudaimonia*, the good life or the life of well-being. In effect, and assuming that MacIntyre, Broadie, and Hursthouse read Aristotle correctly, what makes an action virtuous is not that it is the sort of thing done by virtuous people, but that it enables a person to achieve *eudaimonia*.

Michael Slote[6] offers an insightful and original way of sorting virtue theories, one that I think provides an intriguing way of accounting for the moral merit of certain kinds of avengers. He explicates the differences between what he calls agent-based and agent-focused virtue ethics. A virtue theory, on Slote's account, is agent-based if it treats the "moral or ethical status of acts as entirely derivative from independent and fundamental aretaic (as opposed to deontic) ethical characterizations of motives, character traits, or individuals."[7] In an agent-focused virtue ethics, the aretaic characterization of acts is derived from some other ethical conception, which is independent, or partially so, from the fact that the act is done by a virtuous person.

This distinction may at first seem to be rather complicated and not really worth making. But I think a case can be made that it is an insightful one and extremely important for my purposes. Aristotle's ethics, given the MacIntyre, Broadie, Hursthouse reading, is agent-focused, but book II, chapters 1–4 of the *Nicomachean Ethics* suggests the difficulty Aristotle had in sorting out the distinction.

Book II begins with Aristotle telling us that virtue is the result of habit: "We become just by doing just acts, temperate by doing temperate acts, brave by doing brave acts" (NE 1103a). But what are these virtuous acts? Aristotle admits that there is no single or simple way to describe or prescribe virtuous acts. He tells us that "matters concerned with conduct and questions of what is good for us have no fixity, any more than matters of health" (NE 1103b). He goes on to say that, "the agents themselves must in each case consider what is appropriate to the occasion" (NE 1103b).

Then, however, he shifts to his doctrine of the mean, suggesting that the way to identify virtuous acts is independent of the agent, and that it is accessible by the nonvirtuous person by application of that doctrine. He does add that we can tell when someone (or ourselves) has become virtuous, because the virtuous take pleasure in doing virtuous deeds. The nonvirtuous, apparently, may do virtuous deeds but get little or no pleasure from their doing so. It may cause them some pain, because pleasure for them is typically associated with the excess, for example, in the case of temperance. Hence, for the virtuous person pleasure supervenes on the doing of what is right and good, constituting well-being and the good life (*eudaimonia*).

In chapter 4 Aristotle makes an interesting point, in what Broadie calls "a difficult passage,"[8] that again may confuse the issue of whether his conception of virtue ethics is agent-based or agent-focused. He begins by reminding us that he has not made clear what he means by saying that we must become virtuous by doing virtuous deeds. Are we virtuous when our actions accord with what is virtuous or must they be done because they are virtuous? Is there a difference between doing what a virtuous person would do in the circumstances and acting virtuously in the same circumstances? To make his point, Aristotle draws a distinction between the arts and virtue: "The products of the arts have their goodness in themselves, so that it is enough that they should have a certain character, but if the acts that are in accordance with the virtues have themselves a certain character it does not follow that they are done justly or temperately. The agent also must be in a certain condition when he does them; in the first place he must have knowledge, secondly he must choose the acts, and choose them for their own sakes, and thirdly his action must proceed from a firm unchangeable character" (NE 1105a).

What is Aristotle's point? A work of art, a painting, perhaps one by Jackson Pollock, is a good painting because it has a certain character, it is perceived to have that character by those who observe or study it. All that is necessary to legitimately call it a good painting is for it to have that character, to look the way it does. Presently, I will take up my disagreement with Aristotle on this point, but for now, suppose the Pollock painting qualifies for us as good, "is perceived to have that character." Now suppose that an untrained child of four or five by dripping paint on a canvas produces a painting that satisfies all of the objective criteria we used to evaluate the Pollock masterpiece. On the view Aristotle is suggesting, we should have to regard the child's work as good art.

Broadie writes: "He must mean that we are satisfied with things that are normally produced by art or skill provided they are up to standard, even when they were produced by someone without skill. If we assess what such a doer has done by what he has made, we can say that what he has done is good. Lack of skill implies no defect in what he has done on this occasion, and it might reasonably be claimed that the skill is of value only because whosoever possesses it is more likely to produce acceptable articles."[9] This is, I will say for reasons to be developed later, a truncated aesthetic theory.

Virtue, for Aristotle, is utterly unlike the way he characterizes artistic performance. An action may have, to all observing it, the character of being just or courageous or temperate, but it very well may not be as good as a comparable action performed by a virtuous person. To carry out the disanalogy, the character of actions is only an incomplete sign that they are virtuous. Other conditions in the agent must be present, especially the second and third conditions. That is the basis for Aristotle's famous claim that actions "are called just and temperate when they are such as the just and temperate man would do" (NE 1105b).

Although this discussion sounds like Aristotle is agent-basing, he is not. His conditions that identify the virtuous person are actually independent of the way that virtuous people act. There is a significant difference for him between acting in the way that virtuous persons act and acting as a virtuous person. For Aristotle, one cannot become virtuous merely by mimicking the actions of the virtuous. Following Slote, Aristotle's virtue ethics is agent-focused, not agent-based. The virtuous person is not really "the measure of virtue in action"[10] despite Aristotle's statement to the effect that actions are called just and temperate "when they are such as the just or the temperate man would do."

An agent-based virtue ethics treats the goodness of an action as "entirely derivative from independent and fundamental ethical/aretaic facts (or claims) about the motives, dispositions, or inner life of the individuals who perform them."[11] Agent-based virtue ethics, as Slote notes, would appear to do exactly the sort of thing that Aristotle took pains to guard against with his agent-focused theory. It seems to "obliterate the common distinction between doing the right thing and doing the right thing for the right reasons."[12] But that need not be the case. Imagine an avenger who appropriately visits hostility on a wrongdoer but is solely motivated by malicious hatred. (This is a version of Sidgwick's malicious prosecutor.[13]) Did the avenger act virtuously, do the right thing? An agent-based virtue theory should respond in the negative because the avenger's motive was a bad one and acts are wrong when their motives are bad. But there seems to be something at least vaguely counterintuitive about that outcome, for it suggests that the avenger should refrain from punishing the wrongdoer. However, not to do so, especially if no one else is uniquely in a position to do so, would let the wrongdoer escape unpunished. So it is possible within agent-basing to distinguish between doing the right thing, avenging the wrongdoing, and doing it for the right reasons.

Pale Rider provides a dramatic case in point. The avenger, The Preacher (played by Clint Eastwood), is the only person in the film with the skills capable of taking on the gunmen hired by LaHood, who has been terrorizing, indeed killing, the independent miners of the valley. The Preacher has ordered the miners not to follow him into town as he confronts the gunmen who are led by Stockburn. He kills all of the villains, but we also learn that his motives for doing so are not purely those of moral or retributive hatred. The clear suggestion is that The Preacher is an angel of death, the Pale Rider of the book of Revelations, and that Stockburn was responsible for the multiple bullet wounds in The Preacher's back that are noticed early in the film by the independent miner, Hull Barrett, played by Michael Moriarty. All or most of those wounds should have been fatal. The Preacher has, as he admits, a score to settle with Stockburn. Thus, included in his motives for taking on the gunmen may well be a malicious hatred of their leader.

As Slote understands agent-based virtue ethics, it allows us to "distinguish between doing one's duty for the right reasons and thus acting rightly, on the one hand, and doing one's duty for the wrong reasons and thus acting wrongly."[14] This, however, is not the distinction between acting rightly and doing the right thing. For the agent-baser, an action done for the wrong reasons is wrong. The

Preacher, however, may well have, in fact we are rather sure that he has, mixed motives in doing the right thing: avenging the terrorizing and killing of the independent miners.

The distinctions that then need to be drawn are just as difficult for agent-focused as for agent-based virtue ethics. My own view is that if we can count the right reasons among his motives, then he acted rightly. Total purity of motives is far too high a standard if our ethics is to have any practical value. It might, in cases like that of The Preacher, be reassuring if we could learn that he would have acted in the same way even if the gunmen had been led by someone other than Stockburn, someone utterly unknown to him. Within the film, I think we can be fairly confident that he would have done so. The opportunity to settle an old personal score appears as an added opportunity and not as a primary motive.

Slote raises a second objection to agent-basing that worries about the placing of too much attention on motives. If the moral evaluation of actions derives ultimately or primarily from the inner states of agents, "it would appear to follow that if one is the right sort of person or possesses the right sort of inner states, it doesn't morally matter what one actually *does*."[15] If that is the case, standards would be in danger of disappearing altogether from the moral evaluation of behavior. What role would a moral constraint have to play? Slote's way of dealing with this objection is to remind us that "a view can be agent-based and still not treat actions as right or admirable simply because they are done by a virtuous individual or by someone with an admirable or good inner state."[16] An agent-based theory must avoid the trap of being committed to the view that good people are incapable of performing bad deeds, or the view that just because they do something it is thereby good. Such a simpleminded agent-basing might make some avengers virtuous, but at the cost of destroying the sense of the term "virtuous."

But how are moral restraints to be introduced into an agent-based virtue ethics? In Chapter 3 I argued that retributive hatred, as a motive, is morally good, or at least is morally permissible. I do not claim it is the only such motive that falls into that category. I hope to make the case that a certain kind of honor also is a morally good motive. Actions that express or exhibit morally good motives are good (or right). What does not follow is that persons who are filled with retributive hatred are incapable of acting in ways that do not express it, that it must necessarily become an expressed or exhibited motive. Christians, Stoics, some feminist ethicists, and especially those psychologists who rush to the scenes of terrorist bombings and mass murders in high schools typically urge people who have the emotion not to allow it to motivate their actions. Apparently, most do not.

The moral avenger, motivated by retributive hatred and what I will call personal honor, however, does not shirk the retributive task, although he or she certainly could, and "such refusal and the actions it would give rise to don't count as admirable."[17] Agent-basing an ethics of virtue is not excluding moral standards for actions and placing all the moral weight on having virtuous motivations. Slote sums up the position as follows: "Agent-based views clearly allow for agents to be subject to moral requirements or constraints or standards governing their actions. But those requirements, standards, and constraints operate and bind, as it were, *from within*."[18]

That may seem rather paradoxical; it certainly requires some explanation. The standards that govern the moral judgments of actions in an agent-based virtue ethics are derived from an understanding that certain motivations and not others exhibit or express whatever the position takes to be the most fundamentally good or admirable motivation. If the motive(s) in question furthers that fundamental motivation, then the actions that exhibit or express it are virtuous. Thus, for example, if retributive hatred is a motive, but not the fundamental good or admirable motive, it will have to further or in some way express the more fundamental good motive if actions motivated by it are to be regarded as good or admirable or morally permissible. I do not claim that retributive hatred is such a fundamental good motivation, but I believe it does further another motivation that is fundamental. A further point of clarification: in order to actually exhibit or express fundamental or derivative motivations, an agent will have to seriously take into consideration facts about the world that are external to the agent. Among those facts in the case of vengeance will be conditions of desert and fit. Agent-basing, at least of the sort I have in mind, is not a version of moral autism.

Slote provides two possible ways of formulating agent-based virtue ethics in terms of fundamental motivations. One he calls "cool" and the other "warm." I have little sympathy for what Slote calls warm agent-basing and its basis in benevolence, but his conception of cool agent-based virtue ethics offers distinct possibilities for the conception of virtuous vengeance that I have been developing. A cool agent-based virtue ethics could find its fundamental motivation in the concept of personal inner strength. Slote identifies Plato as the founder of such a virtue ethics because Plato makes the health of the soul the "inner touchstone of all good action."[19] I, however, locate in a certain reading of Emerson's conception of virtue the type of cool agent-basing in inner strength that can accommodate, though Emerson never talks of such things, a virtuous vengeance theory.

Before bringing Emerson into the picture, however, a general issue should be addressed: how is inner strength supposed to relate to actions we would typically regard as morally admirable? What is inner strength and how can it serve as an anchoring virtuous motivation? I would like to think that no one could deny that inner strength is to be held in high regard. It is, in Slote's terms, "intuitively admirable." We admire people who display it, and we show disdain for those who evidence its opposite, parasitism. There is to be found no more repugnant character in literature than Skimpole in Charles Dickens's *Bleak House*. He is the consummate leech who explains his parasitism in the relatively famous lines: "Here you see me utterly incapable of helping myself, and entirely in your hands! I only ask to be free. The butterflies are free. Mankind will surely not deny to Harold Skimpole what it concedes to the butterflies."[20]

Inner strength in a person is generally admired regardless of any consequences it may have with respect to making the person who has it happier or healthier or better off in dealing with "the slings and arrows of outrageous fortune." These, what I regard as indubitable, claims about motivational inner strength certainly support its being treated as a fundamental aretaic assumption about human beings. Do we need some other sorts of arguments to justify treating it as such? I think they would be extraneous; in fact, I not only believe that inner strength is a form of human excellence, but I also believe it to *be* human excellence, a point on which Slote and I disagree. He cannot see how inner strength can be productive of a concern for others that would "direct us away from lying and stealing."[21] I address this concern below.

A person of inner strength might otherwise be described as self-reliant, self-confident, self-sufficient, independent; a person of courage, fortitude, integrity; not self-righteous, but self-assured. To have inner strength is not to be prone to self-deception nor to play the part of the moral chameleon. The inner strength of the agent, in and of itself, can be the goal, the foundational motivation, of a morality of human action. Such a morality would be agent-based, and whatever actions demonstrate or express inner strength, whether directly or because they express or exhibit motivations that are derivative of inner strength, will be meritorious in such a virtue ethics.

Although I used the term "self-sufficient," among others, to characterize the person of inner strength, I do not mean to suggest that inner strength is a version of the Stoic *autarkeia*. The Stoic is far too extreme in defining self-sufficiency as freedom from all pleasures and desires outside of one's direct control to fit the picture I have in mind. Nonetheless, I admit that there is something of the Stoic's egotism in my understanding of motivational (if not achieved) inner strength.

Motivational inner strength, however, need not be solely inner-directed, despite Slote's concern that it cannot provide for the "humane concern for other people."[22] I see no reason why it cannot anchor a moral theory that rules out lying, stealing, and other sorts of interferences with the lives of other people. On some accounts, for example Nietzsche's, it can even produce an outpouring of aid to the underprivileged, not from pity or from a genuine concern about their downtrodden condition, "but prompted more by an urge begotten by excess of power."[23] Plato, in the *Republic*, after setting himself the task of responding to the challenge that there are no very good reasons not to act immorally or unjustly in ordinary human affairs, does not seem to succeed, a point made by Slote.

Plato's response, or what the dialogue leads us to believe is his response, is to work out a theory of justice based on the notion of the harmony of the parts of the soul. But he never gets around to actually addressing the original questions, unless the Myth of Er, at the very end of the dialogue, is intended to do that sort of service. The Myth of Er, as noted in Chapter 3, is a typical karmic story, which is, of course, one way to address the challenge, although it hardly seems a fair one under the circumstances and Plato certainly took a circuitous route to deposit us at that conclusion. Furthermore, it does add credence to the charge that inner strength virtue ethics is at sea in dealing with such issues. It leaves to the karmic powers the punishment of the wicked while encouraging a morality that is very likely to lead one down the garden path to, at best, lack of concern for the lives, property, and integrity of other people. A far more direct and convincing response than what we have in Plato, but firmly anchored in motivational inner strength, is provided by J. B. Books, John Wayne's character in *The Shootist*.

I have elsewhere written at some length about Books,[24] but in this regard it is useful to see how his motivational inner strength would meet the challenge of the *Republic*, though perhaps not satisfy Slote's concern for kindness in human affairs. During a shooting lesson that Books gives to Gillom Rogers, the son of the woman who runs the boardinghouse in which he has taken a room, the following conversation, reminiscent of a shooting lesson in *Shane*, occurs:

GILLOM: How'd you ever kill so many men?

BOOKS: I lived most of my life in the wild country and you set a code of laws to live by.

GILLOM: What laws?

BOOKS: I won't be wronged, I won't be insulted, and I won't be laid a hand on. I don't do these things to other people, and I require the same from them.

GILLOM: How could you get into so many fights and then always come out on top? I nearly tied you shooting.

BOOKS: Friend, there was nobody up there shootin' back at you. It isn't always being fast or even accurate that counts. It's being willing. Now, I found out early that most men regardless of cause or need aren't willing. They blink an eye or draw a breath before they pull a trigger. I won't.

In those few simple words, Books explains how motivational inner strength frames the basis for one's dealings with other people, why those of inner strength do not lie, steal, cheat, and so on. What falls within the category of being wronged surely includes prohibitions against being victimized by thieves, liars, and other harmdoers. Defamation and uninvited invasions of personal space constitute failures of appreciation of the integrity of others. The person of inner strength has no need to belittle or invade the space of others, and so such a person doesn't do such things. The moral leap that Books makes is to treat himself as the model of virtue. But how could he do otherwise? If he were to think that what someone else refrains from doing, though he does not, is more virtuous than his own behavior, he would relinquish some of his sense of inner strength, perhaps to self-doubt. He may no longer be so willing. What he will not do, what he does not do, he expects, requires, of others. The moral requirements on others of the self-reliant person are minimal, but if everyone were to cultivate inner strength, all would meet Books's standards of behavior, and the specific moral concerns raised by the challenge in the *Republic* would not arise. What such a person will not do, he or she will not countenance from others.

Slote acknowledges that an inner strength ethics probably can achieve most of the concerns that moralists might traditionally have about the well-being of other people. He allows that the person of inner strength may find within himself or herself the grounds for criticizing the harming and the failing to contribute to the well-being of others. He states: "The imperative of self-reliance or non-parasitism also connects with the 'deontological' side of our ordinary moral thinking—with our obligations to keep promises, not to be deceptive, to tell the truth, etc. For those who rely on others to believe their promises and who have benefited from others' keeping promises to them would count as parasites upon the social practice of promising if they refused to keep their promises."[25] This sounds remarkably similar to Books's credo.

Self-reliance is the most basic characteristic, the virtue, of those with inner strength. Self-reliance along with its near cousin, self-sufficiency, probably lead the list of the most commonly advocated virtues in American literature, popular culture, and folklore. Ralph Waldo Emerson's essay on the topic is the American locus classicus of the concept. I suspect, however, that "Self-Reliance" is more famous for an oft misquoted line about consistency than for the insights Emerson has to offer regarding "motivational inner strength."[26] Emerson's style is radically different from what today is counted as philosophical exposition. He draws a conceptual portrait of the self-reliant person. However, in his case, and most of the rest of us would do well to pay heed, the conceptual portrait is far more valuable to the attempt to understand what is meant by the notion than the turgid and convoluted prose of what today passes for philosophical argumentation.

Emerson criticizes the standard conception (in his day and ours) of the virtues as separable from the persons who possess them. He writes with scorn: "There is the man *and* his virtues. Men do what is called a good action, as some piece of courage or charity, much as they would pay a fine in expiation of daily non-appearance on parade. Their works are done as an apology or extenuation of their living in the world,—as invalids and the insane pay a high board. Their virtues are penances." To this ringing indictment of what still seems to be the standard picture of moral or virtuous behavior, Emerson responds: "I do not wish to expiate, but to live. My life is not an apology, but a life. It is for itself and not for a spectacle . . . My life should be unique." He tells us that the truly virtuous among us, despite living in the crowd of humankind, "keep with perfect sweetness the independence of solitude." They do not live by "the world's opinion." Conformity is a game of "blindman's bluff."

A person's self-trust is eroded by the fear that he or she will disappoint others unless his or her current actions are consistent with those of his or her past: "Suppose you should contradict yourself; what then? . . . Trust your emotion." Emerson's criticism of foolish consistency might, it seems to me, be understood as a response to those who think of morality in terms of, to use his phrase, "microscopic criticism." By that I think he means to attack moral theories that isolate actions for moral scrutiny and the dissection of lives into moments of moral import, thereby losing sight of the lived life that may well be harmonious despite what appear to be a number of inconsistent specific actions.

Emerson writes: "Your genuine action will explain itself and will explain your other genuine actions. Your conformity explains nothing. Act singly, and what you have already done singly will justify you now . . . If I can be great enough now to do right and scorn eyes, I must have done so much right before as to defend me now. Be it how it will, do right now." "Life," he emphasizes, "only avails, not the having lived. Power ceases in the instant of repose." Life is what matters, is of worth, as it is lived, in becoming, not in having been. Emerson offers the image of a ship sailing from one place to another. Does it sail in a straight line? Probably not, but depending on the wind and other conditions, "the voyage of the best ship is a zigzag line of a hundred tacks." But if we look at the voyage from "a sufficient distance . . . it straightens itself to the average tendency."

Self-reliance for Emerson entails the rejection of the standard moral theories of action and agent evaluation. He recognizes that he is prone to the same charges of antinomianism that I noted earlier with respect to agent-based virtue theories in general. The criticism is that the rejection of traditional moral standards must amount to the rejection of all moral standards or, as Nietzsche put it, to the adoption of a "*laisser aller*" position in place of morality.[27] Emerson denies that this is an implication of the ethics of self-reliance. To reject traditional morality is not to reject self-discipline, a point Philippa Foot makes in her examination of Nietzsche's position[28] and one that is true of Emerson.

There are, Emerson maintains, "two confessionals." He calls them the direct and the reflex ways. The reflex way is the way of the non-self-reliant person who trusts the moral evaluation of his or her behavior to others, to the established standards of the community. The self-reliant person is his or her own direct moral "task-master." It is not that there are no moral standards for the self-reliant. According to Emerson, self-reliance is not "letting go": "I have my own stern claims . . . It denies the name of duty to many offices that are called duties. But if I can discharge its debts it enables me to dispense with the popular code. If any one imagines that this law is lax, let him keep its commandment one day."

Nietzsche's version of Emerson's direct confessional identifies the self-disciplined, self-reliant person with the artist: "Every artist knows how far from any feeling of letting himself go his 'most natural' state is—the free ordering, placing, disposing, giving form in the moment of 'inspiration'—and how strictly and subtly he obeys thousandfold laws precisely then, laws that precisely on account of their hardness and determination defy all formulation through concepts."[29]

Emerson maintains that the direct confessional demands "something godlike in him who has cast off the common motives of humanity and has ventured to trust himself for a task-master. High be his heart, faithful his will, clear his sight, that he may in good earnest be doctrine, society, law, to himself." There is, perhaps rather obviously, the echo of the Kantian moralist giving himself or herself the moral law in this, but Emerson's self-reliance is assuredly not a disguised version of Kantian rational ethics, though one can, Slote suggests, interpret some parts of Kant's ethics as agent-based.[30] That, however, is a stretch I am not prepared to take.

In a stirring admonition, Emerson, not unlike Nietzsche, associates the virtue of self-reliance with the language of art. He writes: "Insist on yourself; never imitate. Your own gift you can present every moment with the cumulative force of a whole life's cultivation . . . Every great man is an unique . . . Shakespeare will never be made by the study of Shakespeare . . . Dwell up there in the simple and the noble regions of thy life, obey thy heart and thou shalt reproduce the Foreworld again."[31]

The association of morality, even agent-based virtue ethics, and art will be, no doubt, dismissed by many moralists. We will be told that there is a radical difference between judgments about works of art and judgments about human actions and characters. Judgments or evaluations of works of art are necessarily singular, and moral judgments about human actions or agents are supposed to be universalizable. Works of art, on the standard accounts, are unique, particulars. The idea is that if one judges a work of art to be good or bad, a success or a failure, one is not thereby committed on pain of logical inconsistency (a pain that little troubles the vast majority of people, including philosophers) to judging a similar work of art similarly.

Humans are, at least in so much as matters to morality as traditionally understood, not unique. Whatever we may be that makes us essentially different from each other is of little concern in ethical theory. Those differences are to be overcome or forgotten behind veils of ignorance, and bland standards and rules that require a uniformity of treatment and evaluation command the moral stage of human evaluation. The liberal project since the seventeenth century has been to make of us atomic individuals that have no individuality, or at least none that is morally considerable. If we judge any person's actions to be good or bad, we are logically bound to make the same judgment of the relevantly similar actions of any other person or of the same person on another occasion. If Julius Caesar acted rightly in crossing the Rubicon, then anyone else in similar circumstances would have acted rightly in fording that river or, I suppose, a similar river or defying a government or whatever one understands Julius to have been up to on the banks of the Rubicon.

When evaluating works of art, creativity and originality command high marks. In the moral evaluation of human actions and characters, the least creative, the least original, grade out on top. The rules and principles of the traditional action-oriented moral theories discourage anything that might pass for "moral originality." In fact, moral originality is, no doubt, thought by many to be an oxymoron. The very idea of moral creativity may be close to impossible to conceive. The test of the rightness of an action is typically that it should be done by any other person (or rational agent) in the circumstances. The identity and the specific circumstances of the agent and all that might entail are not relevant considerations. The rightness of the action is determined independently of the specific person who will be morally evaluated one way or the other depending upon whether or not he or she performs it.

And, as noted earlier, relatively similar actions, irrespective of who performs them, from the moral point of view, are to be judged in the same way. Simply, the standard moral theories encourage copying, duplicating, and replicating. Ethics, as usually understood, responds to our sameness, aesthetics to our differences. If locating relevant similarities is a difficulty in actual cases, ethical theorists invent them in thought experiments. In the evaluation of art works, on the other hand, the relative similarity of two works may or may not be relevant to their aesthetic value. Even if the two works are indistinguishable in all details, they may be judged quite differently. One may be a masterpiece, the other hardly worth artistic consideration. One may be the Turner original, the other a virtually identical copy made by an art student at the Tate Gallery.

We could worry that the dichotomizing of ethics and aesthetics has got ethics wrong and offer agent-based inner strength virtue ethics as a counterexample, which it certainly could be. But I think it has got both ethics and aesthetics wrong. In what sense are works of art unique and judgments about them singular? Artworks are hardly unique when it comes to at least some of the factors that seem to play a significant role in the assignment of aesthetic merit. If "good" in an aesthetic evaluation, as one often hears it uttered by art teachers, refers to a particular choice of color, brushwork, use of shapes and shading, and so on, then such evaluations should be universalizable in a way not unlike Kantian moral judgments or the judgment that inner strength is a fundamental aretaic anchor of virtue. For example, if an original painting is good in this sense, all accurate copies and reproductions must be judged good as well. An accurate reproduction of the *Mona Lisa,* for example, is just as good as the original hanging in the Louvre in this sense of "aesthetically good." In fact, if a forgery were to perfectly copy a masterpiece with respect to the factors involved in this sort of aesthetic judgment, it also must be as good as the masterpiece.

Simply, artworks are not unique with respect to judgments of aesthetic merit that are related to such things as the use of shapes, light and color, themes, and so on. Such judgments are universalizable. To deny the same aesthetic values to works (copies, fakes, reproductions) that are qualitatively identical in regard to what are taken to be the relevant artistic factors would violate the standards of aesthetic evaluation. Qualitative identity with respect to artworks is not numerical identity. T. E. Wilkerson summarizes this point: "If one painting is aesthetically successful because of its use of light and color contrast, then so is any other relevantly similar painting."[32] And isn't the same supposed to be true in ethics?

Such universalizable aesthetic judgments, however, do not exhaust the way artworks are valued, and art history's focus on masterpieces may be responsible for the fact that we generally forget about those sorts of "pedestrian" judgments when we think of aesthetics. In any event, with respect to another sort of aesthetic evaluation, the sort that dominates the fields of art, originality and uniqueness are crucial considerations. Think of the notorious case of van Meegeren's *Meeting at Ammaus*. The painting was done in the style of Vermeer and presented to and accepted by the art world as a Vermeer. When it was taken to be a work of Vermeer, it was interpreted and valued from a certain point of view and within the context of other paintings by the artist. When it was discovered that van Meegeren had forged the painting to pass it off as a Vermeer, its artistic value radically changed. Many of us will wonder how that could happen. The critics, the curators, and the general public were hoodwinked, but when the deception was discovered, why should the aesthetic value of the work plummet? The painting still looks the same. Color, light, and shapes did not change. If it was aesthetically good when it was believed to be an eighteenth-century Vermeer, why shouldn't it still be aesthetically good after we learn it was painted in the twentieth century by van Meegeren?

With respect to the universalizable type of aesthetic evaluations, as noted earlier, it cannot lose its value just because it was discovered to be a fake. The only way to explain its loss of value, I think, is to understand what it is to be a Vermeer as opposed to being a van Meegeren. A painting by Vermeer has a place in the history of art and culture from which it derives a value that a painting in the style of Vermeer forged by a twentieth-century painter never can. According to Wilkerson, "We value Vermeer's works much more highly than van Meegeren's, however similar they may be, because Vermeer was fashioning a new style, while van Meegeren was merely reproducing a style long outdated and well within the competence of a talented modern artist."[33] By the same token, we value a genuine Rubens higher than a painting from the school of Rubens that is not attributable to the master, even though we cannot discern any significant difference in the style, fluid brushwork, use of light and perspective, and so on, between the two works.

Aesthetic judgments of specific artworks in which originality, "fashioning a new style," plays the key role are not universalizable. Simply, when done by X it is good, perhaps a masterpiece, but when replicated by Y it does not have that merit. If, however, the reason the work is aesthetically successful is because it evidences certain features, then the replica must also be aesthetically successful. James Wood, reviewing the final novel of Ernest Hemingway in the *New York Times Book Review*, writes: "Imitation is not original, thus no original writer is ever really imitable . . . The danger of a truly original style, of course, is that it has smooth copiers but does not have rough equals. That which is imitable is neutered by repetition. What cannot be imitated is what is truly original, not necessarily because it was so great but because it was, simply, first; it has a hard and unbreakable primacy . . . What is great in him [Hemingway] is that, as it were, he preceded his own bad influence."[34]

I will call these two sorts of aesthetic judgments that I have identified: presentational judgments and contextual judgments. Presentational judgments are solely focused on the artwork as it is presented to the observer, listener, reader. Hence, they can relate only to such things as use of light, draftsmanship, harmony, rhyme, imagery, plot, and so on. They are, I shall maintain, truncated aesthetic judgments. Contextual judgments make reference, perhaps only implicitly, to the origins of the work and the context out of which it emerges into the history of that sort of art form. It is only in that sense that a work of art is necessarily unique and judgments about it are singular. Works of art are situated in a historical/cultural context. From that perspective they may be viewed as opening a new paradigm, founding a new movement, innovating, introducing a new way of doing things, or conspicuously improving on the current fashion. When works of art can be truthfully said to do those sorts of things, they gain an artistic merit that other works that are qualitatively similar to them, done "after" them, reproduced from them, do not have. Of course, artworks may be failures on every count, consignable only to the dumpster.

Some might be tempted to argue that what I have called contextual aesthetic judgments, "judgments that refer essentially to the genesis . . . of a work," are not aesthetic judgments at all.[35] Wilkerson responds, I think persuasively to this tack, that it is impossible to "sustain the distinction between judgments that concentrate on the content of a work of art, on what we see in front of us, and judgments that concentrate on the genesis, on the historical background, of the work." What is seen in a work of art depends on "giving proper weight to certain features at the expense of others." To do that requires information about the genesis of the work and the historical context in which it was created. And that information tells us something important about the criteria that are appropriate to evaluating the work: "We need to know which details are important, which criteria of success or failure we should use, which artistic gestures are in context striking or not, significant or not, deliberate or not."[36] What Wilkerson means is that the masterful brush strokes of an impressionist like van Gogh should be regarded as anything but masterful if they were spotted in a painting by Giotto.

Do the two types of judgments collapse into each other? Yes and no. No in the sense that when we evaluate a work of art, or what purports to be one, two sorts of things may occur. We might start, as many of us do, with the hope of originality, the hope of experiencing what Robert Hughes called the "shock of the new." There are, of course, two sorts of "new." There is what is new to us, perhaps due to a lack of our own experience, and there is what is new, original, novel, in the genre. To appreciate the latter we need historical/contextual information, and that information will significantly affect the way we see or hear or read the work, the way we are presented with it and the way we should evaluate it. Failing in originality, however, the work can still be evaluated aesthetically in presentational judgments: "Well, at least it works as an arrangement of shapes!" Sadly, most artworks are presentational failures. Throughout the year, but especially during the summer, in small towns and villages as well as in major metropolitan areas, art fairs and sidewalk shows are held. Anyone doubting that most artworks are presentational failures ought to stroll through a few of those shows. However, paintings judged as presentational successes are sold and adorn many a living room or den. Hardly ever does a work of genuine originality appear in such venues.

A further point that supports the "no" answer is that we should expect that works of originality are likely to be judged as failures when evaluated on presentational grounds alone. That is, of course, because the criteria of presentational success are set by the currently dominant style or movement. Works of originality and creative genius might break all of the rules of color, light, and shape, but found a movement. The critical paradigm may then shift and the presentational criteria undergo revision. Of course, the landmarks of previous movements retain their status as works of original genius, and chapters are dedicated to them in the art history texts. But they no longer set the standards against which the pedestrian works are evaluated. Shakespeare, Milton, and Dickens are all artistic geniuses of the first order, and much more important in literary history than Zane Grey, Dorothy Sayers, and John Grisham, but a budding writer today would be ill-advised to imitate their styles, use of phrases, or spelling.

It might be objected that Shakespeare never grows old; Milton and Dickens should continue to demand our careful reading. And it is undeniably true that a great deal is to be learned from the study of the works of the monumental figures in art history. Their works, and those of other "greats," reach out and touch us across the centuries because we recognize in those works what we regard as truths about us and our place in the world. They entertain us and teach us and have import for us because we are products of a specific cultural history. They were key elements in determining in what way our cultural history is taught to us, and thus what we appreciate and regard as worthy of our attention. But they no longer serve as models for the budding artist.

Against the standard view, I have maintained that judgments about works of art can be of at least two different types. One type is universalizable and is similar in structure to ordinary moral judgments as they are described in the traditional ethical theories, such as Kant's. The other type is not universalizable. It makes sense, however, to claim that in the case of some artworks—for example, those that found movements, the true originals—in order to make fair judgments of the first type we need to appreciate the contextual judgment appropriate to them, the second type. Typically, the application of the standards of the first type will be utterly irrelevant to judging their artistic merit. I want to suggest that moral judgments about agents and their actions come in two types, which are analogous to the aesthetic judgments of artworks.

One way to visualize a dual morality might be along lines suggested by J. O. Urmson: "We have to deal in ethics not with a simple trichotomy of duties, permissible actions, and wrong actions, or any substantially similar conceptual

scheme, but something more complicated. We have to add at least the compli-
cation of actions that are certainly of moral worth but that fall outside the notion
of duty and seem to go beyond it."[37] But that is not exactly what I have in mind.
Rather, I want to suggest that action-oriented moral judgments derivative from
deontic ethical characterizations of motives and consequences are universalizable
in the sense that the first type of aesthetic judgments are universalizable. That is,
one is logically committed to making the same moral judgment about all similar
cases. Judgments of the moral status of actions that are entirely derivative of
motivational inner strength (or some other fundamental aretaic fact about the
motives of an individual) are not universalizable. They are contextual. The same
might also be said about agent-focused virtue judgments of actions, for example,
those that might be made by an Aristotelian. One is not logically committed to
making the same moral judgment with respect to replications performed by the
same person or by another. An ethics of two types of moral judgments requires
that we jettison the notion that a uniform code of moral behavior can be constructed.

Today, one hopes, we are likely to reject the view that nothing is art unless it
satisfies a specific definition with respect to form, style, subject matter, mode of
presentation, use of medium, and so on. Of course, throughout the centuries,
that is exactly what many people, critics, art historians, and artists themselves
have tried to do, and in retrospect they seem foolish. We don't have to go back
very far in history to note the reception Duchamp's *Nude Descending a Staircase*
received when first exhibited or the reaction to Picasso's *Les Demoiselles d'Avignon*
on its first showing. Hilary Spurling, in her biography of the early years of the
life of Henri Matisse, writes that in September 1908, Matisse was one of the judges
for the Salon d'Automne exhibition: "George Braque, about to embark on a part-
nership with Picasso that would change the ground rules for all other artists, had
every one of his canvases rejected. Matisse, attempting to describe one of them
to the critic Louis Vauxcelles, sketched an arrangement of converging straight
lines and crossbars: 'It's made of little cubes,' he said in a phrase history never
forget."[38]

The problem that has emerged to all but dominant aesthetics is that we are
now somewhat at sea about how to answer the question, "What is art?" We may
be left with having to accept the position championed by Arthur Danto that
something is to be treated as art if those in the art world treat it as such. Art is
what a gallery owner hangs, what a museum curator exhibits, what an artist displays or performs—something for us to consider and appreciate aesthetically, that
is, from the perspective of aesthetic categories.

Nietzsche, in very much the spirit though not the tone of Emerson, railed
against the notion that there must be a single, uniform moral code for all humans.
He tells us that a uniform moral code that sets the conditions of virtue for all
humans "means that they [humans] should begin to resemble one another in their
needs and demands—more clearly that they should perish. The will of a single
morality is thereby proved to be a tyranny over other types by that type whom

this single morality fits: it is a destruction or a levelling for the sake of a ruling type."[39] According to him, "The demand of one morality for all is detrimental for the higher men; in short, there is an order of rank between man and man, hence also between morality and morality."[40] Nietzsche, though perhaps not Emerson, did not think that all of us were capable of inner strength. He is quite clear about the fact that he believed only a few were likely to have wills strong enough to be self-reliant, self-sufficient, and self-disciplined. For the rest, the herd, the standard moral injunctions were adequate.

Philippa Foot thinks that Nietzsche's insistence that the virtue of inner strength should not be generally promulgated and that his willingness to countenance, indeed encourage, actions that run counter to the standard (for Nietzsche, read "herd") conception of justice indicate that his is not a moral theory at all. "Morality," she tells us "is necessarily connected with such things as justice and the common good, and it is a conceptual matter that this is so."[41] Supporters of Nietzsche, of course, might wonder what argument Foot can offer to defend her conceptual claim. She provides none. But even if she were right with respect to half of her claim, Nietzsche might respond that his multiple moralities do connect to "such things as justice."

With respect to the other half of Foot's claim, he could argue that there is a utilitarian or English bias in her conception of a necessary link between morality and the "common good." Morality might be concerned, even necessarily concerned, with human flourishing without being interested in "the general welfare" or "the common good." Nietzsche writes: "Ultimately they all want *English* morality to be proved right—because this serves humanity best, or 'the general utility,' or 'the happiness of the greatest number'—no, the happiness of *England* . . . None of these ponderous herd animals with their unquiet consciences (who undertake to advocate the cause of egoism as the cause of the general welfare) wants to know or even sense that 'the general welfare' is no ideal, no goal, no remotely intelligible concept, but only an emetic—that what is fair for one *cannot* by any means for that reason alone also be fair for others."[42]

Would Foot have fewer problems with Emerson? I doubt it. Although Emerson appears to be directing his admonitions regarding self-reliance to people in general, he makes little claim on "the common good": "Society everywhere is in conspiracy against the manhood of every one of its members. Society is a joint-stock company, in which the members agree, for the better securing of his bread to each shareholder, to surrender the liberty and culture of the eater. The virtue in most request is conformity. Self-reliance is its aversion. It loves not realities and creators, but names and customs."[43]

Foot does acknowledge that there is something very like a morality in Nietzsche's philosophy. What she identifies is what, following Slote, we should call the agent-focused inner strength virtue ethics of Nietzsche. Nietzschean virtue ethics is founded in his conception of human flourishing and is thereby not strictly agent-based. That is, Nietzsche thinks he knows what conditions are necessary for the flourishing of humans, and he believes that the standard "herd" morality prevents the realization of those conditions. Emerson's position is much more of an agent-based morality of inner strength than Nietzsche's but equally one that could not pass Foot's criteria of a morality. Emerson does have a conception of human flourishing, but it is not the independent foundation, for him, from which the goodness of actions is derived. Emerson's metaphysics places the divine within the soul of every person, and although he does occasionally talk of preestablished harmony and divinely ordained stations, he regularly reiterates: "No law can be sacred to me but that of my nature. Good and bad are but names very readily transferable to that and this; the only right is what is after my constitution; the only wrong what is against it."[44]

Both Emerson and Nietzsche acknowledge that there are two types of moral judgments. For Nietzsche, the universalizable type is the herd morality that he believes is entirely suited to its subjects. Emerson treats herd morality as the morality of conformity, the morality of names, and he regards it as inappropriate and destructive for any human being. He encourages everyone to adopt the virtues of inner strength morality and to free themselves from rule-formulated—that is, name-driven—conformity ethics. The idea, I suppose, is that if the basic categories of moral judgment are merely names, then ethics is nothing more than the derivation of rules for the proper application of names, i.e., right and wrong. There is little or no reference to the lived life of the individual. The self-reliant person, in a way that Emerson is at pains to explain and ultimately refers to as a kind of intuitive vision, has a sense of the good, although it does not seem to be the "common good" nor certainly the "greatest good for the greatest number of people." His American transcendentalism takes the matter into depths I cannot hope to fathom: "That thought, by what I can now nearest approach to say it, is this. When good is near you, when you have life in yourself . . . the way, the thought, the good, shall be wholly strange and new. It shall exclude all other being . . . We are then in vision . . . It is a perceiving that Truth and Right are."[45]

In any event, for Emerson, it seems fair to say that to achieve the proximity to good, a person, any person, must dare moral originality in the face of the pressures of social conformity, and he implies that the outcome will be human flourishing. He writes: "I will have no covenants but proximities. I shall endeavor to nourish my parents, to support my family, to be the chaste husband of one wife,— but these relations I must fill after a new and unprecedented way. I appeal from your customs. I must be myself. I cannot break myself any longer for you, or you . . . I must be myself. I will not hide my tastes and aversions . . . If you are noble, I will love you; if you are not, I will not hurt you and myself by hypocritical attentions . . . I do this not selfishly but humbly and truly. It is alike your interest, and mine, and all men's, however long we have dwelt in lies, to live in truth . . . You will soon love what is dictated by your nature as well as mine, and if we follow truth it will bring us out safe at last.—But so may you give these friends pain. Yes, but I cannot sell my liberty and my power, to save their sensibility."[46]

Slote has usefully summed up what he regards as the four basic facets of a morality of inner strength.[47] I have touched on each of them in the discussion of Emerson, but it should prove useful to spell them out for future reference. The agent of inner strength (self-reliance) possesses the courage to confront the unpleasant facts and dangers of his or her life and the world in which he or she lives. He or she does not hide in self-deception. The person of inner strength is motivationally independent of others. He or she makes his or her "own way in the world." Furthermore, he or she learns to be self-sufficient, which, I suppose, often comes to being able to curb or moderate typical human desires to bring them in line with one's available resources, to resist greedy impulses. Finally, a person of inner strength is not weak of will.

If, despite not having a necessary connection to a conception of the common good, an agent-based inner strength virtue ethics is a morality, as I think it is, then it is conceivable that an inner strength–anchored avenger's moral credentials can be what may be called self-certified. His or her actions in taking vengeance may be an expression of or motivated by his or her inner strength and self-reliance, and under the governance of self-discipline and thereby virtuous, though not universalizable. That is, they may be motivated by retributive or moral hatred and personal honor, and those motives can be instantiations of inner strength and thereby good moral motives. All expressions of inner strength are necessarily morally meritorious without appeal to their consequences, which of course must follow from the fact that inner strength, on the account I have adopted, is the touchstone, the foundation, of virtue in an agent. And I believe I have responded to the charges that it is inadequate to the task of ensuring appropriate treatment of others, fair if not exuberantly benevolent.

The display of moral creativity and originality through acts of revenge can only occur where acts of vengeance are not required by custom and a social conception of justice. For example, acts of revenge in the Mafia are not morally creative acts or expressions of inner strength for the very reason that they are required by the code of the society. They are acts of conformity, regardless of the bravery of the avenger. Acts of virtuous vengeance are not performed to satisfy some accepted canons of justice, but because the avenger's inner strength requires exhibition in that way, and it would be a sign of weakness of will and therefore moral failure not to perform them. Such revenge-taking is not "wild justice"; it is neither wild nor is it a matter of justice per se.

The avenger's retributive hatred, of course, must be stirred by some conception of what is wrongful behavior and an acceptance of the view that wrongful actions should be met by hostile responses. Such notions are not solely, if at all, the products of the avenger's motivational inner strength. As discussed in the previous section, they are conceptual elements, even necessary prerequisites, of morality in general; I think that must be acknowledged. Therefore, we need to clarify how they come to play a motivational role in the cool agent-based virtue ethics of the moral avenger. The answer, I think, is not especially complicated.

If it is the case that the very concept of wrongful action entails that such actions are to be met with hostility, then insofar as the avenger perceives an action to be wrongful, he or she perceives it to require a hostile response. This, of course, says nothing about how the avenger comes to have such a perception, or whether a person of inner strength would regard as wrongful the same actions that an other-oriented (benevolence-directed) virtuous person or a Kantian or a utilitarian would regard as wrongful. What will mark the inner strength virtuous avenger from any other sort, however, will be that the perception of the wrongfulness of the action(s) will emerge directly from his or her sense of self. The constraints and standards governing the avenger's actions "operate and bind, as it were, from within."[48] In Emerson's terms, the standard of judgment will not be a reflexive one. It will be direct. The inner strength avenger's sense of the duty to perform an act of revenge will not be derivative of the "common motives of humanity," nor will such motives ever serve as a basis for justification. In fact, nothing recognizable as a justification or an explanation may be forthcoming. The act, in an important sense, speaks for itself.

In *The Tall T,* a vastly underrated film based on a story by Elmore Leonard, Pat Brennan, played by Randolph Scott, is asked by Doretta Mims, played by Maureen O'Sullivan, why he doesn't just leave the place where they are being held captive. He has killed the two outlaws that the villain, played by Richard Boone, left to guard them when he rode off to collect a ransom for Doretta. They are free. Pat, however, will wait to shoot it out with the villain, he tells her, because "there's some things a man can't ride around." Why can't he ride around the deadly confrontation? Why can't he just let go of, ride around, the matter of the villain having been responsible for killing a family and the stagecoach driver, Rintoon, who were his friends? Why place himself at risk, in jeopardy? He certainly doesn't care that the villain has been enriched by the ransom payment. It's not his money. The answer Pat provides has nothing at all to do with standard moral theories. It implies that his sense of self, his inner strength—reflected also in his conception of personal honor, the direct confessional of Emerson—requires an act of deadly vengeance: "There's some things a man can't ride around." What those things are will vary with the circumstances and with the person. What is crucial is that the criteria reside in the "man," not in a theory of duties to various offices, relations, or community standards or norms. In that sense, his actions may be morally original, expressions of "cool" agent-based virtue.

It might be argued that agent-based inner strength virtue judgments are universalizable if they are stated in general enough terms. Of course, they are and were so stated by Emerson (and in an agent-focused form by Aristotle and Nietzsche). In those terms, they amount to something similar to the directive "It is good to perform acts that express your inner strength." Such a directive is probably comparable to saying something like "Originality and creativity in art are to be encouraged among artists." Such directives, however, are hardly comparable to what is generally meant by "universalizability" in moral theory. The "express inner strength" directive does not say that, because it is morally permissible for X, expressing her inner strength, to do A, doing A is morally permissible for anyone, even in circumstances similar to those in which X did A. A may express the inner strength of X while not being an expression of the inner strength of anyone else.

There are no certified standard expressions of inner strength, just as there are no certified standard expressions of creativity or originality in art. No dependable formulas exist, and in that sense, expressions of inner strength are unique and not universalizable. This point, one hardly needs to be reminded, was made by Aristotle and was noted earlier: "Matters concerned with conduct and questions of what is good for us have no fixity . . . They do not fall under any art or precept, but the agents themselves must in each case consider what is appropriate to the occasion" (NE 1104a). (In the translation by Martin Ostwald, the passage is rendered: "There are no fixed data in matters concerning action . . . And if this is true of our general discussion, our treatment of particular problems will be even less precise, since these do not come under the head of any art which can be transmitted by precept, but the agent must consider on each different occasion what the situation demands.")[49]

What's so valuable about originality, whether in art or morality? We certainly value originality in art and, on the standard ethical theories at least since the Enlightenment, we don't value it in moral matters. I have suggested that it may make sense, given a certain conception of virtue ethics, to place a high value on the moral originality or uniqueness of actions and agents, even though such judgments are not universalizable. I want to be especially clear about the claim I am making when I say that the judgments of acts of moral originality are not universalizable. I am urging a very strict analogy with aesthetic judgments. If the action or agent is being judged good or bad (wicked) because of certain replicable features that it (or he or she) evidences, or if we are only making an extremely general assertion, for example, "expressions of one's inner strength are virtuous," then the judgment is universalizable across the population of moral persons. However, if the moral merit of the action or agent is dependent upon the contextual/historical fact that the agent has expressed his or her inner strength and self-reliance, then the moral judgment is not universalizable.

We are not logically bound to make the same moral judgment of another agent whose actions appear to be relevantly similar to an observer. The same actions may in one case be morally meritorious and in another, of no moral value or even a negative moral value. Such an outcome should not bother Kantians who are committed to the view that actions done from inclination, although externally indistinguishable from actions done from duty, do not accrue to the moral merit of the agent. There is, of course, an enormous difference between Kantian ethics and the inner strength virtue ethics I am recommending. Importantly, for Kant universalization is embedded in the concept of duty: "Act so that the maxim of your actions could, by your will, be a universal law for all mankind." The basic principle of inner strength morality, if it could be said to have one, makes no reference to constraining your actions by considerations of whether or not you could will that all other agents acted in the same way. It tells you to express your inner strength constrained only by considerations of self-discipline, a concept that gains its content from your inner strength.

I still haven't provided any grounds on which to defend valuing originality or creativity. Rationality? I haven't a clue as to how to make a persuasive argument to the effect that it is rational to value originality in art, let alone in morality. In fact, a number of cultures do not value originality in art, let alone morality, and we wouldn't say that those cultures were inherently irrational.

The simple fact is that in our culture we value novelty, originality, and creativity. A defensible way of characterizing our culture, when contrasted with other cultures, is that we are a novelty-oriented people in virtually every element of our lives. Our economy, our entertainment, and most of our daily lives revolve around the search for novelty. Even our religion is not immune. Although some may still cherish "that old-time religion," a significant portion of the population, if it retains interest in religion at all, seems bent on a quest for new forms of worship, new age, even new divinities. Our culture seems to be the embodiment of the Kierkegaardian aesthetic stage. We are forever in search of the unusual, the different, even the shocking and the bizarre. James Burke has written: "In the West . . . we encourage novelty. . . . The sources of modern technology . . . are entirely directed towards the production of the means of constant change. Whereas other societies in the past adopted the same social structures as we do in order to ensure their stability, and others in the contemporary world still do so, we use those structures to alter our society unceasingly."[50] If all of that is true, however, it is still only descriptive. It confirms that we do value originality, but not what is valuable about originality.

The only argument I can think of that might have even a modicum of persuasiveness would be hinged on an Emersonian conception of what it is to be a human being ("Whoso would be a man, must be a nonconformist . . . Nothing is at last sacred but the integrity of our own mind"). But that could well drift into just the sort of argument, premised on a reductive conception of human nature, that produced the universalizability characterization of moral judgments that I have tried to expose as inadequate. The valuing of originality cannot, I am certain, be divorced from its cultural home. It is intimately connected to the constellation of cares that constitute our worldview, but it may be, indeed seems to be, entirely absent from the worldviews of other cultures.[51]

Originality and creativity can be manifested in different ways. In the history of painting there is the originality of Giotto and Braque and quite another sort of originality that can be appreciated in works by Michelangelo and Picasso. Giotto, as Wilkerson notes, "developed a significantly new style."[52] Michelangelo was one of the most conspicuously successful artists in the style originated by Giotto. Braque created cubism, and Picasso painted the most famous and the greatest works in that style. I think a case can be made for a comparable distinction in acts of moral originality. Some constitute the founding of wholly new moral styles; others are significant works within a style. There is, however, something of a problem in providing examples in morals comparable to those so readily available in the history of art; that problem has to do with the way we learn about and write the history of the two fields.

Texts in art history, for example, are typically structured around the landmark accomplishments. The history of ethics is usually focused on contrasting moral theories, whether or not they or their authors represent great moral achievements in individual human lives. No historian of ethics would leave out Kant, though Kant hardly lived the life of a moral original. We have spent very little time in the field of ethics trying to settle some agreement on the moral originals in the way that the historians of art have reached considerable agreement on the great figures, the innovators, the creative geniuses, in their field. Ethics tends to be, under the dominance of the universalizability hypothesis, a rather mundane matter in which we worry about keeping promises and not committing suicide. Of course, with the artists, we have works or bodies of work to judge. With the comparable figures in morality, it would be their biographies, their lives or some part of their lives, even some remarkable actions, that must be considered. I suspect that ethics would benefit from a refocus on the moral originals and their contributions, on acts of moral creativity, on biography. Some writers have turned their attention to extensive fictional examples to augment or correct inadequacies in theory, but few have taken on the lifework of nonfictional morally creative individuals.

There is a problem with the analogy to the history of art and that of moral originality that worries me. When I asked professional artists why they study the works of the great figures in their fields, the answers I got were far from what I had expected. In fact, by and large, I was told that they did not study the works of the acknowledged masters, or that if they did, it was only to satisfy a historical interest. Art history is for historians, not artists, I was told. Some admitted that they might occasionally get some inspiration from the study of the history of their art, which perhaps is all that the study of the biographies of moral originals could provide us. In any event, I am reluctant to offer even a tentative list of candidates as moral originals worthy of consideration in a history of ethics comparable to a history of art. (A few suggestions that would be on my list: Moses, Socrates, Julius Caesar, Jesus of Nazareth, St. Francis of Assisi, Mahomet, Jeremy Bentham, John Adams, Thomas Jefferson, Henry David Thoreau, Sojourner Truth, Harriet Tubman, Chief Joseph, Patrick Pearce, Susan B. Anthony, Rachel Carson, and Malcolm X. Thomas More, Gandhi, and Martin Luther King Jr. stand out as conspicuous contributors in styles founded by the actions or lives of others.) The study of such biographies will not produce rules of moral behavior, formulas for virtuous action, or manuals for the successful expression of inner strength. It can, I suppose, be inspirational, an encouragement to virtue, but the same can be said of the fictional accounts.

I should stress that I am not equating moral originality and creativity with supererogation. The sort of people I have in mind as moral notables were not acting above and beyond the call of duty as understood in some established ethical theory. Like Giotto and Braque in the history of art, they were introducing or creating new moral styles, founding new movements or traditions, altering the way events and actions and agents are conceived in moral terms, redrawing the maps of the moral landscape, or, like Michelangelo and Picasso (in his cubist period), they were, by their actions, living exemplary lives within a style originated by another.

A final point of clarification: agent-based inner strength virtue theories might be either karmic or nonkarmic. I do not intend to suggest that, as the fundamental virtue, inner strength or self-reliance supports a nonkarmic moral theory to the exclusion of a karmic one. That obviously is not the case. Plato, as Slote notes, probably the first inner strength virtue theorist, seems committed to a karmic theory. I want to stress that agent-based morality of inner strength is attractively compatible with a nonkarmic worldview. It lends itself to the development of a virtuous vengeance theory in a less convoluted way than other sorts of approaches, for example, agent-based theories anchored in benevolence or compassion or agent-focused theories of human flourishing and well-being.

HONOR

There is in every breast a sensibility to marks of honor.
Alexander Hamilton[53]

Grieve not, wise man! Mourning is feeble; it avails much more to avenge one's friend. For each of us must the end abide of our course in the world, accomplish what may be glory ere death; to the doughty warrior after life has gone is left but fame.

Beowulf[54]

According to the *Oxford English Dictionary,* the oldest and most frequent uses in English of the term "honor" date to 1375. All pertain to credit, reputation, and a good name. Honor has to do with being worthy of high esteem, even veneration, and carries with it privilege, but it can also relate to nobleness of mind. In fact, one of the definitions of honor in *Chambers Twentieth Century Dictionary* is "self-respecting integrity." I think a great deal can and should be made of those two senses or types of honor. In Chapter 3 I argued that revenge behavior can be a mechanism for the production and maintenance of honor. If or when it is, it will be rational for agents to be avengers, unless the costs of doing so that accrue to the individual avenger far outdistance the benefits, in terms of honor.

In many communities, prominently identified in the anthropological literature with Mediterranean societies but clearly evident throughout the world, there exist norms of honor, misidentified by Elster as norms of revenge, and in such communities vengeance may be an executive virtue. Such a social normative account of honor, however, captures only one type of honor, positional honor or what I will call public or external honor. I think a case can be made that honor also may be private, personal, a fundamental form of private merit. When it is private, acts of vengeance may or may not generate communal approval, depending on whether honor norms also exist in the community and the actions of the agent incidentally satisfy them. Acts of vengeance from within a private honor conception may, independent of public approval or disapproval, promote a sense of integrity, restoration or reaffirmation of worth, and personal merit. Either type of honor, then, can serve as an outcome-oriented end that can render revenge behavior amenable to a directly rational choice interpretation, while public honor can provide the approval/disapproval patterns for a social norm of revenge. In this section, I want to look more closely at the different forms of honor, public (external) and private (personal), and their possible relationship to an agent-based morality of inner strength.

Robert Ashley, the founder of the library of the Middle Temple, London, wrote a treatise, *Of Honour,* somewhere between 1596 and 1603. Although the exact date of publication is uncertain, it must be within that time frame because it is dedicated to Sir Thomas Egerton, Keeper of the Great Seal of England, and Egerton held that post during those years. Ashley's little book is believed to be the earliest attempt by an Englishman to provide a systematic study of the subject of honor. Some years later, Thomas Hooker would write *An Essay on Honour* (1741), and a number of Italian writers tackled the subject before and after Ashley. Dramatists of the period explored aspects of honor in their plays, not the least of which was Shakespeare. It would not be a stretch to characterize most of his *Histories,* especially *Henry IV* (parts I and II) and *Henry V,* as directly concerned with honor, whether as a serious matter or as a source of Falstaff's humor. *Hamlet* and *Romeo and Juliet* are steeped in the concept. But the dramatic literature on honor does not contain, nor should it, systematic treatises on the subject. In England that task was taken up by Ashley.

Ashley, it seems fairly clear from the text, is concerned about two sorts of misunderstandings about honor, one that can be attributed to Falstaff's quips but also to Montaigne, and the other apparently to something he recognizes as a problem among his peers, upper crust late-Elizabethan males. The first is the treatment of honor as merely a name that people bestow on themselves, which is of no real value. The second is the overly ambitious pursuit of honors and social recognition. Ashley takes both to be serious moral mistakes. Each, in its own way, focuses on an extreme with respect to a concept that when properly understood is, he believes, an essential foundation of morality.

Ashley claims that honor is the most divine of attributes because it is offered up both to God and to those who are held in the highest regard among humans. "There ys nothing amongst men more excellent then honour," he writes. He attributes our desire for honor to nature; it is "given vs of nature." It is, as he recognizes, a primitive motivation. He claims that honor is necessarily joined to human felicity and hence is "to be preferred before all other especiall good thinges" such as wealth, health, friends, children, noble lineage, and so on.[55]

Although it is especially evident when Ashley writes about the need for moderation in seeking honor, his debt to Aristotle is clear throughout the treatise. For example, Ashley's placement of honor among those things good in themselves but linked to happiness echoes Aristotle's "honour, pleasure, reason, and every other virtue we choose indeed for themselves (for if nothing resulted from them we should still choose each of them), but we choose them also for the sake of happiness, judging that through them we shall be happy" (NE 1097b). Honor is a good, whether public or private.

Departing from Aristotle, Ashley identifies in honor a special power that the other virtues lack. His insight is that honor has the power to keep people away from all vices. His idea seems to be that honor is in itself desirable, and those who have it gain "all delight of the mind" such that they would not ever want to part with it. To avoid losing it, one must forgo the enticements of all the vices. In fact, Ashley is convinced that without honor, all of the other virtues will perish and people will go about doing "each foule and wicked deed." This is a conception of the moral role of honor that prevails in most honor-driven societies. What it sometimes comes to mean, however, is that deeds that would otherwise be vices are not so classified if done in the name of honor or honor preservation. In societies like the antebellum American South, for example, it also could mean that the commission of acts that would be vices if performed by others are not counted as such when done by "honorable men."[56] The irony of such a use, of course, did not escape Shakespeare; it plays a crucial role in Mark Antony's funeral oration.

Although Ashley only briefly touches on it, the link he seems to have had in mind that works the virtuous magic of honor is shame-avoidance. I will address that matter presently, but it should first prove useful to see where Ashley took his account.

In responding to his ambitious colleagues, he distinguishes between honor and glory. Glory is not honorable. It is a reflection of fame, recognition, and what Ashley calls "magnificence." Honor, however, does involve recognition. It "is a certaine testemonie of vertue shining of yt self geven of some men by the iudgement of good men." Obviously, there are two sorts of recognition, the sort that one gets from the multitude, glory, and the sort that comes from the judgment of good men. The gloss on Aristotle is clear. In reference to the appropriately proud person, Aristotle writes: "It is hard to be truly proud; for it is impossible without nobility and goodness of character. It is chiefly with honours and dishonours, then, that the proud man is concerned; and at honours that are great and conferred by good men he will be moderately pleased, thinking he is coming by his own or even less than his own . . . but honour from casual people and on trifling grounds he will utterly despise" (NE 1124a). The false honor(s) sought by the ambitious is, Ashley thinks, downright evil. His treatise is, in large measure, a caution to his peers to guard against ambition and ostentation. He rails against those who in their attempt to gain honor evidence "a certeine mediocritie . . . For ambitiouslie and insolently to seek after Honour, or to hide ambicion vnder the pretext of vertue, yt ys no lesse faultie then to haue no feeling of Honour at all."[57]

But what is true honor for Ashley? He identifies two necessary aspects of true honor. First, it is a habit of virtue in the honorable person. Second, it is found or judged to be in that person by "good men iudging aright." Ashley explains why the judgment of good men is important: "Because that Honour which ys said to be in any ys not only in him as yf yt depended wholy on him, but also in others, whoe must loue and commend that vertue in him which they seeme to allow of. Therefore the cause of bestowing the honour which draweth vnto yt and requireth approbacion ys in the man which is honored, but the accommodating thereof in those which allow of him for his vertues sake. And do therefore make much of him and esteeme him."[58] Honor, for Ashley, is inseparably personal and communal or public. The communal aspect guarantees shame-avoidance, or fear of ill-repute, that most discussions of the topic take to be essential to the sense of honor. Hence, Ashley's account of honor sets the paradigm that has dominated the topic: although honor may have, at least in the best cases, to do with inner feelings and demonstrable virtues, it is driven by considerations of communal pressure in the form of shame-avoidance.

Honor, as Ashley suggests, may proceed from the display of such habitual virtues as honesty in which an agent may take pride, but it requires an audience, in fact, for Ashley, an audience comprised of those of the highest moral standing. Both Ashley and his contemporary Francis Bacon ("Of Praise") warn that people are prone to value the opinions of the vulgar multitude rather than those of the virtuous, choose the wrong audience, and have only vainglorious popularity to show rather than true honor. Thus, essential to the conception of public honor is a determination of the group that forms one's appropriate audience. Public honor presupposes a definition of the honorable, of one's tribunal of honor. For Bacon, only the noncommon, the socially highest ranking, people are sufficiently honorable to serve as members of that tribunal.

Social stratification seems to be tied up in a Gordian knot with public honor. The way this was typically handled in communities with honor norms was to demarcate classes: "A man is answerable for his honour only to his social equals, that is to say, to those with whom he can conceptually compete."[59] A dramatic way to see how this phenomenon worked is to look at the history of dueling in Europe. Pieter Spierenburg notes that male honor, as revealed in the history of violent rituals such as the duel, "has at least three layers: a person's own feeling of self-worth, this person's assessment of his worth in the eyes of others, and the actual opinion of others about him."[60] Affairs of honor, duels, were never fought across class lines. The insult of someone of a lower class was never a threat to one's honor. Challenges to honor were social station–specific, which does not mean that only the upper echelons of society had honor and so could participate in the ritual violence of dueling to settle disputes and attacks on honor. What it meant was that a person of a lower class could not impugn or diminish the honor of a person of an upper class.

Within classes, various sorts of ritual honor-restoring practices could occur, although those of the lower classes would not be recognized as such by the higher classes. Apologists for upper-class dueling throughout Europe in the nineteenth century maintained that the practice promoted civilized behavior, taught men self-mastery and the proper forms of social interaction, and even established fraternal bonds between the participants. According to Spierenburg, "Having survived it, former enemies are like brothers."[61] He explains: "If we take it at face value, we must assume that the prospect of having to face an opponent in arms restrained men in social intercourse; they thought twice before they said a wrong word . . . The implicit assumption is that honorable men actually do not want to fight at all and do everything to avoid it."[62]

By the second half of the nineteenth century, according to Spierenburg, the middle and the upper classes in Europe "shared a common honor code,"[63] which created the rather roughly defined class of "gentlemen." It excluded shopkeepers and other tradesmen from those who could claim the honor(s) of gentlemen. Hence, the class of those who could legitimately duel in defense of their honor was still restricted. When two gentlemen fought a duel, the courts, controlled by the gentlemanly class, were generally lenient, but should two tradesmen engage in a deadly affair of honor, most likely the courts would treat the victor as a murderer.

With the growth of wealth among the trade classes, the expansion of the class of gentlemen kept pace into the early twentieth century. In fact, there seems to have been a certain amount of recruiting in dueling societies and the like. In 1918 in France, Georges Breittmayer published a new dueling code. He "decreed that anyone of draft age could duel and hence belonged to the same honor group. He only excluded men who had avoided military service or engaged in disreputable activities during the war."[64] Breittmayer's code, however, was utterly without impact in Western Europe because democratizing the social hierarchy had the effect of destroying the social conditions in which affairs of honor made sense. As Spierenburg points out, "If all were honorable, no one would be really honorable."[65]

Public honor requires some sort of social stratification, which also supports what I have elsewhere called a spatial conception of morality.[66] In such a morality human identities are station identities. Personal identity is given almost exhaustively in terms of locations and associations that form and define a social grid. Who one is a matter of where one is within the social structure. F. H. Bradley, a fair candidate as a spatial moralist, makes the point that an individual human being, insofar as he or she is "the object of his [or her] self-consciousness," is characterized and penetrated "by the existence of others." The content of a self is a pattern of relations within a community. As Bradley states, "I am myself by sharing with others, by including in my essence relations to them, the relations of the social state."[67]

The primary moral obligation for Bradley and most other spatial moralists sounds rather like a version of the Socratic injunction to know oneself combined with the Stoic command to realize oneself in one's proper place in the natural/ social order. Self-realization is finding one's position or station and acting accordingly. To find one's place, of course, requires identifying the places of others—not all others, but a significant element of that part of the social grid in which one exists. Bradley tells us that "to know what a man is you must not take him in isolation . . . What he has to do depends on what his place is, what his function is, and that all comes from his station."[68]

In a spatial morality, the primary moral motivation is to measure up and not be seen as inadequate to the tasks that define one's identity. Shame-avoidance propels spatial ethics, which is why public or external honor-based social systems are stratified. It should be recalled that Ashley located in shame, the fear of ill-repute, the social force that works the magic of honor in keeping people away from vices. Plato makes a similar claim for shame in both the *Republic* (465a) and the *Laws* (671c).

A number of contemporary philosophers have provided illuminating studies of the concept of shame. Of note are Gabrielle Taylor's *Pride, Shame, and Guilt*,[69] Arnold Isenberg's "Natural Pride and Natural Shame,"[70] and John Kekes's "Shame and Moral Progress."[71] I have also written on the subject.[72] It is generally agreed that shame, rather than involving transgressions of moral codes or laws, relates to failures, shortcomings, feelings of inadequacy and inferiority, and the unwanted exposure of weaknesses or the fear of such revelations.

When one is ashamed, the normal response is to conceal oneself, to try to mask oneself. Shame has a distinctly visual aspect. It seems to depend, in large measure, on the way one looks to oneself and on the way one wants to be seen by others and the way one thinks or knows one is seen by others. Shakespeare in *King Lear* horrifically portrays the linkage of shame to vision as well as to identity, as Stanley Cavell notes.[73] As the play opens, Gloucester, whose career was built on the creation of an image of respectability and honor in the eyes of others, acknowledges he has fathered a bastard whom he has not properly recognized. He jokes about it to mask his shame, but, as Gabrielle Taylor notes, such an attempt to hide shame "is one way of losing self-respect, for it is one way of blurring the values the person is committed to."[74] Regardless of what Gloucester may have thought he was doing, all he accomplishes is to more deeply implant his son's sense of illegitimacy. That failure returns to haunt Gloucester when his public mask is torn off. Shakespeare marks the association of shame and vision, of avoiding eyes and of having eyes voided, of not letting others see you and of not being able to see them, when Gloucester is blinded and then mocked. It is a grotesque moment, a moment of sheer horror.

Suffering shame is an identity crisis. Shame anxiety, we are told by psychologists, is a feeling of radical isolation from one's social image. It may even be described as an experience of the disappearance of self. Gerhart Piers and Milton Singer claim that shame arises out of a tension between the ego and the ideal ego, and they differentiate it from guilt, which they claim arises out of a tension between the ego and the superego.[75] The ideal ego in a spatial morality is defined by the social conventions that set the expectations for stations, roles, and genders. John Kekes, in a similar vein, notes that "shame is caused by the realization that we have fallen short of some standard we regard as important. Those who are incapable of this emotion cannot be seriously committed to any standard, so they are apt to lack moral restraint. Shame is a sign that we have made a serious commitment, and it is also an impetus for honoring it, since violating the commitment painfully lowers our opinion of ourselves."[76] Honor is typically twinned with shame and mirrors many of its characteristics.

J. G. Peristiany, in a famous anthropological study of the values of Mediterranean societies,[77] echoes Ashley's and Aristotle's accounts of honor as being necessarily both a personal and a public conception of the value of a person. Honor relates, as Peristiany notes, although he could have been quoting from Aristotle, to a person's claim to pride, both as seen by the person and by his or her peer group. The public honor game, played by many different types of people throughout the world, is the game of collecting validations of personal image from those one regards either as one's equals or one's betters and avoiding shame. But the image a person attempts to validate in these games is not one that might emerge from Emersonian inner strength. It is a social ideal that is reproduced in the individual aspiring to personify it and is validated (or not) by its creators and sustainers. If one achieves the "right to pride," one achieves status, but status and the right to pride are elements of the social identity that is not solely, if at all, constructed—though it is internalized—by the individual agent. In effect, it is a type of conformity, the very thing Emerson so vehemently opposed.

Any claim to pride is "mere vanity," according to Peristiany, unless it is granted, validated, certified, by the members of the relevant social unit. Failure of validation constitutes humiliation for the individual and, most importantly, is the basis for shame. As Peristiany notes, "Public opinion forms therefore a tribunal before which the claims to honour are brought, 'the court of reputation' as it has been called, and against its judgements there is no redress. For this reason it is said that public ridicule kills."[78] In a similar vein, John Rawls writes about shame that it "implies an especially intimate connection . . . with those upon whom we depend to confirm the sense of our own worth."[79]

Peristiany makes a clever and, I suspect, correct association of honor with people's heads, one that also plays into the association of shame with vision. Showing respect in most societies involves the head—bowed, covered, or uncovered—and conversely, when a person is honored, typically the head is involved in the ceremony—for example, it is crowned. No doubt, a remnant of the ancient

Celtic fascination with heads survives in these practices. (There are a number of excellent studies of Celtic lore and the role of the head, whether or not severed from the body. I have found John Darrah's *The Real Camelot*[80] useful.) In lineage-based stratified societies—for example, Tudor England—even execution of the most honorable, despite their dishonorable deeds, involved the head. It was chopped off, which as Peristiany notes, is an acknowledgement that it was something worth chopping off. Hence Anne Boleyn, Catherine Howard, Lady Jane Gray, and Mary, Queen of Scots, were entitled to beheading rather than some other, less honorable form of execution. Not to afford them such a penalty would have dishonored not only them but their lineage as well.

Peristiany, Julian Pitt-Rivers, and other structuralist anthropologists postulated a reciprocal honor/shame model to explain the social patterns of the Mediterranean region. The paradigm they elucidated, though hardly of their invention, has had a continuing impact on anthropological studies not only of that region but others as well. According to David Gilmore, the basic idea is that "honor and shame are reciprocal moral values representing primordial integration of individual to 'group.' They reflect, respectively, the conferral of public esteem upon the person and the sensitivity to public opinion upon which the former depends."[81] All societies are what Gilmore calls "face-to-face societies" in which "public opinion arbitrates reputation." Therefore, the reciprocal honor/shame explanatory model, in some form, recommends itself to students of social relations and behavior.

The interpretive use of the reciprocal honor/shame model by anthropologists in cross-cultural studies of the Mediterranean region in terms of male-female relationships or, more specifically sexual contests, however, has provoked a certain amount of controversy. I have no dog in that fight, but it is worth noting how the model, when engaged by Pitt-Rivers, Peristiany, and others, works out the sometimes complex social relations of the cultures that were studied. Honor is understood as an essentially male value, but it is measured by shame, understood primarily in terms of the chastity of women. Put another way, male public or external honor is dependent on the sexual behavior of females. Men are responsible for the shame of their women; his women's chastity is the foundation of a man's honor.

Peristiany explains the sexual-contest conception of public honor and shame with the age-old example of the cuckold, summarizing the symbolism as follows: "The cuckold, *cabron,* literally the billy-goat, is said to 'have horns.' The horns, a phallic symbol, are also the insignia of the Devil, the enemy of virtue . . . The manliness of a husband must be exerted above all in the defense of the honour of his wife on which his own depends. Therefore her adultery represents not only an infringement of his rights but a demonstration of his failure in his duty. He has betrayed the values of the family, bringing dishonour to all the social groups who are involved reciprocally in his honour: his family and his community. His manliness is defiled, for he has fallen under the domination of the Devil and must wear his symbol as the stigma of his betrayal. The responsibility is his, not the adulterer's, for the latter was only acting in accordance with his male nature."[82] If Peristiany's account correctly reflects the public honor and shame conceptions that dominate a number of communities in the studied region, then in those communities masculine virility, concern for reputation, and especially the sexual purity of women are among the highest ethical/social values, and failure to defend one's reputation, as understood in those terms, is shameful and dishonorable.

Carol Delaney, whose anthropological research was done in Turkey, explicates the model primarily in terms of procreation issues: "Minimally, the value of males derives from the social perception of their ability to engender; it is the foundation upon which honor is built."[83] Delaney notes that honor so understood creates high levels of anxiety in the males of the community. Their honor balances precariously on the sexual behavior of the females. With the rural lifestyle of most of the communities as a conceptual background, the female is thought of in terms of a field that is the property of her husband, to be sown only by him. The yield of that field is the source of honor for the man, but only if it is the child of his own seed. Paternity is crucial to honor; a man's honor is lost if he has not been able to unambiguously ensure his paternity. According to Delaney, "Shame is an inevitable part of being female."[84] The only honor a woman can have is by remaining fully aware of her inherent shamefulness and behaving accordingly. However, she does have a certain dominion over her husband's honor. Although she, as Delaney notes, does not possess the "seeds of honor," her sexual behavior can render her husband dishonorable and put him "in the position of a woman and . . . therefore shamed." The ancient pollution doctrine is also invoked to explain the transference of her sexual promiscuity to her husband's shame: "Since seed carries the essential identity of a man, it leaves an indelible imprint which no amount of washing can erase. A woman who has had sexual relations with any man other than her husband becomes physically polluted, and through her, her husband's honor is stained."[85] In discussing the honor/shame culture of the antebellum American South, Wyatt-Brown aptly refers to women as dangerous: "They could present a husband, father, or brother with an illegitimate child and thereby cast doubt on the legitimacy of the line and desecrate the inmost temple of male self-regard. . . . In the American South, it is no wonder that men feared women."[86]

The sort of honor that is the subject of the anthropological research done on the Mediterranean cultures is what I call "public, positional, or external honor" because of its necessary dependence on an audience. When I first conceived of this section, I intended to explicate this notion with references to Hector in the *Iliad*. Hector, as I read Homer, when he takes up the challenge of Achilles, is motivated, if not wholly, then in very large measure, by his concern to protect his public honor, his reputation, his position, in the eyes of the people of Troy: "I could not face my countrymen and the Trojan ladies in their trailing gowns" (Book XXII). However, after reading Wyatt-Brown's account of honor in the

American South, it was obvious to me that, in examining the dominant "psychological and social underpinnings of Southern culture," he had captured the essence of what I mean by "public or positional honor." I will borrow some elements from his explication to complete my sketch of the concept. If he is right, the antebellum white culture of the American South was a fertile field of public honor.

As I earlier noted, public honor requires an ego ideal, a social model, and public evaluation. Wyatt-Brown notes that there were three primary and dependent components of public honor in the antebellum South (I have touched on all three previously, but it is useful to reiterate them): "Honor is first the inner conviction of self-worth . . . Second . . . the claim to that self-assessment before the public . . . [and] third . . . the assessment of the claim by the public, a judgment based on the behavior of the claimant. In other words, honor is reputation. Honor resides in the individual as his understanding of who he is and where he belongs in the ordered ranks of society."[87] All of those conditions were, of course, set forth in Ashley's treatise, which should come as little surprise, because the antebellum Southern whites looked on England and its gentry and upper classes as behavioral and social models.

Wyatt-Brown contends that honor and shame and not conscience or guilt governed the Southern mindset. He quotes William Grayson, who in 1853 proclaimed that Southern honor was not rooted in the very virtue on which Ashley founded it: honesty. Honor, he avowed, was far more a matter of virtue by reputation than virtue qua virtue. "Men of honor," Grayson professed with what reads like a welling pride, "contract debts without intending to pay them," and they may utter falsehoods in gallantry and diplomacy. Swearing, gambling, whoring, even failure to keep the Sabbath are compatible with honor. So, on what was the honorable Southerner's reputation based? The answer is that insofar as the opinion of others was taken to be inseparable from the inner worth of the individual, public or observable traits of character were the sole condition of honor and, by the same token, shame. What mattered was not that one was, for example, honest, but that one was regarded as honest by one's peer tribunal. Above all, the demonstration of one's valor for everyone to witness ensured an honorable reputation. The approbation of the community constituted the highest achievement of virtue. It assured an honored position.

Actually, as Wyatt-Brown argues, public honor in the antebellum South had two forms that existed together, though often tenuously. One had its origins in the European Celtic traditions of external ethics, in which human character was understood to be physically demonstrable "without ambivalence or ambiguity" and in which all judgments of virtue depended completely on appearances, the primal honor of valor. The other form had a Stoic/Christian ancestry and became what Wyatt-Brown calls "gentility." It took the form of "Southern hospitality," a certain "high mindedness," a comfortable knowledge of what were, if rather limited in scope, deemed to be the important literary classics, and, at least, an outward display of piety. With respect to the valorous form of Southern honor, Wyatt-Brown claims that "the following elements were crucial in the formulation of Southern evaluations of conduct: (1) honor as immortalizing valor, particularly in the character of revenge against familial and community enemies; (2) opinion of others as an indispensable part of personal identity and gauge of self-worth; (3) physical appearance and ferocity of will as signs of inner merit; (4) defense of male integrity and mingled fear and love of women; and finally, (5) reliance on oath-taking as a bond in lieu of family obligations and allegiances."[88] Revenge, on such conditions, was usually honorable. Andrew Jackson wrote, in stirring up the "brave sons of Tennessee" to attack the Creeks who had massacred a family of settlers, "we are ready and pant for vengeance."

Probably the most important of Wyatt-Brown's elements of Southern primal honor, the honor of public valor, is the second one, the familiar one: personal identity and self-worth depend on the opinion of others. He further explains: "The opinion of others not only determined rank in society but also affected the way men and women thought. The stress upon external, public factors in establishing personal worth conferred particular prominence on the spoken word and physical gesture as opposed to interior thinking."[89]

The literature on honor and its reciprocal, shame, is dominated by discussions of audience dependence. Recall what Rawls said about shame. One might be led to conclude that there is neither honor nor shame in the absence of a critical audience, a peer group, a tribunal. But if that is the case, then neither honor nor shame could be expected to play a role in a virtue ethics of inner strength. In order to examine whether honor can be personal—that is, whether it can relate to inner strength rather than an audience—I want to first follow a more explored trail regarding the same question in the case of its reciprocal. Does shame really require an audience?

Kekes claims that shame both alerts us to our shortcomings and makes us feel deficient on account of them, shame's painful emotive element. The audience is supposed to be crucial in both of those aspects of shame. As a number of writers have noticed, there are two different judgments that occur in a shame situation. One is the critical evaluation of the audience, and the other is the critical judgment of the agent. The latter is based on whatever standards of behavior the agent has internalized, and they may or may not be similar to those applied by the audience in its judgment of the agent's actions. Douglas Cairns summarizes the situation in the following way: "The critical judgment of oneself which is constitutive of shame is never formally identical with any critical judgment of the audience."[90] That, of course, must be the case, because the agent, as a result of his or her judgment about himself or herself, experiences that painful self-directed feeling.

Whatever judgment the audience makes, it cannot be one of shame, although it may include the judgment that the agent should be ashamed of what he or she has done. A number of different outcomes are possible, any of which can produce shame in the agent. The audience might be positively or negatively impressed by or indifferent to the agent's actions. The agent might, in every case, endorse or reject the audience's judgment. But even if the agent endorses a positive audience response, the result could be that he or she is ashamed. For example, the agent may view the audience's approval as conditioned by their having placed him or her on a social level below what the agent believes to be appropriate to his or her self-image. The agent may agree with the audience and consequently feel shame. If the audience is indifferent, the agent may experience shame at having failed to impress them. In any event, the shame judgment is solely that of the agent, and it is made with respect to or against some standard or ego ideal that he or she has internalized. So, what role does the audience really play in the matter?

Gabrielle Taylor has carefully and convincingly explicated the function of the audience in shame. She notes that "in feeling shame the actor thinks of himself as having become an object of detached observation, and at the core to feel shame is to feel distress at being seen at all."[91] What is crucial in shame is that the agent achieve what Taylor calls a "higher order" critical point of view with which he or she can identify. The concept of the audience, whether real or imagined, affords the agent access to that point of view. The audience itself, then, is not crucial to shame, but the agent's taking up that detached observer point of view is. It is that point of view—of seeing oneself as being seen or possibly being seen in a certain way, as exposed—that motivates the self-critical and self-directed judgment that produces shame reactions. The standard that is internalized in the agent is given content, is "called forth," in the assumption of that point of view. I said earlier that shame is a visual concept. Vision, in this sense, is metaphorical, and so is the role of the audience. Shame crucially involves seeing, but it must be seeing oneself, not as one wants to see oneself, but as one might be seen from the perspective of what Taylor calls "a possible detached observer-description."[92] Further and essentially, to be ashamed the agent must have decided that he or she "ought not to be in the position where (he or) she could be so seen, where such a description at least appears to fit."[93]

The audience in shame is but a conceptual crutch. Rawls and others have been too influenced by the shame-culture discussions of the anthropologists and so look for actual audiences. As Cairns notes, "The proximate source of shame is the self's judgement of the self."[94] It is not, however, that the role of the audience comes to be played by the agent, a mistake made by Cairns.[95] The catalyst of shame is that the agent accesses another visual perspective, one detached from the agent's own, with respect to his or her actions. This is not self-awareness and self-criticism, at least not in the way those notions are usually described. A person can be self-aware without also being aware of the possible descriptions of his or her behavior that might be chosen by a detached observer. I am not sure that this is what Piers means by the audience being "present only as an internalized 'other.'"[96] It certainly involves internalizing a point of view or observational perspective on the actions one performs that is other than one's attached perspective. It is to see oneself as the person who *may* be seen as doing X, though one may not see oneself as doing X at all. That is the cognitive side of shame.

Shame is not only retrospective, but it also may be (perhaps often is) a retarded, delayed, reactive emotion, stalled by the agent's inability to activate its cognitive catalyst. Some time may elapse before a person is able to see himself or herself as possibly being seen to be doing X when he or she was, to his or her mind, doing Y. When he or she is able to see that, to see his or her doing Y in the circumstances as capable of being seen as his or her doing X, to make the self-conscious detached comparison, he or she may feel shame, shame to think that someone like him or her could be seen to be doing X.

The point of view of the possible detached observer, however, is not that of the agent's internal judgment of shame. It is not that the agent says to himself or herself, "I am ashamed, degraded, because such and such an audience could perceive what I have done in such and such a way." If that were the case, if there is no such audience or if the audience could not observe the agent's actions in the circumstances, and the agent knows that is the case, then the agent could not feel shame for what he or she did. Taylor makes the point succinctly: "It is because the agent thinks of herself in a certain relation to the audience that she now thinks herself degraded, but she does not think of this degradation as depending on an audience. Her final judgement concerns herself only: she is degraded not relatively to this audience, she is degraded absolutely."[97] An actual audience, then, is hardly essential to shame. Is that also the case with the reciprocal, honor, despite all of the literature to the contrary? I think it is although that does not mean that the anthropologists and writers like Ashley are wrong about public honor or its motivational capacities.

Imagine that the role of the audience in honor cases mirrors that of the audience in shame cases. Honor standards could be internalized in much the way that detached observer shame judgments are. A person may feel honor, in the sense of self-respecting integrity, in the absence of an audience, or Ashley's "certaine testemonie of vertue shining of yt self geven of some men by the iudgement of good men." The judgment of good men could come to mean not the actual judgment of a tribunal or community, but the judgment a person can make of his or her actions as they could be made by a group of qualified detached observers. Again, vision is the appropriate metaphor. How could I be seen were I seen doing what I am doing? If a likely way I could be seen is under what might be called a "personal honor description," then I may feel that my actions maintain or enhance my sense of self-respecting integrity. What is important is not that others, a tribunal, a community, even one of exceptionally "good men," do in fact so judge me. What is important is that I recognize that I can legitimately see my actions as taking such a description even though I may not, myself, describe them that way. That is what I will call personal or private honor as contrasted with public or external honor.

I am not saying that public or positional honor is to be understood in this way. I am satisfied that public honor does require the actual approbation of others, usually those in an acknowledged peer group. If I am right about this point, then the anthropologists' honor/shame reciprocal model is faulty. Public honor is not the reciprocal of shame, though it might be the reciprocal of public shaming, a distinction that Nathaniel Hawthorne so brilliantly drew in *The Scarlet Letter.* Hester Prynne was publicly shamed for her adultery, but she was not ashamed. Of course, public shaming can be internalized by its object and become shame. By suffering the public display of disapprobation and contempt, being shunned, jeered at, laughed at, cursed, cast out, a person may well adopt the viewpoint and standards of the others, conform, and experience the painful self-directed feeling of shame. Or he or she may not. In personal honor, the audience is also a conceptual crutch that may be returned to its corner when the agent has fully internalized the detached observer perspective on his or her actions.

Personal or private honor is not incompatible with public honor, but it is definitely not the honor of reputation. Personal honor depends on what standards of behavior one, in fact, internalized, against what detached observation point of view one sees oneself as being seen. That point of view could be identical to that of public honor. In that case, one sees oneself as being seen by the public or by some segment of the public, and, of course, one does not want to be seen as the person doing X, where one knows or believes that X is disapproved of by that public. The external elements of personal honor, in such a case, are indistinguishable from those of public honor. One has simply internalized a public honor perspective, treating the positional honors that the public conveys as the only reason to feel honorable. That is non-accidental compatibility of personal and public honor.

Personal and public honor, however, may be accidentally or incidentally compatible in at least three other ways. The detached observational point of view one adopts could be based in deontic values as understood or interpreted in some standard moral theory. For example, it could be Kantian. That is, one might adopt the detached observational point of view of the rational community and derive one's sense of personal honor from seeing one's actions as seen by the members of that community. Insofar as any single member of the rational community is as good an observer/evaluator as any other, to see one's actions as seen by the rational community could be just to see one's actions as seen by oneself when one has adopted the perspective of a rational agent. In Kantian terms, that would be to see one's actions as by one's will becoming a universal law for all people. Incidentally, the actions one thereby identifies as one's duty and therefore honorable could correspond to those admired by the general public or some relevant segment of that public.

Another detached observational point of view that might attract a person of personal honor is one that is based in fundamental aretaic values that are external to the agent, such as the "good life" or Aristotle's *eudaimonia.* This, following on the discussion of the previous section, could be called "agent-focused personal honor." The personal honor comes from seeing one's actions as being seen by those who have a solid grasp of the constituents of human well-being or the good life. I am inclined to say that this may be rather like seeing one's actions as being seen by a discerning Aristotle.

Finally, one might adopt the detached observational point of view of seeing one's actions (or oneself) as seen by one (or by a group) whose fundamental aretaic values are based in inner strength (Slote would add the possibility of fundamental aretaic values based in benevolence). If one takes such a point of view, then one's honor is entirely interior to oneself, which does not, however, mean that one is one's own audience, an audience that is bound to be appreciative. It means that one sees one's actions as seen by those who see the sort of actions one is performing under certain descriptions, as doing Z, where Z either is or is not a description of behavior that evidences inner strength in the agent. Extreme self-criticism and dissatisfaction with oneself may result. On the other hand, personal honor may well up in the person who can see his or her actions as seen as displays of inner strength and self-reliance utterly without regard to what description may be given to one's behavior from any other detached observational point of view. In such a case, the union of a person's honor and sense of personal integrity is complete whether or not one's actions are or would be applauded by the public.

I think that a convincing case could be made that Homer's Achilles (in the *Iliad*) is primarily motivated by "inner strength honor," especially after the death of Patroclus. But John Wayne's character in *The Searchers,* Ethan Edwards, is clearly a prime example of what I have in mind. Geoffrey O'Brien has written that *The Searchers* should be regarded as the "movie of the century."[98] I agree with him but will not reiterate comments about the film I made earlier or in *Cowboy Metaphysics.* I want only to draw attention to a few basic points about Ethan Edwards and his behavior.

Ethan indisputably is a man of honor. When he returns to the Edwards ranch at the beginning of the film, he is wearing both his Confederate cloak and his saber. The war has been over for two years, and what Ethan did during that time is never revealed. We know that he did not go to California and that he has a bag of newly minted Yankee dollars that he does not explain. We are shown a number of scenes that reveal that Ethan and his brother's wife, Martha, share a deep and unrequited love. Even the Reverend Captain Clayton notices Martha's affection for Ethan when he catches a glimpse of her lovingly stroking his cloak. And Ethan, who shows no affection for his brother, sits out on the porch in the evening to avoid observing domestic scenes between his brother and Martha but glances into the house only to see them enter their bedroom and close the door. It is a scene that, we may surmise, tears at his heart. When Ethan returns to the burning ranch house after the massacre of the Edwards family, he searches only for Martha, calling her name. When he finds her, raped and murdered by the

Comanches, his face expresses his anger, his hatred, his loss, and his resolution to revenge the outrage. It is a look that is both maniacal and unforgiving, crazed and committed.

Ethan Edwards never sees himself as seen by an actual external or public audience, never finds it necessary to explain his actions by way of seeking the approbation of others. He does not even seek Martha's support for what he has been doing or will do, presenting himself to the ranch literally out of the blue. He does tell the Reverend Captain that he will not swear an oath to the Texas Rangers because he regards his oath to the Confederacy to still be in effect, but that seems a lame reason and not one that plays any role in the rest of the story. It may, however, fit Ethan's character in one respect, and in that regard it is something of a private joke: the only oath he will acknowledge is to a defeated and dead institution.

Ethan doesn't believe that the "South will rise again" or that he is bound to be at its beck and call. He really is outside of all social organizations, rituals, ceremonies, even his family; he is the epitome of the outsider. In fact, throughout the film he interrupts, or rather disrupts, the cherished social rituals of the community—the funeral and the wedding—in both cases to seek vengeance against Martha's murderers. He also refuses to accept any authority other than his own, only reluctantly agreeing to follow Clayton's orders to sneak up on the tribal camp to try to rescue Martha's daughters, who were kidnapped during the murder raid. His preference is to frontally attack the encampment, killing as many Comanches as possible, even though that could result in the deaths of the girls. He barks at Clayton that if the plan fails, he will never follow another of the Ranger captain's orders: "Don't ever give me another."

Ethan's primary goal is to kill the Comanche chief, Scar, to avenge the horrible death of his beloved Martha. He finds his older niece, Lucy, dead, raped, and mutilated, and when enough time has passed that her sister, Debbie, would have been old enough to be married off to a Comanche, his secondary goal is to kill Debbie. Both are acts that Ethan regards as required by his sense of personal honor. They are probably directly related in his mind, though he never voices the relationship. Instead, we hear from Laurie, who explains to Martin Pawley that Martha would want Ethan to put a bullet in Debbie's brain if she had had sexual relations with a Comanche. In any event, Ethan clearly sees himself as seen by one of inner strength and gauges his behavior accordingly. He makes no apologies for himself but also never justifies himself to others. He is assuredly, from the point of view of the organized community, a very dangerous hero.

After he has scalped Scar, he catches Debbie and, deprived of the opportunity to kill Scar, he will, we all assume, kill the girl who has been one of Scar's wives. Instead, he grabs her and raises her over his head as he would a child. Rather than dashing her to death on the rocks, he gently lowers her and takes her to the Jorgensen's ranch. However, he never enters the house, the symbol of so many of the community values he has rejected. The last we see of him, as the ranch house door closes, he saunters slowly away to "wander forever between the winds" like the dead Comanche whose eyes he shot out. His personal honor is preserved, and vengeance for the death of Martha was partially achieved. The price of inner strength honor, however, is independence, which may mean, as in Ethan Edwards's case, isolation from the community and all of its values and rituals.

It would not be a mistake to say that Ethan is not very changed from the beginning of the film to the end, from when we first see him through Martha's open door until we last see him through the Jorgensen's closing door. Although much has changed around him and through him, he remains the outsider, the man of such inner strength that he relies on no one but himself. We saw him weaken when shot with a poisoned arrow and in the care of Martin, and we saw him change his purpose and restore Debbie to the homesteaders' community. But we never saw him look to an external observational point of view, other than that provided by his own inner strength, to see how his actions are being seen. Much, I suppose, might be made of the fact that Martha must have been responsible in some large measure for Ethan's self-reliant character. In the film, women, especially represented by both Martha and Mrs. Jorgensen, are the core and the strength of the community. Aaron, Ethan's brother, tells him that he would have given up the ranch on any number of occasions if it were not for Martha's refusal to let him quit. Mrs. Jorgensen appears to be the dominant force in that family as well.

Would Ethan have turned out differently if his love of Martha had culminated in marriage? I am confident that he would not, could not, have married Martha, if only for the reason that to do so, he would have had to surrender his personal honor and integrity. I believe we may reasonably suppose that Martha recognized this fact and, despite her deep affection for him and perhaps to sustain a familial relationship to him, instead married his brother. The dubiously coincidental return of Ethan and Martin just in time to prevent Laurie from marrying Charlie McCorry saves Martin from Ethan's lifestyle. Martin will enter the house and the community that Ethan cannot.

Some additional questions about honor remain. Are shame and honor, as suggested by the anthropologists, different sides of the same standard? The idea, typically expressed on a straight-line graph, shows honor at one end and shame at the other. The impression one is to get, I suppose, is that there is a mean that is neither excessive nor deficient regarding a certain sort of behavior; the mean would be neither honorable nor shameful. To be honorable one must exceed the mean, and it is shameful to be deficient with respect to the mean. (Surprisingly, there is no term for the mean!) On some accounts, the mean must contain at least some shame, for to be shameless is a bad thing. Of course, if that is the case, then to be honorable one also must not lack some shame. And the whole dichotomy collapses. In any event, such a view simply is not the one I have adopted. The only standards that are relevant to honor and shame are those that are internalized by the agent in the form of negative or positive reactions to the appreciation of the fact that his or her actions could be (or are) described in a certain way from some detached observer point of view.

Honor, as I describe it, is not a zero-sum game, although in some places, public or positional honor may be, and it certainly is in sections of the *Iliad* where it is a matter of competition. In other places, however, as stressed by Cairns,[99] Homer brings a range of cooperative behaviors into the scope of the honorable. Honor is also not a loss-only game. Certainly it can be lost, and that is an honorable person's primary concern, but it can also be gained in a way that does not necessarily come at another person's cost. Ethan Edwards's honor is not taken from anyone else. His scalping of Scar is not done for the reasons a Comanche might gather scalps of victims, to enhance positional honor. An act of mutilation in retaliation for the rape and murder of Martha, it is the only act of vengeance left to him after Martin has killed Scar. It preserves only his personal honor.

Personal honor and shame (probably also public honor) expand the sphere of human life well beyond what most philosophers are willing to ascribe to morality. That is, both honor and shame encompass much more than is contained in what John Kekes calls the "sphere of choice," which is especially evident in the case of shame. The ploy that takes the form "You shouldn't be ashamed of X, you can't help it" (or "There's nothing you can do about X, you shouldn't be ashamed of it") might only be uttered by someone who has not absorbed even a modicum of the wisdom of Jane Austen. For example, Elizabeth Bennet's family, in *Pride and Prejudice,* behaves at the party at Netherfield in a way that makes her feel so ashamed that she cannot imagine Darcy being attracted to her. Jane Austen writes: "Elizabeth blushed and blushed again with shame. . . . To Elizabeth it appeared that had her family made an agreement to expose themselves as much as they could during the evening, it would have been impossible for them to play their parts with more spirit and finer success." Beyond relations and acquaintances for which one may feel shame, there are natural occurrences and physical deformities. Little wonder we spend so much money trying to hide them.

Helen Lynd noted that in *Of Human Bondage,* Philip Carey, who was born with a clubfoot,[100] is consumed with shame about it and fears his return to school and the taunting of his classmates. A vicar persuades him that if one really believes in God, mountains can be moved. Next to a mountain, what is a clubfoot? So young Philip prays, "Oh God . . . please make my foot all right on the night before I go back to school." The foot is not made "all right," and Philip's reaction is not only to be ashamed of his clubfoot but also to be ashamed of a God that could create a universe in which Philip Carey has a clubfoot and do nothing to make it right.

Similar expansions beyond the sphere of choice apply in the case of honor. As Kekes makes clear, "The domain of morality is wider than the sphere of choice. Morality is concerned with living good lives and there are many constituents of good lives about which we have no choice"[101] (a point to which I will return in

Chapter 6). These elements may include such things as the absence of physical deformities and embarrassing relations. And on the positive side, they may include an enduring feeling of self-reliance and self-respect, of being honorable, of not riding around the things one does not want to see oneself as being seen as riding around.

Personal honor founded in inner strength can provide the outcome orientation for the avenger that makes acts of revenge both rational and virtuous. And in communities with social norms of public or positional honor such as the Mediterranean cultures studied by the anthropologists discussed earlier, revenge can be a "mechanism that may act to support honor."[102] But revenge is not the only way that honor, personal or public, may be produced and sustained. In a social hierarchical system, positional honor can be produced by birth and sustained by the adoption of certain habits of behavior, for example southern gentility. Also, an honor-sustaining "technology" (the term is Hamlin's) that had great influence in the history of Western civilization was chivalry, which was not—or not merely—a vengeance "technology." The heroes of the major Western vengeance films, though occasionally showing signs of what might be identified as chivalrous behavior, are not motivated by the principles of chivalry. Because many of them are displaced Southerners after the Civil War, certain remnants of gentility may emerge in their manner, but they are not "knights without armor," despite what the title song of the old *Have Gun, Will Travel* television series claimed. The point is that although honor is fundamental to rational and virtuous revenge, revenge is hardly the only "mechanism" that supports honor.

Authority

Arbitrary power is like most other things which are very hard, very liable to be broken— and not withstanding all your wise laws and maxims we have it in our power not only to free ourselves but . . . to throw your . . . legal authority at our feet.

Abigail Adams[103]

Imagine the following situation: You were in the woods hunting on a crisp fall morning. You had no luck and walk out into a clearing across from a schoolyard where you parked your car. A scene of carnage and mass murder unfolds before your eyes. Bodies of students and teachers, many dead, some severely injured, lie around the yard. The sheriff's patrol car is on the scene, but as you approach it, you discover that the sheriff and his only deputy have been shot dead beside it. There is absolutely no question that they are dead from multiple gunshot wounds. You spot three adults running by the school. You recognize one as your sister. Suddenly, a gunman jumps from the shadows and fires an assault rifle at the runners, hitting and apparently killing them all. The gunman does not see you, but there can be no doubt that he is the perpetrator of the carnage. In fact, he shouts, to no one in particular, that he is proud of having committed mass murder and fires some shots into the air in triumph. You have your hunting rifle but are in no danger of being spotted as you stalk up behind him. You draw a bead on the back of his head. You shout at him some expression, cluttered with expletives, to the effect that you are killing him for what he has just done, and you squeeze the trigger. He drops to the ground. You approach his body, prepared to fire again if there is any sign of life in him, but the first shot was sufficient. He is dead. Were you morally justified in killing him?

I think the answer is yes, but others may differ with me. Some may say that you had no right to take the law into your own hands. You should have tried to contact other civil authorities. You should have tried to disarm him first. You have no right to act as judge, jury, and executioner. You did not know all the facts. For example, he may be in need of psychiatric help. Perhaps he could not have prevented himself from embarking on his murderous escapade. How can you know the inner workings of his mind? Now we will never know what provoked his assault at the school. You are not a morally legitimate authority with respect to the administration of a capital penalty. You did not kill him in self-defense. Maybe he was out of ammunition. You are a murderer, morally no better than he is.

Those may be reasonable concerns. At least some of them require consideration. My main interest in this section, however, is only with the question of authority—moral authority—to punish, even to kill another human being. The above story may not be a very satisfactory vengeance scenario, although many of those elements are present. For example, you are filled with moral and retributive hatred for the gunman, as you communicate the "vengeance message." You stand in a special relationship to one of the victims, though that may not be an important element of the story. You also may have suffered psychological harm as a witness to the scene and to cold-blooded murder, including the shooting of your sister. You were clearly in an extremely emotional situation. Some might use those facts to excuse your behavior while not allowing that it was morally legitimate. My view is that excuses for your behavior are not necessary; they are out of place when behavior is justified.[104]

I have aligned my account of virtuous vengeance with a retributive position on punishment. So much has been written for and against retributive punishment theories that it would be a monumental task, and probably a waste of space, to survey even a modicum of what is to be found in the literature (see Chapter 7). I am persuaded that consequentialist justifications of punishment usually fail in practice to satisfy our basic human psychological needs to see a penalty exacted for a willful injury regardless of what future effects, if any, the imposition of that penalty may have on the perpetrator or on other would-be perpetrators. More important, however (as discussed in Chapter 3), I am convinced that failure to punish retributively does a gross injustice to the very meaning of the concept "morally wrong." Wrong actions require hostile responses; the very notion of wrong does not otherwise make sense. Those who do wrong deserve punishment. How much they deserve, the fit condition, may be another matter (see Chapter 7). They have, in Nozick's terms, separated themselves from correct values and need to be informed of that fact in no uncertain terms even if rehabilitation is utterly impossible because, for example, they die as the result of punishment. That they did wrong is a sufficient reason to punish them, although it does not mean that they must be punished or that matters in mitigation may not be given serious consideration.

I am not, however, concerned here with the question of desert. My interest is confined to the matter of authority to administer punishment. Although many of those who support retributive punishment neglect the question of authority while concentrating on our intuitions about desert, I agree with Jeffrie Murphy[105] when he maintains that there are three conditions that convert harming someone into punishing him or her. I will phrase the conditions in a slightly different form than Murphy does because his focus is on the legal context more than the general moral one. The first, and certainly no surprise, is the desert condition that identifies the harm as wrongdoing and therefore behavior with respect to which morality requires a hostile response. The second fits the penalty to the wrongdoing, the proportionality condition, a version of which could be something akin to Kant's view that "only the law of retribution (*jus talionis*) can determine exactly the degree of punishment."[106] The third identifies "authorities to enforce sanctions" and needs to specify how we are to distinguish those who have the moral authority to apply appropriate punishments from those who lack that authority. Even if the desert and fit conditions are satisfied, unless someone with moral authority to do so administers it, the hostile response to wrongdoing will not be morally permissible. It will not be punishment, and it will not be an act of virtuous vengeance. It will itself be wrongdoing.

It is rather easy to make a legitimate authority condition intuitively appealing in legal criminal matters because of the structure and its constitutive rules (what I have elsewhere called its "policy and procedural recognitors"[107]). Most of us only need to be reminded of cases where murderers are tried, convicted, and sentenced to death in a court of law, then while awaiting the administration of the sentence and after they have exhausted all appeals, they are killed by prison inmates. The hostile response—death—prescribed by the courts has been carried out, but as most people are likely to acknowledge, it was not punishment because within the legal system the inmates of a prison are not authorized to execute sentences. It is, however, of some interest to my subject that a common public response to such killings in prisons is to regard them, often in vocal approbation, as morally acceptable outcomes. The public's positive response is especially likely when the convict killed was a vicious child molester whose death sentence was commuted to only ten to fifteen years in prison by some sympathetic public official. A similar sense of public approval might be expected to follow the report that a murderer who had used frivolous appeals to seemingly postpone the execution of his sentence indefinitely was killed in prison.

The authority condition is important to moral as well as to legal legitimacy. It is one thing to applaud an outcome that realizes an end that is identical to the one that would be morally appropriate, but quite another for that outcome to have been reached by morally legitimate means, that is by those morally authorized to bring it about.

The authority condition might, on some accounts, be folded into the desert condition by claiming that a wrongdoer deserves not just the penalty but the penalty exacted by a morally legitimate authority. Failure in this second component of the desert condition negates the moral status of the punishment and renders it immoral. My primary objection to formulating the desert condition to include the authority condition is that it places all of the emphasis on what the wrongdoer deserves. But wrongdoers, for reasons I will shortly develop, do not deserve to have their penalties administered by morally legitimate authorities. They deserve their penalties.

I believe that not distinguishing the authority condition from the desert condition is responsible, at least to some extent, for the general neglect in the moral and legal literature of authority issues, the concentration on what the wrongdoer deserves, and the development of lengthy lists of protections against excessive punishments. The literature on capital punishment, for example, regardless of whether it is pro or con, is desert-dominated. I am interested primarily in the administrator of punishment, especially, of course, the avenger. Therefore, the question of legitimate moral authority must be central to my concerns.

Stephen Nathanson offers what seems to be the typical dismissive account of the moral legitimacy of avengers and all individual punishers. He tells us that individuals cannot be morally legitimate authorities when it comes to administering punishments for wrongdoing because, "If morality included a general permission for people to avenge murders by death, then morality as an institution would function less well in protecting people's lives and their well-being."[108] That is a pretty strong claim, but what is the argument? One could look long and hard in Nathanson's book for a supporting argument, but the best he seems prepared to provide amounts to no more than consequentialist conjectures. Even avid avengers, he surmises, might be "unhappy" in a society of self-appointed enforcers of morality. It would be dangerous to let people act on their feelings and interests since their judgments cannot be trusted.

I find Nathanson's conjectures far from convincing. At best they seem to be little more than Locke's inconvenience argument in different dress, though Nathanson does tag on an epistemological worry that requires consideration. His concern about a society of "self-appointed avengers" has the look of another version of the old "what if everyone did that" argument. The most straightforward response to arguments of that type is, "But everyone will not!" Most do not have the inner strength to do so, and if moral constraints on vengeance are adopted, chaos and imminent danger to all of us will not occur.

I do not share Nathanson's intuition that if virtuous vengeance were permitted, morality would fail to protect people's lives. After all, the only ones in danger of a disruption in their lives from virtuous avengers are those who commit offenses, and they deserve to lose their sense of well-being. I suspect that Nathanson imagines that avengers will be haphazard in their administration of punishments and that "good people" will be in constant dread of the berserk avenger knocking at their doors. Avengers of that sort would not have moral authority. Better that he should worry about overzealous, legally authorized squads of enforcers breaking down the doors of good people and protruding into every aspect of their lives. There are, of course, genuine difficulties with what I will call the "too many avengers on this case" problem that need to be addressed presently.

The lack of trust of individuals and the inordinate respect afforded to institutions that are operated by individuals, evidenced in Nathanson's conjectures, never cease to amaze. Unless one opposes the administration of punishment altogether, why should we trust the judgment of, for example, a judge and jury in a courtroom rather than that of an individual person of strong moral character? In a related vein, the adage "Better that the guilty go free than that one innocent person be punished" is regularly repeated to justify the extraordinary lengths to which the legal system has been stretched to protect the "rights of the accused." That protection is something, apparently, that individuals set on vengeance are not believed to be likely to do, but it is a matter that can be addressed by moral constraints that limit moral authorization, as I will suggest presently.

It seems to me that the adage, whatever its virtues with respect to the protection of the innocent, is morally skewed. It is not better that the guilty go unpunished, under any circumstances. Only a karmic moral theory could support such nonsense. In a nonkarmic theory there is no hope of a future rectification of the failures of our institutions to enforce morality. If we do not punish wrongdoers, they are not going to be punished and that erodes morality. What sort of society does the adage encourage? At a minimum, a society that is obsessed with an aversion to risking the conviction and punishment of the innocent encourages the guilty to complicate their cases to such an extent that they avoid or indefinitely delay penalties.

The general confidence of the public, whether or not it is justified in actual cases, in the judgment of institutional arrangements regarding the administration of punishment is hardly a sufficient reason to condemn vengeance. Nor is it an argument for the moral legitimacy of that institutional authority, which is not, of course, to say that a convincing argument that concludes that the state's institutions are morally legitimate authorities in matters of punishment cannot be produced or even that it cannot be premised on treating individuals as morally legitimate exactors of punishment. In fact, that argument is the only sort that I think can succeed in achieving such an end.[109]

As noted in Chapter 1, John Locke tackled these matters. He writes: "And that all men may be restrained from invading others' rights, and from doing hurt to one another, and the law of nature be observed, which willeth the peace and preservation of all mankind, the execution of the law of nature is in that state put into every man's hand, whereby everyone has a right to punish transgressors of that law to such a degree as may hinder its violation."[110] His point is that, if individuals in the state of nature did not have the authority to punish those who violate the law of nature by harming others, the law would not be a law at all. It would be, as he says, "in vain." There are no civil institutions in the state of nature, leaving only individuals to bear the authority. Insofar as the state of nature is a state of equality among individuals with respect to rights and liberties, "what any may do in prosecution of that law, everyone must needs have a right to do."[111]

Locke allows two sorts of rights in the state of nature that legitimize the interference with the property and person of another when he or she has committed a crime, a violation of the law of nature. One is the right of taking reparations (the compensation right), and the other is the right to punish. The first is reserved only for the injured party, the victim of the wrong, or his or her designee. The second is a right held by everyone, whether or not enlisted in the punishment effort by the victim. Consequently, "every man in the state of nature has a power to kill a murderer."[112] Locke suggests both a deterrence and a security argument to support the extension of the punishment right to everyone. He fortresses the latter with the claim that a criminal, especially a murderer, "hath by the unjust violence and slaughter he hath committed upon one, declared war against all mankind, and therefore may be destroyed as a lion or tiger, one of those wild savage beasts with whom men can have no society nor security."[113]

Locke further claims that "the great law of nature" is based on this principle, which he offers in the biblical formula: "Whoso sheddeth man's blood, by man shall his blood be shed." Although he does not identify the source of the quotation, it is from Gen. 9:6 and is a part of God's commandments to Noah after the flood. God is withdrawing from the punishment of criminals, in effect, leaving that business to humans. Nonetheless, God makes clear that the divine creation is the foundation of the ordinance and that the offense is against both God and humans. The complete verse is:"Whoso sheddeth man's blood, by man shall his blood be shed: for in the image of God made he man." Locke also notes that Cain accepts the consequences of the universal punishment right when he says to God, "It shall come to pass, that every one that findeth me shall slay me" (Gen. 4:14). But God, wanting a more drawn-out punishment for the first murderer— one that Cain regards as "greater than I can bear"—marks Cain so that he will be recognized as under the penalty of God and will not be killed, which the great law of nature, later authorized or endorsed by God, would require.

As Nozick suggests, the concept of a right to punish is probably too strong in the circumstances Locke describes. He writes that "the liberty to punish would give Locke much of what he needs."[114] All people in the state of nature should be understood to be at liberty to punish the offender, which means that it is morally permissible for anyone to punish the offender. That liberty of all amounts to an "open punishment" arrangement (the term is Nozick's). There is, however, no reason not to constrain that liberty, and strong moral reasons to do so. In fact, its moral status should be dependent on the imposition of certain reasonable restrictions; intuitively, those should include epistemic considerations. Other considerations that respond to one of Murphy's cautions about vengeance—the one based on the biblical passage about casting the first stone, that is, humility considerations—should probably also be placed on the liberty to punish.

A clear lesson from most of the vengeance Westerns is that the hero (avenger) is not a braggart or filled with what Nietzsche cautioned against: the powerful "impulse to punish." Ethan Edwards, in *The Searchers,* assuredly wants to punish Scar for what he and his Comanches did to Martha and the other members of the Edwards family. It is a driving force, propelling him across the Southwest on his search. But it would be unfair to Ethan to describe him as driven by the impulse to punish for its own sake. He has a very special target and very good reasons to pursue it. He clearly intends to make the Comanche chief pay with death for the rape and murder of his beloved Martha, but not just because of his affection for her. What was done to Martha and the others in the Edwards family was wrong and requires a hostile response. Other characters, especially the Jorgensens, provide the consequentialist justifications for punishing the renegade Comanches: the range will never be safe for families and civilization to thrive. For Ethan it is enough that it was Martha and that it was wrong. Nietzsche was warning against those who evidence the "impulse to punish" for its own sake. They are dangerous, the sort of bullies who made the atrocities of the Nazis possible. I am tempted to call them "professional punishers."

Nozick formulates the epistemic restriction on the liberty to punish as "no one has a right to use a relatively unreliable procedure in order to decide whether to punish another."[115] An unreliable procedure is one that does not regularly and dependably yield, beyond a reasonable doubt, knowledge of who committed the offense and who should be punished for it. If an avenger used an unreliable procedure—for example, flipping a coin, "heads he did it, tails he didn't do it"—then he or she should be excluded from those who are morally authorized to punish that criminal even if the coin toss, on that occasion, correctly identified the culprit who deserves punishment. This restriction may at first seem to be inconsistent with the basic Lockean precept that in the state of nature everyone has the right (read, "is at liberty") to punish a wrongdoer, an offender against the law of nature. It looks as if a right that Locke found in nature is being denied to those who use unreliable methods of ascertaining the identities of wrongdoers who merit penalties.

As Nozick suggests, there are two ways to conceive of how restrictions on the liberty to punish work. The first endorses the view that those who do not know the facts with a high degree of certainty—for example, the identity of the offender—do not have the right, are not at liberty, to punish. The second stipulates that the person using an unreliable procedure still has the natural right to punish, but, because he or she does not really know the facts, he or she would be doing something wrong if he or she were to exercise that right and punish the offender. This will not be affected were it to be the case that the punisher actually "gets" the criminal.

I agree with Nozick that the second formulation is the preferable way to merge the Lockean right to punish with epistemic considerations. In effect, the epistemic considerations set moral constraints on the exercise of the right or liberty. It says that you are at liberty to do it, but if you do not operate within the constraints, you lose the moral authority to do it and that means your doing it is morally wrong. The humility constraints would work in the same way, though I think they are of less moral import than the epistemic constraints. Although the ideal virtuous avenger would operate within both constraints, I cannot think of a good reason to withdraw moral authority from an avenger who satisfied the epistemic requirements but evidenced something less than humility during the administration of punishment. Of course, the two types of constraints typically will work hand in glove since, for example, a lack of sufficient humility is likely to result in slipshod methods of discovery.

The epistemic considerations insist that unless a person has ascertained that the target is the culprit and that the culprit deserves punishment, the person morally may not punish. (Or as Nozick puts it, "If someone knows that doing act A would violate Q's rights unless condition C obtained, he may not do A if he has not ascertained that C obtains though being in the best feasible position for ascertaining this."[116]) Has a wrongdoer who is punished by someone who has not sufficiently ascertained that, for example, he or she is the perpetrator been unjustly punished? I don't see how that can be the case from the moral point of view. Morally speaking, the wrongdoer deserves the punishment regardless of what methods were used. Many of our intuitions in such matters have been shaped by wrongly treating our criminal legal system as a prototype of moral culpability and desert. An offender who is trapped by an illegal operation, such as an unauthorized wiretap, is still an offender by moral standards even if the case against him or her will not "stand up" in a court of law. What the offender morally deserves is an appropriate punishment for the offense, legal rights and procedures notwithstanding. At some level we tend to see the difference, which explains why the public's typical response to cases of this sort is to acknowledge the illegality of the entrapment but, nonetheless, to regard the offender as a proper subject of punishment, as morally guilty if not legally convictable.

An avenger who used unreliable procedures has done something morally impermissible by punishing the offender. Where legal impermissibility in punishment cases is wrapped up in issues of the rights of the offender, moral impermissibility focuses on the lack of authority of the punisher. Morally speaking, offenders do not have the right to be punished only by those who used reliable procedures to determine their targets. But punishers lose what moral authority they would have had if they had utilized a reliable procedure for ascertaining the identity and the desert of the offender. They become wrongdoers and deserve punishment themselves.

Nozick does worry that wrongdoers should have rights against the use of unreliable procedures, but he is not very firm in insisting that there ought to be such procedural rights. As I am reluctant to become entangled in "rights-talk" at all, I will dismiss the concern merely by noting that I cannot imagine what an offender would have to complain about in the case of the use of an unreliable procedure by a punisher. The offender deserves the punishment, and punishment is what he or she got. An unreliable procedure might not have exposed him or her as the culprit, and the offender would have gotten off the hook. If captured by an unreliable procedure, and if the punishment fit the crime, it would be absurd for the offender to admit to being the culprit but argue that because it was only by chance that the punisher caught him or her, punishment was morally improper.

I cannot see why a wrongdoer morally deserves the use of epistemically reliable procedures. Innocent people, however, must be protected from the use of unreliable procedures, which is why the moral authority of the punisher, in no small measure if not entirely, hinges on the use of reliable procedures to ascertain the identity of and other relevant facts regarding the wrongdoer. If the innocent have any "moral rights" in all of this, it is the right not to be subjected to punishers who use unreliable procedures. The way to ensure that right is to remove the moral authority from such punishers, thereby rendering them wrongdoers even if they punish offenders.

Murphy raises a somewhat similar concern that fortifies this epistemic constraint on punishment authority. Citing the biblical passage "Vengeance is mine; I will repay, saith the Lord" (Rom. 12:19 and also in Deuteronomy), he notes, as mentioned earlier, that the sense of the passage may be that humans are never in the appropriate epistemological position to have sufficient knowledge. We could restate Murphy's concern into a claim that defeats the moral authority of all punishers, let alone avengers: humans cannot formulate sufficiently reliable procedures to ascertain the facts relevant to cases of punishment, especially capital punishment. What do we lack? Murphy says that we may lack knowledge of what he calls "deep character": "If we are to punish at all . . . we must be able to have reasonably reliable knowledge of such things as wrongful conduct and the mental states that are generally conceptualized as *mens rea*."[117] As a counter to this position, we could cite the fact that God, in Genesis, was of the opinion that humans could have sufficient relevant knowledge even in capital cases.

Without engaging in a complex analysis of philosophical and criminal psychology, I am prepared to stipulate that we can have the requisite knowledge and that we can formulate procedures that, though probably not perfect, can be called sufficiently reliable to impart moral authority on those that use them. We are used to doing this in the legal sphere, and in this case the access issues would not be substantially different. The notion "beyond a reasonable doubt," for example, as it serves in criminal jurisprudence functions as an epistemic restriction in the determination of *mens rea,* and something comparable in the case of the avenger's moral authority should suffice as well. Unless one wants to argue that all criminal justice proceedings are illegitimate because "deep character" is never accessible, then what works in the justice system of the state should serve for the avenger.

Granted that establishing the existence of a *mens rea* is sometimes a difficult matter, we nonetheless do it. In fact, we are generally comfortable leaving it to the decision of a jury of amateurs who may or may not decide on the basis of "expert testimony" that the accused was in the mental state at the time of the crime that is requisite for punishment, even capital punishment. When the members of the jury choose to ignore "expert testimony" or when they do not sufficiently understand it or are confused by competing experts, they take recourse in their own commonsense understanding of such terms as "intention," "malice," "premeditation," and so on. They examine what they have been shown to be the facts of the case to determine if they can identify what they regard as sufficient evidence of the mental states in the actions of the accused that are requisite for criminality. There is no reason why an individual avenger could not carry out the same sort of investigation. In most cases, despite the movie and television versions of trials, it is not a difficult process, and the deep character of the accused is not so deep as to be unfathomable, at least to a degree sufficient to eliminate reasonable doubt in the mind of an ordinary person.

The defenders of the American criminal justice system place a great deal of stock in the "objective stance" of criminal court juries. Members of such juries are not supposed to know the accused or the victim or have any independent knowledge of the crucial facts of the case before them. There are at least two reasons for this restriction, we are typically told. One is to weed out possible prejudice in favor of either the victim or the accused that might have its roots in previous dealings. The other is to try to guarantee that only the facts as presented in the trial are taken into consideration by the jury as it deliberates about guilt and punishment. The voir dire phase of a trial is intended to ensure the desired impartiality.

The idea of an "ignorant jury" was not the original conception in the history of English law. It was first thought that a jury that was well acquainted with the parties would be better equipped to render a proper decision. In any event, I see no reason why the sorts of concerns that the "ignorant jury" is intended to address could not be satisfactorily handled by the epistemic considerations placed on the moral authority of punishers. Even though the avenger may know the victim, indeed is related to the victim by blood or marriage or is or was in an affectionate association with the victim, if the procedures the avenger uses are reliable, there should be no reason for moral concern.

Open punishment or open vengeance undeniably would be fraught with difficulties and Lockean "inconveniences." One relates to the moral status of the victim. I have already maintained that the offender's actions in violation of moral principles or prohibitions, in effect, bestow on everyone else the moral liberty to do things to the transgressor that would otherwise be forbidden by morality. That moral permissibility neither relies nor relates in any special way to the victim of the offense. The victim, assuming that the offense was not murder, is at liberty to punish the offender but has no more authority to do so than a passing stranger. According to Locke, the victim does have sole authority over matters of compensation, reparation, and the appointment powers to designate someone to act on the victim's behalf in that regard. But when it comes to punishment, the victim is just one among many. This distinction is important in another regard: it helps clarify that vengeance is not victim compensation. Punishing the offender, inflicting pain on him or her, does not compensate the victim for the harm he or she suffered. Ethan Edwards certainly does not believe that, by the killing of Scar, Martha is compensated for being raped and murdered. Hannie Caulder does not believe that she is compensated for enduring gang rape by her killing of the members of the gang.

Avengers typically have a special relationship to the victim, but the victim cannot grant or transfer to them the moral authority to punish the target. And, of course, they don't have to because virtuous avengers already have that authority. When Ethan is told that Martha wouldn't want him to waste his and the other men's lives in the search, he rightly regards that as irrelevant prattle from an overcautious woman. The avenger's moral authority derives from the general liberty of everyone to punish wrongdoers as constrained by the requirement to utilize reliable procedures to ascertain the facts.

The primary concern (which may seem to be a very significant one) that an open punishment or vengeance scheme poses is operational. It is the "too many avengers in this case" problem. If the victim or the victim's next of kin does not have the special right to appoint a specific punisher, if every person wanting to punish is at liberty to do so, how is the punishment of the offender to be coordinated and kept within the bounds of desert, satisfying the desert and the fit conditions? Does the first person to get to the target get an exclusive right to decide what the penalty will be and to execute it? Suppose avenger A administers a penalty on target X that avenger B, who arrives late on the scene, believes is inadequate to the wrong that X did. Can B administer a second and greater punishment? Could X arrange with C, a close friend, to apply a gentle punishment to him before either A or B can catch him? Should that end the matter? X might say, "I've already paid the penalty for my wrongdoing. Leave me alone, on pain of acting immorally yourself."

These and similar coordination and operational issues, according to Nozick, cannot be resolved within the confines of an open punishment scheme. Nozick suggests that the solution to what I have called the "too many avengers on this case" problem could only be accomplished by assuming that "all concerned (namely, everyone) jointly act to punish or to empower someone to punish."[118] However, to accomplish that end would require a decision method among all parties, and such an apparatus is excluded by definition from a Lockean state of nature. The conclusion, according to Nozick, that must be reached is that "there seems to be no neat way to understand how the right to punish would operate within a state of nature."[119] We could put the matter slightly differently by saying that the problem is to explain how open vengeance could function without descending into operational chaos and threatening the moral authority of avengers.

One solution, of course, is the one that Locke and Nozick believe to be the only solution—transforming the open punishment scheme into a controlled one, which has happened in a number of different cultures and communities. We have anthropological studies of some of them, notably those in the Balkan region. Avengers need not be conceived of as existing only in a state of nature, that is, in a state without social norms and decision procedures. In societies in which honor norms (what Elster called revenge norms) operate, the victim or the victim's next of kin typically is given an exclusive right and obligation either to carry out the punishment or to appoint an avenger. Communities of that sort have collectively worked out the operational problems by assigning the power to punish to specific people, one of Nozick's solutions. In such communities, everyone is not at liberty to punish offenders, and although the victim "controls" the extent of the revenge, matters of punishment are kept distinct from those of compensation.

Can we solve the operational problems of morally legitimizing avengers by following suit, declaring open vengeance dysfunctional if not immoral, and extending to victims a special right of vengeance, a right that includes the right to appoint an avenger, albeit one who will use reliable procedures to ascertain the relevant facts of the case? Nothing along these lines will ever be allowable in any society with a legal system comparable to the one that has evolved in, for example, the United States. It will be legally prohibited, no matter how morally acceptable it is, because every legal system claims for itself exclusive punishment authority over the population within its jurisdictional boundaries.

That authority in itself, however, is not a reason to think that victim empowerment would not be a morally permissible way to arrange a vengeance-punishment scheme that worked either in tandem with or as an alternative to the public judicial system, although of course lacking legal authority. People where such a scheme operated, albeit illegally, might come to regard the outcomes it produced as more reliable, more morally appropriate, and faster than those of the legal system, and they might utilize it whenever they were confident that the risks of their running afoul of the legal system were lesser than the benefits they derived, if only in the form of a certain moral satisfaction, from engaging the scheme. The Mafia in Italy and the United States, for example, has operated in this fashion.

There is a major moral problem with victim empowerment in the case of punishment, one that does not matter in compensation cases and one that the criminal law is to some extent intended to address. Suppose the victim or the victim's next of kin does not want the offender punished for whatever personal reasons he or she may harbor. If the sole right to punish resides in the victim or in the victim's next of kin or family (however defined), then a wrong will not be met with a hostile response. Morality would therefore lose its central point. In other words, we cannot leave the future of the authority of morality itself to the whims of victims or their next of kin. It is the business of all of us. That is basic to morality.

But this leaves us in a quandary regarding the virtuous avenger. If appointment by the victim or the victim's next of kin (including self-appointment) is not morally justifiable, and if there are severe operational problems with extending the moral liberty to exact punishments on offenders to everyone inclined to give it a go (open vengeance), is there any way to narrow the field, to identify appropriate avengers? Saint Thomas Aquinas provides a way to eliminate some of the contenders.

In defense of the virtue of vengeance, he distinguishes between avengers whose intention in exacting punishment is "centered chiefly upon the evil done to the recipient," who take "delight in evil done to another," and avengers who use reliable methods to ensure against misapplication of punishment and whose primary intention is "the good to be achieved." Aquinas comes to define that good as "safeguarding the right." In effect, the Thomistic account excludes from moral authority sadists who, even though using reliable procedures, are about the business of punishment because of the kicks they get from causing pain in others, the bullies Nietzsche warned against. The moral authority of the avenger, as Aquinas makes clear, must be built on more than procedural grounds. It requires of the avenger the intention to "safeguard the right," which we may fairly take to mean upholding moral principles. The morally legitimate avenger acts not as the victim's surrogate but in the name of morality, not just to do harm to another but as a way of "repelling a wrong."[120]

The Thomistic account, however, does not solve all of the coordination and operational problems that Nozick showed can plague open punishment. It only narrows the field of morally authorized avengers (again reminding us that legal authority is not ever likely to be officially granted even to the most virtuous avengers—a popular film theme and not limited to Westerns). We are still left with the scenario of two or more virtuous avengers hunting down the same offender. Who should then have the preemptory right to decide the extent of punishment and to administer it?

I was, upon first reaching this point, convinced that Nozick was right. This problem is irresolvable short of creating a separate authority, a dominant protective association or a state, to authorize an avenger. Aside from the fact that such an arrangement will never occur in a mature legal system, if I were to take that ploy, the case for the virtuous avenger would be lost or rather surrendered to the legal authority. Then I realized that Nozick was concocting a problem that does not exist for virtuous avengers, those with moral authority, although it may exist for wide-open punishment in a Lockean state of nature. Aquinas's understanding of virtuous vengeance clarifies the matter and erases the multiple-avengers quandary. We have already denied moral authority to those who use unreliable procedures to ascertain the facts, including the identity of the offender, of the case. We have further refused moral authority to those who, despite the use of reliable procedures, have the inflicting of suffering on the offender as their sole or dominant purpose—sadistic avengers—and we have eliminated those avengers who are acting only as surrogates for victims.

The only avengers who will have moral authority will be those whose motives in seeking vengeance are dominated by the intention to safeguard the right, to ensure that wrongful actions are met with appropriate hostile responses, meaning that conditions of desert and fit or proportionality will have been met. Within such a group of avengers, the first to exact the punishment, in one sense, does preempt the field, because all of the other virtuous avengers would have administered a comparable punishment. They can quit the field satisfied that the matter is properly closed. Once appropriate punishment has been administered, the moral liberty of all virtuous avengers to punish that particular offender for that particular offense is terminated. Of course, if the punishment is death, this is rather obvious. Disagreement among virtuous avengers regarding the appropriateness of punishment or its severity should seldom arise as long as all of the conditions have been met.

But suppose there is disagreement. The condition that is most likely to provoke what disagreement does occur is the fit condition. Suppose that the first avenger does not punish the offender to the extent that the second avenger believes is proportional to the offense. What will the second avenger do? He or she will punish the offender as he or she believes fitting. But this is double jeopardy. Actually, it could become triple jeopardy if the first and second avengers are believed to be too lenient by a third avenger, and so on. Such a punishment, it will probably be objected, is not fair. Not fair to whom? To the offender. Why? If the offender deserves a more severe punishment than is meted out by the first avenger, how can he or she object when it is finally received at the hands of a second avenger? This is morality, not the American criminal legal system!

But the second or the third avenger may be wrong in the estimation of fit. They may err on the side of excess. If any avenger goes too far and exceeds moral proportionality (as will be discussed in Chapter 7), he or she will have committed a wrong that should itself be avenged, that requires a hostile response. Overzealous punishers lose moral authority and become targets. That may be a strong incentive for virtuous avengers to err on the side of lenience, avoiding the impression of excessive punishment, even in the name of safeguarding the right.

In any event, the only difficulty remaining for too many virtuous avengers on the same case will be coordination. Is that an intractable problem for two or more avengers? It would be if one or more believe that they have an exclusive right to administer the appropriate punishment. Virtuous avengers, however, will not believe that to be the case, as not even the victim has assignment rights. They are at moral liberty to punish the wrongdoer; they do not have a right to do so. What is important to them is that the wrongful behavior of the target has met with the morally appropriate hostile response. An avenger's personal honor is not damaged when someone else has administered that response. If public honor is a would-be avenger's goal, he or she should take up another line of work.

The Target:
The Desert Condition

EVIL: AN ASSEMBLAGE

Vengeance is . . . virtuous to the extent that its purpose is to check evil.

Saint Thomas Aquinas[1]

A man said to the universe: "Sir, I exist!" "However," replied the universe "The fact has not created in me a sense of obligation."

Stephen Crane[2]

These are some thoughts about evil. They are an assemblage. I do not pretend that they constitute an argument, but I hope they point to certain conclusions that should be relevant to an appreciation of virtuous vengeance.

Thornton Wilder, the author of what is arguably the "Great American Play" (not the "greatest play by an American playwright"), *Our Town,* also wrote a short novel for which he won the Pulitzer Prize for literature in 1927. Set in the mountains of Peru, he called it *The Bridge of San Luis Rey.*[3] The basic plot is that in 1714, a footbridge, "the finest in all Peru," that spanned a deep gorge on the high road between Lima and Cuzco collapses, killing five people: "The bridge seemed to be among the things that last forever; it was unthinkable that it should break."[4] The problematic of the novel is that Brother Juniper, a Franciscan monk from Italy who is in Peru to convert the indigenous Indians, attempts to prove that the breaking of the bridge was not a mere accident but an act of divine intention; those specific people were intended to die on that bridge.

Wilder explains: "Anyone else would have said to himself with secret joy: 'Within ten minutes myself. . . !' But it was another thought that visited Brother Juniper: 'Why did this happen to those five?' If there were any plan in the universe at all, if there were any pattern in a human life, surely it could be discovered mysteriously latent in those lives so suddenly cut off. Either we live by accident and die by accident, or we live by plan and die by plan. And on that instant Brother Juniper made the resolve to inquire into the secret lives of those five persons, that moment falling through the air, and to surprise the reason of their taking off."[5] Brother Juniper is convinced, of course, that nothing happens by accident: "Pains were inserted into their lives for their own good."[6]

Brother Juniper compiles a great book detailing everything he can gather about each of the five victims of the bridge of San Luis Rey. His book ends "with a dignified passage describing why God had settled upon that person and upon that day for His demonstration of wisdom."[7] He concludes that, in the same event, God was both punishing the wicked and calling the good to an early heavenly reward. When the book is discovered by the local judges of the church, however, it and Brother Juniper are declared heretical and both are burned in the town square.

I will resist the temptation to delve into the intricacies of the plot of Wilder's book. It is the general idea that intrigues me and, indeed, that has kept the novel relatively fresh in my mind for the many decades since I first read it. The underlying conception that sustains Brother Juniper's mission is that there must be a moral order to the universe. When people die nonnatural deaths, and this should be especially evident if they die in what appears to be an accidental disaster such as a bridge collapse, the friar is convinced that it must be for reasons of moral desert. After all, such things are typically referred to as "acts of God." Those reasons should become evident when we expose their lives to moral scrutiny, although, as Brother Juniper learns, "the art of biography is more difficult than is generally supposed."[8]

Wilder limited his focus to the five people on the footbridge. It might be wondered how an event like the sinking of the *Titanic,* with its loss of approximately fifteen hundred lives, would fare if one were to apply to it the general principle of the universe, or an intervening divine power, managing desert. Even if one or two hundred passengers on the *Titanic* morally deserved death for their previous wicked actions or if a handful of the saintly on board deserved an early entry into Heaven, the universe's moral balance would be wildly askew if it, or that divine force, were to kill off an additional thirteen hundred people who did not warrant such a penalty or such a reward, just to punish or reward those who do. But, of course, that result is not what Brother Juniper was intent on proving. If fifteen hundred died when the great ship went down, then at that moment those deaths, every one of them, were divinely ordained, each for its own unique reason. Brother Juniper would have joined with Einstein in attesting, "I shall never believe that God plays dice with the world."[9] (And is that belief also what Anatole France meant when he wrote, "Chance is perhaps the pseudonym of God when he did not want to sign"?[10])

Karmic moral theories, of course, must adopt some version of the notion that the universe is morally ordered, that there is some cosmic moral structure to it that ensures that the wicked are, at least ultimately, punished and the good are rewarded. Saint Augustine wrote: "If there were misery before there were sins, then it might be right to say that the order and government of the universe were at fault. Again, if there were sins and no consequent misery, that order is equally dishonored by lack of equity. But since there is happiness for those who do not sin, the universe is perfect; and it is no less perfect because there is misery for sinners."[11] In fact, Augustine argues that the eternal suffering of sinners adds to the happiness of those in heaven when they observe the tortures of the damned that they do not endure because they led morally good lives, a view later endorsed by Jonathan Edwards.

Nonkarmic moral theories can deny that the universe has any moral attributes or that it is governed by a deity that sees to it that moral desert is served to humans in portions consistent with the moral evaluation of their actions. Although I appreciate the mythic allure of karmic theories and of the idea that there must be a cosmic order in the universe, I cannot think of any really convincing argument to support those fantasies. Certainly, a monumental endeavor like that undertaken by Brother Juniper cannot hope to provide any help along this line. His project presupposes what is most in contention, which is the ultimate irony of Brother Juniper's task. Even Kant's valiant attempt to provide an argument for the karmic element of his moral theory is premised on but a hope and desperate speculations intended to take the motivation of morality beyond mere rationality.

As A. S. Pringle-Pattison once noted about Kant's moral theory: "The real postulate or implied presupposition of ethical action is simply that we are not acting in a world which nullifies our efforts, but that morality expresses a fundamental aspect of reality, so that in our doings and strivings we may be said, in a large sense, to have the universe somehow behind us . . . The universe is a divine moral order, not a power hostile or indifferent to the life of ethical endeavor."[12] Encouraging as that may sound, it is better to face matters squarely and then see how things stand morally. And in matters put straightforwardly, as John Kekes succinctly assesses, "There is no cosmic justice."[13] That is not a comforting conception of the way of things, but, like it or not, it seems the most realistic. We do not live in a moral universe. There are no forces external to humans that ensure justice, that the good flourish and the wicked suffer. Wishing, contrary to the old Vera Lynn song, does not make it so.

When I was an undergraduate at a liberal arts college many decades ago, all students were required to take certain basic humanities courses in the history of thought and literature. In one such course, after covering books from the canon that were required readings in all sections, the instructor was allowed to assign a book of his or her choosing. In the section to which I was assigned, the instructor made what at the time I thought was a perverse choice. Other sections were reading J. D. Salinger or Philip Roth. We had to read a little book (for that I was grateful) by mathematician Norbert Wiener entitled *The Human Use of Human Beings*. I can admit now, despite what I would have said about that book (and indeed about the course) in those days, that much of what concerned Wiener indelibly marked my education.

Wiener was interested in, among a number of other things, what conception of the universe a scientist would have to hold in order to make sense of his or her enterprise. He examined the possibility of science in a Manichean world and rejected that conception because, he argued, a scientist cannot believe that the universe has within it a power of evil, a contrary force opposed to order, that could work against the scientist's attempts to understand it. Scientific error must, he was certain, be due to human failings, not to a malicious universe that deceptively entices the scientist only to crush him or her at the crucial point of the experiment.

The obvious historical alternative to the Manichean worldview, and one that recalled an earlier reading in the course, was the Augustinian universe in which evil exists only as the absence of good. Wiener wrote, "The Augustinian devil, which is not a power in itself, but the measure of our own weakness, may require our full resources to uncover, but when we have uncovered it, we have in a certain sense exorcised it, and it will not alter its policy on a matter already decided with the mere intention of confounding us further."[14] He was fond of quoting an aphorism of Einstein's: "God is subtle, but he isn't simply mean." (Einstein's actual quote was "*Der Herr Gott ist raffiniert, aber böshaft ist Er nicht.*" "Mean" is a fair translation but so is "malicious.") The point was that only in a world in which malignant forces were not working against understanding could the scientific enterprise expect to make serious inroads. Evil, Wiener was convinced, must be Augustinian, an absence of good and definitely not a malevolent force working its vicious will in human lives.

Wiener's universe seemed to be fairly benign. It was not a place with vying (more or less equal) forces of Good and Evil locked in eternal combat and in which humans were usually the cannon fodder. He did not share Mani's vision of Good and Evil, warring independent powers, eternally copresent, creating the world in the midst of their fray. And it really wasn't Augustinian either. It was not a morally bad place, but it also was not a place brimming over with moral goodness. It was just a place. If Wiener's universe had any moral characteristic, it was moral indifference.

But moral indifference is not the sort of trait to be preferred in a universe, as Kant observes. It might be more positive, as Kekes notes, from the moral point of view if the universe were neutral rather than indifferent in moral matters.[15] A morally apathetic universe not only couldn't care less about how things turn out but also about how and why they came to turn out the way they do. A morally disinterested universe is an extraordinarily cold place. If the universe were morally neutral, on the other hand, we might think of it as an interested spectator, perhaps one noting on some cosmic scorecard when immorality occurs and when good deeds are performed (the official moral scorer—neutral, but surely not indifferent). Or the idea of a neutral universe might conjure up the image of a referee in the all too human game of Good and Evil. There is, however, no evidence whatever that either the spectator with the scorecard or the referee image comes close to capturing the moral status of the universe.

The universe is not neutral. It is indifferent, as Stephen Crane so elegantly reminds us. There is no cosmic scorekeeping, no moral referee, and certainly no interference in human affairs to correct for moral injustice, to ensure that humans get their just deserts. Events occur, and as the popular bumper stickers proclaim, "Shit happens!" According to Kekes, "Living a reasonable and decent life is neither necessary nor sufficient for overcoming the moral indifference of nature."[16] People everywhere, in all walks of life, do wicked things, and many of them, perhaps most, get away scot-free. Indeed, not infrequently they financially, politically, socially, and emotionally thrive. The universe is unmoved by the evil humans perpetrate on each other and by the good they do as well. Nothing, no one, external to humans pays any heed, cares, or does anything about injustice, wickedness, malevolence, and all of the other immoral and nasty things we do to each other every day.

Wiener took the reference to God in Einstein's aphorism to "describe those forces in nature which include what we have attributed to his very humble servant, the Devil, and Einstein means to say that these forces do not bluff."[17] Well, they don't bluff, but that is because they have no interest in human affairs, in particular, in moral matters. They are not in the game. Good and Evil is our game. The universe is the venue, nothing more.

The moral indifference of the universe is what Brother Juniper will not allow himself to conceive. Its possibility, however, tantalizes his intellect, and as he burns at the stake he wants to assure his executioners that the Devil had not made use of him to "effect a brilliant campaign in Peru." His sole intention in doing the research and writing the book was "for faith." But he is stymied, as he awaits consummation by the flames, by his inability to locate the pattern in his own life—as he had similarly failed in the case of the five victims of the bridge—that deserves his fate at that time, in that place, in that way. Had he been so good as to deserve an early entry through the Gates of Heaven? Had he been so wicked as to warrant such a death? What good is rewarded, what evil punished?

The reason for Brother Juniper's failure is that he is looking for what cannot be found. And it cannot be found not because things are so utterly complex that it requires a divine intelligence to manage matters of desert, but because it is not and never has been there. It is one thing to pretend that there is a moral order to the universe, but quite another to undertake Brother Juniper's mission of placing theology "among the exact sciences." Doing so, as the Franciscan friar may have realized as he "was given to the congenial flames," exposes the fabric of pretense in which karmic moralists have wrapped the universe.

There is no moral order in the universe. The universe is neither Manichean nor Augustinian. It has no moral character at all, or if indifference to morality is a type of moral character, then it has that. Such a conception should not greatly upset Wiener's scientist, who was more concerned with the possible existence of a powerful malicious force in the universe working against his or her efforts at understanding than with a basically good world functioning in accord with moral principles.

Whatever evil there is in the universe is our doing as well as whatever good. In fact, as Protagoras might have agreed, the universe measures nothing, is the measure of nothing, and so is not the measure or the measurer of what is good and what is evil. If evil is to be identified, measured, and punished or good rewarded, then we will have to do the identifying, measuring, punishing, and rewarding. The universe is not especially amenable to moral goodness or to evil. It just is, which I think is a very difficult thing to admit to ourselves despite the fact that the moral indifference of the universe is displayed for us virtually every moment of every day. Like Brother Juniper, many people want to believe. The events of the world, however, do not cooperate with such a "faith." Good people suffer and die while bad people thrive. Tornadoes and earthquakes devastate the good and the wicked indiscriminately. There is nothing we can do about the natural causes of human pain and suffering other than prepare ourselves for them and weather them the best we can, but we can do something about the wicked people among us. We can punish them.

Humans, their characters and their actions, not the universe, are describable in moral terms, as evil or good or as taking no moral description. One might be tempted to wonder, as a number of writers have, if humans, the species, have an inherent moral character, if they are "by nature" good or "by nature" evil. Volumes cluttering shelf after shelf in libraries have been written on that subject. Theologians and moralists have defended various conceptions of the basic goodness of humans. Evil for them is a corruption of human nature, and it is variously attributed to social forces, mental diseases, genetic elements, cultural factors, and so on, some of which are brilliantly mocked in the song "Gee, Officer Krupke" in the musical *West Side Story*. Wicked behavior, we are told, is the result of deprivations, bad social conditions, innate drives, mental diseases, and unavoidable ignorance.

On the other side are those who find the defects of human society to be the product of deep moral faults in human nature. This view is not, as I understand it, Hobbes's theme, although the idea of the "Heart of Darkness" is not infrequently confused with the Hobbesian story of the progress from the state of nature to the civil state. The two may well share certain descriptions of human behavior when unconstrained by a social power. It would be, however, incorrect on Hobbes's view to use moral language to describe humans who exist in the state of nature, a state that, for him, is premoral. Hobbes describes the state of nature as one in which "the notions of Right and Wrong, Justice and Injustice have no place."[18] Humans will act in the manner he describes in the state of nature because they are self-interested and rational, not because they are inherently evil.

Machiavelli seems to have held that human nature is evil or at least prone to evil rather than goodness. By that he means that we are regularly driven to violence and destruction by folly, depravity, rage, resentment, jealousy, and avarice. He writes, "Anyone who wants to act the part of a good man in all circumstances will bring about his own ruin, for those he has to deal with will not all be good."[19] Maoists transformed Hobbesian and/or Smithian self-interest into evil. They,

Baogang He writes, "believed that self-interest is the source of evil and that moral destruction lies deep in the individual self as a sort of 'original weakness.'"[20]

The Conradian theme of the "Heart of Darkness" is played out in a number of fictional plots, vividly in William Golding's *Lord of the Flies:* "'You are a silly little boy,' said the Lord of the Flies, 'just an ignorant, silly little boy. . . . Fancy thinking the Beast was something you could hunt and kill! . . . You knew, didn't you? I'm part of you? Close, close, close! I'm the reason why it's no go? Why things are what they are?' . . . Simon found he was looking into a vast mouth. There was blackness within, a blackness that spread. Simon was inside the mouth."[21] As E. L. Epstein notes,[22] the vast black mouth is the symbol of the ravenous internal evil of humans, a symbol Conrad used in *Heart of Darkness*.[23] "Lord of the Flies" is a translation of Beezlebub, a name for the devil, and in the "Heart of Darkness" conception the devil not only is in each of us, but it also is humanity at its most basic. Conrad writes: "I understand better the meaning of his stare, that could not see the flame of the candle, but was wide enough to penetrate all the hearts that beat in darkness. He had summed up—he had judged. 'The horror!' . . . It was an affirmation, a moral victory paid for by innumerable defeats, by abominable terrors, by abominable satisfactions."[24]

Laurence Thomas rejects the innate evil conception of humans but admits that humans are responsible for a great deal of evil. He offers an alternative conception of human nature that he calls the "fragility-goodness conception,"[25] an account that owes much of its content to Martha Nussbaum's analysis of Greek tragedy and philosophy in her book, *The Fragility of Goodness*.[26] Thomas claims that humans are not generally disposed either to self-sacrifice on behalf of others or to the harm of others. However, "they are naturally moved by the weal and woe of others, and they want to eliminate suffering."[27] But if that is the case, why is there so much evil? Why are so many people harmed by the actions of their fellows? Thomas maintains that the reason is that human beings are "especially fragile." By that he means we can easily be prevented or diverted from realizing our natural propensities to be moved by the plight of others and not to harm them—we are both good and fragile. If we acted as we should be inclined to act, for example, if the suffering of others were repulsive to us, we would demonstrate our basic goodness. Unfortunately, we are also (and though he does not directly say so, he clearly implies) naturally vulnerable to act in ways that block our own better instincts. We are prone for various reasons, most of which are buried in the complex and conflicted character of humans qua humans, to fail, for example, to be repulsed by the suffering of others. Indeed, under certain circumstances we may even enjoy or revel in it. We do or are complicitous in evil even though we are not innately evil.

But, we should wonder, what inclines us to this fragility, this vulnerability to evil, and what form does it take? With respect to forms, I suspect that Thomas would cite such standard motivations as self-interest, fear, cowardice, and the like. To the question of why we are prone in the manner we are to often resist our deep propensities and act contrary to them, Thomas seems only to say that we are just that way—we are fragile and that is what fragile entities sometimes do: break.

Thomas is right in arguing that his model is somewhat superior to the innate evil model, at least on the grounds that the latter has considerably more difficulty explaining, or explaining away, human goodness, altruism, and the like. After all, we sometimes do demonstrate genuine concern for others and their plights. Some even cross the road and provide succor. For the fragility-goodness model, that is possible, although "difficult to realize."[28] For the innate evil model, no nonconvoluted explanation is forthcoming. A considerable number of adjustments by way of external checks to repress the desire to do evil, typically in the form of social norms or legal restrictions coupled with the fear of punishment or some sort of unwanted social reaction, are usually needed to make the explanation plausible.

I don't think we are by nature evil or, for that matter, good. The endless arguments about the moral nature of human beings are, I think, pointless. I do think we are fragile, if that means we are prone to be weak of will and facilely distracted from doing things that are good. But hardly all evil is the product of weak wills. Admitting that we are vulnerable to the attractions or temptations of wickedness in no way entails that we are also naturally good. A fragility-evil model of human nature that depicts us as innately both evil and fragile might have as much explanatory power as the fragility-goodness model. Our vulnerability to the temptation to occasionally do a good deed could explain why we fail on such occasions to act as villainously as our basic natures would have us.

Rather than adopt and then be embarrassed by the application of one of these models, I suggest that the most we should say is that humans are capable of behaving in ways that we can aptly describe as good and in ways that we should call evil. In neither case does their doing so reflect an innate nature. I am not especially interested in good behavior, except to say that if it is its own reward, as some believe, that will only be because the good person appreciates and enjoys a sense of moral accomplishment. There is nothing especially worrisome about that, but it is a meager reward and hardly one that, at least in my experience, provides a sustaining motivation. If I were interested in the virtues of rewards rather than in those of vengeance, I probably would investigate the need for far more positive reinforcement mechanisms for morally approved behavior. The rewards of virtue, of doing the right thing, may be as pressing as the punishments for wickedness, but it is the latter that has my attention.

I agree with Yan Jiaqi that the sense in which evil is universal is that sense in which all of us have the potential to do evil deeds.[29] Kant, in *Religion Within the Limits of Reason Alone,* talks of the "natural propensity in man to evil,"[30] and he describes that propensity as the basis of our capacity to do evil. Kant sees the propensity to do evil as arising in three different ways or in three different degrees. These are the weakness of the human heart, the impurity of the human heart, and the corruption of the human heart. But Kant also talks about the "seed of goodness implanted in our species,"[31] and that sounds rather like Thomas's fragility-goodness model. Recognizing the potential, even the natural propensity, in oneself to do evil is, as I have elsewhere maintained, crucial to moral maturity.[32] Importantly, however, this recognition is not a consciousness of some universal innate moral nature in humans, even one we often fail, for a variety of reasons, to actualize. It is the awareness, at once both frightening and fascinating, repulsive and seductive, appalling and alluring, horrible and provocative, of one's own capacities to injure, to hurt, to harm, to offend, to victimize. No human nature model is necessary to account for that, and none is wanted.

Human or moral evil, as distinct from what is usually called natural evil—such things as tornadoes and hurricanes, a distinction drawn by Kant in *Religion Within the Limits of Reason Alone*[33]—is behavior that jeopardizes someone's aspirations to live a good life by willfully inflicting undeserved harm on him or her. Human evil (hereafter just evil) can involve such things as the intentional causing of physical and emotional pain and suffering, the unwarranted injuring of people, making them feel helpless, separating them from what they most care about and for, violating their trust, and the like. Evil can be banal, monumental, or casual meanness and caused by big or little imperfections or corruptions of character or by sheer motivated wickedness. Nel Noddings captures a good deal of what I mean by evil when she writes: "The most basic form of evil is pain. Physical pain, when it does not promise a better end state (right here on earth), is an evil we should avoid and relieve. Separation is evil because of the deep psychic pain it causes . . . Helplessness too is associated with psychic pain."[34] Crucially, evil leaves victims who did not deserve the pain, suffering, or deaths they endured at the hands of their victimizers. Evil, we should never forget, regardless of how complex the analyses of the perpetrator's mental states become, is in the first instance about victims. Victimization is the identifying characteristic of human evil.

Mary Midgley has Aristotle characterizing evil people as "vicious people who do wrong contentedly and with conviction."[35] Rawls defines an evil person as a lover of injustice who "delights in the impotence and humiliation of those subject to him and he relishes being recognized by them as the willful author of their degradation."[36] Evil people surely do wrong contentedly and with conviction, and typically relish their roles in the degradation or the destruction of others. Of course, evildoers, as earlier discussed (Chapter 1), might commit their untoward deeds either believing that what they are doing is the right thing to do *or* believing or knowing that it is the wrong thing to do. In either case, they do so contentedly and with conviction.

In the first case (where the evildoer believes he or she is doing the right thing), the usual interpretation is that the evil is perverse; in the second, that it is preferential. (These distinctions, it will be recalled, are owed to Milo and were discussed in Chapter 1.)[37] Perverse evil is the only sort that the ancient Greeks who were committed to the Socratic dictum seemed to think was possible. Kant also rejects the possibility that humans could be preferentially evil. The importance of the distinction for many moral theorists is that perverse evil is supposed to be less wicked than preferential evil because the perversely evil person believes he or she is doing right. He or she then may be quite conscientious, which is something of a virtue or is often thought of as one, in carrying out what he or she believes to be his or her moral duty. The preferentially evil person, well aware that what he or she is doing is morally wrong, has no moral refuge. Also, Kant maintains that a person with an evil heart, a perversely evil person, may have a "will which in general is good,"[38] and that it is only because of human frailty that the "seed of goodness" does not develop "as it otherwise would." The fragility-goodness model again bubbles up to the surface.

As a matter of clarification and a point not made in the earlier discussion, I think there are two types of preferential evil. The first is the type in which the outcome is the intended unwarranted harm of another. The second is when a person believes, *wrongly,* that what he or she is doing is wrong and so acts accordingly without compunction or scruple. In such a case, the person actually does not do wrong, although believes that he or she is doing wrong and prefers doing that to what he or she believes to be right. Doing the right thing or a good thing in such cases is merely accidental. It might be wondered how someone can wrongly believe something is wrong and prefer to do it. One clear way that such a choice is possible is if the person has perverse moral principles and the desire to do evil. Another is because of ignorance of one or the other of the various sorts catalogued by Aristotle. In either event, the evil is preferred. For both types of preferential evil the identifying feature is that the perpetrator prefers doing what is evil or morally wrong to what he or she believes or knows to be morally right.

Throughout the history of moral philosophy there has been a predilection, a testament to the influence of Plato's Socrates, to favor treating human evil on the perverse rather than the preferential model. Kant, for example, writes, "We are not, then, to call the depravity of human nature *wickedness* taking the word in its strict sense as a disposition (the subjective *principle* of the maxims) to adopt evil *as evil* into our maxim as our incentives (for that is diabolical); we should rather term it the *perversity* of the heart, which then, because of what follows from it, is also called an *evil heart.*"[39] Midgley notes that philosophers typically shrink from identifying the most egregious evildoers as preferentially wicked. However, rather than adopting some version of the "madness" hypothesis, they resort to crediting them with having adopted some sort of idiosyncratic, though consistent and well-conceived, alternative moral theory that requires them to perform what we regard as wicked deeds.[40] That approach, of course, makes the evil perverse. Hannah Arendt, however, scotched any such notion with regard to the century's most notorious gang of preferential evildoers, the Nazis. She noted that at the Nuremberg trials, "the defendants accused and betrayed each other and . . . not a single one of them had the guts to defend the Nazi ideology."[41]

I maintained in Chapter 1 that the notion of perverse wickedness, when examined carefully as Milo does, is extraordinarily difficult, if not impossible, to distinguish from preferential wickedness. I am satisfied that most evil people are preferentially, not perversely, wicked. The understanding of evil, however, must not rest on that ground, for it is woefully inadequate to support the requirement of a hostile response.

The focus of accounts of preferential and perverse evil is solely on the mental states of the evildoer. Moral philosophers, dating back at least to Aristotle, seem to be inordinately fascinated with why people do wicked things, and they seem to think that the mental states of the evildoer are the most crucial factor in determining appropriate punishments. Roger Burggraeve's explication of Levinas's analysis of violent evil is a case in point and one that is all the more vivid because of Levinas's well-known concern for "the other." Burggraeve describes Levinas's conception of murder as "a well-determined intentionality . . . to destroy the other totally. . . . Murder . . . renounces absolutely all 'comprehension' of the other, for one no longer wishes to include the other in the 'same,' that is in one's own project of existing."[42]

The evil in the act, on such an account, resides in the mental states of the evildoer. Preferences, wishes, and intentions are identified as the important determinates; the victim is an afterthought. I do not want to suggest that the *mens rea* of the evildoer is not of some importance in the assessment of responsibility and the assignment of punishments. But the mental states of the evildoer are but a piece of the evil puzzle and, though important, are not, I think, as significant a piece as the amount of space devoted to them in the literature might lead us to believe. Typically left out of the equation is the element in harm-causing that actually makes it evil: that there is a victim(s), a person or persons who should be avenged.

If victims were of as little importance as the bulk of the literature suggests, there would be no moral difference with respect to evil between killing someone and intending, or even trying, to kill that person or, better still, between killing a real human being and experiencing the same mental states as in the case of killing a real human but "killing" a virtual entity. With the steady, indeed spectacular, development of virtual technologies, it is imaginable that someone in a virtual setting, equipped with a deadly weapon, could assault and destroy a "virtual human enemy." That person, it seems reasonable to surmise—especially if he or she did not know that his or her enemy was only virtual, a product of technology—may have mental states identical, for all intents and purposes, to those he or she would have had if the virtual enemy were a real person.

No one, of course, would actually be killed. There would be no victim, and the agent would surely not have committed an evil deed. We might be willing to admit that such behavior in a virtual environment indicates a bad or a dangerous character, someone to guard against, but there surely is a great deal of difference between suspecting a person of having bad character traits and identifying him or her as an evildoer. Despite the presence of the mental states, the person has yet to do evil. There are no victims. Intuitively, let alone legally, there is a rather large difference between those who actually kill and those who intend but fail to do so, between those who actually do the deed and those who contemplate doing it, between those who kill real people and those who kill virtual people, even if there is no significant difference in the mental states of the agents.

The rather expansive literature on what is called "moral luck" provides further testimony to the failure to "count the victim." That literature is replete with defenses of the view that one can be held responsible only for what one had within one's control. The favorite example of what Margaret Walker calls the "control condition" theorists[43] is that of two equally negligent drivers, one of whom is lucky enough not to hit and kill a pedestrian, while the other is unlucky and does kill. The standard response is that they both are blameworthy, and the fact that one's negligent driving resulted in a death is a mere matter of luck. The idea, or as Walker puts it, the "troubling assumption," is "that actually causing the harm one risks merits no more blame than merely risking the harm without causing it."[44]

Judith Jarvis Thomson[45] constructs a case in which three different drivers each put their cars in reverse. Two of them do so negligently, not looking where they are going. The third backs out with care. The first and the third each hit and kill a small child. The child, in the third case, could not have been seen because she crept out from a pile of leaves. But the child in the first case could have been seen and the death prevented if the driver had not negligently backed out. In the second case, the negligent driver does not hit or kill a child.

In the comparison between the first and third cases, Thomson says that we will discredit, and blame the driver only in the first case. This view, I suppose, fairly captures our intuitions, but it leaves the bad taste that killing the child "says nothing morally interesting about" the driver in the third case. (I think it does say something morally interesting about the driver with respect to the driver's future behavior, but that is a different story.)[46] We are likely to agree that the driver took the usual and proper precautions and could not have prevented the death. In the first case, however, we will blame the driver because nonnegligent driving would not have resulted in the death. An attentive driver, looking back while reversing, would have seen the child in plenty of time to stop. What then of the comparison between the first driver and the second? The second driver was lucky that no child darted behind the car. Is there a moral difference between the two drivers when the matter seems to turn solely on luck, the first driver's bad luck or the second's good luck?

If the luck factor is ruled out of moral consideration, then, as Thomson maintains, we have a principle of responsibility that reads as follows: "Whatever we do, our doing of it is no more to our discredit than are those purely mental acts by which we do it."[47] This principle points Thomson to the conclusion that whatever moral blame might be appropriate for the first driver would also be appropriate for the second. Whatever moral indignation would be justifiable in the one case would be equally justifiable in the other. It is a principle of this sort, one that places the entire weight of moral blame on the mental states of the agent, that seriously shortchanges the victim of wrongdoing. The victim, in fact, becomes morally immaterial, a victim twice over, first of the harm-causing agent and then of what my colleague Joanne Waugh calls the "tyranny of deontology." I leave the matter of control for discussion in the subsequent section.

In 1974 Jonathan Bennett published a short paper that has provoked considerable discussion and has been widely anthologized.[48] Bennett's analysis of the tortures of Huck Finn as he battles his conscience about whether he should return Jim, the runaway slave, to his "owner" is, I think, cogent. Huck's sympathies for Jim, his affection for him, triumph over the dictates of the morality he was taught. The story goes that, after writing a letter to the runaway slave's owner, Huck tells us that he laid the letter down and started to think of how good it was that he had avoided going to Hell for helping a runaway slave to escape. Then he recalls the raft trip down the river—the good times he had had with Jim and how Jim had cared for him—and he is overcome with sympathy for Jim. He picks up the recently written letter: "I was a trembling, because I'd got to decide, forever, betwixt two things, and I knowed it. I studied a minute, sort of holding my breath, and then says to myself: 'All right, then, I'll go to hell'—and tore it up. It was awful thoughts and awful words, but they was said. And I let them stay said; and never thought no more about reforming . . . as long as I was in, and in for good, I might as well go the whole hog."[49] And we all applaud.

But Bennett goes on to argue, based on the same principle that led us to praise Huck, that Heinrich Himmler is a morally better person than Jonathan Edwards is. Himmler directed the SS and orchestrated many of the atrocities of the Third Reich. He certainly can be credited, as he credits himself, with a considerable amount of the responsibility for the Holocaust. Yet, in some of his speeches, he expressed the difficulty he experienced in restraining his sympathies, as a "decent fellow" would, for the plight of those being exterminated by his orders. He was well aware of the great pain and suffering he was causing, and he believed it necessary for him to sympathize with his victims to—and only to—the extent that he could avoid becoming a "heartless ruffian." Edwards, at least in his sermons, shows absolutely no sympathy, no love or pity, for the damned souls he describes as roasting in Hell. Indeed, he claims that the saved, in whose company he numbers himself, when seeing the "calamities of others" in Hell, will have their sense of enjoyment and blessedness in heaven heightened. (An idea, as noted above, suggested by Saint Augustine.)

Edwards, unlike Himmler, never killed anyone, never ordered anyone killed, but Bennett's account paints him as the more evil of the two. Why? The answer must be that Bennett, like so many other philosophers, thinks that all that really matters in morality with respect to evil is the mental states of the evildoer. Himmler, because he had sympathy for his victims' plight, must be no worse than perversely evil. He was caught up in a perverse morality that dictated his duty to exterminate millions of people (Bennett even makes him begin to sound like a victim himself). Edwards, despite having no victims, is to be despised for his lack of expression of pity for the sinners cast into eternal damnation by God. There is something very wrong here! Victims matter. They matter more than the mental states of victimizers.

Some years ago I taught an undergraduate course in which the primary text was Lewis Carroll's *Alice* books. As a text we used an annotated version called *The Philosopher's Alice.*[50] I recall that one of the most perplexing parts of the text both for me and the students, one that kept our attention for a number of class meetings, was the poem "The Walrus and the Carpenter" that Tweedledee recites in *Through the Looking Glass.* Some years after that course I happened to read a paper by Philip Hallie, published in the *Hastings Center Report,*[51] that not only focused on the puzzling sections of Carroll's poem but also directly criticized the part of Bennett's paper that struck me as utterly counterintuitive. I found that Hallie had arrived, through a somewhat different and less circuitous path, at the conclusions the students and I had reached: that Lewis Carroll had gotten matters right, and that Bennett and most of the recent analysts of evil had missed a major element, the most significant element.

The story of the Walrus and the Carpenter is a simple one. The two convince a number of oysters to take a walk with them on the beach. They rest on a rock and proceed to eat the oysters despite the pitiful protests of the meal. "'Now, if you're ready, Oysters dear, We can begin to feed.' 'But not on us!' the Oysters cried, Turning a little blue. 'After such kindness, that would be A dismal thing to do!'"[52] The Walrus starts to cry and expresses his sympathy for the plight of the oysters. "I weep for you," the Walrus said: "I deeply sympathize." Then with tears pouring down his cheeks, and holding a handkerchief before his eyes, he gobbles up the largest oysters of the bunch. The Carpenter shows no sympathy or pity for the meal and continues to eat. Soon all of the oysters have been devoured. (One wonders whether Himmler had read Carroll!)

Alice and Tweedledum and Tweedledee discuss the poem. Alice, as Bennett would as well, offers that the Walrus is the better of the two beachside diners because "he was a little sorry for the poor oysters." She is reminded that, nonetheless, he ate more of the oysters than the Carpenter did, and he probably held the handkerchief in front of his face to shield his gluttony from the Carpenter. Alice then shifts her judgment: she likes the Carpenter best because he didn't eat as many as the Walrus, although it is pointed out that he ate as many as he could snatch. Alice, as Hallie characterizes it, then "gives voice to a wisdom that is as sound as it is obvious." She declares that they are both no good. Both are evil. What really matters morally is the empty oyster shells. Victims count when one is assessing evil. Indeed, they should count more than the mental gyrations of the perpetrator. Carroll seems to have wanted to make the same point, and nailing it down unambiguously he added additional lines to the poem for the Savile Clark opera *Alice.* They read: "They'd finished all the oysters; And they laid them down to sleep—And of their craft and cruelty The punishment to reap."[53]

Victims count. What a person does to others matters more than why he or she does it. Kewal Krishna Anand, in a book on the concept of karma,[54] summarizes what I take to be the correct position. He writes: "In a nutshell, the value of an action is calculated with reference to the motive of it. But out of the motive and the actual happening if asked which one is to be given more weight, the answer is explicit because what one does after having willed is more important than the mere willing. To kill an enemy is more efficacious and more serious than having a wish to kill him. Hence more is the importance of physical and spoken acts and more is the significance of speech and gesture than that of the mental acts."[55]

Without victims there is no evil. Evil must be punished. Victims must be avenged. Those are basic tenets of morality.

Jean Hampton[56] shifts at least some of the focus in evildoing away from the mental states of the perpetrator and onto the victims. She defines injury as not giving people treatment appropriate to their value or the treatment they deserve. That rather objective aspect of injury typically has a subjective cousin: The victim knows that he or she is being treated in a way he or she does not deserve to be treated. That knowledge usually will produce, minimally, the feeling of being insulted or dishonored or demerited or devalued. The victim is twice victimized, and that situation requires rectification.

I have maintained throughout that the idea that evil, wrongdoing, requires a hostile response is the fundamental principle of morality. People who do evil—simply, evil people—from the moral point of view should be targeted for penalties that are painful to them. Good people must not be subjected to the willful infliction of pain and suffering. But, it may be wondered, why may evil people, from the moral point of view, be treated differently than good people? Why can those who do evil deeds be morally legitimate targets of the infliction of pain and suffering (hostile responses), when inflicting the same sort of things on others is wrong, morally impermissible? The commonsense answer, of course, is that they deserve it, while good people do not. In *Responsibility Matters* (chapter 2), I argue that such a retaliatory rule, or rule of punishment-desert, is fundamental to any morality because it is the glue that holds the moral community together. Also, both karmic and nonkarmic moralists agree that evil people do not deserve the same treatment as good people. But what, morally if not metaphysically, changes in people when they do evil so that we are not prohibited from inflicting pain on them, that doing so is not itself evil?

I want to suggest that the notion of moral merit underlies our sense of a moral change in people, and that it permits hostile responses, the infliction of suffering on evildoers. Simply, evil people merit pain and suffering. Hobbes noted the conceptual link between merit and desert with respect to contracts: "He that performeth first in the case of a Contract, is said to MERIT that which he is to receive by the performance of the other; and he hath it as Due."[57] He generalized the link so that "to merit" is synonymous with "to have it as Due." Hobbes is, I think, correct in associating, indeed identifying, merit with desert. If one merits something one deserves it. If one deserves something, that is what one merits. This seems rather clear in the case of contracts and other sorts of human activities, but does it also hold true for moral merit? Is moral merit the same thing as moral worth?

Kant wrote, "Were no other incentive working in opposition . . . [humans] would be morally good."[58] This innate goodness is, for Kant, the ground of the absolute moral worth of humans as ends in themselves. He captures this notion in the second formulation of his categorical imperative: "Act so that you treat humanity, whether in your own person or in that of another, always as an end and never as a means only."[59] Humans are to be thought of as of equal and absolute moral worth, and this worth egalitarianism is meant to do a rather significant amount of work in moral theories like Kant's. Kekes identifies the practical implication of the notion: "The vicious and the kind, the cruel and the benevolent, and the just and the unjust deserve equal rights to other people's support of their freedom and welfare. Justice, according to the egalitarians, requires that we should ignore the use to which people have and are likely in the future to put their freedom and welfare."[60] Simply, all humans, by virtue of being humans, are endowed with dignity (moral worth) and ought to be treated with respect.

The distinctive intuition of worth egalitarianism is that worth is utterly independent of merit. Regardless of how people have actually behaved toward their fellows or anything else that is morally considerable (such as, perhaps, the environment), there are things that are not to (morally may not) be done to them. To do certain things to them would constitute offenses against their moral worth, their dignity, and also would constitute violations of their moral rights, in effect, disrespecting them or treating them only as means.

The notion that Rudolf Otto praised as "the mightiest and most significant of all ideas that were ever pronounced in the domain of ethical enquiry"[61]—that we are all of equal and inalienable moral worth—is very appealing. It provides a certain amount of assurance that we have value despite what we do or do not do in or with our lives. It serves to set moral boundaries on what others may do to us and we to them, and so it constrains our interactions in what are surely important ways if we are to get along productively with each other. It is too bad that it is fundamentally flawed and actually offends very basic and common intuitions that rest firmly on everyday experience.

Worth connects to value in the way that merit connects to desert, and it may seem that when considering certain kinds of objects, no necessary connection exists between value and desert. The ring is worth so many dollars; its value is so many dollars. The ring, however, may not merit, at least in some sense by some evaluative standards, that number of dollars. Still, it merits the regard with which its owner holds it. Given certain circumstances (its previous ownership, for example), it deserves to be priced at so many dollars. It deserves that value.

The independence of worth and merit, value and desert, very quickly becomes a bit murky. In the case of people, things crumble at least as quickly. A murderer is caught and confesses, and we deprive him or her of his or her freedom and welfare. We incarcerate or even kill him or her in the name of justice. By doing so, are we not failing to respect this person's worth and value while giving him or her what he or she deserves? The typical answer will be that there is a prima facie assumption of moral worth, but if people do such terrible things as commit murder, they can and must be punished, even by deprivation of their freedom and welfare. Such an argument appeals to the merit of the culprit as a condition of the continuation of being treated as having moral worth. Merit and worth thus are not independent. In fact, worth depends on merit, value on desert.

Worth egalitarians will not, of course, like such a characterization, and so, as Kekes has noted, they will offer another tack. They are likely to maintain something akin to the "innocent until proven guilty" doctrine. That is, they are likely to endorse the position that humans are presumed to have equal moral merit as well as equal moral worth. When they commit evil acts, they may reduce their moral merit but not their moral worth. It seems reasonable to grant that people have equal moral merit and worth when they are born. I am not certain what that really means, but I am certain that equality of merit doesn't last very long. Merit is entirely a product of what we do, who we are, who we become, and therefore what we are due.

Kekes provides a valuable analysis of the three "unarticulated beliefs" of worth egalitarianism. I will but briefly endorse his account rather than reiterate it; it does not require augmentation. The three beliefs are that there are two distinct aspects of being a person: the self and the self's possession of various qualities; that worth attaches to universal qualities of humanity, but merit attaches to individual characters that themselves depend on the possession of qualities that people do not deserve; and that the worth of individuals is a distributive consequence of the commitment to the general welfare of humanity. The third belief is, as Kekes notes, derivative of the idea that human nature is, at heart, good. As I have already denied that notion, there is hardly any reason to further consider the third belief.

The first belief of worth egalitarianism is the view that the self is an enduring and continuous entity that is the subject that possesses various qualities. The qualities are changeable and can be developed, acquired, lost, and so on. People are, on this view, necessarily selves, but the qualities they exhibit are contingent. Rawls writes that "the self is prior to the ends which are affirmed by it."[62] You cannot be other than you, but you could be a kinder person, a more caring individual, not so mean to people and cruel to animals. As Kekes notes, the senses of necessity and contingency that are used by worth egalitarians to express their position are rather fluid or imprecise. What is important for them, however, is that moral worth attaches to selves and moral merit to qualities. Insofar as the self is independent of its properties, worth is, or so they maintain, independent of merit.

Basic human rights (whatever they are supposed to be) are bestowed on us independent of the way we behave and the traits of character we exhibit. Apparently, that bestowal is a necessary condition for the development of the qualities that can accrue moral merit to us. In effect, those rights protect the necessary conditions for our choosing what we will do with ourselves. Choice is the key to moral merit, and the basic conditions of choice are assured in worth, which, for all practical purposes, is Rawls's famous stratagem in *A Theory of Justice*. In his conception of justice those conditions of choice, at least with respect to institutions, are supposed to emerge from the ersatz bargaining game of the Original Position in which the persons involved know only their selves as logical subjects but are kept in ignorance of their qualities. The selection of the principles of justice, however, cannot then be the process that might appear to cursory readers of Rawls's famous book. It cannot be a bargaining process; the Original Position is ultimately reducible to the "standpoint of one person selected at random."[63] Michael Sandel refers to Rawls's persons in the Original Position as "radically disembodied subjects."[64] One logical subject is as good as any other when no subjects have any qualities.

What is the problem with worth egalitarianism and the independence of worth and merit? Kekes persuasively argues that the position commits a serious logical error. What the reductionism of Rawls and the other worth egalitarians does is to strip the self of the qualities that mark it as human, making it impossible to maintain that the self that has worth is a human self. Kekes writes: "If the self were regarded merely as the logical subject of which qualities were predicated, then there could be no reason for thinking that the self was a human self. Animals, plants, and material objects also possess logical subjects in this pure sense. But if we go beyond pure logical subjects, so that the kind of logical subjects human beings have could be distinguished from other kinds of logical subjects, then the distinction must be made in terms of some quality or another. In that case, however, the identification of a logical subject as a human self necessarily involves reference to some quality."[65]

The point of this is that if the self is prior to its qualities, moral worth as a human cannot be attributed to it on the sole basis of its being a logical subject. It may not be a human self. But if the logical subject must be a human self to have moral worth, some quality must occur in it that distinguishes it as human, and that would mean that a human self is not prior to its qualities, or at least one of its qualities. Whatever that quality(ies) is(are), it(they) will undoubtedly be related in some basic way to how the human self attains moral merit. The standard candidate for many of the worth egalitarians is the capacity for choice. In any event, the ground for both the ascription of moral worth and merit to a human self is contingent on the logical subject's possession of that quality(ies). If the logical subject possesses any qualities, on the worth egalitarian position, it does so contingently, which would mean, however, that the ascription of both merit and worth are contingent. We should conclude that the human self and its qualities should not be treated as separable for moral purposes, even from the worth egalitarians' point of view.

If worth must be associated with a quality(ies) of humans rather than the qual-ity-less logical subject (the naked self), then worth egalitarians tend to adopt a second belief: that worth attaches to universal qualities of humans, while merit attaches to the qualities displayed individually by people. As noted earlier, a favorite candidate for a universal quality of humans to which worth can be anchored is the capacity for choice. They argue that the mere capacity to choose confers worth on those who have it, and that worth is protected by basic human rights that sustain the conditions in which choice can be exercised. Moral worth, for the choice-worth egalitarian, is not lost even by those who do evil willingly. Our equal worth is based in our natural capacity to choose. We may come to have unequal moral merit, depending on the choices we actually make. Of course, if the evil one does was unchosen, one's having done it should have no impact on either one's moral worth or moral merit.

In defense of a universal quality foundation for moral worth, worth egalitarians typically make the point that moral merit depends in large measure on charac-ter, and that character, at least good character, is dependent, perhaps heavily so, on circumstances and conditions that typically are not within a person's control. As Kekes notes: "Morally good character requires some intelligence, the capacity for self-control, a mental equilibrium that makes it possible to pay attention to others, the absence of brutalizing influences, and not being victimized by extreme poverty, discrimination, or exploitation. People with morally good character must have inherited some good genes, and they had to be raised in at least a minimally hospitable setting."[66] In fairness, such endowments should not be, the argument goes, the bases on which moral worth is laid. They are contingent upon the whims of fortune, and the unfortunate have as much moral worth as the lucky. No one morally deserves the better places at society's table or the native endowments that enable him or her to surpass others socially, economically, or morally. And so worth egalitarians maintain that moral merit must be distinct from moral worth.

Kekes's response to this second belief, one that is evident in Rawls's position in *A Theory of Justice,* is instructive. He points out that worth egalitarians seem to assume that qualities that all humans are supposed to have (such as the capac-ity for choice), that anchor equal human moral worth, are immune from evil, that they are "morally positive forces." But nothing in human experience is so inoculated. As Kekes states, "All aspects of human conduct are subject to the essential conditions of life."[67] Everything involved in being human is vulnerable to corruption.

There is another possible argument in favor of maintaining a strict distinction between moral worth and moral merit. It is the constraints argument, which urges that there be a basis for constraining the way people behave toward each other. Human moral worth serves that purpose. Because humans are beings of moral worth, they have rights, and those rights cannot be violated without moral repercussions being visited on the violator. The underlying notion is again grounded in Kant's second formulation of the Categorical Imperative and is championed by Nozick.[68] It holds that the rights of others, founded in the equal worth of all humans, constitute a constraint on one's goal-directed behavior.

Why should such constraints be worth based rather than merit based? Or, to put the matter slightly differently, why can't worth in a constraint theory be proportional to moral merit? Insofar as desert is related to moral merit, desert would also reflect worth. People who do evil deeds have less moral merit than those who do not. I think we all can agree on that. But if worth is proportional to merit, then people who do evil have less moral worth than nonevildoers, and morality would permit differential treatment: they do not have to be treated with the same respect as good people. We are not as constrained morally in how we treat them as we are in the case of good people.

I have tried to suggest that there are no very strong reasons to insist on the hard-and-fast distinction between moral worth and moral merit. The basic idea of moral worth egalitarianism may be "a deep and independent intuition" and a very significant idea in the history of ethics, but it is only that. As Pepita Haezrahi has shown, proofs of its validity are impossible. It is, as even Kant would acknowledge, "an affirmation of faith in the face of clear evidence to the contrary."[69] Without rejecting its value in morality as a "challenge to our wills"—that is, as a regulative or constraint principle—I think it is at least as intuitively appealing to define worth in terms of moral merit—that is, to break down the barrier between them. On the account I find intuitively appealing, worth (from person to person) varies with merit, and merit is determined by what persons actually do. What they do determines what they are due. A person's moral worth is directly proportional to that person's moral merit.

I earlier asked, "What morally changes in people when they do evil so that we are not prohibited from inflicting pain on them, that doing so is not itself evil?" The answer is that they have less moral merit and consequently less moral worth than good people, and so we are not as constrained in dealing with them as we would be if they were morally worthy. Merit protects worth and worth ensures against the willful infliction of pain and suffering. By that I mean that worth is something like a moral insurance policy. It cannot prevent harm and injury, but it gives the injured party or those who represent that person the moral permit to take revenge, to seek retribution. Those of little or no moral merit have no moral shield against the avenger. They cannot appeal to moral worth to protect themselves from injury or harm or to justify retaliation.

There are, however, some things that should not be done to humans regardless of the way their behavior toward others has reduced their moral merit. (Larry McMurtry seems to have a way of describing such things in vivid detail, as, for example, in the tortures devised by the Black Vaquero in *Comanche Moon*.) However, even stating my notion of restraint in that fashion suggests that there is some basic level of merit that we all have. I do not think that is the case. One's concern for one's own moral merit can be the only restraint on one's retaliatory behavior. Proportionality in punishment is as much a matter of merit retention as it is desert.

Hampton's account of victimization, though I am sympathetic to its basic purposes, rests on a worth egalitarian foundation. She writes: "If I have equal value to that of my assailant, then that must be made manifest after I have been victimized. By victimizing me, the wrongdoer has declared himself elevated with respect to me, acting as a superior who is permitted to use me for his purposes. A false moral claim has been made. Moral reality has been denied."[70] I think that Hampton has moral reality wrong. What the victimizer has done is to decrease his or her own moral merit. The moral merit of the victim, however, is not changed. The act of victimizing has a negative moral value for the victimizer, who is worth less than he or she was worth before the assault on another person. It is not that the victimizer has inflated his or her value vis-à-vis the victim; instead he or she has deflated that value.

The inflicting of a punishment on the victimizer is deserved not to bring the victimizer back to the worth level of the victim, but to give the victimizer what he or she deserves for the actions that were performed. There is no leveling of worth. Worth is driven by merit, and nothing the victimizer can do to the victim can alter the moral merit of the victim. Similarly, nothing the avenger or punisher can do to the victimizer can alter his or her moral merit. Hampton is wrong in maintaining that the avenger "aims to diminish the worth of the offender."[71] The victimizer has already done that by displaying a lack of moral merit and hence moral worth.

To be sure, I am not denying that victimizers often, perhaps typically, act in such a way as to be proclaiming their superiority over their victims. I agree with Hampton that punishment in such cases is a way of setting the record straight, "asserting moral truth." I disagree with her about what moral truth is asserted. She believes that it is the assertion of worth egalitarianism; I believe it to be an assertion of moral merit, hence worth, inequality. Vengeance is not about the elevation of the worth of the avenger or the victim over the victimizer, or a declaration that they are of equal merit or worth. It is about inflicting harm on the victimizer because that is what he or she deserves—merits—while proclaiming that the victim did not merit the injury he or she endured. As noted in Chapter 3, it is the communication of the message of morality to the victimizer, to reconnect him or her to morality. The wrongness of acts of victimization is communicated to the victimizer. It is not a balancing act of the scales of moral worth or merit. The victimizer after punishment is not returned to the same level of moral merit as the victim. Being justifiably punished is not the approved way of accruing moral merit.

Victims deserve to be avenged, to have their victimizers punished. Lately, even the criminal justice system, at least in some jurisdictions, allows victim impact statements to have an effect on the discretionary sentencing of victimizers. As Murphy points out,[72] a reason given in defense of the use of such statements is to allow the victim the opportunity to express his or her response to victimization and thereby try to influence how the victimizer will be punished by the courts.

Although the use of victim impact statements is hardly a substitute for vengeance, it does allow justifiably vindictive emotions and reactive attitudes a role in punishment. Such a legal practice, however, falls short of what could be morally permissible.

THE MORALLY HANDICAPPED AND
THE MORALLY CHALLENGED

Arnold Zuboff writes, "I contend that no agent can be conceived of that could ever be responsible in the way required by retributivism."[73] Zuboff has in mind that an agent cannot be held responsible for his or her actions because he or she cannot be held responsible for his or her own beginnings and so cannot have chosen his or her "own original nature." Nor can he or she be held responsible for any self-improvement or self-corruption that he or she has been able to achieve because those changes that would have been dependent on his or her "original unchosen nature" or would have developed from it. Zuboff writes: "The agent cannot be held responsible in the required sense for any of his actions, whether these are thought of as determined by the nature he essentially did not choose or as bubbling forth somehow undetermined and thus with nothing responsible for them in any sense. I conclude we should cure ourselves of this monstrous mode of judgment that has caused such great suffering in the bitterness of the judge as well as the pain of the needlessly punished."[74] I want to expose certain conceptions that are hidden in Zuboff's position, which, when dusted off, may suggest a rather different outlook than the one he takes.

To buttress our intuitions, Zuboff concocts a story engaging the philosopher's favorite fictive character—a mad scientist. He has us imagine a man who puts pieces of glass in baby food in order to extort money from baby food manufacturers. But the story doesn't end, or rather begin, there. We are to imagine that the baby food contaminator had been assembled, Frankenstein-style, by a mad scientist. This prequel to the story is supposed to ensure that, although we believe that the baby food contaminator is a bad guy and must be prevented from continuing to insert shards of glass into baby food, we will no longer feel that "he deserves to suffer great pangs of guilt as well as what we decent people will do to him." In fact, Zuboff thinks we could be justified in punishing him only on consequentialist grounds, for "in some deep sense" he does not deserve the pain of punishment.

Why do we think that the baby food contaminator is bad? The obvious reason is that putting bits of glass in baby food will, if the food is fed to babies, cause untoward events to occur, and doing so to extort money from the baby food manufacturer is an additional evil. So the action is, and is meant by the storyteller to be understood as, unquestionably wicked. Normally, we would say that anyone who does such things is evil and should be held morally responsible (and should be severely punished) for the actions and their consequences. The prequel to the story, however, is concocted to confuse our original intuitions, to worry us with hints that, if we ignore the new information, we are not being fair or just or caring in our treatment of the evildoer. Learning that the moral monster was "programmed" by a mad scientist to prefer actions such as and including the contamination of the baby food is supposed to be of crucial moral significance. Learning that the evil done by the contaminator, at some level, was not chosen by him, or at least was not chosen in the way generally deemed appropriate for ascriptions of moral responsibility to be justifiable, should exempt him from blame. Zuboff's baby food contaminator labors under a serious moral impediment that alters his status as a proper subject of moral responsibility ascriptions, at least, as far as we know, in the matter of the baby food contamination. He cannot choose his actions in a way that is independent of his programming. To have such a moral disadvantage is to have what looks like safe passage under the guns of moral vengeance.

Consider another type of case: Rod Ferrell, a seventeen-year-old from Kentucky, was tried and convicted in a Florida court for the crowbar murders of a man and a woman. Ferrell is a self-confessed vampire and the leader of a small bloodsucking cult of teenagers. The couple he killed were the parents of a girl who was planning to run away with the cult. Ferrell's defense attorney attempted to persuade the jury that her client lived in a fantasy world created by an abusive, dysfunctional family obsessed with the occult and addicted to drugs. She argued that her client's brutal killing of the couple was, at root, caused by his family's conduct involving him and their general lack of values. His maternal grandparents, in cult rituals, had sexually abused him. His mother was a prostitute who not only shared his involvement in vampirism but also hooked him on drugs. It was unimaginable, his attorney maintained, that Ferrell could be responsible, in the sense that justified punishment, for the murders. It is hard to see, she argued, how someone with his upbringing could have done anything other than turn to a life of depravity, of which the murders were a symptom. Ferrell, at least in the closing statement of his attorney, was made to sound like an actual case of Zuboff's morally impaired monster, with the dysfunctional family playing the role of the mad scientist.

I want to suggest that there are two types of morally impaired people, and the differences between them are crucial for virtuous vengeance, that is, for whether or not they should be held morally responsible and punishable for what they do. Before characterizing those types, however, some preliminaries are in order. In the first place, moral impairment might either be partial or total. The difference is similar to physical impediments, where one might endure limitations on one's physical abilities or be totally disabled with respect to those abilities. Those who are mentally defective or so immature as to have no useful grasp of moral injunctions are morally disabled. With respect to moral accountability, there is hardly anything interesting about them. There is wide agree-

ment about their treatment from the moral point of view, and they are not usually held to be morally responsible or punishable for what they do. A number of
reasons might be provided to explain why this approach is taken with them. For
example, it is argued that we don't punish them because doing so is inefficacious;
it won't deter them from repetitions of the offending behavior. In any event, arguments in defense of the treatment of the totally morally disabled will typically
take the form that we don't punish them because the point of punishment is X
and they cannot grasp X, so X cannot be accomplished by punishing them.

The seventeen-year-old vampire killer, or at least his defense, suggests a rather
different approach. His attorney's attempt was not so much to focus the jury's
attention on the efficacy of punishing her client. It was to argue that the true
description of her client's behavior must be that he could not have prevented
himself from committing the heinous crimes, and because of that incapacity, he
should not be punished. Zuboff's baby food contaminator might have put forth
a similar argument. That defense is a version of the age-old "could not have done
otherwise" argument that crops up throughout moral philosophy, an argument
that depends on what has come to be known in the philosophical literature as
the Principle of Alternate Possibilities (PAP). It is widely believed that, unless
one could have done something other than what one did, unless one had alternate possibilities of action, it is unjust or unfair or morally wrong to hold one
responsible for doing it. Simply, PAP states that persons are responsible for what
they do only if they could have done otherwise in the circumstances. PAP lurks
just barely beneath the surface of Zuboff's position: the contaminator can only
do what the mad scientist has programmed him to do.

PAP incorporates the dictum that "ought implies can." John Kekes interprets
that dictum as "moral accountability . . . presupposes that agents can do or refrain from doing what morality requires of them; that is, it presupposes that they
have a choice."[75] Zuboff's story eliminates choice from the baby food contaminator, and the defense attorney tried, unsuccessfully as it happened, to convince
the jury that Ferrell had no choice in what he did. Kant is quite explicit about
the relevance of "ought implies can" to moral responsibility. He writes: "If a man
is corrupt in the very ground of his maxims, how can he possibly bring about
this revolution by his own powers and of himself become a good man? Yet duty
bids us to do this, and duty demands nothing of us which we cannot do. There
is no reconciliation possible here except by saying that man is under the necessity of, and is therefore capable of, a revolution in his cast of mind."[76]

Harry Frankfurt has famously attacked PAP.[77] He makes the point that "the
fact that a person could not have avoided doing something is a sufficient condition of his having done it. But, . . . this fact may play no role whatever in the
explanation of why he did it . . . It may not figure at all among the circumstances
that actually brought it about that he did what he did, so that his action is to be
accounted for on another basis entirely. Even though the person was unable to
do otherwise, that is to say, it may not be the case that he acted as he did because

he could not have done otherwise . . . If someone had no alternative to performing a certain action but did not perform it because he was unable to do otherwise, then he would have performed exactly the same action even if he could have
done otherwise . . . Thus it would have made no difference, so far as concerns
his action or how he came to perform it, if the circumstances that made it impossible for him to avoid performing it had not prevailed."[78]

Frankfurt's point, or at least one of them, is that if our concern is the ascribing
of moral responsibility, we should not place much, if any, weight on a fact that
is irrelevant to explaining a person's behavior. Only the reasons why a person
did something under the circumstances should matter. That the agent could not
have avoided what he or she did may not be a morally relevant explanation of his
or her behavior under the circumstances so it is not relevant to the ascription of
responsibility. To bring the intuitions that motivate his account to light, Frankfurt created a number of fanciful examples of action overdetermination. Zuboff's
baby food contaminator, however, will serve for illustrative purposes.

To shape the story into a Frankfurt-type case we need to imagine that the contaminator puts the shards of glass in the baby food because that is what he wants
to do. However, if he did not want to do it, a mechanism installed in his brain
by the mad scientist will activate and he will do it nonetheless, which ensures
that he cannot avoid putting the shards into the baby food. Should the contaminator not be held responsible? The intuition that should be started is that what
is important for moral purposes is not that the contaminator could not have done
otherwise, but that in fact, under the circumstances, he put the glass bits in the
baby food because that is what he wanted to do. The lack of alternate possibilities is irrelevant. Put in a slightly different way, he ought not to have put the
shards of glass in the baby food even though he cannot prevent himself from doing
so. "Ought" does not imply can.

Moral responsibility is not necessarily expunged in the absence of genuine
alternate possibilities nor is it undermined by unavoidability. Of course, it may
be objected to the Frankfurt reading of such an example that we still will want to
know why the contaminator wanted to put the shards of glass in the food in the
first place. Perhaps he could not have avoided such wants due to the manipula-
tions of his brain by the mad scientist. Be that as it may, he is not being held
responsible for his wants but for putting the shards of glass in the baby food, and
it is the latter action that, on our story, was unavoidable by him, although done
because it was what he wanted to do. The avoidability or lack thereof of our mental
states is rather a different matter, though one that might be of concern when
mitigation or even leniency in matters of punishment is explored.

The Frankfurt cases illuminate the fact that the lack of ability or opportunity
to do something other than what one does is not in and of itself what John Martin
Fischer calls "a responsibility-undermining factor."[79] What then does undermine
responsibility? Following Fischer, I think that it is the lack of a certain kind of
control of one's behavior.

Fischer identifies two different kinds of control that are relevant to responsibility: guidance control and regulative control. To arouse the intuitions on which Fischer's distinction rests, suppose I am piloting a boat. I want the boat to turn to starboard to avoid a sandbar. I turn the wheel to the right and the boat veers to starboard. I have "guidance control" over the boat's movements in the water if the boat is responsive to my turning the wheel in the way I want it to turn. If I have the power to make the boat turn any way I want it to—that is, if I could have made it turn to port rather than starboard at that specific time—I would have what Fischer calls "regulative control" of the boat's movements. Normally we think that we have regulative control with respect to the movements of our boats when we pilot them around. If I run hard aground on a sandbar that I know blocks the northern entrance to the pass into the bay from the Gulf of Mexico, I feel I am responsible for my plight and will, quite reasonably, offer excuses for my errant piloting to the towboat operator who comes to drag my boat off the bar.

But suppose that I really don't have regulative control with regard to the boat's movements. Suppose, along the lines of the Frankfurt cases, the boat's steering mechanism is such that it works perfectly if I steer to starboard, but, though I am blissfully unaware of it, if I try to steer to port at that moment or to maintain my present direction, the boat will go to starboard. No matter which way I try to steer, the boat will veer to starboard in the same way it does when I steer it in that direction. Of course, that will never happen and I will never learn that it would, because I want to turn the wheel to the right in order to veer the boat to starboard and I do so. Under such circumstances, I have guidance control of the boat, but I do not have regulative control of its movements. I cannot make the boat move in whatever direction I choose at that moment in time. As long as I am turning the wheel to the right, I control the boat's movement to starboard. It goes where I want it to go because I turn the wheel that way. But it would be a mistake to say that I have control over the boat. I can guide the boat to starboard, but I lack regulative control over the boat. Am I responsible for the boat's movement to starboard?

I think the answer must be yes. It doesn't matter that the boat would have veered to starboard regardless of what direction I decided to turn the wheel, since in fact I turned the wheel to the right and the boat responded by veering to starboard. The explanation of the boat's veering to starboard is not that it would do so in any event, but that I turned the wheel to the right; I guided it that way.

The reason for such a response has to do with the causal history of the specific action. The operative principle is that I am responsible for actions that are the result of a reasons-responsive mechanism. As an example, Fischer provides the "unimpaired operation of the human deliberative mechanism."[80] Responsibility is undermined when such a mechanism plays no causal role in the production of the behavior in question. It is important that when thinking about such mechanisms we understand them as not such that their operation entails that a specific action occurs. The human deliberative mechanism satisfies that condition, but the mechanism "deliberating prior to joining the ethnic cleansers in Kosovo" does not.

Fischer writes, "It is very natural and reasonable to think that the difference between morally responsible agents and those who are not consists in the 'reasons-responsiveness' of the agents."[81] In Frankfurt-type cases, if we are persuaded that the agent is responsible, we must believe that the actual mechanism that results in the actions was responsive to reasons. The mechanism that would kick in to cause the same actions but does not do so is not reasons-responsive. Returning to my modified version of Zuboff's example, let us suppose that, in the actual sequence of events, the contaminator puts the shards in the baby food because that is what he wants to do and that mechanism is reasons-responsive. Such an action might mean that the contaminator exercised some normal human deliberative process on the basis of which he arrived at the decision to contaminate the baby food. He might have considered that what he wanted to do was ruin the reputation of the manufacturer that had underpaid him for years and failed to recognize his value to the company. He would make up the difference by extorting money from the company. Had he, counterfactually on my version— not Zuboff's—of the story, discovered that the company was planning a grand celebration in his honor at which he would receive a substantial financial bonus and a package of attractive perks, he would not have wanted to tarnish its image or extort money from it, and he would not have put the glass pieces in the baby food.

But he will put the shards in the baby food because a non-reasons-responsive mechanism will take over, the one implanted by the mad scientist, and he will not be able to avoid doing the heinous deed. The contaminator, in that scenario, does have guidance control with respect to the deed, and the actual-sequence mechanism resulting in his action is reasons-responsive. The contaminator, of course, is not reasons-responsive because, irrespective of reasons, he will put the shards in the baby food; he does not have regulative control. I will call the contaminator who has guidance control but lacks regulative control morally challenged. Those who lack guidance control are morally handicapped. The morally challenged can be held responsible for what they do and so punished when they perform evil deeds. The morally handicapped should not be held morally responsible.

We like to think that most of us have regulative control of our actions, at least most of the time. I am not convinced that we do or that an argument can be mounted to persuade us, once and for all, that we do. I do think that we generally have guidance control. Consequently, we usually are all—at least—morally challenged, which does not mean, contra-Zuboff, that we cannot be responsible in the way required by retributivism. Still, there clearly are different kinds of reasons-responsiveness that might affect the way we judge responsibility.

Fischer points out that there are two senses in which a mechanism may be reasons-responsive, a strong sense and a weak sense. We may say that a mechanism exhibits strong reasons-responsiveness if the agent's awareness of a sufficient reason to do other than it does would lead the agent to choose an alternative course of action and actually do so. Strong reasons-responsiveness, however, is too stiff a requirement to satisfy our basic intuitions about moral responsibility for actions. For example, I may be aware of a sufficient reason for my not doing something other than what I am doing but still choose to do what I am doing. If that occurs, the actual-sequence mechanism, which results in my doing what I am doing, is not strongly reasons-responsive. However, whatever the explanation (I want to explore one in particular below), I should still be treated as morally responsible for doing what I did. Fischer provides a useful example to stimulate our intuitions into agreement with this account.[82]

Imagine that I have a sufficient reason not to spend this afternoon working gratis at the soup kitchen that feeds the homeless. The reason is that I need the time to do the research necessary to finish an article that I have promised to an editor tomorrow. But despite the fact that I have such a reason and consider it a good and sufficient reason not to work in the soup kitchen, I contribute my time to the charity. I suspect that a substantial number of people would praise me for working in the soup kitchen. Insofar as that praise would not be regarded as utterly misplaced, I would be morally responsible for doing so. Some other folks, my editor for one, might blame me for putting charity work ahead of my commitment to get the article in on time. Importantly, however, the actual mechanism that resulted in my working in the soup kitchen was not reasons-responsive in the strong sense.

In typical cases of wrongdoing, a similar lack of strong reasons-responsiveness exists in the actual-sequence mechanism that results in action, yet moral responsibility is assigned to the agent. There usually are sufficient reasons for the agent not to commit the untoward deed, but the actual-sequence mechanism does not respond to those reasons in the strong sense. Nonetheless, the agent is held morally responsible. In effect, when the actual-sequence mechanism is not strongly reasons-responsive, moral responsibility is still not undermined.

Weak reasons-responsiveness, on an account that mirrors Fischer's, requires only that there is a conceivable set of circumstances in which there is a sufficient reason for the agent to do otherwise, and his or her actual mechanism operates and he or she does otherwise. The conceivable set of circumstances, or that possible world, might be remote from the actual world in which the agent acts. All that needs to be imagined, counterfactually, is that there is at least one reason sufficient to provoke the agent's response and that it will result in the agent acting other than the way he or she acted. For example, it is conceivable that a career crook might respond to some incentive not to steal: a guarantee that he or she will be caught and summarily executed. That would be a sufficient reason to prevent the crook from stealing if it were understood by him or her to be a lively possibility. But it is remote and the crook wants to steal; his or her actual mechanism operates and he or she steals. If that occurs, then the crook's actual mechanism that issues in the stealing is only weakly reasons-responsive.

Allegedly, one of the primary purposes of the criminal justice system is to confront would-be criminals with disincentives to engage in felonious lifestyles that they regard as lively and not remote possibilities. It must be believed that, as Fischer puts it, "even an agent who acts against good reasons can be responsive to some reasons."[83] In any event, if the agent's actual mechanism is at least conceivably responsive to incentives to do other than he or she does, he or she can be held morally responsible for the actions that result from that mechanism. Fischer's account produces the following result: if an agent would persist in doing an untoward deed even if he or she were well aware of a good and sufficient reason not to do the deed (e.g., guaranteed death of the agent or his or her family), then the agent lacks even weak reasons-responsiveness and has no control with respect to his or her performance of the deed in question.

Weak reasons-responsiveness, I agree with Fischer, is sufficient for guidance control, and guidance control is adequate for moral responsibility and hence punishability. In fact, as Fischer notes, "Actual irrationality is compatible with moral responsibility."[84] What is crucial is that it is imaginable that the actual mechanism in the agent that results in the actions is at least weakly reasons-responsive. If that condition cannot be met, then the person, on my account, is morally handicapped—not morally challenged—is not a proper subject of moral responsibility ascriptions, and should not be a target of vengeance.

Those who are driven to behavior by irresistible urges, genuine compulsion, non-reasons-responsive mechanisms such as physical diseases, hypnosis, and so on, are morally handicapped, although in cases like hypnosis, only over a range of their behavior and only for a period of time. But if a person acts from a mechanism that is at least weakly reasons-responsive, that person is morally responsible for his or her actions. I leave open for the time being whether the fact that the person has only weak reasons-responsive guidance control when performing an action of wrongdoing is a sufficient reason to lighten punishment.

The morally handicapped and the morally challenged may behave in ways that provoke acts of vengeance. Clearly, on the account I have given, the morally handicapped are improper targets of revenge. The morally challenged, however, do not escape accountability for their untoward deeds. They deserve hostile responses. Suppose then that we consider a possible target of revenge where the issue of whether the provocative actions were the product of a moral handicap or of a weakly reasons-responsive mechanism may be in some doubt. I have in mind people whose characters were formed and nurtured in cultures that are utterly imbued with racial, cultural, and other forms of bigotry and who act on those sorts of beliefs. Consider as examples white American Southerners during the slavery period, Klu Klux Klan members and other white racists following the Civil War and into the present day, witch-hunters in Europe and America in the seventeenth century, medieval crusaders, ethnic-cleansing Serbs, German Nazis, and a wide variety of others who have been raised in cultures of hate, bigotry, intolerance, fanaticism, and so forth.

Let us grant that such people did not choose to be racial and ethnic bigots. Their preferences, and so their characters, are not, or are not fully, matters of choice. Kekes calls their behavior when they are exercising their perverse beliefs "unchosen evil."[85] He writes that "the agents do not decide to cause evil, yet they do so as a regular by-product of their characters and actions."[86] He goes on to characterize them in the following ways: "Human agents cause undeserved harm without being able to do otherwise."[87] "Their evil actions follow from their unchosen vices, they are symptomatic of enduring dispositions, and they occur when they act naturally and spontaneously, in accordance with vices they have developed but without choosing to develop them."[88] "Each (referring to unchosen vices) is brought about by lack of control . . . But whether people are able to exercise control is often not a matter within their control."[89] Although I end up agreeing with Kekes's general view with regard to the responsibility in such cases of unchosen evil, the route that I have already prepared in order to reach that destination is, I believe, more intuitively satisfying in terms of character morality than the one he maps.

Suppose we focus on those whose behavior results from a cultural inculcation over which they had no choice. Provoked by the extensive media coverage of the events in the Balkans, I have in mind the Serbs in Bosnia and Kosovo who committed atrocities against Bosnian Muslims and Kosovar Albanians in the name of ethnic cleansing. They are, however, only an example, and other cases are welcome. I think it is indisputable that the members of prejudiced, intolerant, and bigoted communities, whether ethnic or racial or sexual, regularly reinforce those kinds of views in each other and over many generations. When the vast majority of the members of the community express a singular set of pernicious perverse views and when they are incessantly echoed and enlarged upon by those in positions of authority, even the consideration of questions about the veracity and morality of the dominant views is virtually unthinkable for most community members. It takes a special person with uncommon insight to raise the appropriate concerns. And they can expect not to be heeded, indeed heard, by others.

The perverse preferences of that form of life are among its essential features, and they dominate the characters of those who share that form of life. They are the inescapable mark of belonging to those raised in such a community. The individual members of the community seem to have little or no effective control over their own adoption of those preferences. The process is predominantly one of unconscious habituation rather than rational reflective acquisition. It is likely that the members never have an actual opportunity to alter the course of their character development, "since doing so would have required of them a sustained effort to act contrary to their own predispositions and to the social context that favored their development in a particular direction."[90] The very virtues that might have stood them in good moral stead and withstood the pressures of their culture are exactly the ones that they lack because they were never encouraged or trained in them. Their cultures, their upbringings, are inhospitable to the sort of critical reflection that might encourage them to question the inbred and ingrained preferences they have, to examine and adopt what we would regard as better preferences. Their personal and social identities as well as their self-appraisals and those they make of others are grounded in those preferences.

The Serbian ethnic cleansers, in short, did not choose to be racial and ethnic bigots. They were raised in a centuries-old culture of hatred, distrust, and conflict. (It may be instructive that it was reported that as they carried out the atrocities in Kosovo they often shouted, "Remember the Battle of Kosovo." The Serbs and the Turks fought the Battle of Kosovo in 1388. The Turks won!) In such a culture, the preferences that formed the characters of the ethnic cleansers were cemented. Insofar as acting on those preferences (e.g., performing acts of ethnic cleansing) instead of following moral principles is wicked, their wickedness, at an important level for moral evaluative purposes, was not chosen by them even though it is what they prefer.

Now, imagine a Serb, with a suitably large number of his fellows, on a mission of ethnic cleansing in a village of Kosovar Albanians or Bosnian Muslims. He brutalizes, tortures, rapes, and then murders villagers. Is he to be held morally responsible for his actions in that village? Is he a proper target of revenge for the son of one of the women he has tortured, raped, and murdered? On the account of the Serbian ethnic cleanser that I have provided, it seems natural to describe his behavior as the result of an irresistible impulse, utterly out of his control. But what is such an irresistible impulse? Certain kinds of drug addicts might be described as having literally irresistible impulses or urges when they decide to shoot up heroin. The actual mechanism at work in them that issues in the injection of the drug is not reasons-responsive even in the weak sense. Instead of a deliberative mechanism issuing in the behavior, a physical process takes place in their central nervous system that results in the behavior. As Fischer notes, "When an agent acts from a literally irresistible urge, he is undergoing a kind of physical process that is not reasons-responsive, and it is this lack of reasons-responsiveness of the actual physical process that rules out guidance control and moral responsibility."[91] Is the Serbian ethnic cleanser acting from a literally irresistible impulse or urge?

It is worth noting that recently a Harvard Medical School professor of clinical psychiatry, Alvin F. Poussaint, in a *New York Times* opinion piece, maintained that racism is a mental illness and that those who suffer from it and came to contract it in a manner similar to the way ethnic hatred was ingrained in the Serbian ethnic cleansers are not proper subjects of punishment when their actions issue from this "disease." On an account like Poussaint's, the racist's behavior stems from literally irresistible impulses. Although I have no credentials as a clinical psychiatrist, I have serious doubt that acculturation and other forms of propagandizing yield actual physical or biological processes in people that are not reasons-responsive, at least in the weak sense. I do believe, however, that the actual mechanisms issuing in the Serbian ethnic cleansers' behavior in the Kosovar Albanian village are not strongly reasons-responsive.

Consider a case that approaches these matters from the other side of the moral spectrum. Imagine a woman who has been raised by a morally upright family in which moral behavior and the appropriate moral attitudes and emotions were ingrained and habituated. She never questions whether she is doing the right thing; she never considers doing otherwise. She is firmly committed, for example, to upholding the Ten Commandments, indeed she has a very strong desire to do so. Her behavior is morally impeccable, unassailable, though she is never actually placed in a situation in which she is confronted with a temptation to act other than the way she has been trained, to do something she does not have a strong desire to do. Then, one fateful day, she is approached by her husband's boss and propositioned to commit adultery. Without so much as a moment of hesitation, she firmly but respectfully declines his advances. Does she deserve moral praise for her actions?

She wasn't, as things actually happened, tempted by the proposition. Whatever reasons might be offered to get her to yield to the boss, she was not strongly responsive to them. We sometimes describe such people as steadfast in their convictions. In fact, she is more than steadfast. She is doing what she wants to do, what she desires to do, because that is how she was raised. And, it should be stressed, she had no choice in how she was raised. Nonetheless, no purely physical mechanism has taken over and issues in her actions. We should be comfortable in saying that the mechanism that issues in her actions is weakly reasons-responsive because we can fairly easily imagine a scenario in which she is provided by her husband's boss with a sufficient reason to commit adultery and rejects it. If that is the case, we may praise her rejection of the proposition, and hold her morally responsible for it. Such an account of moral actions is not far removed from Aristotle's conception of moral virtue gained through teaching in which the proper habits are ingrained (NE 1103a). The virtuous person acts habitually but is not without guidance control based in weak reasons-responsiveness. Hence, the virtuous person is worthy of praise.

Considering again the ethnic cleanser, we should say that he has guidance control with respect to his actions in the Kosovar village because he is, at least, weakly reasons-responsive. What sort of reasons? Perhaps only the garden variety that are typically put forth to restrain untoward behavior. It does not matter. He and his like are morally challenged, not morally handicapped. Cultural factors surely are causal determinants of action for the Serbian ethnic cleansers, so it may be much harder for them to resist the urges they have to act out their ethnic bigotry than it is for others to prevent themselves from torturing, humiliating, raping, and murdering those of ethnic groups to which they do not belong. But that explanation does not exempt them from moral responsibility or exclude them as targets of virtuous vengeance.

The *New York Times* reported that after the Sacramento court case that ended in a plea bargain, Dr. Charles Epstein, one of the victims of the Unabomber, Theodore Kaczynski, said: "I looked at him in court and I came to the decision, this is a profoundly evil person. He is really the essence of evil."[92] When Epstein was asked if Kaczynski's mental illness affected his judgment of the man, he replied, "That doesn't take away for me from the fact that he is evil." Epstein captured the essence of a weakly reasons-responsive conception of guidance control and hence of moral responsibility. Even, to paraphrase Epstein, if Kaczynski's mental illness, which Epstein characterized as paranoid schizophrenia, determines the very preferences he has, that he has no effective scope of choice when he is in its throes, he is no less evil, "the essence of evil." He deserves to suffer punishment.

I do not, however, want to suggest that no types of mental illness are moral responsibility blockers. What needs to be demonstrated in specific cases is that the behavior of the person in question issues from physical mechanisms that are not reasons-responsive. I have no idea how mental illnesses might result in such physical mechanisms that produce these literally irresistible impulses, though in heroin addiction we may have a model. On the other hand, recovering heroin addicts, alcoholics, and others have found the capacity to resist the urges, in effect revealing that they are reasons-responsive and so have guidance control. In any event, I am rather certain that racism is not a moral responsibility underminer of the actions that express it. By the same token, the teenage vampire killer, Rod Ferrell, was properly found to be responsible for the murders of the couple in Florida. Zuboff's baby food contaminator (not my revised version of this character), however, may lack guidance control and so should not be a target of retribution. He is morally handicapped. But he is a science fictional entity. We are not.

DESERT

In nature there are neither rewards or punishments—there are consequences.
Robert Green Ingersoll[93]

If pain be added to an evil state . . . the whole thus formed is always better, as a whole, than if no pain had been there.
G. E. Moore[94]

The following statements are foundational to the morality of punishment:

- People who commit acts of willful wrongdoing deserve hostile responses.
- People who are innocent of willful wrongdoing do not deserve hostile responses.

They are not consequentialist, as is Moore's "better on the whole" justification of punishment. They are fundamentally retributive or retributive at their core. There is much more or much less, depending on how you look at it, to punishment than the consideration of consequences.

Although philosophers might spend a considerable amount of time arguing over the precise meaning of "desert," I am comfortable with the ordinary, common use of the term. If I deserve something, then (as previously discussed in the first section of this chapter) I merit it, I warrant it, I am entitled to it, I am worthy of it, I rate it, I've earned it, I have it coming. Deserving something does not mean that I will get it or, in the case of punishment, suffer the pain of it. It only means that I should get it or that someone or some institution that has the ability and the authority to give or administer it to me should do so. Although whole books might be, and have been, devoted to the topic of desert,[95] I see no point here in extending the discussion. I am prepared to let these matters rest, for now, with the two statements above.

I believe that they capture, in sufficient measure for my purposes, what needs to be said on the subject. I have no idea how to justify them other than by appealing to what it means to say that an act is wrong or of willful wrongdoing. In other words, I believe that the very notion of wrongdoing in morality is vacuous unless at least the first statement can be unpacked from it. In this regard, as I have noted earlier, I follow Mackie, who wrote that "the wrongness of an action is thought of as being made up of three elements, its being harmful, its being forbidden, and its calling for a hostile response . . . A wrong action is intrinsically forbidden because it is harmful from the point of view of the universe, and it calls for a hostile response because it is both harmful generally and intrinsically forbidden."[96]

I should point out that the second statement seems to capture a position with which most everyone, except perhaps very hard-core utilitarians, agrees: the punishment of the innocent should be forbidden. Why? Because they do not deserve it. If the absence of desert is an unexceptional sufficient reason not to punish the innocent and we have some way of establishing its absence, should we not also be able to identify the presence of desert? Michael Moore writes: "Neither metaphysical skepticism nor epistemological modesty gets in our way when we use lack of moral desert as a reason not to punish. Why should it be different when we use presence of desert as a reason to punish? If we can know when someone does not deserve punishment, mustn't we know when someone does deserve punishment?"[97]

The first statement does not make reference to the administrator of the hostile response. It does not restrict that role to, for example, a state institution or a divine being, or exclude individuals from playing the role. It does not leave avengers or victims on the sidelines. As Mackie notes, "It is not just from this or that particular person that it calls for a hostile response; rather, it is such that a hostile response *from somewhere* is needed, the situation is somehow generally unsatisfactory if the wrong action gets by without any proportional reaction."[98] Any restrictions on who can fill the administrative role would have to come from a source other than the conception of willful wrongdoing.

The first statement is also neutral between karmic and nonkarmic moral theories.

CHAPTER SEVEN

The Tailored Fit:
The Proportionality Condition

Noxiae poena par esto—Let the punishment match the offense.
Cicero (De Legibus, *III*)

There are in fact two vices against vengeance. By excess there is the sin of cruelty or ferocity, going beyond measure in punishing. The other is a vice by way of defect, as when someone fails to inflict punishment at all . . . The virtue of vengeance means that in redressing wrongs a person keep to a right measure with proper regard for all circumstances.

St. Thomas Aquinas[1]

My object all sublime
I shall achieve in time—
To make the punishment fit the crime.
William S. Gilbert[2]

My account of virtuous vengeance is unabashedly retributive, and over the years, retributivism has come in for a considerable amount of criticism in the philosophical and legal literature, although remarkably there seem to be very few concerted arguments mounted against it. Generally, its detractors prefer name-calling. It is typically deemed barbaric and, presumably, unworthy of a civilized people. Why it is barbaric or why being barbaric is a sufficient reason to dismiss it, however, is seldom explained. More sophisticated attacks have centered on rather practical outcomes—such as the costs versus the benefits to a community—of the adoption of retributivism in a penal justice system.[3] But, despite all of the bad-mouthing, retributivism still seems to appeal to our basic, or gut, intuitions, and of late, various forms of retributivism have been finding their way back into favor in the philosophical literature.

Retributivists punish, in the first instance, because the offender deserves a hostile response. But some retributivists, acknowledging that the inflicting of punishment is to harm the offender, see their problem as that of providing a convincing argument that some significant good is also done in such harming. This is, I suppose, the punishment version of the doctrine of Double Effect. Pure (or what Mackie calls "positive") retributivists, however, punish only because the offender deserves it. The previous wrongful actions of a person are in themselves a sufficient reason to inflict a penalty on him or her. Pure retributivists reject utilitarian and rehabilitative goals that might be piggybacked on retributivism to make it more palatable to the tastes of the morally delicate. Neither the overall good of the community nor the reform of the wrongdoer centrally enters into their justifications of punishment. However, a pure retributivist can respond to the concern that good be done in harming by noting that retributivism is a theory of justice, that justice is a good, and that justice is done when someone gets what he or she deserves. Michael Moore has noted: "Retributivism is a very straightforward theory of punishment. We are justified in punishing because and only because offenders deserve it. Moral culpability ('desert') is in such a view both a sufficient as well as a necessary condition of liability to punitive sanctions."[4]

Less pure retributivists, however, have generally not been satisfied with leaving the desert condition to stand alone in their justifications of punishment. They have modified retributivism in a number of different ways to respond to its critics or to their own worries that desert may not be a defensible sufficient condition. They have looked for additional goods to be achieved by the inflicting of deserved punishment. Broadly speaking, these modified versions might be called Target Retributivisms. (I adopted the term in Chapter 3 from Braithwaite and Pettit.) There seem to be at least three dominant types of Target Retributivism and a number of variations within each of the types. J. G. Cottingham has defined nine varieties of retributivism, but I am comfortable with three basic types, other than Pure Retributivism. I subsume some of Cottingham's "varieties" into more general classifications.[5]

I will call the three types Balancing Target Retributivism, Reprobative Target Retributivism, and Appeasement Target Retributivism. Target Retributivists, when offering a rationale for their position, incorporate some sort of morally desirable goal that the punishment of offenders will promote that exceeds whatever the infliction of pain on the offender is supposed to do in and of itself. It might not be inappropriate to accuse most Target Retributivists of closet consequentialism, though not the utilitarian or rehabilitative versions that they find indefensible. They are still retributivists, and at the core of their view of punishment is first and foremost a matter of desert.

The Balancing Target Retributivists have a certain picture of the moral universe in mind. For them, there is a moral equilibrium of some kind that has been tipped by wrongdoing or by the wrongdoer. Punishment of the offender is understood as reestablishing the proper balance in the moral universe, as adjusting for a wrongdoing that has, temporarily, unbalanced the scales. Kant and Hegel provide classic examples, although on a cursory reading, Kant may appear to be a pure retributivist with no interest in goals. Hegel takes aim at a more clearly defined target.

In the *Metaphysics of Morals (Metaphysik der Sitten)*, Kant writes that punishment "can never be inflicted merely as a means to promote some other good for the criminal himself or for civil society. It must always be inflicted upon him only because he has committed a crime."[6] He invokes a reading of what he calls the "principle of equality" to set the sentencing requirements. He writes that "whatever undeserved evil you inflict upon another within the people, that you inflict upon yourself."[7] It is perhaps of note that Kant does not seem to endorse the obverse principle that "whatever good you provide for others you provide in like measure for yourself." That principle would seem to run counter to his conception of duty for its own sake, although as noted in Chapter 3, the karmic aspects of Kant's moral theory in the *Critique of Pure Reason* might be seen as ensuring that principle as well. The principle of equality when applied to penal sentencing is, for Kant, *lex talionis*. It is arrived at, he is confident, by application of the first formulation of the Categorical Imperative. What you will to be done by you to others, you will as a universal law, and so you will that it be done to yourself. That, of course, does not mean that murder is rationally universalizable. Obviously, the rational person will realize that one cannot rationally will the maxim of action involved in murder as a universal law for all humankind, as its enactment would lead to the destruction of human rationality as well as one's own destruction. Murderers, however, do not, it appears, follow through on the Kantian logic.

Kant's adoption of the "equality of evil infliction principle" (doing it to X is doing it to yourself in like amount) suggests to him the imagery of one kind of Balancing Target Retributivist. He explicates what he means by equality by the parenthetical remark "in the position of the needle on the scale of justice." Evidently, Kant imagines that the offender has unbalanced the scales of justice by his or her deed and that a punishment meted out in accord with *lex talionis* will balance the scales, move the needle back to the midpoint. What is unclear is what those scales are measuring. From his other comments we might surmise that one side of the scales of justice is being weighted down by the undeserved suffering the offender has inflicted on a victim, and that deserved suffering evens the score, returns the scales to an equilibrium balance. That peeks out as a rather odd notion when looked at too closely, suggesting the image of a scale of suffering in the universe, some of which is deserved and some undeserved, that justice must balance. How does deserved suffering balance undeserved suffering? Why should we think that the suffering of the victim is commensurate with the suffering of the offender? Why should we think that an equal amount of deserved suffering balances undeserved suffering? Perhaps it should take twice as much or fifty times as much or a thousand times as much. But, of course, there is the prior question: What actually is being balanced? Suffering is not much like lead weights and mounds of gold dust.

In any event, Kant deserts the image of the needle on the scale of justice and focuses on the offender's will. The victim's pain and suffering or loss, though surely the occasion calling for the balancing act, is less important to Kant than the fact that the offender has willed his or her own punishment. In the remainder of his account, the victim's suffering is not mentioned.

Kant does not treat the desert principle as primitive and so morally and analytically unassailable. As Jeffrie Murphy has pointed out, Kant's retributivism is firmly anchored in his conception of the reciprocity of political obligation. In this sense he is also a Balancing Target Retributivist. Murphy characterizes Kant's position as based in the notion that "if the law is to remain just, it is important to guarantee that those who disobey it will not gain an unfair advantage over those who do obey voluntarily. Criminal punishment . . . attempts to restore the proper balance between benefit and obedience."[8] On this reading of Kant, what is balanced on the scales are advantages within the broader realm of obedience to law. The idea is that the offender gains undue advantage of the lawful obedience of others to aggrandize himself or herself. The inflicting of a *lex talionis*–type punishment takes back that unmerited advantage, thereby rebalancing the scales across the moral community. Such an account virtually excludes the victim even as a benchmark for the application of the talion principle. On its understanding of the balancing act, it is not the suffering of the victim that is balanced; it is the undue advantage that causing the victim to suffer has provided the offender. In fact, it is probably closer to the idea to drop the image of balancing altogether and adopt Hegel's terminology of annulment—the offender's advantage is annulled.

However Kant's balancing act is interpreted, *lex talionis* remains his favored principle of proportionality. But he also recognizes that the talion formula is not appropriate in many cases. In single murder cases there is little difficulty in seeing its applicability; it probably recommends itself to us. However, in the case of serial killers it becomes problematic, for only one of the murders committed by a serial killer can actually be punished by application of the principle. You cannot kill an offender more than once. Of course, throughout the centuries all sorts of grotesque ways of executing the capital sentence in an extended fashion to reflect the seriousness of the crime have been instituted. The old English practice of hanging, boiling in oil, and then drawing and quartering a serious offender, no matter how long the complete process takes and even if the villain is revived after each stage, does not achieve the end of *lex talionis*. My suspicion, in any event, is that penalties of such a theatrical and radical sort were intended more for deterrent than for retributive purposes.

Kant seems satisfied in maintaining that no principle other than *lex talionis* specifies "definitely the quality and the quantity of punishment; all other principles are fluctuating and unsuited for a sentence of pure and strict justice."[9] But he is surely wrong about that when it comes to offenses such as rape and kidnapping, let alone armed robbery. Suppose that an adult kidnaps a baby from its crib and holds the child for three days before returning the child to the parents. What is the appropriate punishment? Suppose further that the parents live in squalor and pay little attention to the baby. They do not provide him with toys nor do they play with him. The kidnapper, on the other hand, lives in a large, beautifully furnished home, lavishes toys and affection on the child, and entertains him throughout the period of the kidnapping. Were *lex talionis* to be artlessly applied, the kidnapper should be taken from his or her home and held in a luxurious house and entertained by his or her keepers for three days. Who would call that an appropriate punishment for kidnapping? And even if the story goes the way most kidnappings do (except for ending in the death of the victim) and the victim is held captive in unpleasant circumstances for a period of days, would sentencing the kidnapper to a like number of days in a filthy jail cell constitute appropriate punishment? Does being raped appropriately punish a rapist?

Kant worries about cases in which the rich are less likely to feel the sting of fines than the poor do, which provokes him to shift the focus of the talion principle from one-to-one matching to similarity matching. He writes: "A fine, for example, imposed for a verbal injury has no relation to the offense, for someone wealthy might indeed allow himself to indulge in a verbal insult on some occasion; yet the outrage he has done to someone's love or honor can still be quite similar to the hurt done to his pride if he is constrained by judgment and right not only to apologize publicly to the one he has insulted but also to kiss his hand, for instance, even though he is of a lower class."[10] Kant does not dwell for long on this matching game, jumping rather abruptly to the case of murder, where he ordains that "if, however, he has committed murder he must die."[11] He will allow similarity matching for other offenses, but it cannot be contrived in the case of murder because there is no similarity between death and life. Executions, however, are to be humanely carried out. He would have opposed drawing and quartering and, probably, boiling in oil. The reason for the constraint is that even though the murderer must die, he or she must be treated with respect and not turned "into something abominable." But, of course, the murderer is "something abominable" and, on Kant's theory, has managed the trick of turning himself or herself that way by an act of will. I suspect that Kant is more concerned about protecting the moral merit of the executioner than the worth of the offender.

Kant's lack of moral concern about killing the murderer is the result of his view that the murderer has willed that punishment on himself or herself. We have the right to punish the murderer, and he or she cannot complain of cruel and unusual treatment when we kill him or her because "'*Per quod quis peccat, per idem punitur et item*' (One who commits a sin is punished through it and in the same way) . . . The only time a criminal cannot complain that a wrong is done him is when he brings his misdeed back upon himself, and what is done to him . . . is what he has perpetrated on others, if not in terms of its letter at least in terms of its spirit."[12] Kant, however, is clear that he does not mean that the murderer wills his or her punishment, but that the murderer has willed a "punishable action." The reason this must be the case is that if the offender wills his or her punishment, then it would not be punishment. Also, and importantly, in the case of murder, the murderer is not willing the taking of his or her own life when he or she commits the crime. In Jeffrey Reiman's terms, he or she is authorizing—not willing—the punishment.[13] This authorization to punish granted by the offender gives us the right to punish him or her, and the similarity principle dictates the type and amount of punishment.

Having a right to punish, nonetheless, generally does not mean that one has a duty to punish. On this point, however, Kant seems somewhat ambiguous. Even though he is typically understood to be a positive retributivist, one who holds that the previous wrong act is in itself a reason for inflicting the penalty and not to do so would itself be a wrong act, two stories he tells may suggest that he was not so clear on this point. The first we can call "The Raft" and the second "The Island."

"The Raft" appears in two of Kant's works, *On the Old Saw: That May Be Right in Theory But It Won't Work in Practice* and *The Metaphysics of Morals.* The plot is that there has been a shipwreck, and two survivors are floating on a small raft or plank. There are provisions sufficient only for one. In order to save his own life, one of them shoves the other, "whose life is equally in danger,"[14] off the raft and he drowns. Kant first denies that the survivor had a right to kill the other person to save his own life: "For I have a duty to save my life only on condition that I can do so without committing a crime. But I have an unconditional duty not to take the life of someone else who is not injuring me nor causing the danger threatening mine."[15] Neither of the rafters caused the dangerous situation in which they find themselves so they both should have an unconditional duty not to take the other's life. Practically speaking, however, each of the rafters could be seen by the other as a genuine threat to his survival, although this is not a clear case of self-defense, as Kant conceives of the story.

On the other hand, the survivor, we may assume, believed that his life was at grave risk by having to share the raft with the other person. There is too little information in the story to confirm why this might be the case, but we might suppose that the raft has only one canteen of fresh water or very sparse provisions, and the survivor ascertains these facts. But Kant tells us that it is "false" to say that the survivor "had a right to do so [to throw the other off of the raft] because of his (physical) need."[16] However, he goes on to say that within the province of law, allowance for such "emergency acts" can be made, and his rather surprising reason is that punishment cannot be appropriately attached to the act because the only appropriate punishment would be death: "And it would be an absurd law that threatened death to one who refuses to die voluntarily in a dangerous situation."[17]

What is Kant imagining? Perhaps that the raft is known by both parties to be provisioned sufficiently for the survival of only one. The choice is up to both parties. Either one may voluntarily jump into the sea and drown so that the other can survive, or one can push the other into the sea so that one can survive. Of course, there is the third possibility that they can split the provisions and last as long as they can in hopes of rescue, but that possibility does not seem to be relevant to the Kantian legal solution; the uncertainty of early rescue is not contemplated. Kant thinks that a law that punished one because "in a dangerous situation" one did not voluntarily sacrifice oneself to allow another to live would be absurd. But what does he mean by "absurd"?

Interestingly, he does not apply the universalization test of the Categorical Imperative or, in fact, any of his moral principles to the case. The proposed law would be absurd because it would be politically foolish, and its administration could severely weaken the power of law itself. He explicitly denies the existence of a *"right of necessity"* when he writes that the "supposed *right* to do *wrong* in extreme (physical) need is an absurdity."[18] The supposed right of necessity would be a moral right. So in *On the Old Saw,* the raft survivor is not to be punished under law, but there is at least the suggestion that what he did was morally wrong.

In the *Metaphysics of Morals,* the raft story is retold and the point is clarified. Kant writes: "There can be no *penal law* that would assign the death penalty to someone in a shipwreck who, in order to save his own life, shoves another, whose life is in equal danger, off a plank on which he had saved himself. For the punishment threatened by the law could not be greater than the loss of his own life. A penal law of this sort could not have the effect intended, since a threat of an ill that is still *uncertain* (death by a judicial verdict) cannot outweigh the fear of an ill that is *certain* (drowning)."[19] Clearly, Kant's appeal is to the practical outcome of the application of such a law: no one would be deterred from performing the act it prohibits in the relevant circumstances. He clearly does not use an appeal to self-defense as a way of justifying his sense of the penal resolution of the matter.

However, although a consequentialist in such matters of legal punishment, Kant returns immediately to form. He writes, "Hence the deed of saving one's life by violence is not to be judged *inculpable (inculpabile)* but only *unpunishable (impunible).*"[20] And he chides the "jurists" who confuse unpunishability with inculpability. The latter is the moral judgment, and it is not consequentialist. Morally, the survivor is culpable for killing the other person on the raft. Kant, as in *On the Old Saw,* also denies the legitimacy of the *"right of necessity.":* "There could be no necessity that would make what is wrong conform with law,"[21] by which he means moral law. Kant's position, carving a deep gulf between moral culpability and legal punishability, is reminiscent of Hobbes's account of the sovereign's situation. Hobbes writes that: "they that have Soveraigne power may commit Iniquity; but not Injustice, or Injury in the proper signification."[22]

There is a relatively famous nineteenth-century legal case that tests Kant's position and our intuitions. It is *United States v. Holmes,*[23] in which a sailor off of the *William Brown,* a sunken passenger ship, was in a longboat that was overloaded with passengers and crew. The boat was leaking, and the gunwale fluctuated from five to twelve inches above the waves. Bad weather was threatening to swamp the boat. Holmes responded to what he took to be a threat to his life and some of the others on board and threw fourteen men and two women out of the longboat into the sea, where they drowned. The passengers did not willingly go to their deaths, and no lottery system was established to determine the order. None of the crew members on the boat were cast into the sea. The next day they were rescued, and Holmes was charged with manslaughter. He was found guilty and received a sentence of hard labor and a fine.

In his defense it was argued that Holmes was innocent of wrongdoing because his were acts of self-defense, and in the longboat he and the others on board existed in a state of nature and were governed only by the "law of necessity," the very law to which Kant prohibits refuge in the Raft Story. The reason the defense invoked the state of nature argument was to counter the prosecution's claim that is well fortified in precedent that sailors bear duties to passengers and cannot save themselves at the cost of the passengers' lives. With regard to the self-defense argument, Judge Baldwin retorted, "The peril must be instant, overwhelming, leaving no alternative but to lose our own life, or take the life of another person."

The judge went on to revirtually retell Kant's Raft Story, maintaining that "neither is bound to save the other's life by sacrificing his own, nor would either commit a crime in saving his own life in a struggle for the only means of safety." In such cases, "the taking of a life is divested of unlawfulness." Judge Baldwin continued that, even if this had been a Raft Story but that one person was a crew member and the deceased a passenger from their sunken ship, the sailor would be guilty of manslaughter if he were to throw the passenger off the raft to save his own life. The *Holmes* case brings a stations and duties ethics to the issue, but the court, by and large, argues that in the Raft Story Kant's account is the correct one: the law should not punish despite moral culpability. The court concludes that Holmes, however, was not in a Kantian Raft Story, and so he is both morally culpable and legally punishable. Consequences of not doing so are also suggested: the breakdown of the duties of the sailor and the loss of the station distinction between passenger and crew member.

Reading the Raft Story, we should regard Kant as something of a consequentialist with respect to legal punishment, though clearly a retributivist from the moral point of view. His retributivism, however, is not pure, for he is willing to forgo punishment in certain cases of moral culpability, those unlikely to produce a deterrent effect. He would likely admit to having the right to punish, but doing so does not become a duty. However, later in the *Metaphysics of Morals,* Kant tells the Island Story, and it may shake our confidence that he is a consequentialist at all. In this story that some writers refer to as "notorious," we are to imagine an island on which exists a community. The community has apparently been in existence long enough to witness murders and to catch and convict the murderers. Murderers are in prison awaiting their executions when the community decides to abandon the island and disperse throughout the world. Kant writes that before the diaspora can begin "the last murderer remaining in prison would first have to be executed."[24]

Given the distinction he drew from the Raft Story and its attendant penal consequentialism, it seems odd that in the Island Story he insists that the penal sentences of the murderers be carried out. After all, the community will cease to exist after the diaspora. What point could there be for the community members to kill murderers who are unlikely to have any further impact on their lives? In the Island Story Kant makes no reference to any deterrent consequences of inflicting the death penalty. He probably realizes that there is no deterrent effect of the administration of capital punishment in a community that will no longer exist. Also, there is no carryover deterrent effect to other communities. Potential murderers are not likely to be deterred from their felonious deeds upon learning that in a now defunct community convicted murderers were executed. One would think that the logic that found the raft survivor unpunishable would hold on the Island as well. But Kant takes a different tack: the murderers must be executed "so that each has done to him what his deeds deserve and blood guilt does not cling to the people for not having insisted upon this punishment."[25]

This account is both retributive and consequentialist. It is consequentialist with respect to the members of the community. One of the two reasons to carry out the punishment is so that the community members will not carry the "blood guilt" with them as they take up residence in other communities. The appeal is clearly to consequences, but what is this "blood guilt" to which Kant refers? At first it might seem that the community members would share in the "blood guilt" of the murderers' crimes because in failing to punish such actions, they would appear to condone them. But that is not exactly Kant's position. He says that the failure can be regarded as an act of collaboration in a public violation of justice. The "blood guilt" is in failing to fit the punishment to the crime according to "the strict law of retribution" and is thereby a failure of moral duty.

Here Kant seems to be arguing that we have a moral duty to exact retribution; it is not just a right, a right that we could choose not to exercise. This is pure retributivism bolstered by the threat of future "blood guilt," which could surely, at least, have karmic consequences in Kant's moral theory. Murderers do not seem only to have a right to be punished either. Clearly, if that were the case, murderers generally would not want to exercise the right. The moral law is the source of the obligation, and the murderer, by authorizing his or her punishment, as it were, also endorses the moral law. Although I am not in full agreement with Jean Hampton's analysis of Kant's Island, I think she is right that Kant took "it as fundamental that to be committed to morality is to be committed to asserting and defending it no matter what the consequences."[26]

The Raft and the Island may be said to differ in a way that matters in that the murderers on the island are not incarcerated because they chose not to kill themselves in a desperate situation. There is, apparently, no ambiguity about their actions in the circumstances. They are both culpable and punishable, and not to punish them would constitute a violation by the members of the community of the moral law, the law of retribution.

Although I have argued that Kant can be read as a Balancing Target Retributivist, and he certainly is a Target Retributivist in the Island Story where the additional target is avoidance of "blood guilt," Hegel provides a clearer case. He holds that criminal behavior unbalances the equality between people. Punishment annuls the wrong and reestablishes the equality. Hegel writes that with regard to punishment "the only important things are, first, that crime is to be annulled, not because it is the producing of evil, but because it is an infringement of the right as right, and secondly, the question of what that positive existence is which crime possesses and which must be annulled; it is this existence which is the real evil to be removed, and the essential point is the question of where it lies."[27] Hegel does argue that the offender has a right to be punished, and not to punish the offender is not to respect him or her "as a rational being." Further, the offender only receives the respect that is due to him or her when the "concept and measure of his punishment are derived from his own act."[28] This, of course, is Kant's talion matching principle: what you do to others you do also to yourself. But what is really important in punishment for Hegel is the annulling of the crime, which is the sense in which Hegel's retributivism is clearly of the Balancing Target variety.

What is it to annul the crime? Reiman, I think correctly, explicates Hegel as claiming that there is an equality among people that the offender has unbalanced by the commission of the crime: "Retributive punishment restores that equality by 'annulling' the crime."[29] If the offender were not punished, we would be attesting to the validity of the injury the offender has visited on the victim. As Reiman notes, "Doing back to you what you did 'annuls' your violation by reasserting that the other has the same right toward you that you assert toward him."[30] Importantly, the victim's injury is not annulled. In fact, the victim gets very little from the Hegelian conception of punishment except, possibly, the satisfaction that the offender has been forced to realize that he or she is not better than the victim is in the moral scheme of things. Restoring the equality of persons that the offender had unbalanced supposedly rectifies the indignity borne by the victim. Reiman states that "a crime . . . is an assault on the sovereignty of an individual that temporarily places one person in a position of illegitimate sovereignty over another (the victim)."[31] The victim has the right to rectify his or her loss of status relative to the offender, which is Hegel's concept of revenge: "The annulling of crime in this sphere where right is immediate is principally revenge, which is just in its content in so far as it is retributive."[32]

But this idea of annulling a crime resists serious examination. How can a past crime be annulled? It cannot be wiped out, made to have not occurred. No penalty can ever do that. I suspect, with Mackie, that Hegel might be carrying over something of Kant's "blood guilt" into the notion of annulment. And Kant's "blood guilt" brings to mind, especially with regard to the Island Story, the pollution doctrine of the ancients discussed in Chapter 1. Is that the target of Hegel's retributivism?

Hegel's balancing conception of retributivism in which punishment's target is to annul the offense by restoring a presumed status quo of equality between the offender and the victim may seem something of a stretch. Nonetheless, Jean Hampton has employed the Hegelian type of Balancing Target Retributivism, although with a modified conception of what is being annulled. She agrees with Hegel that punishment vindicates the relative worth of the victim vis-à-vis the offender. For her, wrongdoers declare themselves to have greater worth than their victims, to be superior to them. They deny the moral reality of the fundamental equality of persons. Punishment sends the offender a different message, an annulment of the declaration of inequality. It "symbolizes the correct relative value of wrongdoer and victim."[33]

Punishment vindicates the victim's relative worth that has been called into question by the actions of the victimizer. Those actions, according to Hampton, amount to evidence of a significant inequality of worth between the two parties. Punishment nullifies that evidence. Her theory, in the same vein as Hegel and Kant, depends on the affirmation of the equality of moral worth of all persons. The offender's actions have assaulted not only the victim but also the doctrine of worth egalitarianism. The victim's moral worth, for Hampton, must be reaffirmed. There is, she seems to recognize, no way to annul the wrongdoer's deed, so all that can be annulled is the "false evidence seemingly provided by the wrongdoer of the relative worth of the victim and the wrongdoer. Or to put it another way, it can annul the message, sent by the crime, that they are not equal in value."[34]

Hampton's position, however, is unsatisfactory. If it is the message that is being annulled, how is that accomplished by inflicting pain and suffering, even death, on the offender? Why can it not simply be stated? The answer seems to be that the original message was delivered by an act of victimization, an act that injured the victim. The inequality message was implied in the act, not stated. Messages of that sort apparently can only be annulled by a talion-like response. The message of annulment is therefore also only implied as the victim inflicts comparable suffering on the victimizer. Still, that is acceptable because it is, after all, retributivism that grounds the theory, and the balancing target is a way to placate those widespread concerns of sensitive folks that pure retributivism is barbaric. The offender is, in the first instance, to be punished because that is what such people deserve. Secondarily, however, morality requires that we annul any and all claims of fundamental inequality among the members of the moral community.

In Chapter 6 I rejected worth egalitarianism, hence the Balancing Target Retributive theories that are based on it are not available to me. George Sher's version of Balancing Target Retributivism moves in a somewhat different direction. He requires a balancing of benefits and burdens among people. He sees the situation as one in which the wrongdoer gains a benefit from his or her deeds against those who practice self-restraint and avoid wrongdoing. The benefit that the wrongdoer secures is freedom from moral restraint, that is, the freedom to get away with the victimization of others. Punishment, on Sher's account, is justified when it is equated with the amount of excess benefit the wrongdoer gained. Sometimes wrongdoers gain a double benefit from their deeds. Sher writes, "The benefits-and-burdens account regards punishment as justified not merely by the wrongdoer's receiving the benefits of others' self-restraint, but by his having these benefits plus the benefit of his own lack of self-restraint." The degree of benefit sets the degree of wrongness, and that sets the amount of punishment required to restore the balance. Proportionality of punishment is measured in terms of net gains in freedom secured by wrongdoing. As Sher notes, "Because the murderer evades a prohibition of far greater force—because he thus 'gets away with more'—his net gain in freedom remains greater. And for that reason, the amount of punishment he deserves seems greater as well."[35]

Sher justifies punishment on the principle that "any unfair advantage enjoyed at an earlier time should be balanced by a corresponding later burden."[36] His "bookkeeping model of justified punishment," however, leads him to worry about "whole life theories of desert" (the term is owed to Gertrude Ezorsky). On such theories it shouldn't matter when in a life one suffered the burdens of undue restraint. All that matters is that when a life is taken as a whole, the benefits and burdens balance. Such a theory, however, should strike us as outrageously counterintuitive. The fact that someone was forced to endure a deprived childhood frequently punctuated with verbal and physical abuse does not give him or her a free pass to commit evil acts on others when he or she achieves adulthood.

Of course, a first pass at such a worry is likely to be that punishment follows the wrongdoing; it does not precede it. Hence, the unhappy childhood cannot count as balancing the adult's gain in the benefits of freedom from moral restraint. In fact, there is a sense of having passed through the "looking-glass" in such a proposal. It might be recalled that the King's Messenger (who is drawn by Tenniel to look like the Mad Hatter) is in prison. The Queen tells Alice, "He's in prison now, being punished: and the trial doesn't even begin till next Wednesday: and of course the crime comes last of all." Alice wonders what will happen if he never commits the crime. "That would be all the better, wouldn't it," the Queen replies and asks, "Were you ever punished?" "Only for faults," says Alice. To which the Queen "triumphantly" retorts: "And you were all the better for it." "Yes, but then I had done the things I was punished for, that makes all the difference." The Queen closes the conversation imperiously: "But if you hadn't done them that would have been better still; better, and better, and better."[37]

Sher notes that the sorts of things being balanced in a whole life approach that lets earlier suffering offset future wrongdoing are not commensurate. In the case of suffering borne before the offense, the amount of lost benefit is determined by the loss of happiness or preference-satisfaction that the person endured. In the case of the commission of an offense, it is the amount of additional benefit in terms of freedom from constraint that the offender has garnered by committing the offense. That benefit is not determined on the scale of the offender's happiness or preference-satisfaction, which is not to say that the offender may not experience greater happiness or preference-satisfaction from committing the offense. Sher's way of putting this correlation is that "the wrongdoer's extra benefit is measured by his act's degree of wrongness, whereas his previous burden is measured on a different scale of preference-(dis)satisfaction."[38] The point is not that the temporal location of the offense and the burden are relevant, but that the scales on which they are measured are significantly different. Sher goes on to explain why the fact that the punishment follows the offense balances the unwarranted benefits.

Punishments are the sort of acts that in the normal course of events are not morally permissible. In everyday life, you cannot go around doing to people what can be done to them when they are punished. People are owed a certain amount of freedom from restraint, and to reduce that amount is to injure them. As long as people act within the boundaries of moral constraint, they enjoy a not insubstantial amount of freedom of action. However, "because the wrongdoer has unfairly gained an extra measure of freedom from moral restraint, the natural way to restore a fair balance is to reduce the protection he ordinarily would have gained through moral restraints on the conduct of others. By treating the wrongdoer in what is ordinarily a forbidden way, we strip away part of the protection that moral restraints on our behavior would ordinarily have afforded him."[39] Sher concludes that in this balancing act we are removing precisely the advantage the offender has wrongfully gained from the commission of the offense. The King's Messenger (the Mad-Hatter) is not being punished in the Queen's prison cell. He is, we might want to say, being tortured or abused.

Michael Davis develops a Balancing Target Retributive position along lines very similar to those used by Sher. He refers to the primary governing principle of his theory as the "unfair-advantage principle."[40] Rather than assessing the imbalance between the offender and the community in terms of benefits and burdens, he uses the language of advantage to make the same point as Sher. But Davis draws attention to a crucial element in the non-harm-based balancing theories that he regards as their strength and I find to be their weakness. He notes that understanding the offender's gain as one of advantage (or benefits for Sher) avoids the need to examine the harm or injury that the offender has visited on the victim. He writes: "The advantage bears no necessary relation to the harm the criminal actually did . . . His crime consists only in the unfair advantage he necessarily took over the law-abiding by breaking the law in question. The measure of punishment due is the relative value of that unfair advantage."[41] In short, non-harm-based Balancing Target Retributivism focuses on what the offender gained by committing the offense, and it ignores what the victim has lost. The victim, other than as a way of identifying that an offense has occurred, plays no role in the determination of appropriate punishment. Rather cavalierly, to my mind, Davis writes that "the damage a criminal actually does is between him and his victim, a private matter to be settled by civil suit (or the moral equivalent)."[42] And what is "the moral equivalent"? Revenge?

This business of repayment for the wrongdoing also is problematic despite the fact that Balancers like Sher and Davis work hard to make their accounts sound plausible. Admittedly, the word "retribution" comes from the Latin "to pay back" (retribuo), but in the first place, paying back is not what the person being punished does. The payback, such as it may be, is done by the punisher, the avenger.

The offender is on the receiving end, not the giving end, of the punishment. Also, if we think of society as the damaged party, as many of the Balancing Target Retributivists do, then it is impossible to conceive of how society is paid back for its loss by having either to foot the bill for the offender's incarceration or the cost of execution. It would seem that society is twice the loser and gains back nothing or very little. And if the victim of a murder was a valued member of society, how is society "paid back" by killing the murderer? Surely the victim is repaid nothing by the state inflicting a punishment, including capital punishment, on a deserving offender.

In *The Dawn* Nietzsche attacks the Balancing Target Retributivists' use of "shopkeeper's scales." He notes that the victim, "quite apart from the question of how this harm might be undone again, . . . turns to the courts for its sake; for the present this maintains our abominable penal codes, with their shopkeeper's scales and the desire to balance guilt and punishment."[43] Nietzsche's solution seems to be to treat wrongdoing as a form or type of sickness and in so doing to remove the connection between it and punishment: "Shouldn't we be able to say: every 'guilty person' is a sick person?"[44]

His idea is that the "number of parasites" a society or an individual can stand is the measure of its strength. In other words, enduring wrongdoing by others is a sign of moral strength in both a community and an individual. Victims who can renounce revenge or any call for the punishment of those who have injured them display their moral power and superiority over offenders. Although Nietzsche frequently attacks the retributive urge because he believes it to be based in unworthy emotions, he also chides a society that becomes "so pathologically soft and tender that among other things it sides even with those who harm it . . . Punishing somehow seems unfair to it . . . 'Why still punish? Punishing itself is terrible.' With this question, herd morality, the morality of timidity, draws its ultimate consequence."[45] And that consequence is that morality renders itself useless and considers itself unnecessary.

Further, Nietzsche does not endorse the Socratic dictum. He claims that Plato was too noble in accepting the view that "nobody wants to do harm to himself, therefore all that is bad is done involuntarily. For the bad do harm to themselves: this they would not do if they knew that the bad is bad. Hence the bad are bad only because of an error; if one removes the error, one necessarily makes them—good."[46] Nietzsche says that this sort of reasoning "smells of the rabble." The clear suggestion from him is that a rehabilitative, indeed any target, even quasi-consequentialist, theory of punishment or response to wrongdoing is morally flawed.

There is another type of Target Retributivism that is not involved in balancing acts, which I will call Reprobative Target Retributivism. Such retributivists regard punishment as an emphatic denunciation of the wrongful action and the person who performed it. There are two sides to punishment, they insist: the hostile response, what Feinberg calls "hard treatment,"[47] and the reprobative symbolism. Both should be painful to the offender. The latter is the additional target, and it is the way in which the wrongness of the offender's action is publicly denounced, reproved, and condemned. Certainly reprobation and denunciation are not insignificant elements of the message communicated in revenge, as discussed in Chapter 3.

A reprobative element of punishment can aim at two sorts of targets. One sort is the intrinsic value of denouncing wrongdoing in and of itself. The other is an unabashedly consequentialist goal, for example, the one argued for by Andrew Oldenquist: making a contribution to "society's identity as a self-respecting community."[48] Some might argue that denunciation could have a deterrent effect (I think this argument could be part of the defense of what I have called the Hester Prynne sanction, though I did not use such a defense when I suggested adverse publicity sanctions in corporate cases[49]). It is hard to imagine that anyone could concoct a persuasive argument against denouncing wrongdoing and those who intentionally do wrong. In fact, morality in very large measure traditionally has been about the business of reproof and prohibition. However, in response to my Hester Prynne sanction proposal, John Ladd argued that "persons . . . ought never to be treated in a degrading fashion . . . To subject a human being to the kind of indignity involved in the Hester Prynne sanction is a violation of the categorical imperative."[50]

Feinberg identified what he called the expressive function as a significant element in punishment, but he noted that criticism would likely be raised regarding the specific forms the condemnatory function might take. I suppose that Ladd's criticism of the Hester Prynne sanction falls in that category. Ladd might grant that denouncing the offender is morally justifiable, while attaching various forms or rituals that may be employed to carry out the expressive function may not. In any event, I am persuaded with Feinberg and Nozick that the message of condemnation is an essential part of morally justifiable punishment. Morality requires not only a firm hand but a loud and clear voice.

With respect to proportionality, the Reprobative Target Retributivists tend to adopt a balancing position. Feinberg, for example, provides two conditions to justify reprobative retributive punishment: (1) "the crime be of a kind that is truly worthy of reprobation"; and (2) "the degree of disapproval expressed by the punishment should 'fit' the crime only in the unproblematic sense that the more serious crimes should receive stronger disapproval than the less serious ones, the seriousness of the crime being determined by the amount of harm it generally causes and the degree to which people are disposed to commit it."[51] It might be argued that the latter condition has the distinct smell of deterrence about it and that it is, in that regard, removed somewhat from retributivism. Of course, it might be argued that condemnation of wrongdoing is good, in and of itself, and that deterrence or improving or sustaining the moral character of the community is a worthwhile side effect, but hardly one that is required to justify reprobative retributive punishment. As discussed in Chapter 3, Nozick's account of the communicative aspect of revenge only requires that the offender understand the message, not that he or she accept it and not that it be generally broadcast to a wider community.

The problem with Reprobative Target Retributivism is that it is utterly unclear whether fitting the condemnatory aspect to the offense will suffice to accomplish the fit that retributivism requires between the penalty inflicted on the offender and the gravity of the offense. Put another way, it is imaginable that the proportionality between offense and condemnation can be achieved while the offender escapes relatively unscathed. Punishment, and especially revenge, is much more than verbal or ritual instruction. It is the inflicting of harm on those whose harm-causing actions merit it.

I noted that there is a third type of Target Retributivism, which is Appeasement Target Retributivism. I can think of two types, suggested by Cottingham's list. One target is placation, the other is satisfaction. Placation generally involves belief in a divine being who has strong retributive views. Punishment is meted out to propitiate the god who will visit terrible things on the community if wrongdoing is not retributively punished. I am not enough of a historian of law and religion to speak with any authority on these matters, but my guess is that the *lex talionis* elements of early law codes are justified by the lawgiver with, at least, hints of placation. Satisfaction theories justify the severity of punishment in terms of a fit with the satisfaction that the suffering of the offender gives to the victim of the offense or to the victim's surrogates. The idea is that the victim must be appeased, so the victim, rather like the god of the placation version, sets the degree of punishment.

The major problem with a satisfaction version of Appeasement Target Retributivism is that it is more consequentialist than retributive and utterly dependent on the whims of the victim. The punishment for an offense could range from death to nothing at all. The victim of a serious injury might be moved by the spirit of turning the other cheek and hence be satisfied by a light reprimand of the offender. In another case, the victim of a minor wrongdoing, a mere slight, might be satisfied with nothing less than the death or mutilation of the offender. After all, the idea of seeking satisfaction for the supposed harms and injuries one has endured is the backbone of the duel. "Will nothing less satisfy you?" is the proverbial question asked of the challenging party.

Retributivism, in all of its forms, requires that wrongdoing be proportionately punished. Pure Retributivism accepts four constraints and sets no additional targets. Braithwaite and Pettit spell out those constraints in the following way: "(1) No one other than a person found to be guilty of a crime may be punished for it. (2) Anyone found to be guilty of a crime must be punished for it. (3) Punishment must not be more than a degree commensurate with the nature of the crime and the culpability of the criminal. (4) Punishment must not be less than of a degree commensurate with the nature of the crime and the culpability of the criminal."[52] A full-fledged or Pure Retributivist requires all four constraints;

what J. L. Mackie calls a Negative Retributivist endorses the first and the third constraints.[53] We should not punish those who are innocent, and we should only punish in proportion to the offense. Of course, the innocent cannot be punished. If harm is inflicted on them it is unwarranted and thus not punishment, but is itself an offense. Strictly speaking, only the guilty can be punished. A Positive Retributivist endorses the second and the fourth constraints: offenders must be punished, and that punishment must not be less than is proportional to the offense. For the Pure and the Positive Retributivists, offenses must be punished. Negative Retributivists permit punishment but do not require it. A Negative Retributivist then can be described as a Permissive Retributivist because permission to punish is granted but punishment is not mandatory.

The view I have taken throughout with respect to virtuous avengers could be classed as a version of Permissive Retributivism. Avengers, on my account, are permitted to inflict hostile responses on offenders, but they are not morally required to do so. Avengers have options. However, that does not entail that the collective "we," society or the community, has such an option. Wrongdoing requires a hostile response, and if it regularly does not receive it, the whole façade of morality will crumble. The need for a hostile response is embedded in the very idea that an action or a person is bad or evil or wicked. It might be wondered why we have a tendency to see wrong actions as calling for hostile responses. Mackie worries about such things, noting that "our basic moral concepts themselves of good and bad, right and wrong, cannot be adequately analyzed unless we include a retributive element."[54] For actions to be morally bad or evil or wrong or wicked is for them to be more than injurious or harmful or even forbidden. Many things are harmful or injurious that are not morally wrong or evil. They are morally wrong when their perpetrators deserve to be treated with hostility by us because they performed them.

Clearly, the natural question that emerges is, why do morally wrong actions deserve hostile responses? But that is the wrong question. In Chapter 3 and elsewhere, I adopted what might be called a predominantly Humean account of the origins of our conception of wrong and its cohort of moral terms. Morality, as Hume maintains, "is more properly felt than judg'd of."[55] What is right is what "we naturally approve of." And what is right tends to render us "proper members of society: While the qualities, which we naturally disapprove of, have a contrary tendency, and render any intercourse with the person dangerous or disagreeable. For having found that such tendencies have force enough to produce the strongest sentiment of morals, we can never reasonably, in these cases, look for any other cause of approbation or blame; it being an inviolable maxim in philosophy, that where any particular cause is sufficient for an effect, we ought to rest satisfied with it, and ought not to multiply causes without necessity."[56] In effect, our sense of wrong, bad, evil, wicked, and the like "proceeds from certain sentiments of . . . disgust which arise upon contemplation and view of particular qualities and characters."[57] The proper question is, why do we naturally see morally wrong actions as requiring hostile responses? Mackie recommends that we look to sociobiological answers that make reference to cooperative strategies. I am satisfied with Hume to accept that this is what it is to be the sort of creatures we are and look for no other causes or explanations.

Society does not have an option with respect to punishment of wrongdoing. All of the retributive constraints on Braithwaite and Pettit's list apply to the collective moral community. Proportionality of offense to punishment, of course, is strictly compelled to ensure that the enforcement of morality is not abused and becomes wrongdoing itself. The virtuous avenger, however, is not compelled to punish; he or she is permitted to punish, which means that the second constraint does not apply to him or her. The permissiveness might be taken to extend to the amount of punishment inflicted by the avenger as well: the avenger *may* punish up to the limit set by the third constraint. The fourth constraint may not, on the other hand, play any role in virtuous vengeance. The problem that may be anticipated is one of coordination. The moral community must punish; the avenger may do so. If the avenger acts and if the wrongdoing is met with a hostile response in the appropriate proportion, as set by the third and fourth constraints, has the moral community's obligation to uphold morality been met? I think that the answer must be yes. Any further punishment of the offender would violate the constraints. On the other hand, should the avenger inflict a punishment that is less severe than the maximum allowed by the third and fourth constraints, the moral community, by activating whatever mechanisms it has instituted for the purposes, ought to inflict further punishment on the offender.

The difficulty in administering the coordination of revenge outcomes and socially instituted penal sanctions, of course, is a practical reason why vengeance is usually discouraged in communities with criminal justice systems. That practical matter does not, however, run to moral considerations. In fact, it is very hard to find any opponents of vengeance who have borne the burden of proving that the deep human emotions that may motivate the avenger are "unambiguously evil or unambiguously sick and that in either case they deserve no place in the moral and legal outlook of civilized people."[58] In fact, I think just the opposite case can be made, which was suggested to me by David Lewis's analysis of the so-called "paradox of deterrence."[59]

Lewis pointed out that "vengefulness is a part of a package deal" in the case of patriots. It is conceptually inseparable from love of country and solidarity with one's countrymen. Lewis writes: "Could a man really be said to love his country if he were not at all disposed to make its enemies his own? Could he really be said to make them his enemies if he were not disposed to harm them?"[60] I suspect that, if we were to examine our loyalties and what we really care about in our lives,[61] we would discover that vengeance is not conceptually separable from many—from most—of them. Morality, our understanding of what is right and what is wrong, is, I believe, in that category. A person cannot really care about morality and not make its enemies his or her enemies and not be disposed to harm them. I have insisted throughout this book that the disposition to administer a hostile response is conceptually inseparable from judging that an action is wrong. The moral concern is, of course, to ensure that the harm one is disposed to do to the enemies of morality is channeled to that end and is not disproportionate or indiscriminate.

I believe that under the constraints developed for virtuous vengeance, concerns about equal protection, due process, and proportionality that might be raised by opponents of revenge can be allayed. Nonetheless, I suppose that the only way that coordination could dependably be accomplished is for the community, through its justice system, to have, as it were, first crack. However, should the community fail in its moral duty to satisfy the four retributive constraints, the virtuous avenger would not lack moral justification.

In circumstances in which no community system for the administration of appropriate penalties exists or in which such a system is corrupt, the virtuous avenger is the last best hope of morality. He or she empowers morality as long as the penalties that are imposed satisfy the proportionality constraints. Unfortunately, the third and fourth proportionality constraints leave open how the avenger is to determine what level of punishment is commensurate with the nature of the offense and the culpability of the offender. It sounds as if balancing is again in the offing, but I think that need not be the case. What is wanted is fit. The punishment is supposed to, as the Gilbert and Sullivan song goes, "fit the crime." The notions of fit and balance are not substitutable. We talk of clothes fitting their wearer, the music befitting the situation, the square peg not fitting in the round hole, a meal fit for a king, and so on. Fit, but not balance, has to do with suitability, tailoring, proper sizing. Something is said to fit the situation or the circumstances when it is well adapted or suited to them, when it is just the right size. In the case of punishment and offense, fit might have more to do with shaping or molding the punishment to the moral contours of the offense than to balancing it.

I have no idea what balances rape, for example. I am certain that *lex talionis,* a rape for a rape, is utterly unsatisfactory. But when I start to think of what might be a suitable punishment, my attention is drawn to the moral contours of rape and so to the victim's experience. What is it to be raped? It is to have one's physical space trespassed violently, to be violated, to be emotionally and physically assaulted, to have one's very sense of self ripped from one's control. It is to have one's integrity maligned, spit upon, trampled. It is to be enslaved. Perhaps the most moving piece written by a philosopher that I have ever read is Susan Brison's account of the rape and attempted murder she endured in France. She writes: "I had been grabbed from behind, pulled into the bushes, beaten, and sexually assaulted. Feeling absolutely helpless and entirely at my assailant's mercy, I talked to him, calling him 'sir.' . . . He called me a whore and told me to shut up . . . I instinctively fought back which so enraged my attacker that he strangled me until I lost consciousness. When I awoke, I was being dragged by my feet down into a ravine . . .I wish I could convey the horror of losing consciousness while my animal instincts desperately fought the effects of strangulation . . . I was sure I was dying. But I revived, just in time to see him lunging toward me with a rock. He smashed it into my forehead, knocking me out, and eventually, after another strangulation attempt, he left me for dead."[62] Brison goes on to describe her ordeal in the hospital and the fears for her safety that she continued to experience for some time after the attack. She notes: "I didn't want people to know that I had been sexually assaulted. I don't know whether this was because I could still hardly believe it myself, because keeping this information confidential was one of the few ways I could feel in control of my life, or because, in spite of my conviction that I had done nothing wrong, I felt ashamed."[63]

What punishment fits rape? Nothing annuls rape or the message the rapist implicitly (sometimes explicitly) delivers to his victim. What sort of punishment is suitable or apt? What sort of punishment can be styled to the moral contours of rape? Asked in that way, we are not so tempted to wonder how much pain, suffering, or deprivation of freedom balances the offense or annuls it or its message. The punishment will fit the offense if it is tailored to the moral contours of the offense, and that qualification will set the outer limits on justifiable retribution. To sustain a moral community, that limit will be the amount of punishment that must be inflicted on the offender, no more, no less. The virtuous avenger may not inflict more punishment but may inflict less. In the case of rape, the tailored fit for the offense, in my view, is death.

It will surely be objected that death is too severe, even for a rapist. Perhaps a convincing nonconsequentialist argument can be devised that identifies a punishment that is a better fit to the moral contours of rape. It might involve continual torture and long-term incarceration, perhaps for life, in absolute solitary confinement. It might involve the forced feeding of substances that produce all manner of ghastly physical and mental reactions. Such things are fertile grounds for fiendish imaginations. Dante, of course, set the bar on such inventiveness (recall the discussion of Count Ugolino in Chapter 1). Death, however, seems to me to have less of a moral impact on the punisher. We could imagine a future in which all of the appropriate nasty business is administered by robots or androids, taking the sting out of it for the human punisher. Admittedly, there is an emotional, if not a moral, price to pay in the administration of deserved punishment. I am reminded of Carl Sandburg's poem about the hangman at home:

What does the hangman think about
When he goes home at night from work?
When he sits down with his wife and
Children for a cup of coffee and a
Plate of ham and eggs, do they ask
Him if it was a good day's work
And everything went well or do they

Stay off some topics and talk about
The weather, baseball, politics
And the comic strips in the papers
And the movies? Do they look at his
Hands when he reaches for the coffee
Or the ham and eggs? If the little
Ones say, Daddy, play horse, here's
A rope—does he answer like a joke:
I seen enough rope for today?
Or does his face light up like a
Bonfire of joy and does he say:
It's a good and dandy world we live
In. And if a white face moon looks
In through a window where a baby girl
Sleeps and the moon-gleams mix with
Baby ears and baby hair—the hangman—
How does he act then? It must be easy
For him. Anything is easy for a hangman,
I guess.[64]

Tailoring the fit might appear to depend on the moral sensitivity or intuitions of the punisher(s). When is the fit "just right?" When does a suit of clothes fit? When it feels right? Yes, but also when it looks right to the wearer and to others. There are conditions but no mechanical formulas. Despite the movement in criminal law toward nondiscretionary sentences, from the moral point of view, that approach would be comparable to insisting that all suits on the rack are perfect fits for all customers; no alterations allowed. The moral contours of offenses typically are not perfectly patterned to preestablished models. Morality is an art, not a science.

Tailoring the fit involves, though not exclusively, the making of what I will call appreciative judgments. These are not verdicts, and they certainly are not mere judgments of fact. Although neither true nor false per se, they are prone to infelicity. A fit is apt or inappropriate, good or bad, suited or ill-suited. My first inclination was to endorse for fit something rather like the radical nonconditions-governed account Frank Sibley provides for aesthetic concepts.[65] Certainly there is no precise set of mechanical rules or a definitive set of conditions that determines whether or not fit has been accomplished, whether or not a particular punishment is felicitous. Precedents are also of only modest help. However, though I think that there must be a rather open list of relevant conditions for fit from case to case, I think fit in the case of moral punishment is what H. L. A. Hart once called a defeasible concept.[66] A concept's application is defeasible if we cannot contrive a complete list of sufficient conditions of its felicitous application because any or some member of such a set is always open to a defeating condition that would void the concept's use (make it inappropriate or infelicitous) in the circumstances. We can comfortably offer a list of conditions for such a concept's application only if we conjoin with that list a caveat indicating that the presence of certain features in the circumstances voids the applicability of the concept. Later, in *The Concept of Law*, Hart refers to this "indeterminacy of concept application" as "open-textured."[67]

The defeasible conditions for fit punishment could range over descriptions of relevant factors regarding the offense, the authority of the punisher, the age of the offender, and so on, and would include what I suspect is a dominant defeasible condition: the inability of the offender to understand the message of punishment. In Chapter 6 I mentioned the work of Norbert Wiener, who was concerned with the transfer of information, communication. He noted that semantically significant information has a tendency to be dissipated and not gained during attempted transmissions. He referred to this as "the cybernetic form of the second law of thermodynamics."[68] Semantically significant information is information that is both received and processed by the receiver of the information. Only semantically significant information is successfully communicated from one person to another. The most likely information to be received and processed without loss is information already expected by the recipient, information the recipient does not have to expend much time or effort in deciphering. Simply, there is less likelihood of loss in transmission of the communication of clichés than there is of complicated purple prose. Clichés, we might say, are unambiguous. It is difficult to misunderstand them or to lose their sense in the circumstances. In other words, if getting the message across is the point, then the message ought not to be subtle, filled with nuances, cluttered with well-honed turns of phrase.

The communication condition can be seen as defeating fit punishment in a number of different ways. If the offender is incapable of understanding the message, fit is voided. If the avenger is unable to deliver the message in a way that is unambiguous to the offender, fit is not achieved. There are a number of different ways in which the offender may lack the ability to understand the message, which might include diminished mental capacity, mental illness, physical impairment, language incompetence, and so on. On the other hand, the fault may lie with the punisher, who may fail to deliver the message successfully in a variety of ways or for a plethora of simple or complex reasons.

A final point: the tailoring of the fit is open to disputation, and punishers—avengers—must be prepared to explain how their choice of punishment suits the offense being punished. This is not a futile business. Critical conversation intended to persuade others of the presence or absence of morally relevant factors in the case is in order. The discussion should typically turn on the question of whether or not the case or the offender evidences certain features and how those features should be seen from the moral point of view. Some of those questions, the relatively uninteresting ones, can be classed as matters of fact. But once the facts are more or less settled, the fittingness of the punishment may be anything but settled. The serious discussion may have only just begun, and it is a discussion in which the moral community should always take a serious interest. We all need to be engaged in the process of assessing fit. Sometimes that discussion will lead to the expansion of the scope of the defeating conditions, sometimes to the narrowing of that scope. However, because previous cases can only serve as suggestions, in a crucial sense, each case, let alone each type of case, is a moral challenge both to the avenger and to the moral community at large. In that sense, the virtues of vengeance are regulated through the moral dialogue of the community.

NOTES

PREFACE

1. Peter A. French, *Cowboy Metaphysics* (Lanham, MD: Rowman and Littlefield, 1997).
2. Jeffrie Murphy, "Two Cheers for Vindictiveness," *Punishment and Society* 2, no. 2 (2000): 131–43.

CHAPTER ONE. SOME LITERARY FOUNDATIONS: A SURVEY

1. *Agamemnon, The Oresteia*, trans. by Robert Fagles (London: Penguin Books, 1975).
2. Francis Bacon, "Of Revenge," in *Essays*, 1625.
3. Charlotte Brontë, *Jane Eyre*, 1847.
4. Pietro Marongiu and Graeme Newman, *Vengeance: The Fight Against Injustice* (Lanham, MD: Rowman and Littlefield, 1987), p. 9.
5. Sigmund Freud, *Totem and Taboo*, trans. A.A. Brill (New York: Random House, 1918).
6. See Hesiod, *Theogony, Works and Days*, trans. Apostolos Athanassakis (Baltimore: Johns Hopkins University Press, 1983).
7. A point made by Marongiu and Newman, *Vengeance: The Fight Against Injustice*, p. 17.
8. All references to the *Iliad* are to Homer, *The Iliad*, trans. E.V. Rieu (London: Penguin Books, 1950).
9. Jon Elster, "Norms of Revenge," *Ethics* 100 (July 1990): 868.
10. Ibid., p. 869.
11. Ibid., p. 867.
12. J. L. Austin, *Philosophical Papers* (Oxford: Oxford University Press, 1961), p. 84.
13. Hans Jochen Boecker, *Law and the Administration of Justice in the Old Testament and the Ancient East* (Minneapolis: University of Minnesota Press, 1980), p. 174.
14. Friedrich Nietzsche, *Ecce Homo*, 10, trans. Walter Kaufmann (New York: Random House, 1969).
15. See Peter A. French, *Responsibility Matters* (Lawrence: University Press of Kansas, 1992), chap. 4.
16. See Harry Frankfurt, "Alternate Possibilities and Responsibility," in *The Importance of What We Care About* (Cambridge: Cambridge University Press, 1988), chap. 1.
17. Ibid., p. 8.
18. Ibid., p. 9.
19. References to the *Oresteia* are to Aeschylus, *The Oresteia*, trans. Robert Fagles (London: Penguin Books, 1975).
20. Fagles and Stanford, "The Serpent and the Eagle," *The Oresteia*, pp. 13–97.
21. Ibid., p. 89.
22. Jean Paul Sartre, *The Flies*, in *No Exit and Three Other Plays* (New York: Random House, 1955).
23. Marongiu and Newman, *Vengeance: The Fight Against Injustice*, p. 45.
24. Fagles and Stanford, "The Serpent and the Eagle," p. 81.

25. Susan Jacoby, *Wild Justice* (New York: Harper and Row, 1983), p. 31.

26. Ibid., p. 83.

27. See Jeffrie Murphy, "Two Cheers for Vindictiveness," *Punishment and Society* 2, no. 2 (2000): 131–43.

28. References to the *Inferno* are to Dante Alighieri, *The Divine Comedy,* translator unnamed (Garden City, NY: Doubleday, 1946).

29. Graeme Newman, *Just and Painful: A Case for the Corporal Punishment of Criminals* (New York: Macmillan, 1983), pp. 64–65.

30. Ronald Milo, "Wickedness," *American Philosophical Quarterly* 20, no. 1 (January 1983): 69–79.

31. Ibid., p. 69.

32. Following Milo; ibid., p. 70.

33. Plato, *Gorgias,* trans. Robin Waterfield (Oxford: Oxford University Press, 1994), 509e.

34. Milo, "Wickedness," p. 69.

35. Ibid., p. 70.

36. Ibid.

37. Patrick Nowell-Smith, *Ethics* (London: Penguin, 1954).

38. See for example, Owen Flanagan, *Varieties of Moral Personality* (Cambridge, MA: Harvard University Press, 1991), pp. 91–92.

39. Milo, "Wickedness," p. 71.

40. Ibid., p. 73.

41. Ibid., p. 72.

42. Ibid.

43. Nowell-Smith, *Ethics,* pp. 266–67.

44. See Milo, "Wickedness," p. 73.

45. Jacoby, *Wild Justice,* chap. 2.

46. Ibid., p. 35.

47. Ibid.

48. Ibid., p. 43.

49. Johann Wolfgang von Goethe, *Wilhelm Meister: Apprenticeship and Travels,* trans. R. O. Moon (London: Foulis, 1947), pp. 211–12.

50. Ibid., p. 212.

51. John Locke, *An Essay Concerning the True Original, Extent and End of Civil Government,* the second of the *Two Treatises of Government,* 1690, chap. 2.

CHAPTER TWO. THE WESTERN VENGEANCE FILMS

1. Lord Byron, *Don Juan,* canto 1, stanza 124, 1818.

2. John Milton, *Paradise Lost,* 1667.

3. Ibid., book 4.

4. Philip French, *Westerns: Aspects of a Movie Genre* (New York: Oxford University Press, 1977), p. 195.

5. See J. L. Austin, "Pretending," in *Philosophical Papers,* 2d ed. (Oxford: Oxford University Press, 1970).

6. Jeanine Basinger, *Anthony Mann* (Boston: Twayne Publishers, 1979), p. 101.

7. Ibid.

8. Ibid., p. 99.

9. Jim Kitses, *Horizons West* (Bloomington: Indiana University Press, 1969), pp. 59–60.

10. Cesare Beccaria, *On Crimes and Punishments,* trans. Henry Paolucci (1764; reprint, Indianapolis: Bobbs-Merrill, 1963).

11. Robert Cumbow, *Once Upon a Time: The Films of Sergio Leone* (Metuchen, NJ: Scarecrow Press, 1987), p. 74.

12. Phil Hardy, *The Western* (New York: William Morrow, 1983), p. 350.

13. Scott Eyman, *Print the Legend* (New York: Simon and Schuster, 1999), p. 384.

14. See Roger Ebert, *Ebert's Video Companion* (Kansas City, MO: Andrews and McMeel, 1996), p. 927.

15. Robert Frost, *The Death of the Hired Man,* 1914.

16. Arthur M. Eckstein, "Darkening Ethan: John Ford's *The Searchers* (1956) from Novel to Screenplay to Screen," *Cinema Journal* 38, no. 1 (Fall 1998): 3–24.

17. Ibid., p. 14.

18. J. A. Place, *The Western Films of John Ford* (Secaucus, NJ: Citadel Press, 1974), p. 164.

19. Eckstein, "Darkening Ethan," p. 17.

20. Geoffrey O'Brien, "The Movie of the Century," *American Heritage* (November 1998): 22.

21. Alasdair MacIntyre, *After Virtue* (Notre Dame: University of Notre Dame Press, 1984), p. 175.

22. Friedrich Nietzsche, *On the Genealogy of Morals,* trans. Walter Kaufman and R. J. Hollingdale (New York: Random House, 1967), p. 38.

23. Ibid., p. 39.

24. Ibid., p. 36.

25. MacIntyre, *After Virtue,* p. 128.

26. Jean-Paul Sartre, *The Flies,* in *No Exit and Three Other Plays* (New York: Random House, 1955).

27. John Rawls, *A Theory of Justice* (Cambridge, MA: Harvard University Press, 1971).

28. D. H. Lawrence, *Apocalypse* (New York: Knopf, 1931).

CHAPTER THREE. THE CONCEPT

1. William Shakespeare, *The Merchant of Venice,* act 3, scene 1, 1597.

2. Robert Nozick, *Philosophical Explanations* (Cambridge, MA: Harvard University Press, 1981), pp. 366–70.

3. See Nigel Walker, "Nozick's Revenge," *Philosophy* 70 (1995): 581–86.

4. Nozick, *Philosophical Explanations,* p. 367.

5. Ibid.

6. Ibid., p. 368.

7. Ibid.

8. See Peter A. French, *Responsibility Matters* (Lawrence: University Press of Kansas, 1992), chap. 5.

9. Bruce Reichenbach, *The Law of Karma* (Honolulu: University of Hawaii Press, 1990), chap. 2.

10. *Bhagavad Gita,* trans. Juan Mascaro (London: Penguin Books, 1962), p. 13.

11. Ibid., p. 39.

12. Ibid., p. 80.

13. See Aristotle, *Nicomachean Ethics,* book 3.

14. Reichenbach, *The Law of Karma,* p. 79.

15. Ibid., chap. 6.

16. See John Passmore, *Philosophical Reasoning* (New York: Basic Books, 1961), p. 40.

17. Reichenbach, *The Law of Karma,* p. 97.

18. S. Radhakrishnan and C. A. Moore, eds., *A Source Book in Indian Philosophy* (Princeton: Princeton University Press, 1957), pp. 380–81.

19. Sankaracarya, *Commentary on the Vedanta-Sutras,* trans. George Thibaut (Delhi: Motilal Banarsidass, 1904), p. 38.

20. Ibid., p. 183.

21. Plato, *Republic,* trans. Paul Shorey, in *Plato: The Collected Dialogues,* ed. Edith Hamilton and Huntington Cairns (1930; reprint, Princeton: Princeton University Press, 1961), pp. 841–43.

22. Rene Descartes, *Meditations on First Philosophy,* trans. Laurence J. LaFleur (Indianapolis: Bobbs-Merrill, 1951), p. 3.

23. See F. H. Bradley, *Ethical Studies* (1876; reprint, Oxford: Clarendon Press, 1989), chap. 4.

24. J. B. Schneewind, "Autonomy, Obligation, and Virtue," in *The Cambridge Companion to Kant,* ed. Paul Guyer (Cambridge: Cambridge University Press, 1992), p. 332.

25. Immanuel Kant, *Kant's Critique of Practical Reason and Other Works on the Theory of Ethics,* trans. T. K. Abbott (1873; reprint, London: Longmans, Green, 1909), p. 218.

26. Ibid., p. 206.

27. Immanuel Kant, *Religion Within the Limits of Reason Alone,* trans. Theodore Greene and Hoyt Hudson (Chicago: Open Court Publishing 1934), p. lvi.

28. Ibid., p. lvii.

29. Kant, *Critique of Practical Reason,* p. 209.

30. Ibid., p. 210.

31. Ibid., p. 211.

32. Ibid., pp. 220–21.

33. Schneewind, "Autonomy, Obligation, and Virtue," p. 333.

34. Kant, *Critique of Practical Reason,* p. 227.

35. Immanuel Kant, *Opus Postumum,* ed. Erich Adickes (Berlin: De Gruyter, 1920), p. 806; translation provided by Theodore Greene.

36. John Stuart Mill, *Utilitarianism,* 1861, pp. 15–16.

37. Nozick, *Philosophical Explanations,* p. 369.

38. Peter Strawson, "Freedom and Resentment," in *Freedom and Resentment and Other Essays* (London: Metheun, 1974).

39. Ibid., p. 5.

40. Ibid., p. 15.

41. Ibid., p. 16.

42. J. L. Austin, *How to Do Things with Words* (Oxford: Oxford University Press, 1962), pp. 152–54.

43. Ibid., pp. 154–55.

44. Elizabeth Beardsley, "A Plea for Deserts," *American Philosophical Quarterly* 6, no. 1 (1969): 33–42. See also William Alston, "Moral Attitudes and Moral Judgments," *Nous* 2 (1968): 1–23.

45. J. Braithwaite and P. Pettit, *Not Just Deserts* (Oxford: Clarendon Press), 1990.

46. See J. L. Austin, *How to Do Things with Words.*

47. Nozick, *Philosophical Explanations,* p. 372.

48. Ibid., p. 373.

49. Ibid., pp. 374–80.

50. Ibid., p. 382.

51. Walker, "Nozick's Revenge," p. 585.

52. Nozick, *Philosophical Explanations,* p. 378.

53. Immanuel Kant, *Groundwork of the Metaphysics of Morals,* trans. Lewis White Beck, in *Foundations of the Metaphysics of Morals with Critical Essays,* ed. R. P. Wolff (Indianapolis: Bobbs-Merrill, 1969), p. 54.

54. Nozick, *Philosophical Explanations,* p. 378.

55. Michael Walzer, "Political Action: The Problem of Dirty Hands," *Philosophy and Public Affairs* 3 (1973–1974): 160–80.

56. Michel de Montaigne, *Essays,* trans. by J. M. Cohen (New York: Penguin Books, 1958), p. 351.

57. John Rawls, *A Theory of Justice* (Cambridge, MA: Harvard University Press, 1970), p. 310.

58. Ronald Dworkin, *Taking Rights Seriously* (Cambridge, MA: Harvard University Press, 1971), p. 182.

59. Gregory Vlastos, "Justice and Equality," in *Social Justice,* ed. by R. B. Brandt (Englewood Cliffs, NJ: Prentice-Hall, 1962), p. 43.

60. Alan Gewirth, *Reason and Morality* (Chicago: University of Chicago Press, 1978), p. 206.

61. See Rawls, *A Theory of Justice,* p. 311.

62. John Kekes, *Facing Evil* (Princeton: Princeton University Press, 1990), p. 111.

63. Immanuel Kant, *The Metaphysical Principles of Virtue,* trans. J. W. Ellington (Indianapolis: Hackett Publishing, 1983), chap. 2, paragraph 9.

64. William Ian Miller, *Bloodtaking and Peacemaking* (Chicago: University of Chicago Press, 1990).

65. Jon Elster, "Norms of Revenge," *Ethics* (July 1990): 867.

66. Ibid., p. 870.

67. Milovan Djilas, *Land Without Justice* (London: Methuen, 1958), pp. 86, 105–7.

68. J. Bussquet, *Le droit de vendetta et les paci corses* (Paris: Perdone, 1920), p. 358.

69. See Philip Pettit, "Virtus Normativa," *Ethics* 100 (1950): 725–55.

70. David Hume, "Of Self Love," *An Enquiry Concerning the Principles of Morals,* 1751, appendix 2.

71. Elster, "Norms of Revenge," p. 875.

72. Ibid., p. 873.

73. See H. L. A. Hart, *The Concept of Law* (Oxford: Oxford University Press, 1961).

74. See Robert Nozick, *Anarchy, State, and Utopia* (New York: Basic Books, 1974), p. 1.

75. See Alan P. Hamlin, "Rational Revenge," *Ethics* (January 1991): 374–81.

76. Elster, "Norms of Revenge," p. 283.

77. Hume, "Of Self Love," appendix 2.

78. Jeffrie Murphy, "Two Cheers for Vindictiveness," *Punishment and Society* 2, no. 2 (2000): 131–45.

79. Paul Hughes, "Moral Anger, Forgiving, and Condoning," *Journal of Social Philosophy* 25, no. 1 (Spring 1995): 103–18.

80. Ibid., p. 104.

81. Joseph Butler, *Fifteen Sermons Preached at Rolls Chapel,* 1726.

82. Hughes, "Moral Anger, Forgiving, and Condoning," p. 117.

83. See French, *Responsibility Matters,* chap. 1.

84. See Peter Strawson, *Freedom and Resentment* (London: Methuen, 1974), p. 14.

85. Ibid., p. 15.

86. Ibid., p. 16.

87. See G. E. Hughes, "Moral Condemnation," in *Essays in Moral Philosophy,* ed. A. I. Melden (Seattle: University of Washington Press, 1958).

88. Adam Smith, *Theory of the Moral Sentiments,* 1759, p. 2, sect. 1, chap. 1.

89. Ibid.

90. J. L. Mackie, "Morality and the Retributive Emotions," in *Persons and Values, Selected Papers,* vol. 2 (Oxford: Clarendon Press, 1985), chap. 15.

91. Ibid., p. 214.

92. See French, *Responsibility Matters,* chap. 2.

93. Peter Danielson, "The Moral and Ethical Significance of TIT FOR TAT," *Dialogue* 25 (1986): 454.

94. See Peter A. French, *Corporate Ethics* (Fort Worth, TX: Harcourt Brace, 1995), pp. 79–90.

95. Murphy, "Two Cheers for Vindictiveness," pp. 131–43.

96. Strawson, *Freedom and Resentment*, p. 14.

97. Ibid., p. 23.

98. David Hume, *A Treatise of Human Nature* (1739; reprint, Oxford: Clarendon Press, 1978), p. 367.

99. Ibid., p. 367.

100. Ibid., p. 368.

101. Jeffrie Murphy and Jean Hampton, *Forgiveness and Mercy* (Cambridge: Cambridge University Press, 1988), pp. 60–87.

102. Ibid., p. 71.

103. Ibid., p. 78.

104. Ibid., p. 61.

105. Ibid., p. 80.

106. See Kekes, *Facing Evil.*

107. Murphy and Hampton, *Forgiveness and Mercy*, p. 82.

108. Ibid., p. 100.

109. Edmund Pincoffs, "The Practices of Responsibility Ascription," *Proceedings and Addresses of the American Philosophical Association* 61, no. 5 (June 1988): 825–39.

110. Michael Moore, "The Moral Worth of Retribution," in *Responsibility, Character, and the Emotions,* ed. Ferdinand Shoeman (Cambridge: Cambridge University Press, 1987).

111. See French, *Responsibility Matters,* chap. 18.

112. Murphy and Hampton, *Forgiveness and Mercy*, p. 107.

113. See Jeffrie Murphy, "Getting Even," *Social Philosophy and Policy* 7, no. 2 (1990): 209–25.

CHAPTER FOUR. THE CONDITIONS

1. "Third Annual Message," December 6, 1887.

2. J. L. Austin, *How to Do Things with Words,* ed. J. O. Urmson (Oxford: Oxford University Press, 1962), 1965.

3. Ibid., p. 15.

4. Ibid., pp. 19–20.

CHAPTER FIVE. THE AVENGER: THE AUTHORITY CONDITION

1. George Bernard Shaw, *Major Barbara,* 1907, act 3.

2. Sarah Broadie, *Ethics with Aristotle* (Oxford: Oxford University Press, 1991), p. 57.

3. Ibid.

4. Alasdair MacIntyre, *After Virtue* (Notre Dame: University of Notre Dame Press, 1981), p. 148.

5. Rosalind Hursthouse, "Virtue Theory and Abortion," *Philosophy and Public Affairs* 20 (1991): 223–46.

6. Michael Slote, "Agent-Based Virtue Ethics," *Midwest Studies in Philosophy* 20, (1995): 83–101.

7. Ibid., p. 83.

8. Broadie, *Ethics with Aristotle,* p. 82.
9. Ibid., p. 83.
10. Slote, "Agent-Based Virtue Ethics," p. 83.
11. Ibid., p. 84.
12. Ibid.
13. See H. Sidgwick, *Methods of Ethics,* 1874, p. 202.
14. Slote, "Agent-Based Virtue Ethics," p. 85.
15. Ibid.
16. Ibid., p. 86.
17. Ibid.
18. Ibid., p. 87.
19. Ibid.
20. Charles Dickens, *Bleak House,* 1853, chap. 6.
21. Slote, "Agent-Based Virtue Ethics," p. 89.
22. Ibid., p. 88.
23. Friedrich Nietzsche, *Beyond Good and Evil,* trans. Walter Kaufmann (New York: Random House, 1966), no. 260.
24. See Peter A. French, *Cowboy Metaphysics* (Lanham, MD: Rowman and Littlefield, 1997), chap. 5.
25. Slote, "Agent-Based Virtue Ethics," p. 90.
26. Ralph Waldo Emerson, "Self-Reliance," in *Essays* (1841; reprint, New York: Thomas Y. Crowell, 1926).
27. Nietzsche, *Beyond Good and Evil,* no.188.
28. Philippa Foot, *Virtues and Vices* (Oxford: Basil Blackwell, 1978), p. 90.
29. Nietzsche, *Beyond Good and Evil,* no. 188.
30. Slote, "Agent-Based Virtue Ethics," p. 84.
31. Emerson, "Self-Reliance," pp. 60–61.
32. T. E. Wilkerson, "Uniqueness in Art and Morals," *Philosophy* 58, no. 225 (July 1983): 307.
33. Ibid., p. 308.
34. James Wood, "Review of Hemingway Book," *New York Times Book Review,* July 11, 1999, p. 15.
35. Wilkerson, "Uniqueness in Art and Morals," p. 308.
36. Ibid., pp. 308–9.
37. J. O. Urmson, "Saints and Heroes," in *Essays in Moral Philosophy,* ed. A. I. Melden, (Seattle: University of Washington Press, 1958), pp. 204–5.
38. Hilary Spurling, *The Unknown Matisse* (New York: Knopf, 1998), p. 419.
39. Friedrich Nietzsche, *Will to Power,* trans. Walter Kaufmann (New York: Random House, 1967), no. 315.
40. Nietzsche, *Beyond Good and Evil,* no. 228.
41. Foot, *Virtues and Vices,* p. 92.
42. Nietzsche, *Beyond Good and Evil,* no. 228.
43. Emerson, "Self-Reliance," p. 35.
44. Ibid., p. 36.
45. Ibid.
46. Ibid., p. 53.
47. Slote, "Agent-Based Virtue Ethics," p. 91.
48. Ibid., p. 87.
49. Aristotle, *Nicomachean Ethics,* trans. Martin Ostwald (Indianapolis: Bobbs-Merrill, 1962).
50. James Burke, *The Day the Universe Changed* (Boston: Little, Brown, 1985), pp. 13–14.

51. See Peter A. French and Mitchell Haney, "Changes in Latitudes, Changes in Attitudes," forthcoming, for a discussion of incompatible worldviews based on the idea that worldviews are collections of cares, not beliefs.

52. Wilkerson, "Uniqueness in Art and Morals," p. 312.

53. *Federalist Papers,* no. 40, paragraph 13, p. 263.

54. *Beowulf,* trans. Gordon Hall Gerould (New York: Ronald Press, 1920), p. 51.

55. All quotes are from Robert Ashley, *Of Honour,* ed. Virgil Heltzel, (San Marino, CA: Huntington Library, 1947), which is a printed version of his handwritten paper book of twenty-six leaves.

56. See Bertram Wyatt-Brown, *Southern Honor* (New York, Oxford University Press, 1982).

57. Ashley, *Of Honour,* p. 56.

58. Ibid., p. 52.

59. J. G. Peristiany, *Honour and Shame* (Chicago: University of Chicago Press, 1966), p. 31.

60. Pieter Spierenburg, *Men and Violence* (Columbus: Ohio State University Press, 1998), p. 10.

61. Ibid., p. 11.

62. Ibid., p. 9.

63. Ibid., p. 11.

64. Ibid.

65. Ibid.

66. See Peter A. French, *Responsibility Matters* (Lawrence: University Press of Kansas, 1992), chap. 5.

67. F. H. Bradley, *Ethical Studies* (1876; reprint, Oxford: Clarendon Press, 1989), p. 173.

68. Ibid.

69. Gabrielle Taylor, *Pride, Shame, and Guilt* (Oxford: Oxford University Press, 1985).

70. Arnold Isenberg, "Natural Pride and Natural Shame," in *Explaining Emotions,* ed. A. Rorty (Berkeley: University of California Press, 1980).

71. John Kekes, "Shame and Moral Progress," *Midwest Studies in Philosophy* 13 (1988): 282–96.

72. See French, *Responsibility Matters,* chap. 5, and "It's a Damn Shame," in *Freedom, Equality, and Social Change,* ed. C. Peden and J. Sterba, (Lewiston, NY: Mellon Press, 1989).

73. Stanley Cavell, *Must We Mean What We Say?* (Cambridge, MA: Harvard University Press, 1969), chap. 10.

74. Taylor, *Pride, Shame, and Guilt,* p. 83.

75. Gerhart Piers and Milton Singer, *Shame and Guilt* (New York: W. W. Norton 1971).

76. John Kekes, *Facing Evil* (Princeton: Princeton University Press, 1990), p. 282.

77. Peristiany, *Honour and Shame.*

78. Ibid., p. 27.

79. John Rawls, *A Theory of Justice* (Cambridge, MA: Harvard University Press, 1971), p. 443.

80. John Darrah, *The Real Camelot* (London: Thames and Hudson, 1981).

81. David Gilmore, *Honor and Shame and the Unity of the Mediterranean* (Arlington, VA: American Anthropological Association, 1987), p. 3.

82. Peristiany, *Honour and Shame,* p. 46.

83. Carol Delaney, "Seeds of Honor, Fields of Shame," in *Honor and Shame and the Unity of the Mediterranean,* p. 40.

84. Ibid.

85. Ibid., p. 42.

86. Wyatt-Brown, *Southern Honor,* p. 54.

87. Ibid., p. 14.

88. Ibid., p. 34.

89. Ibid., pp. 46–47.

90. Douglas Cairns, *Aidos* (Oxford: Oxford University Press, 1993), p. 15.

91. Taylor, *Pride, Shame, and Guilt,* p. 60.

92. Ibid., p. 66.

93. Ibid.

94. Cairns, *Aidos,* p. 17.

95. Ibid., p. 18.

96. Piers and Singer, *Shame and Guilt,* p. 67.

97. Taylor, *Pride, Shame, and Guilt,* p. 68.

98. Geoffrey O'Brien, "The Movie of the Century," *American Heritage* (November 1998): 17–22.

99. Cairns, *Aidos,* pp. 83–87, 140.

100. Helen Merrell Lynd, *On Shame and the Search for Identity* (New York: Harcourt Brace 1967).

101. Kekes, *Facing Evil,* p. 285.

102. Alan Hamlin, "Rational Revenge," *Ethics* 101 (January 1991): 377.

103. *Letter to John Adams,* May 7, 1776.

104. See J. L. Austin, "A Plea for Excuses," in *Philosophical Papers* (Oxford: Oxford University Press, 1960).

105. Jeffrie Murphy, "A Paradox in Locke's Theory of Natural Rights," *Dialogue* 8 (September 1967). See also H. L. A. Hart, "Prolegomenon to the Principles of Punishment," in *Punishment and Responsibility* (Oxford: Oxford University Press, 1968).

106. Immanuel Kant, *Metaphysical Elements of Justice,* trans. John Ladd (Indianapolis: Bobbs-Merrill, 1965), p. 101.

107. See Peter A. French, *Collective and Corporate Responsibility* (New York: Columbia University Press, 1984).

108. Stephen Nathanson, *An Eye for an Eye* (Lanham, MD: Rowman and Littlefield, 1987), p. 118.

109. See, for example, Robert Nozick, *Anarchy, State, and Utopia* (New York: Basic Books, 1974).

110 John Locke, *Second Treatise of Government,* 1690, chap. 2, sec. 7.

111. Ibid.

112. Ibid., chap. 2, sec. 11.

113. Ibid.

114. Nozick, *Anarchy, State, and Utopia,* p. 138.

115. Ibid., p. 106.

116. Ibid., p. 107.

117. Jeffrie Murphy, "Two Cheers for Vindictiveness," *Punishment and Society* 2, no. 2 (2000): 131–43.

118. Nozick, *Anarchy, State, and Utopia,* p. 139.

119. Ibid.

120. Quotes are from Saint Thomas Aquinas, *Summa Theologica,* vol. 2, question 108, trans. Fathers of the English Dominican Province, 1911.

CHAPTER SIX. THE TARGET: THE DESERT CONDITION

1. Saint Thomas Aquinas, *Summa Theologica,* vol. 2, trans. Fathers of the English Dominican Province, 1911.

2. Stephen Crane, *War Is Kind,* 1899.

3. Thornton Wilder, *The Bridge of San Luis Rey* (1927; reprint, New York: HarperCollins, 1998).

4. Ibid., p. 5.

5. Ibid., p. 7.

6. Ibid., p. 8.

7. Ibid., p. 9.

8. Ibid., p. 115.

9. Philipp Frank, *Einstein, His Life and Times* (New York: Knopf, 1947).

10. Anatole France, *Le Jardin d'Epicure,* 1894.

11. Saint Augustine, "On Free Will," in *Augustine: Earlier Writings,* ed. J. H. S. Burleigh (Philadelphia: Westminister Press, 1953), 3.9.26.

12. A. S. Pringle-Pattison, *The Idea of God in Modern Philosophy* (Oxford: Oxford University Press, 1920), p. 35.

13. John Kekes, *Facing Evil* (Princeton: Princeton University Press, 1990), p. 23.

14. Norbert Wiener, *The Human Use of Human Beings* (New York: Da Capo Press, 1954), p. 35.

15. Kekes, *Facing Evil,* p. 24.

16. Ibid.

17. Wiener, *The Human Use of Human Beings,* p. 35.

18. Thomas Hobbes, *Leviathan,* 1651, chap. 13.

19. Machiavelli, *The Prince,* trans. David Wootton (Indianapolis: Hackett, 1995), p. 48.

20. Baogang He, "Designing Democratic Institutions and the Problem of Evil: A Liberal Chinese Perspective," in *The Just Society,* ed. Ellen Frankel Paul, Fred D. Miller Jr., and Jeffrey Paul (Cambridge: Cambridge University Press, 1995), p. 302.

21. William Golding, *Lord of the Flies* (New York: Putnam's Sons, 1954), pp. 132–33.

22. Ibid., "Notes," p. 192.

23. Joseph Conrad, *Heart of Darkness and the Secret Sharer* (1902; reprint, New York: Bantam Books, 1981).

24. Ibid., pp. 119–20.

25. Laurence Thomas, *Vessels of Evil* (Philadelphia: Temple University Press, 1993), p. 15.

26. Martha Nussbaum, *The Fragility of Goodness* (Cambridge: Cambridge University Press, 1986).

27. Thomas, *Vessels of Evil,* p. 15.

28. Ibid., p. 21.

29. See Yan Jiaqi, *Wode sixiang zichuan (My Intellectual Autobiography),* trans. D. S. K. Hong and Denis Mair (Honolulu: University of Hawaii Press, 1992).

30. Immanuel Kant, *Religion Within the Limits of Reason Alone,* trans. Theodore Greene and Hoyt Hudson (New York: Harper, 1960), p. 24.

31. Ibid., p. 50.

32. See Peter A. French, *Responsibility Matters* (Lawrence: University Press of Kansas, 1992), chap. 3.

33. See, for example, p. 15.

34. Nel Noddings, *Women and Evil* (Berkeley: University of California Press, 1989), p. 118.

35. Mary Midgley, *Wickedness* (London: Routledge, 1984), p. 59.

36. John Rawls, *A Theory of Justice* (Cambridge, MA: Harvard University Press, 1971), p. 439.

37. See also Ronald Milo, *Immorality* (Princeton: Princeton University Press, 1984).

38. Kant, *Religion Within the Limits of Reason Alone,* p. 32.

39. Ibid.

40. Midgley, *Wickedness,* p. 61.

41. Hannah Arendt, *Eichmann in Jerusalem* (Hammondsworth, UK: Penguin Books, 1963), p. 175.

42. Roger Burggraeve, "Violence and the Vulnerable Face of the Other: The Vision of Emmanuel Levinas on Moral Evil and Our Responsibility," *Journal of Social Philosophy* 30, no. 1 (Spring 1999): 38.

43. Margaret Walker, "Moral Luck and the Virtues of Impure Agency," in *Moral Luck*, ed. Daniel Statman (Albany: State University of New York Press, 1993), pp. 235–50.

44. Ibid., p. 237.

45. Judith Jarvis Thomson, "Morality and Bad Luck," in Moral Luck, pp. 195–216.

46. See French, *Responsibility Matters*, chap. 1.

47. Thomson, "Morality and Bad Luck," p. 199.

48. Jonathan Bennett, "The Conscience of Huckleberry Finn," *Philosophy* 49 (1974): 123–34.

49. Mark Twain, *The Adventures of Huckleberry Finn* (1884; reprint, Cambridge: Riverside Press, 1958), pp. 179–80.

50. Peter Heath, *The Philosopher's Alice* (New York: St. Martin's Press, 1974).

51. Phillip Hallie, "The Evil that Men Think—and Do," *Hastings Center Report* (December 1985).

52. Lewis Carroll, *Through the Looking-Glass,* chap. 4, 1871.

53. See Roger Lancelyn Green, ed., *The Diaries of Lewis Carroll,* vol. 2 (London: Cassell, 1953), pp. 446–47.

54. Kewal Krishna Anand, *Indian Philosophy* (Delhi: Bharatiya Vidya Prakashan, 1982).

55. Ibid., p. 13.

56. Jeffrie Murphy and Jean Hampton, *Forgiveness and Mercy* (Cambridge: Cambridge University Press, 1988).

57. Hobbes, *Leviathan,* chap. 14.

58. Kant, *Religion Within the Limits of Reason Alone*, p. 31.

59. Immanuel Kant, *Foundations of the Metaphysics of Morals,* trans. L. W. Beck (Indianapolis: Bobbs-Merrill, 1969), p. 54.

60. Kekes, *Facing Evil*, p. 108.

61. Rudolf Otto, *Notes to Kant's Grundlegung zur Metaphysik der Sitten* (Gotha: L. Klotz, 1930), p. 199.

62. Rawls, *A Theory of Justice,* p. 560.

63. Ibid., p. 139.

64. Michael Sandel, *Liberalism and the Limits of Justice* (Cambridge, MA: Harvard University Press, 1982).

65. Kekes, *Facing Evil,* p. 112.

66. Ibid., p. 115.

67. Ibid., p. 116.

68. See Robert Nozick, *Anarchy, State, and Utopia* (New York: Basic Books, 1974).

69. Pepita Haezrahi, "The Concept of Man as an End-in-Himself," *Kant-Studien* 53, no. 2 (1961–1962): 209–24.

70. Murphy and Hampton, *Forgiveness and Mercy,* p. 125.

71. Ibid., p. 137.

72. Jeffrie Murphy, "Two Cheers for Vindictiveness," *Punishment and Society* 2, no. 2 (2000): 131–45.

73. Arnold Zuboff, "Morality as What One Really Desires," *Midwest Studies in Philosophy* 20, (1995): 159.

74. Ibid., pp. 159–60.

75. Kekes, *Facing Evil,* p. 89.

76. Kant, *Religion Within the Limits of Reason Alone,* p. 43.

77. Harry Frankfurt, "Alternate Possibilities and Moral Responsibility," *The Importance of What We Care About* (Cambridge: Cambridge University Press, 1988), chap. 1.

78. Ibid., p. 8.

79. John Martin Fischer, *The Metaphysics of Free Will* (Oxford: Blackwell, 1994), p. 162.

80. Ibid.

81. Ibid., p. 163.

82. Ibid., p. 166.

83. Ibid., p. 167.

84. Ibid., p. 168.

85. Kekes, *Facing Evil*, p. 83.

86. Ibid., p. 70.

87. Ibid., p. 66.

88. Ibid.

89. Ibid., p. 83.

90. Ibid., p. 75.

91. Fischer, *The Metaphysics of Free Will*, p. 174.

92. *New York Times* wire story carried in *St. Petersburg Times*, January 24, 1998, p. 1A.

93. Robert Green Ingersoll, *Some Reasons Why*, 1896.

94. G. E. Moore, *Principia Ethica* (Cambridge: Cambridge University Press, 1903), p. 214.

95. See, for example, George Sher, *Desert* (Princeton: Princeton University Press, 1987), and Wojciech Sadurski, *Giving Desert Its Due: Social Justice and Legal Theory* (Dordrecht: D. Reidel Publishing, 1985).

96. J. L. Mackie, *Persons and Values, Selected Papers* (Oxford: Oxford University Press, 1985), p. 213.

97. Michael Moore, "The Moral Worth of Retributivism," in *Responsibility, Character and the Emotions*, ed. Ferdinand Schoeman (Cambridge: Cambridge University Press, 1987); page references here are to the reprint of Moore's paper in *Philosophy of Law*, ed. J. Feinberg and J. Coleman (Belmont, CA: Wadsworth, 2000), p. 750.

98. Mackie, *Persons and Values*, p. 213.

CHAPTER SEVEN. THE TAILORED FIT: THE PROPORTIONALITY CONDITION

1. Saint Thomas Aquinas, *Summa Theologica*, vol. 2, trans. Fathers of the English Dominican Province, 1911, question 108.

2. William Gilbert, *The Mikado*, act 2, 1885.

3. See Russ Shafer-Landau, "The Failure of Retributivism," *Philosophical Studies* 82 (June 1996): 289–316.

4. Michael Moore, "The Moral Worth of Retributivism," in *Responsibility, Character and the Emotions*, ed. Ferdinand Schoeman (Cambridge: Cambridge University Press, 1987); page references here are to the reprint of Moore's paper in *Philosophy of Law*, ed. J. Feinberg and J. Coleman (Belmont, CA: Wadsworth, 2000), p. 747.

5. See J. G. Cottingham, "Varieties of Retributivism," *Philosophical Quarterly* 29 (July 1979): 238–46.

6. Immanuel Kant, *The Metaphysics of Morals*, trans. Mary Gregor (Cambridge: Cambridge University Press, 1996), p. 105.

7. Ibid.

8. Jeffrie Murphy, *Kant: The Philosophy of Right* (London: Macmillan, 1970), p. 142.

9. Kant, *Metaphysics of Morals*, p. 106.

10. Ibid.

11. Ibid.

12. Ibid., p. 130.

13. Jeffrey Reiman and Louis Pojman, *The Death Penalty: For and Against* (Lanham, MD: Rowman and Littlefield, 1998), p. 91.

14. Kant, *Metaphysics of Morals,* p. 28.

15. Immanuel Kant, *On the Old Saw: That May Be Right in Theory But It Won't Work in Practice,* trans. E. B. Ashton (Philadelphia: University of Pennsylvania Press, 1974), p. 68.

16. Ibid.

17. Ibid.

18. Ibid.

19. Kant, *Metaphysics of Morals,* p. 28.

20. Ibid.

21. Ibid.

22. Thomas Hobbes, *Leviathan* (1651; reprint, London: Penguin Books, 1986), p. 232.

23. 1 Wall Jr. 1 (Circuit Court Eastern District, Pennsylvania, April 22, 1842).

24. Kant, *Metaphysics of Morals,* p. 106.

25. Ibid.

26. Jeffrie Murphy and Jean Hampton, *Forgiveness and Mercy* (Cambridge: Cambridge University Press, 1988), p. 131.

27. G. W. F. Hegel, *The Philosophy of Right,* trans. T. M. Knox (Oxford: Oxford University Press, 1952), p. 70.

28. Ibid., p. 71.

29. Reiman and Pojman, *The Death Penalty,* p. 89.

30. Ibid.

31. Ibid., p. 90.

32. Hegel, *The Philosophy of Right,* p. 73.

33. Murphy and Hampton, *Forgiveness and Mercy,* p. 125.

34. Ibid., p. 131.

35. George Sher, *Desert* (Princeton: Princeton University Press, 1987), pp. 80, 82.

36. Ibid., p. 83.

37. Lewis Carroll, *Through the Looking-Glass,* 1871, chap. 5.

38. Sher, *Desert,* p. 84.

39. Ibid.

40. Michael Davis, *To Make the Punishment Fit the Crime* (Boulder, CO: Westview Press, 1992), chapter 3. See also Robert Solomon, *What Is Justice?,* with Mark C. Murphy (New York: Oxford University Press, 1990), and *A Passion for Justice* (Lanham, MD: Rowman and Littlefield, 1995).

41. Ibid., p. 45.

42. Ibid.

43. Friedrich Nietzsche, *The Dawn,* trans. Walter Kaufmann, in *The Portable Nietzsche* (New York: Random House, 1954), p. 86.

44. Ibid., p. 87.

45. Friedrich Nietzsche, *Beyond Good and Evil,* trans. Walter Kaufmann (New York: Random House, 1966), p. 114.

46. Ibid., p. 103.

47. Joel Feinberg, *Doing and Deserving* (Princeton: Princeton University Press, 1970), chap. 5.

48. Andrew Oldenquist, "The Case for Revenge," *Public Interest,* 82, (1986): 72–80.

49. See Peter A. French, *Collective and Corporate Responsibility* (New York: Columbia University Press, 1982), chap. 14.

50. John Ladd, "Persons and Responsibilities: Ethical Concepts and Impertinent Analo-

gies," in *Shame, Responsibility and the Corporation,* ed. Hugh Curtler (New York: Haven Publications, 1986), pp. 94–95.

51. Feinberg, *Doing and Deserving,* p. 118.

52. J. Braithwaite and P. Pettit, *Not Just Deserts* (Oxford: Oxford University Press, 1990), p. 34.

53. J. L. Mackie, "Retributivism: A Test Case for Ethical Objectivity," in *Philosophy of Law,* pp. 780–787.

54. Ibid., p. 785.

55. David Hume, *A Treatise of Human Nature* (1739; reprint, Oxford: Oxford University Press, 1978), p. 470.

56. Ibid., p. 578.

57. Ibid., p. 581.

58. Jeffrie Murphy, "Getting Even: The Role of the Victim," *Social Philosophy and Policy* 7, no. 2 (1990): 210.

59. David Lewis, "Devil's Bargain's and the Real World," in *The Security Gamble: Deterrence Dilemmas in the Nuclear Age,* ed. Douglas MacLean (Lanham, MD: Rowman and Littlefield, 1985), chap. 10.

60. Ibid., p. 144.

61. See Peter A. French, *Cowboy Metaphysics* (Lanham, MD: Rowman and Littlefield, 1997), chap. 1.

62. Susan Brison, "Surviving Sexual Violence," *Journal of Social Philosophy* 24, no. 1 (Spring 1993): 5–6.

63. Ibid., p. 6.

64. Carl Sandburg, "The Hangman at Home," in *Smoke and Steel* (New York: Harcourt, Brace, 1920).

65. Frank Sibley, "Aesthetic Concepts," *Philosophical Review* 67 (1959): 421–50.

66. See H. L. A. Hart, "The Ascription of Responsibility and Rights," *Proceedings of the Aristotelian Society,* 1948–1949.

67. H. L. A. Hart, *The Concept of Law* (Oxford: Oxford University Press, 1961), p. 124.

68. Norbert Wiener, *The Human Use of Human Beings* (New York: Da Capo Press, 1954), p. 78.

INDEX